Censoring Sex

Censoring Sex

A Historical Journey Through American Media

John E. Semonche

ROWMAN & LITTLEFIELD PUBLISHERS, INC.
Lanham • Boulder • New York • Toronto • Plymouth, UK

ROWMAN & LITTLEFIELD PUBLISHERS, INC.

Published in the United States of America
by Rowman & Littlefield Publishers, Inc.
A wholly owned subsidiary of The Rowman & Littlefield Publishing Group, Inc.
4501 Forbes Boulevard, Suite 200, Lanham, Maryland 20706
www.rowmanlittlefield.com

Estover Road
Plymouth PL6 7PY
United Kingdom

British Library Cataloguing in Publication Information Available

Library of Congress Cataloging-in-Publication Data

Semonche, John E., 1933–
  Censoring sex : a historical journey through American media / John E.
Semonche.
    p. cm.
  ISBN-13: 978-0-7425-5131-2 (cloth : alk. paper)
  ISBN-10: 0-7425-5131-8 (cloth : alk. paper)
  ISBN-13: 978-0-7425-5132-9 (pbk. : alk. paper)
  ISBN-10: 0-7425-5132-6 (pbk. : alk. paper)
    1. Censorship—United States—History. 2. Sex in popular culture—United
States. I. Title.
  Z658.U5S46 2007
  363.31—dc22   2007004347

Printed in the United States of America

∞™ The paper used in this publication meets the minimum requirements of
American National Standard for Information Sciences—Permanence of Paper
for Printed Library Materials, ANSI/NISO Z39.48-1992.

Contents

Acknowledgments   vii

Introduction   1

1   Books and Periodicals: Seduction by the Written Word and
Maybe a Picture or Two   9

2   Dirty Pictures, Naked Statues, Etc.: You Call That Art?   55

3   The Movies: Teaching the Wrong Lessons and in the
Dark as Well   95

4   Music and Dance: Stirring the Senses and
Unleashing the Beast   137

5   Home Invaders: Radio, Television, and the Internet   177

Epilogue   223

Endnotes   231

Index   275

About the Author   301

Acknowledgments

One of the joys of academic life is that one can continue to learn new things, and one of academia's most closely guarded secrets is that one can often learn as much from one's students as they learn from him. Some legal history, my specialty, can be found in the following pages, but also much can be found that is not. Although the study of popular culture has blossomed in many disciplines, including history, during the last generation or so, it has not been an area that previously occupied my research interests. The freedom, then, to move into this area, not as a specialist, but as a researcher relying on the wide-ranging work of others, has indeed been a learning experience. As with all students, I am indebted to so many others who helped me navigate what at times was strange and alien territory. That indebtedness is reflected in the notes that can be found at the back of the book. I have not tried to become a popular culture specialist but an interloper, who hopefully can communicate with others. I have made no attempt to write a definitive or complete history of sex censorship; instead I have sought to convey the nature of the struggle between competing forces over time and to extract episodes in that struggle that capture the human interest inherent in it.

Despite the fact that I chose not to repeat myself or to be content with remaining on secure ground in my work, I probably would not have undertaken this task had it not been suggested as a collaborative effort by a former doctoral student. After getting her PhD in history, Margaret A. (Peggy) Blanchard went on to a distinguished career in the School of Journalism and Mass Communication at the University of North Carolina at Chapel Hill (UNC-CH). She earned a chair and became not only a caring teacher but a sought-after expert on the First Amendment. Her suggestion that we collaborate on a study of censorship launched this project. Unfortunately, her later years were absorbed with her supervision of graduate students, and she was only able to write a single chapter dealing with Anthony Comstock, a man whose name became synonymous with a desire to stamp out all sexual speech. Before she could finish that chapter and move on, she was struck by cancer. She struggled to make sure her students finished their work before she died in May 2005. I worked with her chapter to make it an independent entity, and it was published under both our names in a special summer 2006 issue of *Communication Law and Policy* paying tribute to her work and professional life.

In addition to my indebtedness to all the writers that have illuminated our understanding of popular culture and censorship and to Peggy, I want to thank Lloyd Kramer, Chair of the History Department here at UNC-CH. He reminded me that the time had come to enjoy the benefits of a semester's sabbatical in the fall of 2006. An earlier sabbatical had given me the opportunity to get a good start on the research and writing for this book, and the recent one gave me the opportunity to put the finishing touches on the manuscript. Without these two semesters freed from teaching and committee responsibilities, this book would have taken much longer to complete.

Except for a year at the University of Connecticut in Storrs, my professional life has been spent at Chapel Hill. After receiving my law degree at Duke University to go with my PhD in history, a spot was grooved out for me in Chapel Hill's History Department. I have never been tempted to leave, having found the university and department quite congenial and supportive.

The folks at Rowman & Littlefield did such a nice job with my last book, *Keeping the Faith: A Cultural History of the U.S. Supreme Court*, that when it came time to find a publisher for this volume the choice was not difficult. I want to thank all of them, both those who have left and those still onboard, who had a hand in contracting for and then transforming the manuscript into an attractive book.

Finally, I want to thank the two women in my life. First, thanks to my wife, Barbara, a librarian with an international reputation, for her unfailing support, for her help in tracking down some elusive articles and books, and for acting as a sounding board. Second, thanks to our daughter, Laura Jones, who writes a biweekly newspaper column on personal fitness and owns and operates an art gallery, for making an exception to her unerring judgment in believing that her dad is one of the smartest people she knows.

Introduction

[A] sizable portion of the American public accepts censorship as an imagined "quick fix" solution to moral drift and other social ills. . . . Fears of unbridled . . . sexuality, of a world without clear moral compass, and of the impact that a gigantic multimedia universe is having on our children, have contributed to the continued scapegoating of speech in America.[1] (Marjorie Heins, 1998)

All censorship incidents are the result of cultural or political tensions, and they often serve as a means by which the powerful choose to impose their sensibilities upon those who lack power.[2] (Peter Blecha, 2004)

The activity of censoring not only permits but moralizes and glorifies the preoccupation with sex.[3] (Horace M. Kallen, 1930)

As a result of our ignorance, apathy, and fear, sex has to a great extent become by default the intellectual, moral and legal property of politicians, clerics, and ideologues.[4] (John Heidenry, 1997)

In all likelihood a desire to censor emerged with the creation of human society, and the species' interest in sex most assuredly antedated that time. Modern censorship, however, comes with the invention of Johannes Gutenberg, that fifteenth-century troublemaker who gave us movable type. He could hardly have anticipated the sweeping significance of what he had done. Robert Freidman, in his book, *The Life Millennium*, called Gutenberg's creation the "most far-reaching" technological innovation of the millennium,[5] and readers of the Sunday *Times* and viewers of A&E's *Biography*, saw the German printer placed first in a list of the most influential figures of the last one thousand years. Movable type not only launched an ever-continuing

1

information revolution, but it also freed men and women from the prisons of their own ignorance.

As both readers and reading material increased, all institutions were threatened. Reading was recognized as a subversive activity that could only be controlled by limiting what was published. That is why, early in the battle for a free press, licensing laws, which imposed such prior restraint, provided the primary target. The fear, of course, was that people would get the wrong ideas; they would challenge the status quo; and they would act upon impulses that endangered the community. Thus, a new urge to censor was unleashed.

Well before the industrial age, those persons and groups who sought to control the masses were alerted to the problems they faced. And, when words were joined with pictures, and then, when those pictures moved and finally talked, the concern only grew. Industrialization brought to the United States new media that bypassed preexisting channels and authority structures, whether the subject was politics, economics, education, religion, or sex. The target was vast audiences, among which children were especially willing and eager receptors.[6]

Although the new censors were worried about more than sex, it, along with sin, occupied much of their efforts. In fact, some students of censorship have concluded that heresy and treason, predominant worries of earlier times, would inevitably be succeeded by worries about sex.[7] Forbidden fruit was more than that apple that tempted Eve in the Garden of Eden; it had something to do with sex. It was God's ultimate joke: the act necessary to preserve the human race was potentially sinful. Ever after sin and sex would be entangled, as the history of the United States from the time of the Puritans up to the present demonstrates. Because the sex drive was so strong and so many persons were seen as undisciplined, censors worked to preserve a precarious moral status quo. That status quo was based on a conception of the family that not only gave to husband and wife and mother and father certain closely defined roles, but also gave to children a special status that displaced their earlier characterization as little adults. Since the well-regulated adult mind, by definition, could resist subversive influences, censors claimed that their aim was to protect children and those adults who, for one reason or another, lacked that well-regulated mind.

As present-day attempts to regulate the sexual content of the Internet have clearly shown, the ability to draw a line based either on who the viewer is or what the content is has been exceedingly difficult. This frustration explains why censors in earlier times sought to suppress all such communication. For instance, keeping people ignorant about the sexual functioning of the human body or about how to prevent pregnancy was as much an aim, as was the banning of titillating sexual material. Early censors were well aware of the danger of attempting to draw lines distinguishing among sexual materials, and they had the advantage of working in a nineteenth-century environment in which the protection of free speech and of a free press was far from fully realized.

When, in the latter decades of the nineteenth century, millions of immigrants from Southern and Eastern Europe, most of whom were Roman Catholic and Jewish, arrived with different attitudes toward sex, the censor's task only expanded. These new immigrants seemed more resistant to the melting pot, less willing to embrace preexisting middle-class norms. Not only did this increase in population add to the potential market for sexually explicit material, but also the immigrants, themselves, were viewed as purveyors of such writings and pictures. Purity crusaders would seek to prevent the immigrants' access to what they saw as passion-fueling material, and for those who peddled such wares, legal mechanisms would be put in place to prosecute them.

Censors quickly learned that laws were their best weapons in the fight to morally cleanse an impure society. State and federal laws were enacted that broadly defined what was obscene. Even when such laws were in place, purity crusaders also used social pressure to limit public access to sexual material. Businesses that sold suspect merchandise were warned and urged to regulate themselves to avoid unfavorable publicity that could threaten their very survival.

Censorship occurs because important values are perceived to be under attack. Moral guardians assume that individuals cannot be trusted to make the right choices. In the commercial marketplace, companies that produce products that do not sell are weeded out; the same holds true in the marketplace of ideas. Censors knew that there was a market for sexual expression; they wanted to prevent it from being stocked, confident in the belief that they knew what was best for others.

A certain irony is involved in the censor's work in that it calls attention to objectionable material, thus giving it a visibility that in most cases it would not otherwise have. Censors become, in fact, publicists for the very work that they want to hide from public view. And, at times, creators or purveyors of sexually explicit material deliberately provoke the wrath of moral guardians, well aware that increased public interest will be generated.

Censors often proceed with the view that the evil is in the book, the picture, or the film rather than in the society the medium reflects. Those censors on the right who question whether government can ever succeed in overcoming poverty, ending racism, or distributing better the benefits of an affluent society find nothing inconsistent in expecting government to improve people's morality. In recent years, however, censorship has not been the exclusive preserve of those on the right, for people at the opposite end of the political spectrum have been "lured to the bonfires" by the illusion of creating a better society. "Get rid of bad pictures and one is rid of bad

acts. . . . The social benefit rationale for censorship has smoothed a progressive patina over older, religious sanctions against sex. It makes the banning of books and movies seem reasonable to many Americans who would
laugh at threats of brimstone and hellfire."[8]

In a very real sense we are all censors, sometimes discriminating ones,
sometimes not. We decide what we find objectionable or disgusting and
what we wish to avoid. Furthermore, we seek in various ways to persuade
others to share our tastes, to follow our lead. Problems arise when we seek
to impose our tastes upon others, not by argument or example, but by restricting their freedom of choice. When we seek to deny to others the opportunity to choose for themselves, we become censors in the sense that the
term is used here.

Censorship occurs at the very start of the creative process, when creators
limit or self-censor what they produce. Societal limits on sexual speech
clearly can have a chilling effect on the creative process. Once something
is created, however, that, in itself, does not assure any public visibility. The
work has to be exhibited, published, or made available in some way. So,
the artist may create but not find an outlet for the work—no publisher, exhibit space, airtime, etc. This prior need to rely upon middlemen to reach
the public is what has made the development of the Internet, with its direct communication between the creator and the public, a revolutionary
development in communications. Such ready communication also explains why the Internet so quickly attracted the attention of government
regulators. When the hurdle of publication or exhibition is cleared, however the product is not necessarily free to circulate. It may then have to survive legal examination, pressure applied by various groups, the decisions
of timid administrators, etc.

At times self-censorship is adopted to head off more disturbing alternatives. Unlike the self-censorship we all engage in, when a medium becomes
its own censor it limits the choices available to its customers. The result may
hamper creativity more than if a law were enacted, for limits are placed
upon governments that do not restrain private parties and organizations.

Today those persons and groups who seek to limit the availability of or
accessibility to certain material deny that they are acting as censors. They are
protecting children; they are seeking to create a welcoming environment in
which sensitive persons are not made uncomfortable; or they are simply opposed to using public funds to support that which offends many in society.
Such attempts to frame how their opposition is characterized are challenged by those who provide alternative frames that expose a lack of trust
in the ability of individuals to choose for themselves—the very root of the
censorial urge.

Despite excursions deeper into the past, the stories told here largely begin in the latter decades of the nineteenth century when capitalism has ac-

celerated and messages have become commodities. Censorship for reasons of religious and political orthodoxy, though hardly absent in modern times, tends to be supplanted in periods of relative calm by a search for moral orthodoxy. This search is coupled with a perceived need to protect the mentally weak, the less than well-regulated persons in the community.

Today, sex censorship, except for the proscription against obscenity that continues to limit what adults may obtain as well, is justified almost exclusively in terms of protecting children. How and why this is so and how it has reconfigured the battleground between supporters and opponents of censorship is explained in the pages that follow. No matter how different the progression to the present has been with various media, how and why this battlefield has been confined and the implications of such confinement constitute much of what is to be found here.

The pages that follow deal with both government censorship and that of industries, groups, organizations, and private individuals, all of whom seek to prevent the communication entirely, to modify it, or to restrict its availability or accessibility. Although censorship is serious business, its history is not without humor. This book is organized around popular culture and the way in which concerns about sex have led to censorship. Four chapters on books, pictorial art, movies, and music and dance are followed by a final chapter on electronic media. Each chapter traces censorship over time and is complete in itself. Although each story is different from the others because censorship has come in different ways and at different stages in the creative process, the concerns that led to censorship and the resulting battles are strikingly similar.

Books and other printed material constituted the first medium to attract the attention of censors of sexual speech in the modern age. It is the arena within which the law of obscenity would be developed. Book censorship on sexual grounds evolved from proof of obscenity by assertion and common sense to the development of a legal test that sought to protect speech about sex in American society. The censorship involved was often that of the heavy hand of government, something that bookends the treatment of censorship found in this volume. Presently censorship in this area tends to be localized and to center on what children are reading or have access to in public schools and libraries. The chapter also introduces Anthony Comstock, the intrepid censor of the late nineteenth and early twentieth century.

A move to pictorial art again encounters Comstock and his successor at the New York Society for the Suppression of Vice. The chapter considers the role of the federal government as censor both in regard to its authority over the mails and over the admittance of goods into the country. Yet many of the incidents in the chapter deal with local efforts to censor art, efforts that continue to the present. The censorship of art tends to be more local and isolated than censorship in the other areas simply because images are not generally widely reproduced. When photography was used to reproduce images of nude pictorial art, it became a target of censors. Only later was photography itself recognized as an art form.

In no medium was self-censorship institutionalized as it was in the motion picture industry. Censors were convinced that motion pictures, even before sound, constituted the greatest threat to the moral well-being of society. Beginning with the earliest and most primitive moving pictures, crusaders against the industry were active. To limit protests, local and state legislation, and threats of federal action, the industry created the Production Code. From the early 1930s until the late 1960s, its rigorous enforcement sexually sanitized American movies, creating a substantial disconnect between what viewers knew and what they saw on the screen. Not until the Production Code was scrapped and a ratings system instituted was the American cinema released from this form of bondage. The new system did not end all movie censorship, but it gave producers room to refine an art that had languished and fallen behind its European competitors.

In dealing with popular music, one deals with lyrics, which have been an ongoing target of censors. The bawdy lyrics of the colonial period have survived to this day. Only recently, however, have they been collected and published, though many a reader has probably heard them before. Present-day lyrics make the earlier earthiness look somewhat quaint. More is involved than words, for censors targeted both music and dance. Ragtime and jazz were seen as detrimental influences on the young long before rock and roll became the agency of youth rebellion. Beginning with the scandalous waltz, social dancing moved from the animal varieties of the 1920s through those that accompanied the beats of the rock-and-roll and post–rock-and-roll years.

The final chapter covers electronic media: radio, television, and the Internet. The scarcity of the bandwidth led to federal governmental regulation of both radio and television, but with the proviso that such regulation was not to become censorship. Despite this attempted bar, censorship in the area of radio and television was present from the very start. Station licenses had to be renewed periodically, and the federal agency had to make a determination as to whether the license holder was serving the public interest and not filling the airwaves with objectionable matter. Furthermore, license holders, sensitive to the need to satisfy the controlling agency, engaged in self-censorship. How else was renewal to be assured and further governmental regulation to be avoided? In regard to the Internet, the federal government has been an eager censor seeking to regulate the sexual content cyberspace makes available.

In the eighty-plus years that free expression claims have received serious judicial attention, Americans have won the right to discuss almost everything without restriction. The exception has been sex. Legal and social barriers have been lowered but never removed, as incursions into that innermost sanctum of human existence continue to meet resistance. Sexual speech may, in fact, constitute the last frontier for freedom of expression to conquer. The pages that follow show just how difficult and elusive that quest has been.

Mingo, [Trojan Horse commenting on "Clean Books" Bill]. ca. 1920s cartoon. The cartoonist presents the campaign for clean books as a stalking horse for political censorship. Picture Collection, The Branch Libraries, The New York Public Library, Astor, Lenox and Tilden Foundations

1

Books and Periodicals

Seduction by the Written Word and Maybe a Picture or Two

No argument for the suppression of "obscene" literature has ever been offered which, by unavoidable implication, will not justify, and which has not already justified, every other limitation that has ever been put upon mental freedom.[1] (Theodore Schroeder, 1911)

As long as there have been books, there have been books suppressed. . . . [S]ex censorship . . . [may well be] merely a changing form of the control of the State over opinion, a phase of its evolutionary development.[2] (Morris Ernst and William Seagle, 1929)

Censorship is to the book business, what the flea is to the dog.[3] (H. V. Kaltenborn, 1930)

I have never yet heard of a girl being ruined by reading a book.[4] (Jimmy J. Walker, 1923)

The comment that reading books did not threaten a young woman's virginity was uttered by Jimmy Walker, who, in 1923, sought to expose the hypocrisy of his colleagues in the New York legislature. He noted that those senators who supported the Clean Books Bill and who were so intent on protecting "little girls" from "salacious books" were among the chamber's "best tellers of shabby stories." He added that the present issue reminded him of Prohibition in that many legislators were inclined to "vote one way and drink another."[5]

New York City was commonly viewed as a moral cesspool, not at all representative of the other sections of the large state. The New

York legislature, sitting in Albany, was often receptive to moral crusades and often insensitive to free speech concerns. That may be why John Sumner, Anthony Comstock's successor at the New York Society for the Suppression of Vice, had such bright hopes that his recent lack of success in the courts might be reversed by the enactment of new legislation. Support seemed to be growing for the suppression of much of the new writing that challenged what many considered to be the boundaries of good taste. The postwar period had carried forward the literary experimentation that had characterized the century's early years. Clerics and other guardians of the public morality could be expected to be supportive of censorship attempts, but surprisingly many publishers, booksellers, and librarians seemed to agree.

Sumner, whose earlier idea of a book jury to clear books for publication was rejected, now eagerly supported the Clean Books League. Its guiding spirit was a New York Supreme Court judge, John Ford, who had become incensed when he found that his sixteen-year-old daughter was reading D. H. Lawrence's *Women in Love*. She had borrowed the book from a private lending library. Ford drew upon his wide-ranging contacts to put together a coalition to seek a new law that would modify the state's criminal code. The bill would have allowed prosecutors to base an indictment on an isolated passage in a book and then deny the admission of any other portion of the book into evidence. In the belief that juries were more trustworthy than judges, the bill provided for a mandatory jury trial and the barring of any expert testimony. The drafters did not want literary experts confusing the sensibilities of the average juror. Finally, the excerpt did not even have to be sexually stimulating, as long as it met the test of being "filthy" or "disgusting."

Only after the proposed legislation had been passed in the lower house by a substantial majority and was well on its way to a similar outcome in the Senate did opponents organize. With the bill posing "the most far-reaching challenge to American literary freedom in the 1920s, if not in this century,"[6] a group of publishers, authors, booksellers, and librarians mounted a challenge. A number of New York City newspapers cooperated by condemning the proposed legislation. For instance, the *New York Times* called it "the worst censorship bill that has ever been proposed."[7] Within these groups there was antagonism toward the new literature that prevented the massing of a united front against suppression, but those who challenged the bill developed arguments that slowly eroded the bill's support. The alliance that formed in opposition labeled the proposal "revolutionary," as much a kiss of death in the time period as any appellation could be. It further argued that the bill would "empower laymen, whipped and driven by fixed prejudices and opinions, to shackle knowledge at its source, in the name of social welfare, morality and religion." To those persons unimpressed by such arguments, opponents warned that, should the bill pass, the publishing industry would move to New Jersey. When John Ford, the leader of the Clean Books movement, attacked literary critics and accused publishers of seeking to protect "the dirty profits from their own filthy books," he saw his support erode further.[8] Even Sumner's gift to each committee member of a dozen sealed envelopes containing salacious passages from recent publications could not stem the tide. The bill was defeated in the Senate by a thirty-one to fifteen count.[9]

When similar bills were introduced in the 1924 and 1925 sessions of the New York legislature, not only had support dwindled but professional organizations had also seemingly resolved their internal differences. The anticensorship position had lost its radical tinge and had become the new norm. One can notice the difference even in *Publishers Weekly*, which straddled the issue in 1923 but came out strongly against subsequent bills. The same is true for the National Association of Book Publishers and the American Booksellers' Association.[10]

Since Gutenberg's invention of movable type made the printed word increasingly accessible, the printed word has been the favored target of censors. When the masses could decipher the printed word, the worry about the effect of this development grew. Concern about sex was an evolutionary development, for early censors were first concerned about religious orthodoxy and then political orthodoxy. One can see a clear evolution in focus "from heresy to treason to obscenity."[11] A religiously diverse, politically free, and individualistic society inevitably turns its attention to threats to the secular social order. Not surprisingly, many of the perceived threats were related to sex.

Of course, the most effective way to ban books was to prevent their publication in the first place. That was the purpose of the *Index Librorum Prohibitorum* (Index of Prohibited Books), first published in 1557 under the direction of Pope Paul IV.[12] It was designed to inform censors as to what could be published; printers could only offer work that had been given official approval. Such licensing laws existed in England until 1695. Their abolition was hailed as freeing speech from prior restraint. Free speech certainly did not mean freedom from punishment for subsequent publication. Book censorship by licensing was replaced by a second method in England

and the United States beginning in the eighteenth and early nineteenth centuries. It involved punishing the publication, sale, or transportation of certain books. Clearly this method did not prevent publication, but it did make it hazardous and it did send sellers and buyers underground.

In dealing with repression in American society, the tendency has been to blame the Puritans, those seventeenth-century dissenters from the Church of England who came to America to establish a New Zion.[13] To be repressive became "puritanical." To ignore the influence of the Puritans in the evolution of American society would be wrong. However, the suspicion of joy, the attack on art in its many forms, and the struggle for sexual control, associated with them, was part of the evolution of a secular society that had its counterparts in other countries as well. Yet the Puritans did contribute to a tradition of censorship in assuming that what was written and therefore read would influence the reader's conduct. The depiction was bad not in itself but rather because of its potential effect on the weak individual. Later censors often would stress the harmfulness of targeted material on the young or the weak, but at other times they seemed to believe that the material itself, independent of any readership, was harmful.

Sex censorship was first recorded in the American colonies in Massachusetts Bay in 1668. It involved a fictional journal titled *Isle of Pines*. Authorities looking for unlicensed publications found a copy in a printer's workshop, but the fine of five pounds was remitted when the printer repented. The book recounted the adventures of a shipwrecked mariner cast adrift on an island with three white women and a black female slave. His sexual prowess led to the production of 565 children, grandchildren, and great-grandchildren.[14]

The difference between targeting the publication instead of the conduct of the reader can be seen in the concern of Jonathan Edwards, a leading figure in the First Great Awakening. In the 1740s, when ministering to his flock in Northampton, Massachusetts, he became alarmed at the effect a late seventeenth-century British publication was having on some young men in the town. The book, which apparently circulated widely in colonial America, was *Aristotle's Master-piece*. It was in part a sex manual with information on the human body, both male and female. Edwards's concern was not about the book and its contents, though he did talk about it being "unclean to be read." What he centered on was the conduct of the young men who referenced the book's contents while teasing young women. Edwards held a formal church inquiry into the conduct and found the young men less than contrite.[15] This centering on conduct rather than text would change with the new century.

Despite the tendency to blame the Puritans for sexual repression in the United States and despite sumptuary laws against fornication and adultery in the colonies, the worry about sexual speech, as such, seems largely absent from colonial America. Benjamin Franklin, a founding father and the nation's first postmaster general, would have run into difficulty a century later had he put some of his writings in the mails.[16] No, the worry about sex, along with other concerns brought in the wake of a diverse mass society, seems to be a product of nineteenth-century not eighteenth-century America. Fueled by moral and religious concern, the campaign against lewd books, however, would last well into the twentieth century.

Those concerns were highlighted in the Second Great Awakening that lasted over a half century from the late 1790s until the mid–nineteenth century. Early in the nineteenth century the principal Harvard University commencement speaker warned of the "indecencies and moral dangers of novel reading." And the *Ladies' Visitor*, a Boston publication, in its first issue in 1806 promised its readers that it would not contain anything that "might cause the crimson fluid to stain the cheek of unaffected modesty."[17]

That the first obscenity trial concerning a book recorded in the United States took place in Massachusetts should occasion no surprise. The subject was the erotic classic of the previous century, *The Memoirs of a Woman of Pleasure*, commonly referred to as *Fanny Hill*. It details the sexual experiences and the observations of Fanny. In 1749, a year after the novel's publication, John Cleland, the book's author, was prosecuted and convicted for "corrupting the King's subjects" in England. The book had circulated in expurgated form in the American colonies, but only after its publication in full in 1821 did it excite censors.[18] Peter Holmes, its publisher, was tried and convicted under the common law for the corruption of youth and for offending the peace.[19] Holmes appealed the conviction, noting that the jury had not been allowed to see the book. Judge Isaac Parker of the Massachusetts Supreme Court saw no deficiency in this procedure, saying otherwise the state would "give permanency and notoriety to indecency."[20]

The earliest instance of an attempt to censor a work that would become a permanent part of the American literary canon involved Nathaniel Hawthorne's *The Scarlet Letter* published in 1850. Literary critics praised the work, but clergymen and religious publications considered it "a dirty story" belonging only in a brothel's library. Hester Prynne, the female character who had a child as a result of her affair with the minister, Dimmesdale, simply did not suffer enough. Much later the book would be seen as unfit for assignment to high school students, but the immediate effect of the local outrage was Hawthorne's decision to move his family from Salem to a house in the Berkshire Mountains.[21]

The Scarlet Letter continued to circulate, which was not true of Walt Whitman's *Leaves of Grass*, a collection of poetry that he self-published in 1855.

The following stanza reveals some of the sensuality and earthiness that led some critics to find the collection obscene and immoral:

> Copulation is no more rank to me than death is.
> I believe in the flesh and the appetites,
> Seeing hearing and feeling are miracles, and
> each part of me is a miracle.

One bookseller refused to distribute the book, and when Whitman did find an outlet, sales were weak, and booksellers, worried about prosecution, eventually returned the copies to the author. The president of Yale University found the poems akin to "walking naked through the streets." The book was unavailable in New York and Philadelphia bookstores, and Boston took legal action against it. Only one library, the Library Company of Philadelphia, purchased a copy; all others refused. When in 1865 Whitman's supervisor at the Department of the Interior discovered that his employee had written "an indecent book," the poet was fired. Ralph Waldo Emerson praised the work, but then suggested that the poet agree to an expurgated edition. Whitman refused even with the lure of increased sales, saying that he considered expurgated volumes the really "dirty" books. He only relented shortly before his death in 1892.[22]

Whitman's resistance to expurgation introduces a form of censorship that has disappeared in recent times but was quite common from the early nineteenth century until well into the twentieth. In fact, Thomas and Harriet Bowdler's attempt to rid William Shakespeare's works of indecency gave the process a new name—to bowdlerize. Some favorite English subjects, in addition to Shakespeare, were the Bible, and the works of Geoffrey Chaucer and Jonathan Swift. The early target in the United States was the dictionary. American publishers distinguished their dictionaries from English ones, because the latter often "lacked delicacy and chastity of language" and contained words "highly offensive to the modest ear."[23] Eventually American bowdlerizers would tackle the classic English and European authors, but an American target was Benjamin Franklin. Some of his essays, such as "Advice to a Young Man on the Choice of a Mistress" in which he suggests that a young man choose an older, and therefore grateful, woman, were simply not republished until the twentieth century. But his *Autobiography*, probably because of its moral lessons, was used in schools and was usually expurgated. One episode in which Franklin makes a rejected overture to the mistress of a friend is treated differently by the expurgators. Some leave it out entirely; others make attempts to sanitize it.[24] Often bowdlerizers did not acknowledge what they had done. At other times blank spaces were left where words or phrases were excised.

The absence of statutory law to punish obscenity was gradually remedied as Vermont led the way in 1821. Over the next century all the states, except for New Mexico, enacted obscenity laws. Congress entered the picture in 1842 to ban the entry of obscene pictorial art into the country. In 1873 an 1865 law regulating the mailing of obscene materials was strengthened and became known as the Comstock Act. The new legislation was attributed to Anthony Comstock, the purity crusader. As an agent for the YMCA, he had come to Washington armed with examples of obscene material to convince legislators of the need for toughening the law. The new statute also added obscene printed matter to the list of what the Customs Service was now to bar from entry into the country.[25] With strong laws now in place, there was a concerted campaign against the printed word. Comstock was especially active as an unpaid enforcer of the postal censorship act.

Some members of Congress had indicated concern that postmasters and customs officials would become censors, but the fact that the 1873 act was passed in the wake of the Crédit Mobilier scandal tended to make the people's representatives eager to jump aboard a moral crusade. Whether Congress ever intended to authorize censorship by customs officers and postmasters is not clear. Offensive material could be seized in conjunction with a criminal indictment, but could government officials simply bar such material from entry or circulation? In 1890, Attorney General Charles J. Bonaparte gave his blessing to the local practice, thus giving official sanction to government censorship. Although such seizures could be challenged, the cost tended to be prohibitive. Even when the claimant could afford the challenge, the courts were little inclined to overrule the judgment of the government official.[26] The decisions then of local censors around the country and at ports of entry most often concluded the matter.

Although obscene material was now barred from entering the country and from the mails, there was one remaining loophole to be closed—internal circulation by means other than the United States mail. The loophole was closed in 1897 when Congress criminalized the action of depositing "any obscene, lewd, or lascivious book, pamphlet, picture, paper, letter, writing, print or other matter of indecent character" with an express company or other common carrier for transport to another state or territory. Birth control and abortion material was likewise proscribed.[27]

One effect of the tariff law, as with all tariffs, is to spawn a domestic industry, and apparently that was true of the ban on indecent and obscene materials. Critics differ on who wrote the first American pornographic novel but all agree that the industry was well underway by the mid–nineteenth century. These early ventures were sexually explicit in the *Fanny Hill* sense. Large, milky breasts were fondled, and penises were at the ready. These books circulated quite widely but underground.[28]

Booksellers caught by Comstock and his ilk often accepted the confiscation of their material and even incarceration, perhaps acknowledging that the books they peddled exceeded the moral boundaries of the Victorian age.

Titles such as *The Lascivious London Beauty, Love on the Sly*, or *Peep behind the Curtains of a Female Seminary* might not lead one to challenge their assessment. After arresting a number of booksellers in 1872, Comstock decided to go to the root of the problem, the publishers of such titles.[29]

Before the 1840s pornography was imported, but in 1846 an Irishman, William Haines, began publishing in New York. By 1871 he is reputed to have made available 320 different works, with a single title selling as many as one hundred thousand copies. Eager buyers had made his business quite lucrative.[30] He was one of four publishers that Comstock targeted. When warned that the purity crusader was determined to end his lucrative business, Haines apparently committed suicide. Comstock was able to seize the offending books and the plates for new titles. Financed by Morris K. Jessup, president of the YMCA, the purity crusader paid Haines's widow the sum of $450 to compensate her, in part, for the loss. Two of the remaining publishers were also pursued successfully by Comstock, one turning over his stock to the purity crusader and the other fleeing south. Their deaths shortly thereafter were included in the accomplishments the crusader proudly tallied for the press.[31]

Sporadic prosecutions earlier in the century involved attempts to communicate information about birth control or other sexual information. For instance, Dr. Charles Knowland was fined in one town in Massachusetts and imprisoned in another for publishing *Fruits of Philosophy: An Essay on Population* in which he wrote about the physiology of sex and birth control.[32] Such books would continue to attract the censor. For instance, Comstock targeted a number of sex manuals. He kept up a running battle with Margaret Sanger and her husband and their attempts to publicize birth control methods. He also sent Ida Craddock to an early grave when she could not face another term in jail for selling her advice to newlyweds, titled *The Wedding Night*. Comstock and other censors made no distinction between books designed to inform readers about sex and books designed to stir their lustful urges. Neither was there any immunity for the classics nor for what critics called literature. *The Lustful Turk, The Decameron*, and Walt Whitman's *Leaves of Grass* were all equally objectionable.[33] Near the end of his forty-year-plus reign of censorship, Comstock took credit for destroying "160 tons of obscene literature."[34]

By the end of the nineteenth century worries about assimilating the new immigrants from Southern and Eastern Europe fed the censorial urge. At the same time, the content of the American novel was taking on some of the European coloring that had made Emile Zola, Gustave Flaubert, and other writers so objectionable to American censors. Comstock, for instance, said much of this writing was "little better than histories of brothels and prostitutes, in these lust-cursed nations." The result, he continued, was to sow "the seeds of lust" by putting "vile thoughts and suggestions into the minds of the young."[35]

Although the post–Civil War period saw purity crusaders increasingly turn to the law to aid them in their efforts, censors operated from publishers' offices without any help from outsiders. These internal censors either refused to accept manuscripts that challenged the moral status quo or required deletions of offensive material. Critics worried whether this type of censorship would cut off the flow of ideas and stifle creativity. At times a moral ending in which sinners suffered for their sins made an otherwise objectionable narrative acceptable, but far too often the presence of an erotic passage or two was enough to damn the entire work. Not until the genteel tradition was challenged by naturalistic writers, such as Stephen Crane, Theodore Dreiser, and Frank Norris, however, did book censorship become a major problem. Stephen Crane had to bear the cost of publishing *Maggie: A Girl of the Streets*, a novel dealing with a prostitute. Only after *The Red Badge of Courage* gained literary attention did the earlier work find a publisher and then only after some offensive prose was deleted.[36]

From that early prosecution involving *Fanny Hill* in 1821 the intervening seventy-plus years is devoid of cases involving works of fiction. Things would change, in part based upon what was going on in the former mother country. Lord Campell's Act of 1857, one of a number of antiobscenity measures passed by Parliament, set the stage for an important decision that would have profound ramifications across the Atlantic. The case involved the seizure of copies of a pamphlet by Henry Scott, a Protestant author, titled *The Confessional Unmasked: Shewing the Depravity of the Roman Priesthood, the Iniquity of the Confessional and the Questions Put to Females in Confession*. Scott appealed the seizure to the recorder of London, Henry Hicklin, who would give his name to the case. The recorder decided in favor of the author on the basis that he did not intend to corrupt public morals, but Hicklin's decision was overruled by Chief Justice Alexander Cockburn. He etched into law the following rule: "The test of obscenity is whether the tendency of the matter charged as obscenity is to deprave and corrupt those whose minds are open to such immoral influences and into whose hands a publication of this sort may fall." Any vagueness in the so-called Hicklin test tended to be resolved in the United States by using the most susceptible individual as the guide.[37]

Although prosecutions increased in the 1890s, the subjects of attack involved either erotic classics or books by contemporary European authors. Classics, such as *The Decameron* had long been available, but the worry was that such books were now more generally available. Also, as the censors looked at the material, it still had more sexual content than did most contemporary fiction. In fact, this content, to Victorian era censors, was precisely what distinguished the refinement of the present age from the crudity of the distant past. Their regard as classics did not deter the purity crusaders, but the fact that they had stood the test of time would eventually become a factor that judges considered as they determined whether a book was obscene.

For instance, an 1894 case brought before the court the question of whether some of these erotic classics, including *The Decameron, The Heptameron, The Arabian Nights, Tom Jones,* and Rabelais's *Gargantua and Pantagruel* could be sold for the benefit of creditors. Judge Morgan J. O'Brien did more than favor the creditors. He said that "to condemn a standard literary work, because of a few of its episodes, would compel the exclusion from circulation of a very large proportion of the works of fiction of the most famous writers of the English language." O'Brien essentially ignored the Hicklin rule, which not only judged what harm the work could do to the most susceptible reader, but also was interpreted to allow selected passages to meet the test of obscenity. Although the judge anticipated a future rule that would be slow in gaining acceptance, he also said that such "rare and costly books" would neither fall into the hands of children nor "be bought nor appreciated by the class of people from whom unclean publications ought to be withheld."[38]

A subsequent New York case, again in an unusual posture for an obscenity determination, involved a man who had contracted to purchase a forty-two-volume set of Voltaire's works for two hundred dollars. He sought to renege on the purchase on the basis that, since two of the volumes were immoral, the contract was illegal. A trial court agreed with him, but the case was reversed on appeal. Judge Samuel Seabury for the Supreme Court of New York ruled that the ban on "the sale of immoral publications cannot be invoked against those works which have been generally recognized as literary classics."[39] Apparently the judge was assuming that an eighteenth-century work published in the twentieth century had met the standard for literature. The Voltaire works claimed to be immoral were the *Philosophical Dictionary* and *The Maid of Orleans.* In the latter work, King Charles seeks a virgin to save France, despite the fact that he is told there are no virgins in France. Judge Seabury said that immorality should be judged by contemporary standards that ordinary people, not experts, could easily determine. Apparently the time contemporary writing took to become literature was relatively short, for the judge christened Whitman's *Leaves of Grass* a literary classic, despite its troubles with censors.

Censorship of the written word was the arena in which courts would be asked to clarify what was obscene and what was required to adequately inform a defendant of the crime for which he was charged. The United States Supreme Court, which had given its blessing to federal postal censorship,[40] was asked in 1896 to determine what fell within its parameters. In a 5 to 4 decision, the majority agreed that an article in a Kansas newspaper was "exceedingly coarse and vulgar, and . . . plainly libelous." However, the justices continued, they could not find within the piece "anything of a lewd, lascivious, and obscene tendency, calculated to corrupt and debauch the mind and morals of those into whose hands it might fall." Although these words indicated that the Court had accepted the Hicklin rule for determining obscenity, they also narrowed the scope of the legislation. Although it would take the Court many years to attempt a definition of obscenity, here it extracted the term from the murkiness that had defined its earlier existence. Henceforth, obscenity would be limited to sexual expression designed "to corrupt and debauch the mind and morals of those into hands it might fall.[41]

However, in the same term of Court the justices approved two practices that were regularly attacked by defendants in obscenity cases. The first involved the claim that a defendant was denied his constitutional right to be informed of the charges against him because the indictment did not contain the specific material alleged to be obscene. The majority of the justices approved the practice of not defiling the public record with such material and said that the defendant was sufficiently informed of the charge against him. Finally, the Court dismissed the claim that the defendant had been entrapped because the offending paper was put in the mails in response to a decoy letter. The justices said that precedent had determined that such a fact did not make a violator of the law any less guilty. So, although the High Court would not expand the range of what was obscene to include nonsexual material, it tended to allow room for prosecutors to follow practices that seemed less than fair. In fact in the latter case, two justices dissented on grounds that the defendant's right to be informed of the charge against him had, in fact, been violated.[42]

Censors did not ignore the classics as the nineteenth century became the twentieth in part because of such decisions. For instance, as late as 1930, the Customs Service was still banning works such as Aristophanes's *Lysistrata*, Honoré de Balzac's *Droll Stories*, and some of Daniel Defoe's novels. However, as judges coped with the cases, they expressed the belief that the survival of the works indicated that they possessed some social value.[43]

New material on the horizon seemed to provide an easier target, as contemporary authors sought to test the limits of the permissible. These new works that invited obscenity prosecutions in the twenty-five years before the First World War strike the modern reader as a rather strange lot, hardly at all sexually explicit. The sexual revolution was a rather mild one and still partially wrapped up in worries about attacks on the institution of marriage and on religion. Furthermore, publishers were still the most active censors, standing at the gates and imposing their Victorian views on authors.

The resort to law, however, would prove to be a double-edged sword, as seen in these early obscenity cases. Although some judges would do the censor's bidding, others had ideas of their own that challenged common prosecutorial assumptions. In fact, the American law of obscenity, the foundation of which was laid by the Hicklin case, would largely evolve as courts struggled with obscenity prosecutions concerning the written word. Comstock, for instance, was unconcerned about the literary reputation of a work as a factor in determining whether a work was obscene or not, a determination the purity crusader said the average person was qualified to make. Some judges were unsure.

For instance, when a Philadelphia vendor was arrested for selling Leo Tolstoy's *Kreutzer Sonata*, the judge was unimpressed by the fact that the book had been censored by both the czar of Russia and the United States Post Office. Judge Martin R. Thayer responded that "neither . . . has ever been recognized in this country as a binding authority in questions of either law or literature." By painting "lewdness and immorality in the most revolting colors," the judge said, Tolstoy intended to encourage chastity.[44] Although Thayer found the work devoid of interest and literary merit, he concluded, it was not obscene.

Comstock, himself, was involved in the second of these prosecutions, based upon his purchase of a copy of Gabriele d'Annunzio's *Triumph of Death*. Both the clerk who sold the purity crusader the copy and the clerk's father, the owner of the shop, were defendants in the New York City case. Academics and literary critics were prepared to defend the work, but the court ruled that such testimony was inadmissible. The three judges for the Court of Special Sessions, however, did consider more than the special passages that had been marked for their inspection. On that basis, the judges found the defendants not guilty. An irate Comstock accused the court of overruling precedent in the area by not limiting their inspection to the selected passages.[45] He took his campaign against the book to New Jersey where he hoped to find a more acquiescent court. As with many of Comstock's later battles, the result was not legal success but rather financial success for the author of the book. As the *New York Times* put it, "Until that illustrious maker of reputations took the matter in hand the Italian's books were a drug in the market."[46]

Although New York tribunals were growing suspicious of these obscenity prosecutions,[47] Boston censors seemed to find more accommodating judges. The Watch and Ward Society, which Comstock had helped found as the New England Society for the Suppression of Vice, had successfully banned Elinor Glyn's *Three Weeks*. Its New York publisher sought to test the ban by supporting the sale of the book to a member of the Boston Police Department. In the resulting indictment, the grand jury concluded that some of the offending language was too "improper to be placed upon the court records." Despite the author's discretion in dealing with adultery and in limiting physical contact to kissing, the seller was found guilty.[48] In rejecting the appeal, the unanimous appellate court said: "An author who has disclosed so much of the details of the way to the adulterous bed" cannot complain when a jury finds that he has appealed more to the reader's animal, rather than spiritual, instincts.[49]

The appeal had been taken to challenge the trial judge's instructions on the meaning of obscenity and the relevance of the intentions of the author. Dismissing the argument that obscenity and impurity are legal terms, the court said that they are common words that can be easily understood by people on a jury. Furthermore, the court ruled that the purpose of the author in writing the book, a factor that had saved other works from being banned, was irrelevant. If the work gave rise to impure thoughts it could be censored.[50] This 1909 opinion would serve censors well, but being banned in Boston would become somewhat of a badge of honor.

Today Glyn's work would be classified as a romance novel, quite different from the other prewar novels that led to obscenity prosecutions. Those novels were part of a literary movement, at times called naturalism, which portrayed characters, usually drawn from the lower rungs of society, meeting new circumstances and responding in unconventional ways. The result was an encounter with themes that themselves caused concern among the literary traditionalists. They were being challenged by authors writing realistically about the world about them—a world that included prostitutes, mistresses, and adulterers. Simply writing about such persons alarmed censors, for the errant characters were not presented as admirable people. Most often they suffered and were morally condemned. Passion and sexual longing were recognized and implied, but description was not explicit. For instance, the following passage is as risqué as any found in the novels that got the attention of censors prior to World War I: "[S]he, utterly helpless in his grasp, intoxicated by the cataclysmic enormity of her first real entrance into the secrets of sexual passion, clung to him, returning throb for throb, pulsation for pulsation; while through the light fabric of her thin silk skirts she could feel the warmth of his body penetrate into her own."[51]

Daniel Carson Goodman's *Hagar Revelly*, the novel that contained these words, was the first American work of fiction to be subjected to an obscenity prosecution, and it was also a special target of the aging Anthony Comstock. This relative absence of prosecutions was partially the result of publishers asking authors to eliminate certain passages in their submitted manuscripts. Still, what found its way into print disturbed the custodians of the public morality, perhaps feeling that if what circulated was not challenged then authors and publishers would simply go further.

Goodman's novel was sent by mail to a buyer. The sender was tried for the offense, but the trial jury found the defendant not guilty. What was more significant was the opinion by Judge Learned Hand. Although he said that the Hicklin test meant that the prosecution could proceed, he suggested that the test might be outmoded. Its compatibility with "mid-Victorian morals," he said, "does not seem to me to answer to the understanding or morality of the present time, as conveyed by the words, 'obscene, lewd, or lascivious.'" He would use obscene "to indicate the present critical point in the compromise between candor and shame" in the community of today. In other words, the judgment as to what is obscene must be made in terms of contemporary community standards. The judge could not believe that his fellow Americans would support treating sex in terms suitable for "a child's library." He added that a sense of shame should not be interposed to prevent an "adequate portrayal of some of the most serious and beautiful sides of human nature."[52]

Goodman might not make his way into college courses on American literature, but censorship was not reserved for the less worthy. Theodore Dreiser's *Sister Carrie* was accepted, and then rejected, by Doubleday. In 1900 when Dreiser insisted that his contract be honored, Doubleday printed one thousand copies but then refused to distribute them. Such problems indicated how substantially the crusade against offensive literature had permeated the American psyche. Books that later generations would praise were condemned simply because of their topics and censored at various points in the publishing process. Book censorship in the late Victorian period was really quite extensive, considering "the sum total of countless small decisions by editors, publishers, booksellers, librarians, critics, and—occasionally—vice societies, all based on a common conception of literary propriety."[53]

Dreiser had been affected by the episode and for a while ceased to write. A decade would pass before he published another novel, and then he ran into new difficulties with his work, especially *The "Genius."* The novels that immediately preceded it, *The Financier* and *The Titan*, were only published after pages of "woman's stuff" were eliminated. *The "Genius"* was published in 1915 and had sold about eight thousand copies before it came to the attention of John Sumner, Comstock's successor at the Society for the Suppression of Vice. What bothered him about Dreiser's novel was its central character's obsession with sex and his values—values that challenged traditional morality. Yet, the language was suggestive, not explicit. Citing seventy-five lewd passages, Sumner convinced the new publisher, John Lane Company, to recall the remaining copies of the novel. Dreiser obtained the printing plates to assure that they would not be destroyed and then sued his publisher for a breach of contract. The suit dragged on and was finally dismissed in 1918 on the grounds that there was no case or controversy in that no formal charge of obscenity had ever been brought against the book.[54]

What was significant, however, is that, despite the lack of support Dreiser received from his publisher, he amassed considerable encouragement from others. This was the beginning of a movement that would pay considerable dividends in the future. As long as authors were dependent on publishers who refused to support them and as long as the literary community saw no common interest in fighting censorship, the censors won. Now, under the leadership of that iconoclast, H. L. Mencken, the literary community was energized and mobilized behind Dreiser. Five hundred signatories protested such censorship, including traditionalists, such as Robert Frost and Willa Cather. Still, almost another decade would pass before Dreiser published a new novel, and *The "Genius"* was not reprinted until 1923.[55]

American entry into the Great War seemed to strengthen the moral fervor of the censors. The world was to be made safe for democracy and the nation would be purged of immorality. Men in uniform would be protected from both the evils of alcohol and prostitution. "Refreshed by the spiritual exaltation of the war, exempt for the moment from legal criticism, and instructed by the official coercion which had silenced dissent and controlled public behavior . . . , the vice societies" saw Utopia just around the corner. However, what was just around the corner was a massive assault on the traditional values upon which their Utopia had been built, an assault that was mirrored in the vital literature of the postwar period.[56]

The censor's faith would be sorely tested. In 1918 John Sumner purchased a copy of Théophile Gautier's *Mademoiselle de Maupin* from a bookstore clerk, Raymond D. Halsey. The novel, first published in France in the 1830s, was a broad, scandalous attack on middle-class sexual morality. When Halsey was acquitted of the charge of selling an obscene book, he sued the New York Society for the Suppression of Vice for malicious prosecution. All three courts considering the case decided in favor of Halsey, ruling in effect that the society had no reasonable grounds for believing that the book was obscene. Judge William S. Andrews for the majority of the New York Court of Appeals said that the book must be considered as a whole, not on the basis of a few paragraphs. He called attention to the danger "of a censorship entrusted to men of one profession, of like education and similar surroundings." That is why, he said, that a jury composed of people of different means was better equipped to determine "the currents of public feeling."[57] Halsey was awarded the sum of twenty-five hundred dollars in one of the many setbacks the society would face in the postwar years.[58]

Such setbacks, however, did not deter crusaders who desperately tried to capture their lost world by launching an intense book censorship campaign. Support in the broader community for vice society activity was waning, as was the willingness of publishers to heed the censor's call and condemn new and daring authors. Authors, such as Meneken, Sherwood Anderson, Floyd Dell, F. Scott Fitzgerald, Sinclair Lewis, and John Dos Passos, "were engaged in a massive assault upon the comfortable assumptions with which most Americans had grown up." One literary critic referred to this literary outpouring as a "literature of disillusion."[59] When the old publishing houses were not receptive to this literature, new publishers were. The new work was largely devoid of "joy and adventure, wholesome physique and sane mentality, clear vision and buoyancy, genial criticism, and whimsical humor," characteristics that Sumner prescribed for literature.[60] As had his predecessor, Sumner lumped together these new authors and their mainstream publishers with pornographers. For those censors who sought to suppress such work, the above ground circulation of sexual matter was probably more to be condemned than that of less literary merit that circulated underground.

Despite an outpouring of naturalistic literature, Sumner's first obscenity prosecution involved a prominent American author working in a different genre. James Branch Cabell with his *Jurgen: A Comedy of Justice* eschewed realism for fantasy. The title character was a pawnbroker-poet searching for perfection in a series of romantic adventures with mostly mythical women. Book sales were modest until one critic pointed out the double entendres and not-so-hidden sexual content of the novel.[61] In one instance, a bride is dressed in a tunic with "twenty-two openings, so as to admit all imaginable caresses."[62] Cabell's use of a magic sword as a phallic symbol is illustrated in the following exchange between Jurgen and one of the queens he encounters on his quest:

> "It is undoubtedly a very large sword," said she: "oh, a magnificent sword, as I can perceive even in the dark. . . . There is something in what you advance."
>
> "There is a great deal in what I advance. I can assure you. It is the most natural and most penetrating kind of logic: and I wish merely to discharge a duty."
>
> "But you upset me, with that big sword of yours, you make me nervous, and I cannot argue so long as you are flourishing it about. Come now, put up your sword! Oh, what is anybody to do with you! Here is the sheath for your sword," says she.[63]

What had been published had been toned down, but Guy Holt, Cabell's editor, was still worried. The author simply assumed that readers would not understand the book's "phallic hints and references." In fact, Cabell thought some day he might provide a concordance to decipher the "many private jests" his writings contained.[64] The review that brought *Jurgen* to Sumner's attention appeared in early January 1920. With a warrant on January 14, agents for the New York Society for the Suppression of Vice seized the plates, copies, and sheets of the book from the publisher's offices. The publisher and editor were charged with publishing and distributing a "lewd, lascivious and indecent book" in violation of New York law.[65] The defendants pled not guilty and requested a jury trial.

After copies of the book had been seized and the editor and publisher indicted, an Emergency Committee was formed to protest the action. Those who signed the protest constituted a who's who of American letters. Over one hundred notables signed the protest without any reservations, and another sixty, most of whom had not read the book, agreed in principle with the protest. One of the unequivocal supporters was Theodore Dreiser, who offered to contribute one hundred dollars if others would join him in providing a defense fund to be used by writers and publishers who fell into the net of the censors.[66]

The trial did not get underway until October 1922. After three days, the judge directed the jury to find the defendants not guilty. Since the indictment had listed the pages of *Jurgen* that contained the offending material, the brief submitted by the defendants' lawyer took each instance and explained why the material could not be considered obscene.[67] In a brief opinion, Judge Charles C. Nott conceded that "certain passages therein may be considered suggestive in a veiled and subtle way of immorality," but he added that "these suggestions are free from the evils accompanying suggestiveness in more realistic works." His conclusion was that the book "is one of unusual literary merit" and contains nothing that would meet the requirements of the state obscenity statute.[68]

John Sumner and the New York Society for the Suppression of Vice did have one success in prosecuting the *Little Review* for publishing an erotic excerpt from James Joyce's *Ulysses*. Other attempts to prosecute new publishers, such as Thomas Seltzer and Horace Liveright, for their publications led to judicial rebukes. For instance, Magistrate George W. Simpson in considering some Seltzer publications praised them for the contribution they made to contemporary literature and said "that the policy of pouncing upon books too frank for contemporary taste . . . is objectionable and should be curbed." And Magistrate Charles A. Oberwager in exonerating Liveright, concluded that no individual nor no organization should be endowed with "general powers of censorship over literary works."[69] Seltzer's prosecution led him to summon support from a press that was beginning to ask whether selected passages should be used to prove obscenity charges; whether expert testimony was relevant; and whether a book should be banned because of its potential effect on the most susceptible of readers.

Despite Sumner's lack of success in the courts, the society's campaign against books still engendered considerable respect. Publisher Alfred A. Knopf often capitulated when threatened by Sumner. For instance, when Knopf published *Janet Marsh* by Floyd Dell, with its frank depiction of free love and abortion, Sumner got the publisher to withdraw the book.[70] The literary community was still split about the new literature, as were the publishers. For instance, only seven of the thirty publishers asked to sign the *Jurgen* protest did. The critic of all he surveyed, H. L. Mencken, often presented as the arch foe of all censorship, said that publishers who risked prosecution for their publications were "simply silly." Furthermore, in one of the stranger episodes of 1920s, we find Mencken, at the request of Theodore Dreiser, sitting down with Sumner to expurgate *The "Genius."* After weeks, negotiations ended when Liveright agreed to publish an expurgated edition.[71]

Sumner's first attempt to tap such support was his book jury plan in which citizen panels would pass on the suitability of manuscripts for publication. Lack of support caused the vice crusader to try another approach. If the New York legislature could be persuaded to strengthen state law, results in the courts could be expected to be more favorable. Sumner could not have foreseen how this campaign would backfire with the formulation of what had been absent earlier—"an articulate anticensorship coalition."[72]

That coalition would defeat "the most sustained and formidable attempt in the 1920s to convert the obscenity law into a fool-proof instrument for the emasculation of serious literary expression." It would also survive so vigorously that even the most conservative literary critics could no longer express sympathy for any legal suppression. By the end of the decade, authors, publishers, booksellers, librarians, and their professional organizations left behind their earlier differences and were now committed to fighting censorship. The vice societies were on the defensive, successful only in attacking underground pornographic books, such as *Fanny Hill* and Frank Harris's *My Life and Loves*. In desperation, Sumner substituted fear for his earlier rationale of community well-being to justify his continued campaign.[73]

One renegade bookseller, Bernard Guilbert Guerney, was not impressed as he, in an issue of his tabloid, printed a cartoon of the vice crusader with the identifying line "John S. Smutrat: Vicesnoopia Filtheatia." Sumner responded by trying to get an indictment of the bookseller for criminal libel, but the grand jury refused. Guerney countered by suing Sumner for inciting the distributor of the tabloid to break his contract. When *Publishers Weekly* reported the affair, Guerney took the opportunity to criticize his colleagues, referring to "this flea-circus of a trade." He added: "[I]f booksellers would show a little 'guts' when harassed by purity racketeers, instead of rolling over with their paws in the air and their tails dutifully tucked between their legs, the fight against censorship might really make headway."[74]

Sumner would have been well-advised to stick to the pornography that was being pumped out during this interwar period. One critic, however, paid tribute to these publishers of erotica because they "helped liberate the popular imagination and furthered democratic principles of freedom of speech and action. Hard driving entrepreneurs, these bookmen and bookwomen catered to American needs in a society where sexual repression and prurience were commonplace." In fact, he argued, censors needed pornographers. "[T]he blunt fact of their existence provided antivice crusaders with the public enemy they needed to show how fascination with sex was indeed a moral offense exploited by people with contempt for purity." And, of course, the pornographers needed the censors to advertise the work to potential consumers, making the relationship a symbiotic one.[75]

The attack on censorship of literary work spread to Boston, where the Watch and Ward Society had effectively determined what books would be made available. The dominant ethnic group, the Irish Catholics, and the old Yankee families agreed that this new literature from the New York publishing houses posed a threat to the moral values of the city's population. In 1915 a Boston Bookseller's Committee was established with three booksellers and three members of the Watch and Ward Society to review current novels. If the book passed this scrutiny, it could be sold with impunity; if not, its sale made the seller vulnerable to a Watch and Ward prosecution. Boston's newspapers neither advertised nor reviewed condemned titles. The editor of the *Harvard Crimson* expressed his frustration with the "constant repression of creative work."[76]

This repressive system was given national attention by articles in Mencken's *American Mercury* in 1925. The society sought to retaliate, but its attempts to prove that an issue contained an obscene article failed. When Mencken sought to obtain an injunction preventing the society from interfering with the magazine's distribution, he was successful. Judge James M. Morton found the coercive tactics used by the Watch and Ward Society illegal and denied that it could impose its views on others by threats of prosecution. The whole affair was well publicized and the authority of the society was weakened.[77]

Four years later the society was dealt an even more severe blow. In October John S. Sumner alerted the Watch and Ward Society to the purchase of five copies of D. H. Lawrence's *Lady Chatterley's Lover* by Cambridge bookseller James A. DeLacey, a former Yale librarian, who had Harvard University's students and faculty among his clientele. After arranging for the purchase of the book, the society initiated legal proceedings against DeLacey and his clerk. Despite strong support from the Harvard contingent, the convictions were upheld by the appellate court. DeLacey was devastated by the experience, and he lost both the bookstore and his wife. The aftermath for the society, however, was no better, for, as a result of the episode, it lost much of its financial support.[78]

However, the society was far from alone in its desire to protect the morals of the people of the Bay State. In 1927 a district attorney told booksellers that they could be prosecuted for selling Sinclair Lewis's *Elmer Gantry* and Dreiser's *An American Tragedy*. This time even the Watch and Ward Society joined the city's press in condemning the district attorney. Alfred Harcourt, the publisher of Lewis's book, decided against a test case, but Horace Liveright was ready to fight. One of the publisher's cohorts was arrested after he sold a copy of *An American Tragedy* to a police lieutenant. The judge paid no attention to Dreiser's literary reputation nor to the fact that the book was assigned reading at Harvard. Despite the unfavorable press Boston was receiving, the jury found the seller guilty. The state supreme court upheld the conviction.[79]

By the time of the appeal in April 1929, much had happened and an attempt to reform Massachusetts law on obscenity was making real headway.

Anticensorship advocates realized that the problem was a broad-reaching, indiscriminate censorship law. It condemned any publication "manifestly tending to corrupt the morals of youth," or "containing obscene, indecent, or impure language." Although reformers were unable to change the portion of the law protecting the morals of youth, they did purge the law of the impure language provision.[80]

New York and Massachusetts were major battlegrounds on which censors and their opponents clashed in the 1920s, but book censorship was also a matter of federal law. Obscene books had been made nonimportable by changes in the tariff law in 1873, and until 1930, local customs inspectors generally made binding decisions. They, as well as postal inspectors, were aided in 1928 when the Customs Service and Post Office Department agreed on a list of seven hundred books that were both nonimportable and nonmailable. On that list were both classics and the work of contemporary writers, such as James Joyce, D. H. Lawrence, and George Moore.

When the tariff law came up for reconsideration in 1929, a proposal was introduced in the United States Senate to widen the ban on nonimportable material.[81] Senator Bronson M. Cutting from New Mexico took exception not only to the proposed modification but also generally to the prohibition on obscene publications. Cutting abhorred government interference with the arts and saw no justification for governmental officials protecting people from themselves. His impassioned speech led the Senate to drop obscene books from the banned list.[82] Eventually guardians of morality and patriotism counterattacked and the Senate voted to retain the prohibition. However, important changes were made in the provisions that became part of the Hawley-Smoot Tariff of 1930. Books were to be judged as a whole and for their effect on the average person. Also the secretary of the treasury was given discretionary authority to admit materials judged obscene if they were "so-called classics or books of recognized and established literary or scientific merit . . . when imported for noncommercial purposes."[83] Seized books were to be brought to a federal district court by a U.S. attorney to get a judicial determination on the claim of obscenity, and importers were given the right to a jury trial.[84]

As Senator Cutting focused attention on the censorial power of customs inspectors, a particular decision by postal inspectors brought their largely unchecked power to public attention in 1929 as well. In the previous decade, Mary Ware Dennett had written a pamphlet entitled *The Sex Side of Life—An Explanation for Young People*, initially for the edification of her two sons. It was graphic in its descriptions of the sex organs and their functions, and it presented sexual intercourse as pleasurable and masturbation as undesirable but not harmful. The pamphlet was originally published in a medical journal and then widely circulated by the YMCA. As early as 1922, the Post Office Department judged it to be nonmailable, but Dennett continued to send it as sealed first-class matter. After responding to a decoy request, she was charged with mailing obscene material. In April 1929, when Dennett was found guilty by a jury and fined three hundred dollars, there was a public outcry.[85]

Contrasting censorship of *An American Tragedy*, which had been found to be obscene in a Boston trial, with *The Sex Side of Life*, the *New Republic* said the latter suppression constitutes a "frightful injury not only to a principle, but to the children of the nation and to society itself." The journal not only paid lip service to Dennett's work but also published a segment of it.[86] The American Civil Liberties Union (ACLU), which had been more concerned with the suppression of political speech, now agreed. The organization set up a "National Mary Ware Dennett Defense Committee" to support an appeal of her conviction.[87]

In March 1930 Judge Augustus N. Hand in federal district court overturned the conviction. To meet the statutory test that the pamphlet be "obscene, lewd, or lascivious," he began, it must "tend to deprave the morals of those into whose hands the publication might fall by suggesting lewd thoughts and exciting sensual desires." Hand found no precedent for holding obscene "a truthful exposition of the sex side of life," concluding that the trial judge should have so ruled. He added that Dennett's treatment "tends to rationalize and dignify such emotions rather than to arouse lust. . . . It also may reasonably be thought that accurate information, rather than mystery and curiosity, is better in the long run and is less likely to occasion lascivious thoughts than ignorance and anxiety."[88]

Success in the Dennett case led the ACLU to create a National Council on Freedom from Censorship. The council mounted an attack on postal censorship with the support of Senator Cutting, who introduced a bill that, among other provisions, would have made the new customs law changes binding upon the Post Office Department as well. However, with the mounting depression plus the upcoming 1932 election the bill never made it out of committee.[89]

Meanwhile, the United States Supreme Court was considering whether Minnesota could stop the publication of a scandal sheet by declaring the newspaper to be a public nuisance. Obviously states had considerable power to classify threats to the public safety as nuisances, but could a state stop a publisher from printing by simply declaring that what he printed was a nuisance. Jay M. Near published the *Saturday Press* and nine issues were cited as "malicious, scandalous and defamatory." His targets included public officials, the city's two major papers, and the Jewish race. The prosecutor asked the court to order Near not to publish any future issues. Having previously ruled that the First Amendment's protection of free speech and free press binds the states, the Court found the Minnesota law in violation of Near's rights. Near certainly could be held responsible for what he published, but to stop him from publishing was just the type of restraint that the guarantee of a free press had been designed to prevent.[90] Attempts are made in the future to use nuisance laws to restrict the availability of sexual materials, and although this 1931 case does not conclusively decide that issue, it does indicate that attempts to muzzle speech in such a manner tend to be viewed with considerable suspicion by the courts.

Anticensorship groups had been making considerable progress. Operating under the law's new classics exemption in 1931, the Customs Service removed a number of books from the nonimportable list, including *The Arabian Nights*, Boccaccio's *The Decameron*, Casanova's *Memoirs*, and Rabelais's *Gargantua*.[91] In the Southern District of New York, Judge John M. Woolsey responded favorably to challenges mounted against the actions of the Customs Service. The new tariff provisions of 1930 provided for proceedings to be instituted against the books themselves. Two such cases in 1931, dealing with books written by Dr. Marie C. Stopes, *Married Love* and *Contraception*, came before Judge Woolsey. Although he rejected the claim that the new provision in the tariff law violated the First Amendment's protection of the press, he found neither book obscene nor immoral. Characterizing the first book as "a considered attempt to explain to married people how their mutual sex life may be made happier," Woolsey said, "instead of being inhospitably received, it should . . . be welcomed within our borders."[92] In the second case, although he acknowledged that many persons oppose birth control, he found nothing in the book that would "stir the sex impulses of any person with a normal mind." Instead, he said, "the sufferings of married women due to ignorance of its teaching," can only arouse "feelings of sympathy and pity."[93]

The new customs law was also tested in a case involving a modern work of fiction that was steadily gaining a reputation in literary circles—James Joyce's *Ulysses*. One of the new publishers, Random House, headed by Bennett Cerf, had obtained the rights to publish the work. To clear it of obscenity charges, Cerf arranged to have a copy of the work imported. When it was seized by customs officials, Morris Ernst, the foremost attorney in the censorship field, represented Random House. He took the opportunity of his friendship with Judge Woolsey, to supplement the judge's reading of the book with helpful explanations of the prose, the technique, and with book censorship generally.[94]

In a well-crafted and sensitive opinion, Woolsey cleared the book of obscenity charges. Considering the work in its entirety, he found nowhere "the leer of the sensualist," and concluded that it was not pornographic. As to the many "dirty words" it contained, Woolsey said they are familiar Anglo-Saxon words that "would be naturally and habitually used" by the people Joyce is describing. To widen the consideration beyond himself he asked two "literary assessors" whether lustful thoughts arose as a result of their reading the book. Their negative response bolstered his conclusion that the book did not meet the obscenity test, for "nowhere does it tend to be an aphrodisiac."[95] The opinion was widely circulated, as Cerf included it in the Random House publication of *Ulysses*.

On appeal, the Second Circuit Court of Appeals in a 2 to 1 decision reached the same conclusion Woolsey had, and in the process discarded the old Hicklin rule. For the majority, Judge Learned Hand posed the crucial question as "whether such a book of artistic merit and scientific insight should be regarded as 'obscene.'" That determination he said must be made on the dominant effect of the work as a whole. The objectionable parts, which he admitted were "coarse, blasphemous and obscene," were clearly relevant to the theme. Contrary to other judges who ruled that the critical reputation of a work was irrelevant, Hand gave that factor considerable weight. In dissent, Judge Martin T. Manton, who believed fiction should "cheer, console, purify, or ennoble the life of people," saw no reason to abandon the Hicklin test.[96]

Hand's ruling received considerable attention, and although its principles of decision were anticipated earlier, their reiteration and consolidation here was significant. Two years later the same circuit court, in a case involving postal censorship of books without the literary significance of *Ulysses*, censured the trial judge for adhering to the Hicklin standard and for refusing to allow reviews of the works into evidence. Judge Hand, again writing the opinion, said a new trial was necessary because the trial judge had invaded the jury's province.[97]

In 1934 as a further indication that the heavy hand of censorship had been lifted, the secretary of the treasury hired Huntington Cairns to determine the fate of challenged books. Cairns was a lawyer who had opposed censorship and was respected by civil libertarians. By 1935 the head of the ACLU, Roger Baldwin, was delighted with the relaxed policy on imported books that Cairns had instituted. Despite its failure to change the law on postal censorship, the ACLU also noted a "far more liberal attitude in the Post Office Department."[98]

Writing was on its way to being liberated from moral censorship. The judiciary deserves some of the credit, but the simple fact was that the nineteenth-century belief "that writing wields immediate force upon its reader" did not survive. The new battleground again became the earliest one, for the first human "pornographers did not write, they drew pictures." Pictures in a multitude of varieties would assume "the quasi-magical aura" with which words had been invested.[99]

This new liberalism, however, did not extend to works of fiction that dealt with homosexuality. For instance, *The Young and Evil*, by Charles Henri Ford and Parker Tyler, a fictional treatment of homosexual life during the Depression in Greenwich Village, New York, could not find an American publisher.[100] Only forty-two years later was it published in the United States by Arno Press as part of a series of books dealing with gays.

Homosexuality was kept undercover, but increasingly magazines dealing with sexual themes proliferated. In 1879 Congress provided a special mailing rate for magazines "originated and published for the dissemination of information of a public character, or devoted to literature, the sciences, arts, or some special industry."[101] This special rate coupled with the economy new technology provided saw magazine production proliferate. Magazines, such as the *Police Gazette* and *Munsey's* regularly ran pictures of women in tights, swimsuits, or in outfits with décolletage. Other magazines followed, and by 1915 "cheesecake" was added to the American lexicon. It referred to pictures of partially clad women, found in various places, including "girlie magazines."[102]

Newsstands in the 1920s were filled with magazines that "trafficked heavily in borderline obscenity, pornographic and quasi-pornographic fiction, and photographs of nude and seminude females."[103] Periodically, such vendors became targets in clean-up campaigns in various cities and states throughout the 1920s and 1930s. For instance, in the mid-1920s Chicago, Omaha, Washington, and Kansas took action against such titles as *Artists and Models*, *Hot Dog*, and *Snappy Stories*. In the 1930s, New York City police warned vendors that selling such periodicals endangered their licenses and ordered them not to display some fifty-nine periodicals. One publisher was fined and sentenced to three months in jail for shipping such titles across state lines. The Post Office Department warned publishers that their second-class mailing privileges were in danger, and Congress held hearings on pornography in magazines, comics, and paperbacks. Such censorship activity had little effect on the availability of such products, for the demand remained and filling it was not expensive.[104]

Although cheap girlie magazines with photographs of near-naked women on pulp paper were abundant in the 1930s, Arnold Gingrich felt that the time was right for a classy men's magazine. The first issue of *Esquire*, dated October 1933, was priced at fifty cents and printed on oversized glossy paper with about a third of its pages in color. It was the first mainstream publication to advocate a shameless sexuality. Seeking to appeal to the urban middle-class male, the first issue was a great success. Articles on men's fashion and fiction by authors, such as Ernest Hemingway and John Dos Passos, were grouped with George Petty's creation, the Petty Girl, who appeared in sexually tinged cartoons. Here was a high-class pinup that the magazine celebrated with the following paean: "Every hour she is different. Her demands, her form, the movements of her rippling limbs, the spasmodic play of her wayward moods, give an infinite variety to her sparkling beauty. When you tire of her, you tire of life." By the end of 1941 the Petty Girl was displaced by the Varga Girl, the creation of artist

Alberto Vargas. Vargas's renditions became the quintessential pinups of World War II.[105]

Challenges to the legitimacy of postal and customs censorship were mounted from the very beginning, but the United States Supreme Court did not give such claims much of a hearing before World War II. When it began to inspect the decisions made by postal authorities, however, the Court increasingly overrode their decisions. Postmasters sought to purify the mails of obscene material using three approaches: the denial of second-class mailing privileges; the purging of such materials from the mails; and the prosecution of those individuals who sought to distribute nonmailable materials.[106]

In 1943 Postmaster General Frank C. Walker sought to use the first of these tools against *Esquire*. He contended that some of its jokes, cartoons, pictures, and articles were "morally improper" and had "dangerous tendencies and malignant qualities."[107] Varga Girls constituted almost a quarter of the ninety items cited by the postmaster general.[108] He conceded that the content was not obscene and therefore the magazine could be mailed. However, since he found the content "indecent, vulgar and risqué," he argued that *Esquire* had not met its "positive duty to contribute to the public good and the public welfare."[109] With this argument, Walker sought to deny the magazine's second-class mailing privileges, which, if the denial stood, would have delivered a deathblow to the periodical.

A little over two years later, the United States Supreme Court unanimously repudiated Walker's view. From an inspection of the items brought to the Court's attention, Justice William O. Douglas, for the Court, concluded that Congress had not given the postmaster general the power "to prescribe standards for the literature or the art which a mailable periodical disseminates." To uphold the order to revoke the second-class mailing rate, Douglas continued, would "grant the Postmaster General a power of censorship. Such a power is so abhorrent to our traditions that a purpose to grant it should not easily be inferred."[110]

As the courts were easing censorship restraints in the United States, authoritarian governments in Europe were administering blows to literary freedom.[111] When the United States joined the war against the Axis powers, anticensorship advocates worried whether a heightened moral concern that inevitably came with wartime conditions would lead to further censorship. After all, the first postal censorship law came as a result of the Civil War, and the World War I period and its immediate aftermath saw a demand for conformity that stifled free expression. But the attempt in World War II to distinguish a democratic United States from its totalitarian foes generally kept down an insistence on consensus at any cost.

During World War II, William Arnold, a Roman Catholic, was the head chaplain, and he kept meticulous records on the moral depravity of the

nation's fighting men, in part revealed by their chosen reading material. His complaints were usually ignored, but chaplains were recruited by the National Organization for Decent Literature to oversee the magazines available on base newsstands. On the hit list were titles such as *True Love, Modern Romance, Breezy Stories,* and *Scarlet Confessions.*[112]

World War II had just ended with the Japanese surrender in the Pacific when the high court in Massachusetts issued its opinion that *Strange Fruit* by Lillian Smith was an obscene book. The depressing story of an interracial love affair that ends tragically was generally well received by literary critics. However, the Massachusetts court counted at least four scenes of sexual intercourse and found objectionable material on about every fifth page. The governing statute proscribed work that "manifestly tends to corrupt the morals of youth," and the majority had no difficulty finding that *Strange Fruit* did just that. A dissenting judge concluded that youthful readers would not be attracted to the book were it not for the publicity that the censors had given it.[113]

The next target in the Bay State became the very popular *Forever Amber* by Kathleen Windsor, a book the critics hated but the public loved. Set in seventeenth-century England, it told of the sexual adventures of Amber. It depicted a totally amoral society, but the sexual liaisons were described in general terms. Massachusetts had passed a new law allowing civil actions to be initiated by the attorney general against a book on obscenity grounds. If the trial court decided there were grounds to make such a finding, anyone wishing to dispute such a finding could appear within thirty days. Also the new law provided for the admission of testimony regarding the literary merits of the book. Apparently the literary expert provided by Macmillan, the publisher, had some effect, as the court mentioned the book's historical accuracy as an important factor in making its decision. It also cited the absence of realistic detail in the book's sexual descriptions as contributing to its finding that the book was not obscene.[114]

Some observers read too much into the Amber decision, for the Massachusetts high court had not been converted to a more permissive attitude toward literature that dealt with sexual matters. That observation was confirmed when a court confronted Erskine Caldwell's *God's Little Acre* in the same type of civil action. This comic novel set in rural Georgia dealt with the sexual affairs of the Walden family. Earlier John Sumner and the New York Society for the Suppression of Vice had targeted the book. In New York a magistrate concluded the state law was aimed at pornography, which he defined as work "where all other incidents and qualities are mere accessories to the primary purpose of stimulating immoral thoughts." Acknowledging the support Caldwell's work had received from literary critics, the magistrate condemned Sumner's attempt to dismiss such evidence:

This court cannot subscribe to Mr. Sumner's opinion of the capacity for fair judgment of these leaders of American literary and educational thought. . . . The court is of the opinion . . . that this group of people, collectively, has a better capacity to judge of the value of a literary production, than one who is more apt to search for obscene passages in a book than to regard the book as a whole.[115]

Also, a Pennsylvania court had included Caldwell's book with other challenged mainstream publications and ruled that the books were not obscene. Although the Massachusetts high court noted these decisions, it then dismissed them as irrelevant. A court that had found no realistic detail regarding sexual affairs in *Forever Amber* now found it in abundance in Caldwell's work, saying that at times the author was producing "outright pornography." Differing with the trial judge who relied heavily on the literary critics, the appellate court said that art and sincerity could not immunize obscenity.[116]

The Pennsylvania case that the Massachusetts court cited was decided a little over a year earlier. In addition to the Caldwell volume, it involved James T. Farrell's *Studs Lonigan Trilogy* and *A World I Never Made*, William Faulkner's *Sanctuary*, Calder Willingham's *End as a Man*, and Harold Robbins's *Never Love a Stranger*. Judge Curtis Bok in dismissing the indictments wrote extensively because of his belief that this was the first case in Pennsylvania dealing with contemporary literature and the state penal code. Saying that the novels were attempts to "show life as it is," he said "frank disclosure cannot legally be censored." He continued: "I believe that the consensus of preference today is for disclosure and not stealth, for frankness and not hypocrisy, and for public and not secret distribution. That in itself is a moral code." To the question of would he expose his three daughters to such writing, he responded that he would prefer that they "meet the facts of life and the literature of the world in my library than behind a neighbor's barn." Recognizing that the state was not ready "to discard censorship altogether," Bok would find a book in violation of the law only when a clear causal connection could be established between the book and criminal behavior and when the proof of this connection was established "beyond a reasonable doubt." What the judge was doing was taking First Amendment law as it had been established by the United States Supreme Court, strengthening its clear and present danger test, and then applying it to the area of obscenity.[117] He left little room for obscenity prosecutions, but he was only one state judge.

Meanwhile, despite the rebuff the Post Office Department received in the *Esquire* case, it received new authority in its campaign against obscenity. The postmaster general was given authority in 1950 to return mail to the sender when convinced that the firm that sent the mail was distributing obscene materials. This new law supplemented an earlier one that allowed such action only when the firm used a fictitious name. In 1955 phonograph records were included in the category of nonmailable material, the prohibition now reading: "Every obscene, lewd, lascivious, indecent, filthy or vile article, matter, thing, device, or substance." Then, the following year, the postal service was afforded the power to impound offending mail. Finally, in 1958 Congress acceded to the desire of postal authorities to allow the trial of offenders in places where the material was received not simply in the jurisdiction from which it had been sent. This change in the law gave the department the opportunity to choose more sympathetic venues in which to bring suit.[118] Postmaster General Arthur E. Summerfield, who served during the administration of President Dwight Eisenhower, was determined to rid the mails of obscenity. He zealously pursued sexual material, especially photographs, but lower federal courts were generally not sympathetic to his initiative.[119]

When the postwar period saw women's breasts and bottoms regularly pictured in various media, the sexual content of magazines began to change. The content of the prewar years had been rather traditional and uncomplicated. Now, however, magazines with titles such as *Wink, Keyhole,* and *Picture Fun* began to explore sex in its myriad varieties. The bosomy nude was still there, but now there was sadism, masochism, fetishism, and other so-called perversions.[120] In this atmosphere, Hugh Hefner, who worked on *Esquire* in its early years, felt that the time was right to launch a new men's magazine. It was grounded in heterosexual sex and despite its breaking new ground with nudity, it was clearly in the old *Esquire* tradition. Hefner got Alberto Vargas to strip away more clothing from the Varga Girl. A nude centerfold was the magazine's contribution to the evolution of the pinup, the one in the first issue being the famous nude calendar photo of Marilyn Monroe.[121] From Monroe forward these nude centerfolds destroyed the ban on nudity in the mails. Religious and civic groups targeted *Playboy* and the imitators it spawned by seeking to rid the newsstands of all such magazines. Such efforts to censor the magazine through pressure on retailers would continue into the future.[122] In 1955 the Post Office Department, on the basis of three issues, sought to deny *Playboy* second-class mailing privileges. It was no more successful than it had been with *Esquire* earlier, as a court overturned the denial.[123]

Rebuffed on the second-class mailing privilege issue, the department tried to ban the November 1958 issue from the mails. It contained semi-nude photographs of the French actress, Brigitte Bardot. They were stills from her movie, *And God Created Woman,* which opened with the camera lingering on the naked backside of Bardot. The district court judge responded by issuing a restraining order forbidding postal officials from taking any such action for five days and requiring them to distribute the magazine as second-class matter. A panel from the federal appeals court rejected staying the order, which meant that the issue would be distributed and the case rendered moot. The failure to provide *Playboy* with a hearing on the finding of obscenity had defeated this attempt to censor.[124]

That the United States Supreme Court would have to confront obscenity prosecutions seemed inevitable in the post–World War II period. The Court as constructed by Franklin D. Roosevelt had gone out of the business of protecting the property right and taken up the task of assessing governmental action, at both the state and federal level, against claims that it invaded personal liberty. Doubleday and Company was convicted under New York's obscenity law for distributing Edmund Wilson's *Memoirs of Hecate County*. The Court divided evenly, four to four, meaning then that the conviction would stand.[125]

Still, the Court's new willingness to hear challenges to state censorship boded well for those who sought a federal constitutional hearing on book banning.[126] First the Court took on the question of whether a state could use children as the basis for determining whether a book could be sold. As it reversed the conviction of a bookseller, the Court said "to reduce the adult population of Michigan to reading only what is fit for children," is akin to burning "the house to roast the pig."[127] The old Hicklin standard, the Court ruled, was just not compatible with the United States Constitution.

Four months later in 1957, the Court was ready to tackle the remaining issues dealing with obscenity prosecutions. Pennsylvania's Judge Bok's view that obscenity should only be proscribed when it resulted in criminal conduct was supported by Judge Jerome Frank on the Second Circuit Court of Appeals, who had heard one of the cases the Supreme Court was now considering. In an extensive appendix to his concurring opinion, Frank argued that the federal postal law under which the defendant had been convicted was constitutionally suspect given the decisions of the Supreme Court on the First Amendment over the past twenty-five years. The problem with obscenity law, Frank said, was that no evidence exists to tie obscenity publications to the type of antisocial conduct that deprives an adult individual of First Amendment protection. Secondly, Frank continued, under the statute, "punishment is apparently inflicted for provoking, in such adults, undesirable sexual thoughts, feelings, or desires—not overt dangerous or antisocial conduct, either actual or probable."[128]

Most Court observers were well aware that, after stirring up the nation with the school desegregation decisions in 1954 and 1955, the justices were not about to give irate segregationists a new opportunity to gain converts in their campaign against the Court. In companion cases dealing with the federal postal law, *Roth v. United States*, and a California law against obscenity, *Alberts v. California*, the Court upheld both obscenity laws. To rule obscenity nonspeech, as the Court did, when it bore all the characteristics of speech, posed a problem. By declaring purveyors of obscenity outside the protection of the First Amendment, the Court was forced, for the first time to define obscenity. Dissenters William O. Douglas and Hugo Black had no such problem since they believed that all obscenity statutes violated the First Amendment's free speech and free press guarantees. John Marshall Harlan would have upheld the state prosecution but reversed the federal one on grounds that the federal government had no authority in the area. Chief Justice Earl Warren was worried about sweeping language in the Court's opinion that might interfere with speech that should be protected. He would limit the reach of the decision to the defendants here, who, he said, "were plainly engaged in the commercial exploitation of the morbid and shameful craving for materials with prurient effect."[129]

The five-person majority in an opinion written by Justice William J. Brennan, Jr. said that "sex and obscenity are not synonymous," and that the "portrayal of sex . . . in art, literature and scientific works, is not itself sufficient reason to deny material the constitutional protection." The justice paid tribute to the freedoms of speech and press, saying that they "have contributed greatly to the development and well-being of our free society and are indispensable to its continued growth." Their protection, he continued, should not be eroded either at the state or federal levels. Rejecting the Hicklin test as unconstitutionally restrictive, Brennan then formulated the modern test as follows: "whether to the average person, applying contemporary community standards, the dominant theme of the material taken as a whole appeals to the prurient interest."[130]

In suppressing obscene literature, the Court majority accommodated the community interest, noting that all states had laws addressing the matter, but the dissenting duo of Justices Douglas and Black were incensed that the morals of a majority should override First Amendment rights. Douglas said that the "legality of a publication in this country should never be allowed to turn either on the purity of thought which it instills in the mind of the reader or on the degree to which it offends the community conscience. By either test the role of the censor is exalted, and society's values in literary freedom are sacrificed." Concluding that the majority had established a new standard— appealing to a prurient interest—Douglas found it deficient. It "does not require any nexus between the literature which is prohibited and action which the legislature can regulate or prohibit."[131] Judges Bok and Frank had won two converts, but the odds were stacked against them.

Although the Court left room for the prosecution of obscenity after *Roth*, it indicated that its new interest in the area would require both the states and the federal government to adhere to the new constitutional standard.[132] In subsequent terms it reversed lower court obscenity convictions by simply referring to *Roth*, and in 1959 the Court ruled that California could not convict a bookseller for having obscene material in his stock without proving that he had knowledge of that fact.[133]

One type of distinction that was relatively common at the time was between hardbacks and paperbacks, the idea being that relatively cheap paperbacks got into the hands of children and others who were not mature enough to deal with sexually oriented material. Rhode Island sought to endow nine appointed citizens with the task of protecting the morality of youth by educating the public and recommending the prosecution of those persons violating the state's obscenity law. The commission the nine citizens formed notified a state wholesaler, Max Silverstein, that some of the paperbacks he was distributing, including Grace Metalious's 1956 bestseller, *Peyton Place*, had been placed on its "objectionable" list. The list was to be forwarded to local police for possible prosecution. Silverstein received thirty-five such notices, and to avoid trouble he decided not to distribute the books. Then the publishers brought suit, and although they lost in the Rhode Island courts, the United States Supreme Court by an 8 to 1 count agreed with them and declared the law establishing the commission unconstitutional. Justice Brennan, for the Court, ruled that the commissioners operated "a scheme of state censorship effectuated by extralegal sanctions; they acted as an agency not to advise but to suppress" and without the normal protections of the criminal processes.[134]

With the Court delimiting what material could be found obscene, Grove Press decided that the time was ripe for an unexpurgated edition of D. H. Lawrence's *Lady Chatterley's Lover*. Since its first appearance in the 1920s, it had been acclaimed as a masterpiece, though few readers had the opportunity to read the book as Lawrence wrote it. When it had been published, it was expurgated, and even in that form it was often subjected to prosecution. It detailed with precision the unlikely but intense sexual relationship between Lady Chatterley and the estate's gamekeeper, Mellors. The following passage is illustrative:

> "Th'art good cunt, though, aren't ter? Best bit o'cunt left on earth. When ter likes! When tha'rt willin'!"
> "What is cunt?" she asked.
> "An' doesn't ter know? Cunt! It's thee down theer; an' what I get when I'm i'side thee; it's a' as it is, all on't."
> "All on't," she teased. "Cunt! It's like fuck then."
> "Nay, nay! Fuck's only what you do. Animals fuck. But, cunt's a lot more than that. It's thee, dost see: an' tha'rt a lot besides an animal, aren't ter? even ter fuck! Cunt! Eh, that's the beauty o' thee, lass."[135]

Grove Press not only made the book available but sent out advertisements for it through the mails. When the postmaster general ruled that neither the book nor the advertisements could pass through the mails, Grove Press challenged the order. It sought an injunction against enforcement of the order and a ruling that the book was not obscene.[136] Judge Frederick Van Pelt

Bryan acknowledged the literary reputation of Lawrence and compared his task with that of Judge Woolsey in the *Ulysses* case. He came to the same conclusion, saying that the postmaster general's action was "contrary to law and clearly erroneous." Neither the four letter words, nor the fact that sex was a major theme, Bryan continued, made the book obscene. As to community standards, he said, the book "does not exceed the outer limits of the tolerance which the community as a whole gives to writing about sex and sex relations." To illustrate how far the judiciary had come since its ready dismissal of expert opinion and assessments of literary reputation, the judge concluded: "A work of literature published and distributed through normal channels by a reputable publisher stands on quite a different footing from hard core pornography furtively sold for the purpose of profiting by the titillation of the dirty minded."[137] Judge Bryan's ruling was appealed. With no more regard for the postmaster general's taste than that shown by the trial court, the Second Circuit Court of Appeals responded with a resounding NO to the question it saw the case posing: "[S]hould a mature and sophisticated reading public be kept in blinders because a government official thinks reading certain works of power and literary value is not good for it?"[138]

Grove followed up its success by publishing Henry Miller's *The Tropic of Cancer* in 1961. The postmaster general again banned the book from the mails, but before a court challenge could be instituted, he lifted the ban.[139] Grove Press had agreed to defend booksellers against possible suits, and there were more than sixty cases in twenty-one states.[140] In 1964 the United States Supreme Court in a per curiam decision reversed a Florida conviction and in effect brought the cases against the book to a halt.[141] When Grove Press published Miller's *The Tropic of Capricorn* in 1962, it encountered no legal problems at either the state or federal level.[142]

Depictions of seminaked and naked females had a substantial history and even social acceptance,[143] but depictions of the naked male form, except for classical sculpture, generally lacked both. Such magazines were generally seen as catering to homosexual males. Was the U.S. Supreme Court's definition of obscenity broad enough to cover such magazines? The justices answered that question in 1962 when it reviewed a postal order that *MANual*, *Trim*, and *Grecian Guild Pictorial* were obscene and therefore nonmailable. Although the seven-person Court could not agree on a majority opinion, six of the justices voted to reverse the Post Office Department's finding.[144]

Apparently the worry about nudity in the mails still had not dissipated, for when the June 1963 issue of *Playboy* contained eight pages of nude photos of the blond actress, Jane Mansfield, in boudoir and bath, postal authorities took notice. What apparently had caught their attention were the photos in which a fully dressed man sat on the edge of the bed as Mansfield was writhing and gyrating in an attempt to distract the man from his reading. Heffner insisted upon a jury trial. In this first and only attempt to find *Playboy* obscene, the Post Office lost. The jury, composed of eleven women and one man, divided 7 to 5 against the prosecution. The government did not retry the case.[145]

In the same year it made *The Tropic of Cancer* available, Grove Press published William Burroughs's *Naked Lunch*. The book was attacked in Los Angeles and Boston for its forthright depiction of sexual orgies and its scatological language. It was cleared of obscenity charges in Los Angeles, but not by the trial court in Massachusetts. On appeal, however, after important United States Supreme Court rulings in 1966, the Massachusetts high court found that the book had some redeeming social importance; the absence of any such value was now a part of the constitutional test for obscenity.[146]

In cases since *Roth*, the Court refined the definition of obscenity. In 1959 it said that material could not be characterized as obscene simply because it dealt with sex.[147] The prurient interest part of the test was modified in 1962 to require that the appeal be "patently offensive."[148] Finally, two years later the Court ruled that the material had to be "utterly" devoid of social importance."[149] Brennan wanted this determination made according to national standards, but whether he commanded a majority for that view was unclear. The redeeming social importance prong of the test was at the heart of the Court's opinion in a case that had come from Massachusetts. It involved the book that first gave rise to an obscenity prosecution in the United States—John Cleland's *Memoirs of a Woman of Pleasure* or *Fanny Hill*. Grove Press had emboldened old-line publishers to become more adventurous, and G. P. Putnam's Sons responded by bringing out the Cleland book. Unlike other work that had considerable literary support, *Fanny Hill* was always thought to be the exemplar of what was obscene. Its author had no literary reputation and its erotic scenes constituted the book's core. In New York it was eventually cleared of obscenity charges by the state's highest court, but not in New Jersey and Massachusetts.[150] An amicus brief filed in the case argued that finding *Fanny Hill* to be protected speech would further close "the gap on the community of 'Sodom and Gomorrah.'"[151]

Agreeing to hear the Massachusetts case, the Supreme Court decided six to three to reverse the decision though only two others joined Justice Brennan in his opinion announcing the judgment of the Court. Justices Black and Douglas added concurring opinions reiterating their position that obscenity laws were totally inconsistent with the free speech and free press guarantees of the First Amendment. Justice Stewart simply said that *Fanny Hill* was not "hard-core pornography." Despite the lack of a Court opinion, Brennan's insistence that a book must be "*utterly* without redeeming social value" to be declared obscene became a part of the new definition of obscenity.[152]

On the same opinion day, the Court upheld the conviction of Ralph Ginzburg for violating the postal obscenity law. He had sent through the mail three separate publications: *Eros*, a high-priced, hard-backed quarterly exploring "the joy of love;" *Liason*, a biweekly newsletter devoted to sexual matters; and *The Housewife's Handbook on Selective Promiscuity*, a woman's account of her sexual adventures. Unlike the trial court, the justices did not find any of the items obscene, but the majority upheld the conviction on the basis that Ginzburg had advertised them in such a manner as to appeal to his customers' prurient interest. For the first time, the Court held that how material was advertised and disseminated were relevant considerations in establishing a violation of the obscenity law. To illustrate how the publisher pandered to the prurient interest, the Court noted his attempt to mail the items from Intercourse, Pennsylvania.[153] How much this new wrinkle in obscenity law would intrude upon its growing liberalization was unclear at the time.

Two years later the Court seemed to answer the question as it accommodated New York in upholding a law that sought to prohibit selling material that was "harmful to minors" to those persons under the age of seventeen. What was harmful was defined as follows: material "patently offensive to prevailing standards in the adult community as a whole with respect to what is suitable material for minors."[154] Despite, then, no finding of obscenity in the "girlie" magazines involved in the case, the Court upheld the conviction of Sam Ginsberg, the seller. As long as states stuck to the formula approved in this case, the Court nodded its approval. Also the decision gave the states room to restrict the display of nonobscene magazines and books on grounds that the protection of children justified such action. The result, of course, was to make such material less accessible to the adults who did not want to visit back rooms or ask for a key to open a locked display. When booksellers challenged such laws, they did have some success in narrowing the material that could be judged "harmful to minors."[155]

What was clear was that, despite the Ginzburg and Ginsberg decisions, sexually explicit materials continued to gain greater public visibility. The judicial response to the type of pulp fiction that had long circulated underground is illustrative. From 1957 to mid-1964, obscenity convictions involving such material were appealed nine times, and in no case was the determination reversed. Things would change, however, after the United States Supreme Court decided in favor of *The Tropic of Cancer*. For instance, Illinois's high court reversed a bookstore owner's convictions for selling titles, such as *Campus Mistress* and *Born to be Made*, saying they were no worse than *The Tropic of Cancer*, nor were they devoid of any redeeming social importance. In subsequent cases, the court cleared titles such as *Instant Love, Love Hostess*, and *The Sex Addicts*. It drew the line, however, on *Lust Campus, Passion Bride*, and *Crossroads of Lust*, which involved cunnilingus, flagellation, lesbian intercourse, rape, and varieties of sadism and masochism. The Second Circuit Court of Appeals agreed with the Illinois high court in overturning a conviction based on a publisher selling titles such as *Men in the Ladies Room* and *Girls Concentration Camp Ordeals*. The court said that, were the publisher to go to jail for such publications, he might well be horrified to find *Fanny Hill* or *The Tropic of Cancer* in the prison library.[156]

As the lower courts realized the need to separate obscenity, which was not protected, from speech, which was protected, required drawing a line. This task proved to be quite difficult indeed. To avoid limiting speech, the chaff would have to be admitted with the wheat. The United States Supreme Court agreed, for in 1967 it concluded in a per curiam opinion that the pulp novels and magazines involved in three combined cases from three states were not obscene. The New York case, *Redrup v. New York*, under which the combined decision was announced, involved two pulp novels, *Lust Pool* and *Shame Agent*.[157] In the same year the Court reversed eleven convictions of sellers of pulp novels dealing with sex by citing *Redrup*, a practice it would follow into the 1970s.[158]

With sexually explicit material circulating freely, Congress took a different approach to regulation by giving postal recipients new authority to cleanse their mailboxes of sexually oriented mail. Under what was referred to as the Pandering Act, a section of the Postal Revenue and Federal Salary Act of 1967, a patron could fill out a form at the local post office claiming that a specific company's mail was "erotically arousing or sexually provocative." Postal authorities would then notify the offending firm that it could not send mail to that party. In the other piece of legislation, referred to as the Goldwater Amendment to the Postal Reorganization Act, mail recipients could fill out another form indicating that they did not wish to receive sexually oriented mail from any party. The postal service then would notify all companies known to send such mail of the existence of the list containing the names of such patrons, which it then required the companies to purchase. Henceforth, the companies were precluded from sending any mail to the objecting parties, regardless of its content.[159] Both provisions were upheld against free speech claims by courts in 1970 and 1971, the former by the United States Supreme Court. Chief Justice Warren Burger, for the unanimous Court, rejected the claim, ruling that "a mailer's right to communicate must stop at the mailbox of an unreceptive addressee."[160]

Whether the decisions resulted from agreement with social conservatives or worry about personal liability, some printers have refused to print copy submitted to them. In 1973 a Minnesota printing establishment refused to print two pictures included in the June edition of *Folio*, a trade magazine for the publishing industry. Both were taken from *Playboy*. The edition appeared with two blank pages carrying the following explanation: "Unfortunately, the printer of *Folio*—the Brown Company—has refused to print this illustration." One picture was described as a "nude scene," and the other as an "orgy scene."[161] When the editor of the *Art Journal* decided to do an issue on censorship and include controversial photographs by Robert Mapplethorpe, he found the journal's regular printer unwilling to print the photos. Another printer was found and the issue with Mapplethorpe's photos reached the public.[162]

Convinced that women were not really informed about their own bodies, the Boston Women's Health Collective in 1971 published a 112-page newsprint book for thirty-five cents. Its popularity led both to further editions and increasing controversy. In 1977 Phyllis Schlafly and her Eagle Forum, noting the growing availability of the book, sought to ban the book, saying that it encouraged everything from masturbation to premarital sex to lesbianism. They had success with school libraries in Helena, Montana, when the district attorney threatened librarians with charges of contributing to the delinquency of minors. Jerry Falwell, televangelist and founder of the Moral Majority, joined the campaign when he sent out a fund-raising letter in 1981 printing excerpts from the book and calling upon recipients to demand the removal of the book from classrooms and libraries.[163]

Worries about sexual permissiveness moved beyond single titles. In fact, one critic noted that best-seller lists were filled with books "that once . . . would have put their publishers in jail." To counter this development, Charles H. Keating Jr., an attorney in Cincinnati, founded Citizens for Decent Literature, whose membership grew in three hundred chapters throughout the nation.[164]

The Court seemed to respond to complaints about the widespread circulation of sexually charged material in American society. By a 5 to 4 count the justices in *Miller v. California* in 1973 reaffirmed that obscenity was beyond the pale of First Amendment protection. In the Court opinion, Chief Justice Warren Burger replaced the "utterly without redeeming social value" requirement with "whether the work, taken as a whole, lacks serious literary, artistic, political, or scientific value." Marvin Miller had sent out a mass mailing advertising four books, among which was one titled *Sex Orgies Illustrated*, and a video. Justice Douglas protested that the majority was allowing Miller's conviction to stand under new standards that "until today's decision were never the part of any law."[165] Also, the majority agreed that the community standards used could now be those of the local community, rather than those of the national one. On the same decision day, the same majority concluded that the proprietor of the Peek-a-Boo Bookstore could be found guilty of selling an obscene book. The title of the pulp book was *Suite 69* and according to the Court it was composed "entirely of repetitive descriptions of physical, sexual conduct, 'clinically' explicit and offensive to the point of being nauseous."[166]

Chief Justice Burger in another decision reached the same day gave the Court's blessing to those groups in American society who were protesting the new sexual permissiveness. He held "that there are legitimate state interests at stake in stemming the tide of commercialized obscenity," and its purveyors could not hide behind the absence of empirical data "that would conclusively demonstrate that exposure to obscene material adversely affects men and women or their society." Nor, Burger ruled, does the right of privacy immunize consenting adults from state regulation.[167]

Justice Brennan, who authored the opinion in *Roth* that placed obscenity beyond the pail of First Amendment protection, now dissented. Justices Potter Stewart and Thurgood Marshall joined him. The time has come, Brennan said, to recognize that the Court's attempt to distinguish protected sexual speech from obscenity has failed. Rather than accept the substantial damage to protected rights that the majority opinion encouraged, he would instead rule that "in the absence of distribution to juveniles or obtrusive exposure to unconsenting adults," both state and federal governments are prohibited from suppressing "sexually oriented materials on the basis of their allegedly 'obscene' contents."[168] Justice Douglas added his own dissent, reiterating the position he had first taken in *Roth*.

Four members of the Supreme Court were committed to doing away with obscenity as a special and unprotected category of speech, but that would be the largest minority the Court could assemble. New appointments to the Court were in the offing, and the new members, drawn from an increasingly conservative society disturbed by the widespread circulation of sexually explicit material, were not inclined to follow in the footsteps of Douglas, who would leave the bench in 1975. The circulation of such materials expanded and became a leading target in the subsequent cultural wars. A federal pornography study in 1970 had called for an end to censorship, but a new study in 1986 called for new legislation, convinced that danger lurked in the circulation of such material.

Prior to issuing its report, the commission sent letters to retailers who sold erotic magazines, such as *Playboy* and *Penthouse*, saying that they had been named as purveyors of pornography and would be so cited in the forthcoming report unless they changed their ways. Although a federal court would later require the commission to send letters retracting the threat, some retailers, such as 7-Eleven and Rite-Aid stores, discontinued the sale of such magazines.[169]

Clearly, the desire to censor had not ebbed. In fact, the administration of Ronald Reagan had called for the second study and was partly indebted to a number of socially conservative groups that put a high priority on dealing with the sexual permissiveness they saw in modern society. Reagan's attorney general, Edwin Meese, in addition to heading the new pornography investigation, created the National Obscenity Enforcement

Unit in 1987. Its aim was to eliminate all sexually oriented material, whether within or without the orbit of First Amendment protection. In 1984 Congress amended the Racketeer Influenced and Corrupt Organizations Act (RICO). Originally passed to deal with organized crime, RICO now applied to purveyors of obscene materials. A husband and wife were indicted and found guilty of transporting about one hundred dollars worth of obscene materials in interstate commerce. The government then put on evidence of similar convictions of the couple to establish a pattern of criminal conduct that met RICO's definition of racketeering. The jury decided that all the property used in the couple's business should be forfeited, which included three bookstores and nine video rental shops, resulting in an estimated loss of two million dollars.[170] The Supreme Court refused to hear the case.[171]

In addition to expanding the use of RICO, the federal government has not been averse to arranging prosecutions before friendly courts, called forum shopping. An egregious example of this type of persecution involved the prosecution of Adam & Eve (PHE Inc.) that sold, in addition to printed material, adult sex toys, videos, garments, etc. In fact, the actions of the Justice Department were so neglectful of constitutional guarantees that it endured judicial censure. The federal government threatened multiple prosecutions that surely would have driven the company out of business. In its prosecution of PHE in the friendly climes of Utah, initially the government was successful in countering a plea of prosecutorial misconduct. However, PHE did get an injunction that restricted the government from filing any suit until the litigation in Utah was concluded. When the Justice Department sought reversal of the order, the Tenth Circuit Court of Appeals found "an extensive pattern of prosecutorial conduct dating back some five years that appears to suggest a persistent and widespread campaign to coerce [the defendants] into surrendering their First Amendment rights." Eventually, after seven and a half years of government threats, a settlement was reached in late 1993. The government promised not to seek any further indictments and in return the company pled guilty to one felony count. That charge related to an advertisement for sexually explicit videos in which the description of contents was not in large enough type and not placed in the proper place on the envelope.[172] PHE Inc. was not driven out of business, but the threat of both forum shopping and multiple prosecutions as attempts to censor remains in the federal government's arsenal.[173]

In large part because the Supreme Court's interpretation of the First Amendment's protection of speech and press has made the task exceedingly difficult, the drive to censor books has ebbed. What remains is the censorship that occurs by the refusal to publish a work, and a censorship that seeks to protect a particular demarcated group from exposure to sexual materials.

The belief that children are sexual innocents who can be harmed by exposure to sexually explicit materials is so deeply engrained in our society that it is difficult to gain a hearing for a contrary view.[174] Just ask writer and founder of No More Nice Girls, Judith Levine, about the difficulties she encountered in finding a publisher for her book, titled *Harmful to Minors: The Perils of Protecting Children from Sex*. She eventually found an academic publisher willing to present her views to a largely resistant public. A quotation from the book's conclusion may help explain why:

> To be moral about children and their sexuality is to realign our idea of what promotes their best interests and what truly imperils them. . . . [A]s children move out into the world, protecting them from sex will not protect them from those dangers that have little to do with sex but may ultimately make sex dangerous.
> Sex is not harmful to children. It is a vehicle to self-knowledge, love, healing, creativity, adventure, and intense feelings of aliveness. There are ways even the smallest children can partake of it. Our moral obligation to the next generation is to make a world in which the needs and desires of every child—for accomplishment, connection, meaning, and pleasure can be marvelously fulfilled.[175]

She went on to say that sex between teenagers and adults should not necessarily be condemned.

Before the book appeared, word leaked out about its approach and contents. The reverberations were heard throughout the country. Tim Pawlenty, house majority leader in Minnesota who would subsequently be elected the state's governor, called upon the University of Minneapolis Press to stop its publication. Some protestors saw the book endorsing pedophilia. The university responded to the political turmoil by seeking an external review of the press's decision. That review concluded that the book had been published in accordance with proper academic standards. The public outcry resulted in increased sales. Within a year nineteen thousand copies had been sold, a substantial total for a university press title. In April 2003 it won a *Los Angeles Times* book prize, Levine being cited for producing "a cogent and passionate critique of the war against young people's sexuality." Both she and the press, the award read, "deserve the highest praise for launching a necessary, overdue debate." The director of the press appreciated the good news, saying that the most controversial item on the present season's list was a memoir of a woman waging war against the beavers around her house.[176]

In regard to the censorship of a particular, demarcated group other than children, the best example involves those persons subjected to military regulations. Military authorities have long had an ongoing concern for the moral welfare of servicemen going back at least to the Civil War. In 1996 Congress passed the Military Honor and Decency Act that prohibited the secretary of defense from permitting "the sale or rental of sexually explicit material on property under the jurisdiction of the Department of Defense." The legislation defines "sexually explicit material" as "an audio recording, a film or video recording, or a periodical with visual depictions, produced in any medium, the dominant theme of which depicts or describes nudity, including sexual or excretory activities or organs, in a lascivious way."[177] Under the law an eight-member Resale Activities Board of Review was established to review items for sale that might run afoul of the legislation. One hundred and fifty-three magazines were placed on the banned list. *Playboy* would be available, but *Penthouse* would not.[178] When the publishers of *Penthouse,* among others, brought suit, a trial court ruled against the ban on First Amendment grounds. Its ruling, however, was reversed by the Second Circuit Court of Appeals.[179] The most recent challenge to the act saw the federal district and circuit courts in California in agreement with the Second Circuit Court of Appeals. Military bases, said the courts, were not public forums.[180]

Book censorship remains a problem in twenty-first-century America primarily in libraries and public schools.[181] Books written for children have always been censored, but that censorship had been imposed either by the authors themselves or their editors at the publishing houses. With the 1970s came books that began dealing with hitherto taboo subjects in language with which children certainly were familiar but that had not previously appeared in such literature. Educators saw in the new literature challenging material that would encourage students to think for themselves. In the latter half of the decade, this new breed of children's book began to attract the attention of censors.[182] Although the primary concern was sexuality in one form or another, once the censorial impulse surfaced, even American literary classics, such as John Steinbeck's *The Grapes of Wrath,* Ernest Hemingway's *A Farewell to Arms,* and Aldous Huxley's *Brave New World* became suspect.

The American Library Association (ALA) has been a leader in publicizing and, at times, combating censorship attempts; it sponsors a Banned Books Week every September to call attention to the issue.[183] In the ALA's list of "The Most Frequently Challenged Books of 1990–2000," most of the activity came in public schools and in public libraries and involved books specifically intended for adolescents. Despite the attacks by fundamentalist Christians on the immensely popular Harry Potter books because of the series' paganism and mysticism, the primary concern behind the challenges has been sex. The top reason, which accounted for almost 20 percent of the challenges, was that a book contained "sexually explicit" material. However, almost three-quarters of the challenges were based on sexual content, such as nudity, "offensive language," sex education, "promoting homosexuality," and "unsuited to age group."[184]

Of course, it comes as no surprise that sex should figure so prominently in this arena of censorship. Going back to Anthony Comstock, a prime motive of concerned adults was to save children from being harmed by their exposure to sex in written or pictorial form. The ALA takes quite a different perspective, introducing its list with a quotation from one of the most challenged authors, Judy Blume: "[I]t's not just the books under fire now that worry me. It is all the books that will never be written. The books that will never be read. And all due to the fear of censorship. As always, young readers will be the real losers."[185]

On ALA's list are five books by Judy Blume, all dealing in realistic fashion with an adolescent girl's anxieties in dealing with puberty and attendant concerns.[186] Her *Forever* about a teenage romance involving sexual activity has often been the subject of parental concern.[187] In 2004 the National Book Foundation honored her with its annual medal recognizing her contribution to American literature. She was surprised but happy that the foundation had recognized that writers of children's books had a contribution to make.[188]

Another author who has often been targeted is Phyllis Reynolds Naylor for her series dealing with an adolescent, Alice McKinley. In *Alice on the Outside*, Alice is in the eighth grade and worrying about her boyfriend as she copes with a crush that another girl has on her. *Alice in April* deals with puberty and the bodily changes it brings. And in *Alice Alone*, the ninth-grader is forced to deal with the sexual abuse of a classmate. Naylor's books headed the ALA's 2003 list of the ten most challenged books in the nation. This brief synopsis of their contents affords some glimpse into the type of material that is disturbing censors.

Robert Cormier's *The Chocolate War*, rated by the ALA as a "Best Book for Young Adults" has been a recurrent target for both its language and sexual content. It was number one on the 2004 list and remains among the top five on the 2005 list. The story concerns a teenager at an all-boys Catholic school who refuses to sell chocolate bars to raise funds. His decision incurs the wrath of both the administration and his fellow students. Aside from strong language, the book's treatment of masturbation and homosexuality has disturbed critics.[189]

One should not be misled by the relatively low number of challenges specifically characterized as opposition to sex education, for that issue continues to percolate in the school environment. Typical of the genre and ranking at the top of the challenged list in 2005 is Robie H. Harris's *It's Perfectly Normal: Changing Bodies, Growing Up, Sex, and Sexual Health*. In issuing the new list, the ALA noted that attempts to remove such books from library shelves dropped to the lowest number since the early 1980s when the ALA started compiling such lists. Books actually removed also hit a new low with forty-four, compared to two hundred in 1982. In trying to explain the decline, the director of the ALA's Office for Intellectual Freedom, Judith Krug, said that librarians have been better able to summon community support, and would-be censors seem now to have focused their attention on content available on the Internet.[190]

The illustrations in Harris's book, done in watercolor and pencil, illustrate many nude body types, as the book seeks to explain the many changes that come with puberty and deals, among other things, with homosexuality. In fact, Annie Proulx's *Brokeback Mountain*,[191] which chronicled the homosexual relationship between two sheepherders, so bothered donors of a three-million-dollar gift to a private school in Austin, Texas, that they requested that it be withdrawn from a list of optional reading for seniors. School authorities refused, and the gift was withdrawn. Authors of books for teenagers were so impressed with the school's decision that they formed an organization, Authors Supporting Intellectual Freedom (AS IF!), and donated signed copies of their books. As 2005 drew to a close, sixty books had been received for the "Freedom Library," some having considerable value.[192]

The challenges to books dealing with homosexuality and lesbianism are on the rise. As might be expected, with same-sex marriage a divisive issue in American society, such challenges can only be expected to mount. That in fact was a conclusion reached by the Texas chapter of the ACLU in its report on the 2003–2004 school year. Naylor, for her Alice books, was the "most frequently banned author" for the second year in a row. The ACLU chapter began to issue yearly reports on banned and challenged books in the state beginning with the 1995–1996 school year. In its 2004 report, the chapter concluded that religious fundamentalists were especially active in targeting sexual content and were working in opposition to the need to reduce Texas's high teenage pregnancy rate.[193]

Texas and California are the two states that exert the most influence over textbook content. For various reasons, sexuality has not been a substantial factor in the textbook wars. To gain adoptions, publishers are their own censors in this area. Matters concerning religion and the treatment of minorities fuel the textbook controversies, though worry about the presentation of alternate lifestyles and challenges to traditional sexual roles has been a part of the concern.[194]

Challenges to books in schools and libraries, whether successful or not, rarely make it into the judicial system, but when they do the results can be surprising. A United States Supreme Court decision is illustrative. Four members of the Court must vote to hear a case, and the four who voted to hear an appeal from a school board's decision to remove nine books from the school library were eager to reverse a lower court decision rejecting summary judgment in the board's favor. The school board had made its decision on the basis that the library books were "vulgar, immoral, and in bad taste, making them unsuitable."[195] The titles were all by well-received authors, and some of the books did contain the sexual content that often invited censors. To the four, Chief Justice Warren Burger, and Justices Lewis F. Powell, William H. Rhenquist, and Sandra Day O'Connor, taking the case would give the Court the opportunity to deny judicial interference with the discretion of the local school board.[196] They only needed one more vote to use the case to so inform school authorities throughout the nation. The four, however, ended up in dissent, as the other five members of the Court, Justices Brennan, Byron R. White, Thurgood Marshall, Harry A. Blackmun, and John Paul Stevens believed that the protesting students had the right to have their suit tried.

Most decisions made by local authorities are final because the challenging process is so costly and time-consuming, but not always. A relatively recent Texas case is instructive. As already indicated, much censorial effort in recent days has been directed against books dealing with homosexuality or lesbianism, especially when the author seeks to present the same-sex relationship as normal or accepted. In 1997 the Wichita Falls, Texas Public Library purchased two copies each of Leslea Newman's *Heather Has Two Mommies* and Michael Willhoite's *Daddy's Roommate*. Both picture children with gay and lesbian parents. Linda Hughes, the library administrator, saw the books as an important addition to the library's collection in that they explained "to children that you may live in a different lifestyle, but the important thing is people love you." Eventually in May 1998 the books came to the attention of Reverend Robert Jeffress of the First Baptist Church. He checked all copies out of the library and refused to return them, but then eventually agreed to pay for them on the condition that the library not replace the books. The Library Advisory Board decided that the books should be replaced; they were placed in the reading section for ages nine to thirteen. Reverend Jeffress and his supporters did not give up. Eventually they got the city council to pass a resolution giving three hundred adult library card owners the right to have material removed from the children's area and placed in the adult sections of the library. In July, when presented with the petition to relocate the two books, the library administrator complied. A group of citizens sought an injunction against the enforcement of the resolution that was granted by U.S. District Court chief judge Jerry Buchmeyer. The judge issued a memorandum opinion in which he summarized the evidence, called the library administrator "the real heroine of this unfortunate story," and found several fatal constitutional defects in the city council's resolution. The resolution and the removals, he said, "burden fully protected speech on the basis of content and viewpoint and they therefore cannot stand." Furthermore, the censorship activity burdened the plaintiffs' right to receive information, provided for no timely review, and delegated governmental power to private individuals.[197]

This little case is instructive in that it shows both the power of a determined group to get the city to do what it wishes and the countervailing power of another determined group to invoke the agency of the court to undo the result of successful political pressure. The record is filled with such stories that justify the faith many Americans place in the judicial branch of government.

In dealing with the written word, especially books, this chapter has shown how what was considered obscene was initially determined by a taken-for-granted social consensus. Over time concern for an amorphous public harm was replaced by an assessment of individual harm, the stirring of lustful impulses in the reader. Some critics, including Supreme Court justices, wondered why such stirrings were condemned. But condemned they were and are today.

Sexually explicit books and magazines, however, are readily available, thanks in large part to the inherent difficulty in protecting sexual speech, while trying to carve out an exception. The free speech argument is a powerful one and to take it seriously, as courts began to do in the 1930s, meant that eventually some of the barriers that had been imposed on books and magazines were destined to fall. Zoning and display laws seeking to regulate sexual materials do have some effect on adult availability, but generally the battle today takes place in school districts and public libraries, where attempts to suppress are now being met by resistance.

Attorney General John Ashcroft speaking to employees in front of the statue of The Spirit of Justice in the Great Hall of the Department of Justice in Washington, D. C. on November 8, 2001. AP images/Kamenko Pajic.

2

Dirty Pictures, Naked Statues, Etc.

You Call That Art?

[T]he history of eroticism is neither more nor less than a reflection . . . of the history of art. . . . [M]ost erotica of the past survives . . . under the rubric of "art."[1] (George N. Gordon, 1980)

One of the significant roles of art and the First Amendment is to protect the right of individuals to push the envelope and challenge the values of society.[2] (Kent Willis, 2000)

Let the nude be kept in its proper place, and out of reach of the rabble, . . . and its power for evil will be far less. The fault may be in the minds of the weak ones, but we must take the world as it is, not as we wish it might be. Many a youth inherits tendencies to lust and intemperance and . . . ought not to be exposed to temptation.[3] (Anthony Comstock, 1887)

I [have] . . . a fundamental belief in the goodness of the American people and the ability of the society to right itself. I leave with the belief that this eclipse of the soul will soon pass . . . and with it the lunacy that sees artists as enemies and ideas as demons.[4] (John Frohnmayer, 1992)

Statues have long adorned public buildings, and when a home for the Department of Justice was being planned, it seemed especially appropriate to include human representations of justice. In 1932 C. Paul Jennewein, a German émigré and sculptor of increasing stature, was chosen to do all the sculptural work for both the exterior and interior of the building. Among the works were statues for the Great Hall, a two-story reception area that would be used for ceremonies and public speeches. Working within the art-deco style

of the times, Jennewein created two twelve-and-a-half-foot aluminum figures. The *Spirit of Justice* was the female figure, draped in
a toga, but with the area from her right breast down to her upper
thigh exposed. The *Majesty of Justice* was the male figure naked to
the waist with a sculpted cloth draped over his right leg covering his
sexual organs. Jennewein had not always displayed such modesty
in his work. For instance, the Darlington Memorial Fountain he
made for Washington's Judiciary Park left not only the fawn naked
but the nymph as well. As some moral custodians pondered this
display of the female form, they suggested that she be adorned with
a frock. The artist rejected the idea, saying that "she was straight
from the hand of God, not from the hand of a dressmaker."[5]

Jannewein created a total of fifty-six architectural sculptures for
the Department of Justice Building, which he executed with such
skill that the unified design of the pediments, reliefs, stand-alone
sculptures, and decorative elements was widely praised for its "ex-
quisite beauty." By the time of his commission from the Department of Justice, Jennewein had compromised by covering up some
of what the hand of God had created. When the nudity of some of
his figures caught the attention of the Fine Arts Commission, the
artist agreed to place fig leaves in appropriate places. When the
commission suggested he enlarge the fig leaves, he suggested that
the Department of Agriculture be consulted to determine the
proper size of a fig leaf.[6]

For years the statues in the Great Hall attracted no special notice
in a capital city festooned with statues of human figures in various
states of undress. With the proliferation of press conferences that
came with the extended activity of modern government, officials at
the Department of Justice thought the best place to put a podium
in the Great Hall was in front of the sculptures. The problem with
this decision was graphically illustrated in 1986 when Attorney
General Edwin Meese held a press conference to release a thou-
sand-page report on pornography. Press photographers were quick
to see the possibility of a revealing photo. By getting close to the
floor, they could catch Meese holding up the volumes castigating
pornography with the bare breast of the *Spirit of Justice* clearly visible behind his head.[7] If the pictures that appeared the next day embarrassed Meese and the administration, they were wise enough to
ignore them.

Such was not the case with one of Meese's successors at the Department of Justice. John Ashcroft had been defeated in his campaign for a second term as a senator from Missouri by a Democrat
who was killed in a plane crash before the election. President

George W. Bush's nomination of him to be attorney general was a controversial choice because of the nominee's outspoken social conservatism and his lack of sympathy with civil liberty claims. Nonetheless, he was confirmed. In his press briefings in the aftermath of the terrorist attacks of September 11, 2001, he was disturbed by pictures of himself against the backdrop of the *Spirit of Justice's* naked breast. On certain occasions, such as the naming of the building after Robert F. Kennedy, the statues were draped to hide them from public view. The cost to rent the drapes was two thousand dollars. Apparently someone in the department became convinced that such drapes should be bought and hung permanently. When the purchase of the drapes for over eight thousand dollars was revealed, newspapers and other media outlets took aim, talking about cover-ups, prudery, censorship, sexual hang-ups, and so forth. Barbara Comstock, whose surname is the same as that late nineteenth and early twentieth century crusader against vice, said that Ashcroft had nothing to do with the decision and that it was not made to hide the statues from view but rather to provide a better backdrop for television.[8] ABC news had reported otherwise, and other observers quickly pointed out that, had the decision not been made with Ashcroft's implicit approval, he would have reversed it. Furthermore, the *Daily News* in New York City obtained e-mails confirming that the primary purpose of the new drapes was to cover up the embarrassing statues.[9] The attorney general, a fundamentalist Christian minister, certainly felt more comfortable without the large aluminum breast perched above his head.[10]

For the twenty-first century to commence with worries about a female statue's naked breasts, especially after the public, near the end of the previous century, was exposed to intimate details of oral sex at the highest level, is indeed quaint. The episode, however, is eloquent testimony to a long history of discomfort with nudity and sex and its portrayals both on canvas and in three-dimensional forms.

Jannewein's retort to the art commission's request to enlarge the fig leaves cleverly sidestepped the real issue, which was not the botanically correct fig leaf size but the exposure of the male's sexual organs. The earliest recorded instance of alarm at the public exhibition of plaster casts of naked ancient sculptures came in 1784, only one year after the peace treaty with Great Britain had signaled the success of the American Revolution. An English portrait painter had imported a plaster replica of an undraped Venus, hoping to put it on public exhibit. Responding to claims of indecency, he put it in a case and showed it only to those persons who specifically asked to see it.[11]

When the Pennsylvania Academy of Fine Arts was established in 1805 as the first institution in the country devoted to fine art, one of its founders, Charles Willson Peale, a well-regarded portrait painter, began a battle that lasted for fifteen years. He was determined to triumph over local prudery with regard to the exhibition of nude classical sculpture. In an initial exhibit of fifty such sculptures in the following year, the statues were draped when ladies' days were scheduled.[12]

Philadelphia, the city of brotherly love, earned further notoriety when in 1815 it gave birth to the first obscenity case tried in the courts of the United States. Although no statute dealing with obscenity existed, the Pennsylvania Supreme Court found six men guilty of the common law crime of corrupting morals by exhibiting an obscene painting. They had shown the painting to curious spectators in return for a fee. The court described the offending picture as "a certain lewd, wicked, scandalous, infamous, and obscene painting, representing a man in an obscene, impudent, and indecent posture with a woman." When the defendants objected that the description was vague and insufficient, the court said that the description was sufficient, given the need to pay "some respect to the chastity of the records." A Massachusetts court later agreed, saying "obscene matter need not be set out in the indictment lest the court should give permanency and notoriety to indecency."[13] Thus began a judicial tradition that gave preference to the purity of the court record over the right of defendants to have the elements of their crime precisely identified. To paraphrase a Supreme Court justice over a century later, as he tried to cope with defining what was obscene, the keepers of the public morals knew what corrupted when they saw it.[14]

Although art museums were not immune from the surveillance of censors, easily obtained reproductions of certain holdings or mass-produced work generally constituted the targets. So-called high art would be viewed by self-disciplined people in the proper setting; the other work would be viewed by those whose passions were less disciplined. As in all censorship, the art variety was premised on such class thinking and categorizing.

American artists regularly ran into difficulty in drawing the human form from life. Certainly the form was there, but it was well covered and not truly available. This fact led many such aspiring artists, as early as the later eighteenth century and through most of the nineteenth century, to travel to Europe where the artistic study of human anatomy was possible.[15]

Before long the desire to censor art was etched into statutory law. Beginning in 1821 three New England states passed laws proscribing obscene material, but the first federal law dealing with sexual matters and the first national statute censoring material concerned only pictures. Passed with no recorded debate, Congress in a provision of the Tariff Act of 1842 prohibited the "importation of all indecent and obscene prints, paintings, lithographs, engravings, and transparencies."[16]

Customs officials were to confiscate such material and then initiate court action to authorize its destruction. Because the cost of challenging such determinations was substantial, there were few contested cases. In the first reported contest under the new law, paintings on nine snuffboxes led to the destruction of an entire shipment of goods. Only one of these paintings was seen by the jury, and its offending portion had been obliterated with ink.[17] Fifteen years after its first enactment, the tariff act would be amended to include other "obscene articles," which covered three-dimensional representations along with photographs.[18] In fact, photographs, of partially clad or naked women, had been and would continue to be smuggled into the country, duplicated and offered for sale.[19]

When the eighteenth annual exhibition of the National Academy of Design ran into controversy over the exclusion of a painting from the exhibition, a painting that had been exhibited without controversy in Boston, a defender of the ban denied that censorship was involved. But then, he said, if its exclusion was the result of its sexual content, the National Academy was only protecting the public's morals. The academy would not "be prostituted to please the 'salacious' cravings of libertine fancies."[20]

A nineteenth-century fascination with classical sculpture brought Americans into contact with anatomically correct depictions of the human body, male and female. How they responded to this exposure is interesting indeed. For instance, a bare chest caused alarm when it was exposed in a sculpture of George Washington. Horatio Greenough was commissioned to do a statue of the Father of the Country in 1832 for the Capitol rotunda. He based his work on a sculpture of a seated Zeus and left the upper half of Washington's body unclothed. Cries of "outraged purity and patriotism" greeted its installation.[21] In 1843 Hiram Powers sculpted a naked woman with her chained hands covering her pudendum. Powers explained the moral message of the *Greek Slave,* saying it was not her person but her spirit that stood exposed. When a committee of Cincinnati clergy gave their approval, the statue was not only exhibited but also extensively copied in miniature and proudly displayed in American homes for the next century.[22]

No one claimed that Powers was ill informed about a woman's anatomy, but that was precisely the reason given by jurors for failing to give a commission to a woman sculptor. Anne Whitney had won a blind contest to sculpt a likeness of Senator Charles Summer of Massachusetts. When the male jurors discovered her gender, they used the excuse that a woman would not be sufficiently familiar with a man's anatomy to do a proper job. Was this their reason or were they simply "protecting patriarchal production and control of the arts," something feminist critics would say has not disappeared from the American art scene.[23]

Supervisors of the public morals would have much to worry about when the Civil War extracted young men from the communities that had overseen their behavior. Added to the moral dissipation that came with drinking and gambling was the circulation through the mails of obscene writings and pictures. One of the offending books was John Cleland's *Memoirs of a Woman of Pleasure,* a spicy narrative that would grace the record of the United States Supreme Court a century later.[24] Apparently members of Congress became convinced that the young men serving the Union needed protection from such salacious material. Although some senators expressed concern that a bad and dangerous precedent was being set, a law was passed barring such material from the mail and providing for criminal sanctions. So, for the first time, government control of the mails was used to justify censorship.[25] The law provided that "no obscene book, pamphlet, picture print, or other publication of a vulgar and indecent character, shall be admitted into the mails of the United States." Violators could be fined up to five hundred dollars and/or sentenced to serve a prison term of up to one year.[26]

In early March 1872 Anthony Comstock successfully began his forty-year campaign against the corruption of youth when he purchased sexual material from some New York City stationery stores. He had both a salary and an expense account furnished by the YMCA and financed by eminent New Yorkers. On the basis of the evidence seized, three employees of the stores were convicted under state law and sentenced to terms running from three months to a year. A little over a year later Comstock was instrumental in getting Congress to tighten its postal obscenity law by providing for more severe penalties. Forbidden material now included advertisements, devices, and information about contraceptives. Furthermore the new law, now known as the Comstock Act, banned printed, as well as pictorial, materials from entering the country. The law's namesake was charged with enforcing the law as a special unpaid agent of the Post Office Department.[27]

The law was further strengthened in 1876. One change simply cleaned up some sloppy drafting that left the circulation of some obscene material out of the penalty phase, but of most importance was the provision that stated specifically that such obscene material was deemed "non-mailable matter, and shall not be conveyed in the mails."[28] Whether offending material could simply be seized or whether a criminal prosecution had to be instituted first was unclear. In 1890 the attorney general interpreted the law to eliminate the need for any prior charge, thus authorizing post office censorship. Again, the cost of challenging any particular determination usually meant that the views of the particular governmental official ruled.[29]

A unanimous U.S. Supreme Court in 1878 conferred its blessing upon the authority of the postal service to deny certain material access to the mails. In the decision, which involved lottery materials, the Court specifically cited the Comstock Act as an illustration of what Congress constitutionally could do to bar "matter deemed injurious to the public morals" from the mails. The Court did, however, exclude letters and sealed packages from the reach of the censor.[30] This protection was worth less than one might imagine, as Comstock and other zealots simply ordered the suspect material. When it arrived sealed, the agent to whom it was addressed simply broke the seal and used the contents to convict the sender.

Comstock had appeared in Washington as a lobbyist for the YMCA's Committee for the Suppression of Vice, shortly to become the New York Society for the Suppression of Vice. Its charter assumed the organization's responsibility for "the enforcement of laws for the suppression of the trade in, and circulation of obscene literature and illustrations, advertisements, and articles of indecent or immoral use." To understand the power of the society, one must realize that it, and similar societies in the latter nineteenth century, literally took the law into their own hands. Convinced that the official law enforcement bodies were either not doing, nor interested in doing, the job, these vigilante bodies filled the enforcement gap. They justified their extralegal action in the name of staving off moral degeneracy. Such societies assumed governmental functions, and "employed extralegal measures in regulating private and leisure-time behavior." They were no less than "'private' states, vigilantly preserving their own sexual and moral code."[31] The Society for the Suppression of Vice, under Comstock's leadership, took full advantage of such power. Trumpeting his success under both state and federal law two years after his campaign began, Comstock said he had seized 134,000 pounds of books and destroyed 194,000 pictures and photographs.[32] The purity crusader found an ally in the New York Supreme Court when it upheld the conviction of a man for selling photographs of paintings that had been publicly exhibited both in the United States and abroad. Rejecting claims that this fact, the intent of the seller, and who the buyer was were relevant, the court said that the law was designed "to suppress the traffic in obscene publications and to protect the community against the contamination and pollution arising from their exhibition and distribution."[33] Comstock was especially pleased with the court's rejection of expert testimony on the basis that the average adult could judge "whether a picture tends to awaken lewd thoughts and impure imaginations in the minds of the young."[34]

Comstock was far from alone when he saw the immigration of Slavs, Jews, Italians, and Greeks from Southern and Eastern Europe as posing a new threat to public morality. The Society for the Suppression of Vice was organized in New York City in May 1873 with the sponsorship of prominent businessmen, such as J. P. Morgan, and its agents were given the authority to search, seize, and arrest in their arduous pursuit of vice. Three years later, the New England Watch and Ward Society was formed to protect the public by suppressing lewd books and censoring art displays.[35]

Such class bias did not prevent the purity crusader from hounding reputed and well-regarded art dealers, as when, acting for the Society for the

Suppression of Vice, he raided M. Knoedler & Company and seized photographs and engravings of French art. He charged the firm with endangering youth and corrupting morals. The fact that prominent artists challenged Comstock's prudery only convinced the crusader that his work was necessary. Even a reluctant court felt compelled to agree with Comstock in regard to a few of the pictures. The *New York Telegram* published the pictures, mostly of nude women, on the front page of four issues and dared the purity crusader to take action. Comstock, instead, decided to "discharge a sacred duty" by taking his crusade to Philadelphia, where he met further resistance. Rebuking the purity crusader, the judge freed the defendants that Comstock had brought before the court.[36]

In a pamphlet entitled *Morals vs. Art,* the purity crusader answered his critics, saying that there was a proper place for art where it could be viewed by "cultured minds." His target was the cheap photographic reproductions obviously produced for the "eyes of the uncultivated and unexperienced."[37] If Comstock's crusade drew jeers and opposition from some, he continued to have influence in the halls of Congress, for in 1888 the national legislature tightened the ban on mailing "obscene, lewd, or lascivious" matter. The legislation now provided for a fine up to five thousand dollars and for imprisonment at hard labor for up to five years.[38]

Comstock's lack of success in Philadelphia came, in part, as a result of the failure of such reformers to connect sexual depravity with dirty politics, a link that served the antivice societies of Boston and New York quite well. Philadelphia had its own purity crusader in the person of Josiah W. Leeds, who until his death in 1907 sought, often unsuccessfully, to root out the sources of sin. His campaign against art is a case in point. In March 1891 the Philadelphia Academy of Art held its annual exhibit of modern art. Among its six hundred pieces were many nudes that stirred the attention of Leeds. Five hundred Christian women protested the "flagrant indelicacy" of some of the pictures, saying that their womanhood was offended and that the exhibition of the art attacked "the delicacy of our daughters and the morality of our sons." The committee that hung the exhibit and to whom the protest had been directed denied any attempt to corrupt community morals. Then, it took the offensive: "Heaven forbid that the delicacy and morality of children be so poorly established as to be in danger of overthrow by the contemplation of the pictures you have selected for censure. . . . [W]e cannot refrain from expressing our sincere pity for that man or woman who finds in all the beauty and purity of the human form nothing but immodesty, indelicacy, and, alas, indecency." Although no paintings were removed from the exhibit, the director of the academy assured Leeds that "you are not likely to have so much cause for disapproval in future exhibitions." The *Philadelphia Inquirer* seemed to straddle the issue, supporting the offended ladies in print but then in a cartoon suggested hypocrisy by depicting them exposing their bodies in both formal balls and on the beach.[39]

As previously noted, American state courts had established the rule that the court record would not be sullied by the inclusion of the specific material that was the subject of an obscenity prosecution. The United States Supreme Court ruled that since the defendant could be presumed to know what was deemed objectionable or could find out through requesting a bill of particulars, there was no failure to inform him of this key element of the offense. What was involved in the Supreme Court case was a twelve-page tabloid, Lew Rosen's *Broadway*. On three of its pages were pictures of women "in different attitudes of indecency" only partially obscured by lampblack that could readily be erased with a piece of bread.[40] In the preceding year the Court had ruled that the fact that a post office inspector under an assumed name had requested the obscene material did not save the defendant from prosecution. This was not entrapment, the Court said, because the official did not solicit the commission of a crime; he was only seeking to determine whether the individual was engaged in a lawful business.[41] Such official conduct continues up to the present. FBI agents, in their attempt to gather evidence to prosecute the purveyors of such material, are possibly the biggest buyers of child pornography.

Anthony Comstock had always maintained that naked statues were acceptable in museums, but when the director of the Metropolitan Museum of Art provided a home for Frederick MacMonnies's *Baccante and the Infant Fawn*, leaders of the American Purity Alliance and the Women's Christian Temperance Union (WCTU) disagreed. The statue of a naked woman holding a bunch of grapes in one hand and an infant with the other hand had originally been installed in the garden of the Boston Public Library. A Harvard art professor had called the woman captured in bronze shameful and "blatantly licentious," and a WCTU representative added that the sculpture was "an outrageous insult to pure American motherhood." The museum director, however, held firm.[42]

Comstock, however, continued to prowl the streets making sure that the windows that fronted them were freed from nude images. His tolerance for nude pictures or sculptures within the confines of the gallery did not extend to art students and art schools. For instance, when an issue of the magazine of the Art Students' League of New York contained photographic images of the sketches students had done in life study classes, he had the issue seized and destroyed.[43] Such activity drew increasing opposition not only from artists and their patrons but from critics and the general public as well. The avoidance of the nude in art, said one critic, has created a suspect art resting "on sentimentality and facile prettyness."[44]

Still, the new century had not brought an end to the campaign against nude classical statues. In Buffalo, the Board of Alderman sought to get the

Albright Art Gallery either to drape the statues or put them in a special room where they would not be inadvertently viewed by visitors. The Roman Catholic clergy had pushed for the action, believing that the public display of nudity "was demoralizing and harmful especially to the immature." This was so because "pure thoughts may suffer blight." The School Protective League in Boston agreed, as it criticized the Art Museum of Boston for displaying "questionable art that has such a bad effect on the morals and manners of children as well as upon people of mature years."[45]

Anthony Comstock's reputation as a censor of licentious art led one promoter, Harry Reichenbach, to use that reputation to his financial benefit. The subject was a painting by Paul Chabas entitled *September Morn*. It depicted a naked woman modestly wrapping her arms around herself ankle deep in a lake. Earlier that year Chicago police sought to ban its public display. Reichenbach had purchased the painting and now sought to parlay his purchase into a small fortune. He displayed the picture in a window and hired some young boys to gather in front of it and make comments. He then alerted Comstock to the display, and although the crusader found "too much maid" and "too little morning" in the picture, he decided it was neither immoral nor obscene. However, the publicity generated by Comstock's visit created a huge market for all sorts of reproductions of the painting. When postcard reproductions were banned from the mails, the appetite of the public for *September Morn* only increased. Almost a half century later, after being rejected by the Philadelphia Museum of Art, the painting would be accepted by the Metropolitan Museum of Art and exhibited in the Great Hall.[46]

This episode occurred in 1913, the year in which Americans were introduced to modern art at the famous National Guard Armory show in New York City. Although critics attacked the show and the press ridiculed the works, the art world would be forever changed. Some four hundred works, including those of Cezanne, van Gogh, Redon, Gauguin, Matisse, and Picasso, were on display. Many of the visitors had trouble finding the nude in Marcel Duchamp's cubist painting, *Nude Descending a Staircase*. Difficulty in deciphering the nude did not prevent the painting, along with one that depicted prostitutes, from sparking an Illinois state vice inquiry when the exhibit moved to Chicago. One critic called the exhibition "nasty, lewd, immoral, and indecent."[47] Apparently the fact that the viewers had to call upon their imagination to reconstruct the lewdness in Duchamp's work was no bar to its condemnation.

In this same year before the Great War would challenge the progress of civilization, the United States removed the 20-percent duty that had been placed on works of art in the 1897 tariff act. The new legislation also allowed two reproductions of the work to enter duty free.[48] Obscene or indecent art, however, was still completely banned from the country, and any domestic production could not be shipped in the mails or in interstate commerce.

With the movement of the United States to war with the Central Powers in early 1917, the concern of censors moved from nudity and sex to antiwar sentiments, but the postwar period would bring the old targets back. In an interesting twist of fate, George Creel became chairman of a newly established group, the National Council to Protect Freedom of Art, Literature and the Press. Heading the country's propaganda machine, the Committee for Public Information, during the war, he had done his best to suppress errant political views. Now he called censorship a menace to both liberty and enlightenment. Condemning the "bigotries of personal prejudice," he said censorship condemns itself by "its unfailing stupidity and inevitable futility." His organization sought to abolish all censorship laws in the United States.[49]

Comstock died in 1915, but the term "Comstockery," coined by George Bernard Shaw in his verbal tussles with the purity crusader, lived on.[50] John S. Sumner, secretary of the Society for the Suppression of Vice, carried on Comstock's campaign against photographs "flaunted as art." He noted, though, that the moral backlash from the success of the prohibition campaign made convictions for the public display of indecent art more difficult. Apparently it was easier to obtain convictions of individuals who possessed such materials, at least if the conviction of Lorenzo Dow Covington, a noted Egyptologist, is any indication. Covington had purchased a collection of pictures, he said, to better study human nature. His collection was searched by Sumner after a few of the pictures turned up in a prosecution of two men who said they bought them from Covington. Sumner seized two hundred pictures, and had the man arrested. After Covington was deemed sane, he was convicted of possessing obscene material and sentenced to a term of no less than six months and not more than three years.[51]

Sumner was just as personally active in policing the city for indecent work as his predecessor had been. He proudly summed up the work of his organization in 1924, saying that, since its founding a half century earlier, the society had confiscated an average of sixty-five thousand pictures and postcards a year, making a grand total of three million since 1874. Two years later, however, the society criticized the press, judges, postal authorities, and the Department of Justice for a deluge of indecent and immoral material flooding the country. And when Sumner sought to prosecute a retailer who was selling reproductions of nude paintings by artists, such as Rembrandt and Goya, he was rebuked by a judge who dismissed the charges. Sumner appeared undaunted as he challenged gallery owners with moral turpitude for exhibiting in a display window a reproduction of Tintoretto's *Susanna*. They responded that the painting depicted its subject "clothed exactly as the Bible had described her when certain prurient minded elders gazed on her." The result of Sumner's concern was to bring new viewers to the exhibit. When Sumner celebrated his silver anniversary with the Society for the Prevention of Vice, he defended his work, which he described as suppressing images of "degraded 'objects d'art'" that supplied "an illegitimate thrill to old fools and to young boys and girls."[52]

Sumner especially disliked the drawings of Clara Tice, which adorned many illustrated editions of famous erotic works. Illustrated erotic books had been brought into the country and placed in private libraries, but not until the twentieth century did American editions appear. One of the most famous of these naughty illustrators was Tice, whose line drawings pictured naked women with pudenda and all. In 1928 Sumner raided the Gotham Book Mart, which had been known as a place where one could find erotica, and confiscated several copies of one of Tice's illustrated editions.[53]

During the looser morality of the 1920s and 1930s, Sumner would lose both financial support and court cases. However, the U.S. Postal Service, with its national reach and its ability to summon widespread support, continued its censorial activities. Still the challenge to censorship was growing and what was considered obscene and therefore nonmailable was shrinking.[54]

Modern art had won a victory that pleased some, but not others, including the American Artists Professional League, composed of a couple thousand members, who lobbied for the reimposition of a tariff on contemporary foreign art. Why, they asked, is the American artist not "entitled to the same protection as the American steel or textile manufacturer"?[55] The answer was simple; the artists had less clout and their plea went unheeded in the highly protective Hawley-Smoot Tariff of 1930. The tariff act, when it was finally passed, did respond to those inside and outside the artistic community who had been seeking to ease the censorship on imported goods. The final say on whether suspect material was obscene or immoral and therefore subject to destruction would be transferred from the Treasury Department and its Customs Service to the district courts. In these courts defendants were entitled to a trial by jury.[56]

Such protection, however, was costly, and customs officials still made the initial decisions, often quite inconsistently. For instance in 1931, customs officials seized a postcard containing pictures of Michelangelo's nude frescos in the Sistine Chapel, but a similar decision two years later was overturned by superiors in the Customs Service. The collector of customs in Chicago, however, was upheld when he confiscated etchings by Anders Zorn and James Abbott McNeil Whistler. Although the etchings had been regularly exhibited in art galleries, this fact did not make them fit for sale.[57] Nudity, no matter how artistically depicted, was still considered indecent if not obscene.

When Congress freed works of art from any duty, customs officials had to determine just what was a work of art.[58] A major case involved Constantin

Brancusi, a Rumanian abstract sculptor, whose metal works, according to a number of art experts, "left too much to the imagination" to be considered art. For customs purposes, the Treasury Department defined sculptures as an "imitations of natural objects in their true proportions of length, breadth, and thickness." The case arose over *Bird in Space*, a sliver of polished bronze standing over four-feet tall and mounted on a six-inch circular base. Since it bore little resemblance to a bird, it was classified as a manufacture of metal, and, as such, dutiable at 40 percent. The Customs Appeals Court rejected the representational requirement, though it would remain on the books until the late 1950s. The piece, the court ruled, was the work of a professional sculptor that was "beautiful and symmetrical in outline, . . . pleasing to look at and highly ornamental," and, as such, a work of art.[59]

Although no one accused Brancusi's sculpture of being a phallic symbol, the advent of modern art seemed to revive the interest of censors. For instance, the board of the Oakland, California, Public Library wanted to pre-censor art exhibits in the building because a recent exhibit had not only contained nudes, "but distorted nudes" at that. To escape such censorship, the art gallery was moved to a new location.[60]

As we have seen, the federal government in conjunction with the construction of public buildings at times commissioned artists, usually sculptors. Not until the New Deal, however, did the federal government, as part of its work relief programs, substantially subsidize the creation of art. Musicians, writers, actors, and visual artists were all paid for their work. Such governmental support for the arts brought with it the threat of censorship: if the government is paying, should it not be able to determine what it wants to pay for? Actually visual artists had much less difficulty than did the people involved in the Federal Theatre Project where there was great concern about the spread of radical ideas. Except for those artists doing public murals, where the work was present for all to see, most artists worked in relative obscurity with limited opportunity to show their work. Despite such lack of visibility, the Chicago project director cautioned artists to avoid "nudes" and "dives," among other things.[61] Although arts' supporters hoped that such federal support would survive the Depression, it did not.

Supervisors of the public morality did not take a vacation during the Great Depression, but increasingly public authorities seemed less concerned about sex in art. Certainly, Hitler's campaign to purify German art made censorship much less appealing. In 1934 Secretary of the Treasury Hans Morgenthau sought a thoughtful and balanced individual to deal with the widely varying and often unduly harsh customs decisions regarding materials dealing with sex. He chose Huntington Cairns, a lawyer and classical scholar who had won a case against a censorship decision, in part by getting the Court of Custom Appeals to consider expert testimony.

Cairns would serve as legal adviser in the area into the 1940s. At times he supported test cases to challenge wholesale bans that the statutory language imposed.[62] Cairns more liberal views resulted in few challenges to his rulings.[63]

Although decisions in the Customs Service were now more standardized under an intelligent and sensitive leader, the postal service was still decentralized and filled with the uninformed bureaucrats that Cairns criticized in a 1938 article.[64] For instance, in the late 1930s the postmaster in New York halted the mailing of *PM*, a graphic arts magazine, because it contained nude drawings by Abner Dean and Peter Arno. And when an issue of *Studio*, a well-respected Anglo-American art journal, was ruled obscene by the New York postmaster because it contained images of nudes, it was banned and the magazine's second-class mailing privileges were suspended. Postal authorities in Washington reversed both decisions on grounds that the publications were highly regarded and took a "serious approach to art."[65] A federal appeals court added its voice to the general discussion when it said that nudity was not synonymous with obscenity, insisting that the portrayal must be intended "to promote lust or to produce libidinous thoughts."[66]

In addition, the nation's highest political authority, President Franklin D. Roosevelt, lent his support to artistic freedom. In a speech at the Museum of Modern Art in New York City, he said: "Crush individuality in society, and you crush art as well." Artists, he continued, have "complete freedom from the strictures of dead artistic tradition or political ideology," and should not be "limited in method or manner of expression."[67]

Such official tolerance did not necessarily spread widely in the country. For instance, when George Grey Barnard, a highly regarded sculptor, gave fifty of his pieces to the Kankakee, Illinois, Central High School, the unclothed sculptures of human figures caused alarm. The sculptor finally agreed that the school board could hire another sculptor to craft trousers for the male figures, but he was able to get the board's agreement to accept the female figures as they were. And as sculptures were being constructed for the Golden Gate Exposition in 1939 in San Francisco, the director got involved in a fig leaf controversy that summoned up Jennewein's troubles with regard to the male figure in the Department of Justice building. Titled *The Bounty of the West*, the exhibition director said, the figure might well be called "a failure of the fig-leaf crop,"[68] referring to the depiction of the male's testicles and penis.

Still, censors were finding their targets more resistant. For instance, when the art committee at the University of Southern California sought to ban nude models in life drawing and sculpting classes, the opposition forced a lifting of the ban. And in the same January of 1940 the trustees of the Milwaukee Art Institute issued a resolution on the freedom to exhibit, equating the exhibition of art to the freedom to speak and publish.[69]

Greater artistic freedom may have been the result of political dissent becoming more of a concern of censors in the days before the nation's entry into World War II, but after Pearl Harbor, when such dissent all but disappeared, concern over sexual material reemerged. Issues of *Life* were banned in Boston in 1942 and 1943 because they contained pictures of nude paintings by contemporary artists. Elmer Plummer's painting of a stripper was displayed as part of the annual watercolor society exhibition in San Francisco, but when the exhibit moved south to the City of Angels it was "secluded from the public eye" in a back room at the Los Angeles Art Museum. An artist in Trenton, New Jersey, was asked by representatives of the USO branch to paint a mural in the auditorium they were using. When he finished, his fourteen by eleven foot nude rendition of *The Spirit of Freedom* was rejected. Servicemen, the critics said, should not be exposed to "nudity." The artist wondered how these moral supervisors intended to protect servicemen from the nude statues and paintings they would encounter when reaching Rome.[70]

Others were more worried about college women, especially those at Smith College. The college had been the beneficiary of a fresco by the noted Mexican artist Rufino Tamayo. Elizabeth Cutter Morrow, a future trustee and interim president of the college, had commissioned the work. When Tamayo had completed the fresco, some viewers were more than a little disturbed by the nine by forty-three-foot picture of naked figures. The most prominent of the five figures was a huge reclining cubist woman with a tiny head, four breasts and a large splash of public hair. The artist said the woman of heroic size "lies in an attitude of surrender, to symbolize abundance and generosity." School officials stood firm against would-be censors, at least until 1970 when a decision was made to either sell or destroy the work. Tamayo, who noted the uproar on the fresco's completion, now smelled "a Puritan plot." Officials took refuge behind the fact that the library building was scheduled to be torn down for the construction of a fine arts center. Whether the offer to sell had no takers or whether there were second thoughts about discarding the huge work of art, the mural was removed and mounted on panels and loaned to the Clark Art Institute.[71]

Still, such worry was not shared by most authorities in the federal government during World War II, who, instead, seemed to encourage male interest in the female form. Whether stirred by a concern about homosexuality or not, officials in and outside the military gave their implicit support to "nose art" and "pinups." Nose art referred to the paintings of scantily clad women on the nose of fighter planes. Pinups were given that name during the war because the illustrations or photographs of beautiful women were pinned up wherever servicemen could find a surface. Beginning with the Varga Girl, illustrations painted by Alberto Vargas for *Esquire*, pinups encompassed provocative and sensual photographs of attractive women, including movie stars, such as Betty Grable and Rita Hayworth. The pose of Betty Grable captured in the most famous of World War II pinups was credited with making her a film star. The fantasies such images stirred, authorities believed, would strengthen the morale of the fighting men.[72]

The end of World War II brought not the peace so many had sought but rather the Cold War, in which the hunt for communists not only found artists but their art as well. Artists were often viewed as social deviants, and clearly some were sympathetic to socialism and communism. Because their products were never as socially visible or influential, they never became the targets of Congressional investigating committees as did persons in the movie industry. The worry about artists with communist sympathies would continue in Dallas, Texas, long after it had subsided elsewhere.[73] Some politicians saw in abstract art itself a threat to democracy. For instance, Congressman George A. Dondero, a Republican from Michigan, made the exposure of this connection his personal crusade. Even Congressman Richard M. Nixon, who would go on to become vice president and then president, jumped on the bandwagon, suggesting that a Congressional committee be appointed to remove from governmental buildings "all that is found to be inconsistent with American ideals and principles."[74] Had these politicians really investigated the situation, they might have been surprised to find that the Communist regime in Russia had long condemned modern art as "bourgeois."

Three prominent American museums joined together to combat the notion that modern art was subversive. Calling the attack "reckless and ignorant," their spokesmen said that aesthetically innovative art should not be perceived as "socially or politically subversive, and therefore un-American."[75] Certainly modern art was culturally and artistically subversive, but one could argue that was its very purpose.

This worry about abstract art may seem strange given the fact that usually censors were most concerned about what was clearly represented in the picture or sculpture, what could not be missed by the most casual of observers. One writer sought to capture the rationale behind the censorship of modern, abstract art. Nonrepresentational art, she said, is "blasphemous, indecent, or frankly pagan," because it deviates from picturing God's creation. Instead it exhibits "private pleasures in shapeless and distorted forms," and, as such, is "a diabolical creation reproducing man's depravity."[76] Here the merger of sex with sin cannot be missed. If this article, reprinted in *Catholic World*, did not make the point clearly enough, Pope Pius XII in an address to the First International Congress of Catholic Artists in 1950 added to the condemnation. Such immoral art, he said, seeks to "lower and enslave the spiritual powers of the soul to carnal passions."[77]

Despite this excursion that brought art into what was essentially a matter of political censorship, moral guardians felt more comfortable dealing with representational images. The Post Office Department's campaign against nudity led the Eastman Kodak Company to develop its own censorship policy. In film sent to the company for developing, prints were inspected and ones that might run afoul of the postal laws were not returned to the sender. If the sender provided a sufficient explanation that satisfied Kodak, the disputed pictures would be sent. One customer found out about this policy when his photograph of a reproduction of Goya's *Duchess of Alba* was not printed by Kodak.[78] In looking at *Duchess of Alba*, one is hard-pressed to find the problem. The duchess is fully covered except for her face, throat, and upper part of her chest with precious little décolletage.

The Post Office Department apparently sought to obtain a ruling on nudity in the mails by banning postcards of another Goya painting, *The Naked Maja*. United Artists Corporation had sought to advertise its motion picture of the same name by sending out twenty-three hundred postcards. After six months, the Justice Department conceded that the image was not obscene and that the postcards should be delivered, to the dismay of post office officials. Postal authorities had argued that, although the painting itself was not obscene, color reproductions for commercial purposes were.[79]

In Fall River, Massachusetts, *Life*'s tenth anniversary issue was banned because of the reproduction of two paintings of couples in the country, one titled *Noon* and the other more descriptively titled *Lovers in the Cornfield*. The ban was widened when police chiefs in the Southern District, "under penalty of imprisonment or of fine, or both" were directed to follow suit. A critic in the *New York World-Telegram* commented, "No age has a copyright on damn fools."[80] When a later issue of *Life* appeared with fourteen photographs of famous nude statues and paintings, police, after citizen complaints, ordered the magazine off the newsstands in Fall River and Lowell.[81]

Mother Earth's Fertility, a reclining nude sculpture on the wall of an annex to New Mexico's capitol became the subject of a bitter dispute between artists and local churchmen. The sculptor said the piece was "wholly without sex appeal," but the spokesman for the Ministerial Alliance, a Protestant group, found the figure "extremely suggestive." When the building's architect had the nude chipped away, the newly established Committee for the Preservation of Cultural Freedom cried censorship. And in New Orleans, city workers removed a recently installed life-size bronze of a family after it sparked much controversy and had been labeled "pornographic rather than artistic" by a priest and some public officials.[82]

The fact that art had stood the test of time did not save it from the censors. Police in Pittsfield, Massachusetts, banned the November 26, 1951, issue of *Time* because it contained a picture of Pieter Brueghel the Elder's *The Wedding Dance*.[83] Although the male erections were not exposed, no one could miss what the artist was representing. Also, officials in Dubuque, Iowa, seized a book entitled *The Pocket Book of Old Masters*. Too many of the images contained nudes and, as such, were "obscene and offensive to public morality."[84]

Executive officials and courts had not defined obscenity, assuming, one imagines, a certain confidence in the ability of persons to know it when they saw it. For instance, customs officials in Baltimore seized over a hundred prints of ancient artifacts that had been mounted on cards because they were obscene. The pictured vases, lamps, statues, etc., were decorated with images depicting various erotic activities "including acts of sodomy and other forms of perverted practice." At least that was the way the district court described the images. The importer had sought to convince the court that the prints were part of a scholarly exploration in archaeology, but the court rejected the categorization and found them obscene. A trustee of the Peale Museum, also in Baltimore, came to the same conclusion about a work included in an exhibit of life in the city. The watercolor pictured a nude couple lying in bed. The trustee's complaint led to the removal of the piece from the exhibit. Its new location, the director's office, became a popular spot, as over three hundred people requested a viewing.[85]

Only in 1957 did the United States Supreme Court begin to wrestle with squaring the prosecution of obscenity with the protection of free speech in the Constitution. The Court upheld federal and state obscenity laws by classifying obscenity as nonspeech, thereby placing it outside the boundaries of the First Amendment's protection. To classify as nonspeech what certainly looked like speech, forced the Court to try to define obscenity. It said "the test of obscenity is whether to the average person, applying contemporary community standards, the dominant theme of the material appeals to prurient interest."[86] Although some critics would question what was wrong with appealing to prurient interest and others would wonder if the more restrictive test would allow the suppression of sexually explicit material, the test, though tinkered with, was never repudiated. The result of its use was to unleash a torrent of sexual material for social digestion in the years that followed.

Sex, as a subject of scientific study in the United States, got its start with Indiana University's Institute for Sex Research under the leadership of Alfred Kinsey. After Kinsey's seven-year battle with U.S. Customs, he found a sympathetic district judge. In allowing pictures depicting Chinese artworks with erotic subjects into the country, the judge said that "what is obscenity to one person is but a subject of scientific inquiry to another." When the Treasury Department decided against an appeal, the federal government ended its long-running feud with the institute.[87]

In 1958, members of Congress introduced legislation responding to the pleas of art importers to broaden the definition of what was a work of art so they could avoid paying any duty. The Customs Service had been classifying the pieces as manufactures for purposes of levying a duty but then valuing the pieces as works of art. The new law now permitted free entry for all fine art made of any material and in any form.[88]

Images in *Playboy* that had recurrently stirred censorial interest had their counterparts in the area of fine arts. Reacting against abstract expressionism, a new generation of artists revived representational art. Beginning with the pop artist Tom Wesselmann's *Great American Nudes* with their focus on a woman's erotic zones in the very early 1960s to the pornography featured in the work of David Salle and Eric Fischl, the nude was back in favor. As with books, the line between what was pornography and what was art was getting difficult if not impossible to draw. At first the depiction of naked women in seductive positions was interpreted as heralding a new frankness in sexual matters. With the rise of the new feminism in the 1970s, however, the work of such male artists was condemned for its objectification of women.[89] Furthermore, Salle and Fischl were special targets as their paintings seemed, to such female critics, to be deliberately insulting and humiliating.[90] At any rate, pornography was now finding its way into the high temples of art—the museums.

The sexually permissive 1960s—the time before herpes and HIV gained public attention—saw an interesting trial of a gallery owner and his salesman in San Francisco, who were charged with offering "lewd objects for sale." From discarded automobile parts Ron Boise had constructed eleven figures "engaged in various forms of sexual intercourse." The defense cited the long tradition of sexual expression in art, going back, at least, sixteen hundred years to the Indian classic on sexual pleasure, the *Kama Sutra.* In fact one expert referred to the figures under scrutiny as "*Kama Sutra* sculpture." And to show how the society had progressed, the experts noted that erotic art by Leonardo, Michaelangelo, Rembrandt, and Picasso was repeatedly pictured and readily available in any bookstore. One observer saw in the jury's verdict of not guilty considerable doubt that "the law may validly ban the *public* showing of any creative work without regard to its aesthetic appeal."[91]

That opinion received reinforcement almost a year later in another California trial, this time in municipal court in Beverly Hills. An art instructor and president of the Los Angeles Printmaking Society was arrested for "preparing and exhibiting obscene matter, possession of obscene matter, and commission of an act 'which openly outrages public decency.'" The drawings involved were referred to as "genitally oriented." A first trial ended with a hung jury; the second, using the record of the first and held before a judge, resulted in a finding of not guilty. The ruling, however, did not prevent the instructor from losing his job at the Chouinard Art Institute.[92]

Apparently it was not only the Department of Justice that had difficulty with artists, for the State Department in 1965 removed a surrealistic exhibit from its Exhibition Hall. The wife of the first secretary of the Belgian Embassy had created the paintings. Among other images, her anatomical work showed a female breast emerging from an egg, bosoms suspended on a hook, and a woman's torso on a hat rack.[93]

Los Angeles Country Art Museum officials refused to remove two life-size sculptures that were deemed pornographic by the Los Angeles Board of Supervisors, but they arranged a compromise by closing the exhibit to viewers under eighteen years of age unless accompanied by a parent or a teacher. Edward Kienholz, the artist, constructed assemblages or environments. The first of the offending pieces *Back Seat Dodge—'38* depicted young lovers visible through one of the rear doors of an automobile. The second piece featured *Five Dollar Billie*, a prostitute in an establishment called "Roxy's." She was made less visible as a result of the protest, but both assemblages remained on exhibit.[94]

With the overabundant use of sex in advertising, gallery owners found it difficult to generate public attention for erotic work. Sidney Janis tried to do this in regard to an exhibit he opened in his gallery under the title Erotic Art '66. Instead of the censorship he anticipated, he got bad reviews. John Canaday, the well-regarded art critic, said that by closing the exhibit to those under the age of eighteen, Janis eliminated the audience that might have found some sexual stimulation in the show. Both Janis and the artists, Canaday continued, "failed to recognize a primary truth about eroticism, which is that pictorial description of genitalia, the representation of intercourse, either normal or perverse, and all the rest of the physical and visual paraphernalia of sex, are not erotic per se."[95]

The Chicago Art Institute ran into an embarrassing problem when it held the 70th annual Chicago and Vicinity Show in 1967 and awarded the first prize of fifteen hundred dollars to an artist who had created a six-foot-square painting titled *Events*. The large square was divided into 108 smaller ones, many of which depicted human sexual activities. Although the museum's curator called the painting a "happy and humorous thing," other persons at the institute called it shocking. The prize-winning painting was returned to the artist, with the explanation that the work was not appropriate for public display. Local art dealers speculated about an escalating price for the work, "since it was certified . . . by the institute judges and banned by the institute moralists." Leanne Shreves, the artist, however, was furious and talked of legal action.[96]

Nudity continued to bother some in this permissive decade. In the heartland, vice detectives in Des Moines, Iowa, removed a painting of a nude in a nightclub, saying it was "too realistic." It was one of a number of pieces done for the club by the wife of the rector of an Episcopal church in the city. A year later the city council voted to remove five pictures from the 20th Annual Iowa Artists Exhibition in the Des Moines Art Center. The art center compromised by moving the pieces to a separate room and admitting only adults. When a sculptor used his front yard, not too far from a busy high-way, to display life-size statues of naked male and female nudes in erotic poses for sale, he was charged and convicted for "offering obscene images for sale."[97]

On the West Coast, protests were less successful. For instance, in Cypress, California, at Forest Lawn Memorial Park, a twenty-two-foot replica of Michelangelo's *David* was displayed without the marble piece that had covered its genitals since 1937. Protests by some local residents did not dissuade park officials, who claimed that times had changed and "nudity is no longer something to be covered up."[98] Also, farther south in Los Angeles, David Stuart succeeded in attracting attention, unlike Sidney Janis in New York, with his Erotic Art '69 show. He was charged with sixteen misdemeanor counts of displaying obscene art. The curator at the County Museum of Art said the prosecution of an art dealer was outrageous in a "town full of sexual permissiveness." A first trial ended without a verdict, but in the second one expert witnesses carried the day and Stuart was acquitted of the charges.[99]

Public display was one thing, but private viewing was another, especially after the United States Supreme Court found a right of privacy in the Constitution.[100] In *Stanley v. Georgia* in 1969 the justices ruled that the private possession of obscene material could not be prosecuted, for it was protected by a federal right of privacy. "Whatever the power of the state to control public dissemination of ideas inimical to public morality," the Court ruled, "it cannot constitutionally premise legislation on the desirability of controlling a person's private thoughts."[101]

Federal judge Frank A. Kaufman, who earlier found "redeeming social importance" in a batch of erotic paintings designed for exhibit in the United States, now probed the implications of the *Stanley* ruling. To him, it meant that "consenting adults may send obscene material to one another through the mail for their personal and private use."[102] Another lower federal court had found a portion of the customs regulations prohibiting the importation of obscene material unconstitutional, saying that if a person is constitutionally protected in being able to view the pictures, he cannot be barred from importing them without violating his freedom under the First Amendment. This court also found that the failure to provide time limits in the governing statute was a fatal defect. The Customs Service was ordered not to enforce the statute and to return the seized photographs.[103] A year later another federal appeals court came to a similar conclusion about importation of obscene materials for private use but did not address the provision in the tariff law criminalizing the importation of such material for commercial use.[104]

Agreeing to review the matter, the United States Supreme Court cured the procedural defect by writing into the law a time limit of sixty days within which to institute a forfeiture proceeding. Although four members of the Court wanted to rule that the decision in *Stanley v. Georgia* did not prevent the government from prohibiting the importation of such material for private use, they could not get the needed fifth vote. They had to be content with ruling that since the photographs were imported for the specific purpose of incorporating them in a book, this was importation for a commercial purpose and therefore could be barred by the law. The dissenters called attention to the Herculean efforts that the patched together majority had made in an effort to defer "to popular passions and what it perceives to be the temper of the times."[105] On that same opinion day in May 1971, a majority decided to reverse a lower court decision that would have extended the *Stanley* ruling. A postal inspector seeking to cleanse the mails of obscene material had answered an advertisement for the material. The Supreme Court ruled that the right to possess such material did not confer any right upon another to sell and deliver it.[106]

The more conservative environment to which the Supreme Court dissenters had alluded was nowhere more evident than in the reception the new administration in Washington would give to a report from a committee formed in the prior administration. The more permissive sexual environment in part encouraged by the free speech decisions of the United States Supreme Court had created growing concern about the distribution of sexually explicit material in society. In 1967 President Lyndon Johnson had obtained authorization from Congress to create a Commission on Obscenity and Pornography. In 1968, less than two years after its inception, the committee had spent almost two million dollars. Two hundred bills concerning the traffic in pornography had been introduced in Congress.[107]

As the nation waited for the report, a number of incidents captured the public's attention. Thomas Forcade, projects coordinator for the Underground Press Syndicate, delivered his criticism not only in words but also by shoving a cream pie in the face of a member of the commission. His intent, he said, was to protest "this unconstitutional, illegitimate, unlawful, prehistoric, obscene, absurd keystone committee."[108] Forcade could not know that the commission would come in with the startling recommendation that all obscenity laws should be removed from the statute books.

Leaks, however, did indicate that the commission was marching to a different drummer than were many in society. A psychologist in Salt Lake City called the draft report "rigged." Representative Robert N. C. Nix (D-PA) was horrified to learn that the commission had sponsored an experiment at the University of North Carolina that involved twenty-three young men watching stag movies. The conclusion the three researchers reached was that repeated exposure to pornography results in boredom.[109] And Charles H. Keating Jr., the only appointee of President Richard M. Nixon and the founder of Citizens for Decent Literature, took exception to the majority's conclusion that pornography did not cause sex crimes. He urged the president to fire the commissioners and form another panel.[110]

Keating, who in another decade would be convicted and sent to prison in connection with the savings and loan scandal, now sought to restrain publication of the commission's report. He won a ten-day court order to halt publication on the basis that his fellow commission members had not shared the report with him and therefore he was hindered from responding to it in dissent.[111] On the last day of the month, the report finally appeared with its radical, and quickly neglected, recommendation. Much more attention would be paid to the recommendation that governments at the state level consider legislation specifically directed at pictorial displays that could be seen by children and penalizing the sale of erotic material to children without parental consent. Some of Keating's sentiments were visible in the dissent that accused the majority of protecting the obscenity business and called its report "a shoddy piece of scholarship that will be quoted ad nauseum by cultural polluters and their attorneys."[112]

That the atmosphere of the country had changed by the time the report was issued, was well illustrated by the political reaction it met. By a 60 to 5 vote, the United States Senate repudiated its findings, saying that the commission had "failed to carry out the mandate of Congress and its statutory duties."[113] President Nixon pronounced the report's recommendations "morally bankrupt." Instead of supporting the repeal of laws prohibiting the sale of obscene material to adults, he urged their proliferation. He continued: "The warped and brutal portrayal of sex in books, plays, magazines and movies, if not halted and reversed, could poison the wellspring of American and Western culture and civilization."[114] The report was made available through the Government Printing Office and it encountered no difficulty with postmasters. An illustrated version, however, led to the indictment of the publishers for sending obscenity through the mails in both Dallas and in San Diego.[115] Pictures still seemed more threatening than words.

A new commission appointed by President Ronald Reagan in 1985 not surprisingly came to very different conclusions. Headed by Attorney General Edwin Meese, its stated purpose was to assess the connection between pornography and illegal behavior. One year after its formation, the Meese Commission on Pornography made its report. Contending that sexual materials and sexual behavior are linked, it recommended more stringent regulation of such sexually explicit material.[116] Its recommendations, though satisfying social conservatives, had no more effect than those of its predecessor.

The turmoil of the 1960s brought with it ideas of sexual liberation and eventually a feminism that was at times aggressively sexual. Female artists challenged both tradition and artistic constraints in experimenting with new ideas and techniques. In the process of so doing, they substituted their own views on sexuality for male fantasies and made the erotic a central focus. The most noted of these feminist artists is Judy Chicago, in part because of her continued production, her ability to reduce to prose her artistic thoughts and methods, but most of all for *The Dinner Party*. This massive construction is in the shape of a triangular dinner table honoring thirty-nine women in history with ceramic plates, thirteen to each side. In addition, the attached tile floor includes the names of 999 additional women. All told, some four hundred people worked on various aspects of the construction, which in addition to the substantial porcelain work, included much needlework as well. Although praised by many women and certainly recognized as a most significant piece of modern art, the piece had its critics. For instance, Chicago's concentration on the vagina, albeit in semiabstract forms, in the design for the plates was criticized by those feminists who felt that concentrating on the biological differences between men and women limited the empowerment of women. The project began in 1974 and was not completed until 1979 when it was first shown at the San Francisco Museum of Modern Art. Either because of or in spite of its being labeled pornographic, record-breaking crowds streamed in to see the exhibit.[117]

Despite the availability of various venues for the exhibition of the construction, including ones in Great Britain and West Germany, Chicago sought a place for its permanent installation. *The Dinner Party* had been in storage for a couple of years when she thought she had found it a permanent home. She agreed to its being permanently housed at the University of the District of Columbia, which planned to make it the centerpiece in an old library renovated as a multicultural art center. When the *Washington Times* divulged the plans, congressmen reacted, calling the work "ceramic 3-D pornography" and "weird sexual art." Supported by district and federal funds, the university was targeted by the House of Representatives. It voted to cut the university's appropriation by slightly less than the bond money appropriated for the art center. When students protested the proposed cut, Chicago withdrew her offer.[118] Only in the new century did the Brooklyn Museum of Art provide a permanent home for *The Dinner Party*.[119]

Judith Bernstein ran into opposition when she was chosen to be included in a large Philadelphia exhibit entitled Women's Work—America '74. The civic center's museum director responded to her twelve-and-a-half-foot charcoal drawing of a screw, by ordering its removal, saying "it's a penis." Lawrence Alloway, the *Nation*'s art critic, lamented the failure of the jurors to protest as a group, though protest flowed from various sources. He did not deny the phallic imagery but saw it as a part of an art movement that combined technological and anatomical references, the most visible practitioner of which was the noted artist, Claes Oldenburg. Alloway concluded that Bernstein's recent work had a similar architectural robustness.[120]

Censors seeking the removal of art from public view had mixed success. When a Maryland official in June 1973 demanded that an "obscene and objectionable" nude painting be removed from the Annapolis Invitational Art Show, ten of the artists withdrew their work in protest and the director of the exhibit resigned.[121] A year later in Evanston, Illinois, the home of Northwestern University, the director of the art center refused to respond to criticism and remove paintings of male nudes done by a local artist.[122] Some adults appeared to be embarrassed by the paintings, but when the claim could be made that children would be exposed to the artwork, the result was different. That was the case in South Charleston, West Virginia, where three nude paintings were removed from an exhibit because the venue, the town's recreational center, was often visited by children. A painting of a woman nursing a child remained in the exhibit, because children knew that most babies were breast-fed.[123]

As photography became more respected as an art form, the display of photographs became more common, as did complaints about the images. Women artists in an art cooperative in 1977 voted to remove all their work from a scheduled showing in the John Hancock Center in Chicago when one artist had eight photographs removed from the exhibit. Jane Wenger had taken photographs of parts of her body, including her breasts, buttocks, and pubic area. A spokesman for the company said they were unsuitable for viewing by children. Protesters responded that the photos were hardly erotic, measured by the images that were readily available in the magazines for sale in the lobby. Wenger concluded that the episode provided "wonderful publicity" for her and the cooperative galley.[124]

More than photographs were targeted by police officials in Providence, Rhode Island, spurred on by a new state antipornography law. From a show titled Private Parts, they removed forty-three items by students and faculty of the Rhode Island School of Design. One member of the city council was incensed by such disregard for community standards under the banner of art, but the city solicitor said that the raid was "absurd" and the statute unconstitutional.[125]

In Philadelphia, Pennsylvania, U.S. District Court judge Joseph S. Lord was disturbed to find an art exhibit in the federal courthouse that included paintings of female nudes. He wanted them removed. Lord found them offensive because he "detected in them a theme of lesbianism" and because the courthouse was a place frequented by "nuns, priests, and children." The General Services Administration, responsible for all federal buildings, removed the nudes and hung them elsewhere.[126]

Artist Kyra Belán found that, despite the fact that 90 percent of her work depicted male nudes, only her female nudes won prizes, were accepted for nonfeminist shows, and garnered her professional recognition. She could only conclude that the arts establishment found it difficult to accept male nudity on a par with female nudity. Belán lamented that such entrenched opposition had caused some of her female colleagues to turn to other subjects.[127]

One group of feminists, who called themselves Guerilla Girls, the Conscience of the Art World, carried on the protest in more visible ways, through demonstrations, posters, and advertisements. One ad began "Do women have to be naked to get into the Met. Museum," referring to the disproportionate number of female nudes compared to the number of male nudes in the museum's collection. They sought to call attention to what they claimed was the sexism of the art establishment and its institutions.[128]

In late 1980 public officials in Jenkintown, Pennsylvania, informed a gallery owner that he was violating a zoning ordinance that prohibited store window displays of pictures depicting "human genitals in a state of discernable sexual stimulation" within one thousand feet of a church. The etchings were part of Picasso's erotic series. The wife of one of the councilmen warned that she might take a brick to the offending window.[129] She at least recognized the artist's work, which was not the case with the police in Orlando, Florida. An original Picasso print was lumped together with some confiscated pornographic videos and nearly burned. It was saved from the flames because the city property manager was attracted to the frame that housed it.[130]

Where art is displayed is often the motivation for a form of censorship. For instance, the nudes of the noted artist Philip Pearlstein were hung at the University of Tennessee in the Concourse Gallery in the University Center, a seemingly proper place. However, the chancellor was worried that homecoming weekend would bring donors to the campus who might be offended by the display. Therefore, he had the exhibition moved to a less trafficked area. He denied that his action constituted censorship, but 250 faculty members disagreed, as they signed a petition condemning the chancellor's action. On Monday following the weekend, the exhibition was rehung in its original place.[131]

Supervisors of the public morality seemed especially active in Dallas, Texas. For a second year the city's chapter of the Texas Fine Arts Association ran into trouble with paintings of nudes. Although the female nudes included in the exhibit at the Plaza of the Americas were pictured from the back and although one of the works won a prize, the works were again removed from the show. A private gallery showed the three works, along with four others subsequently removed for a similar reason.[132] When, in the same year, another gallery in Dallas put on a display of photographs, under the exhibit title of Overexposed, board members found that some photos met the show's title far too literally. Robin Milsom had entered photographs of her sexually aroused naked husband. The dim light was not enough to hide his erection. Faced with the choice of removing or covering up the photos, Milsom removed the offending photos. In her parting shot, she noted that photos of naked women had long been exhibited without question.[133]

Protests against nude paintings or photographs in places of public access are usually resolved by the removal of the offending pieces or by the cancellation of the exhibit. When county officials in Scranton, Pennsylvania, ordered the removal of Joseph Ray's charcoal drawings of nudes, he complied. Ray, however, then sued the county officials for violating his right to free expression. He found a sympathetic federal judge, Edwin M. Kosik, who directed county officials to display the nude drawings. The judge said the gallery in the courthouse had long been established and could not now be censored.[134]

That censorship attempts attract public interest cannot be disputed, for nothing is more appealing than the forbidden. This observation was confirmed in one of the art capitals of the country—Santa Fe, New Mexico. A gallery sought to attract local interest during the low tourist season by staging a showing of erotic art. A gun barrel in the shape of a penis was displayed with an abstract painting of nudes in a window seen by passersby. Saying that the pieces violated the city's obscenity ordinance, a local police officer ordered the gallery to remove them from public display. The gallery responded by taking the pieces out of the window and covering the window with a sign indicating that what had been on display had violated the city's code. The city manager intervened and apologized to the gallery owner, saying that the ordinance had been misapplied. No apology was needed, for the episode had brought more than two thousand visitors to the gallery to see what the fuss was all about.[135]

Back in Ohio, the Toledo Friends of Photography were less than friendly when they removed two juror-selected photographs from their annual show at the gallery of Owens-Corning, Inc. They believed that a photo that zeroed in on the photographer's erect penis and one of a partially clad couple photographed from the front might offend the corporate sponsor. The Malaysian citizen, who had submitted the graphic self-portrait, said he knew the work would be censored in his home country, but he had expected more from a country that professed a belief in free expression. The show's juror added that he had seen much more offensive work in magazines and on television.[136]

As the 1980s became the 1990s, some concerned citizens worried that the First Amendment was under "national assault." That was the position of the San Francisco Board of Supervisors when it called attention to "a dangerous state of hysteria and repression" descending upon artists. The supervisors were supporting a highly regarded artistic photographer, Jock Sturges, who had been targeted by the FBI and local police for producing child pornography.[137] The officials seized one hundred thousand negatives, his computer, and business records. After an extensive investigation by the FBI that lasted a year and a half, a federal grand jury refused to indict Sturges.[138]

Other amateur and professional photographers have found that nude pictures of children were matters of high priority for the FBI and other police units. As one critic has suggested, "the intensity of public sentiment about pedophilia and child pornography, fed by a sensationalizing media machine, has heated up to the point where it far exceeds the relative weight of the problem."[139] She and a colleague put together a collection of articles dealing with censorship, one of which detailed the personal stories of four women who came to the attention of the police because of nude photos they had taken. One grandmother considered suicide as her granddaughter was quizzed by the Division of Youth and Family Services. The granddaughter served a year of probation. Another woman, an assistant professor of photography at Cornell University, lost her job. A third lost custody of her child, and the fourth, while teaching in London, found the former mother country no more able to make what seemed to be commonplace distinctions when nude children were the subject.[140]

Although Sally Mann of Lexington, Virginia, a well-regarded professional photographer, was not threatened with criminal prosecution for an illustrated lecture she delivered at the Virginia Museum of Fine Arts, she did provoke the attention of the state's governor. In a letter to the museum's director, Republican Jim Gilmore complained about the showing of "lewd pictures with children in graphic and compromising positions" to an audience that included "students and even a small child." The museum, he said, should establish policies "that will prevent these kinds of displays from occurring again on state owned property." Mann had used the pictures, almost as an afterthought, to help define the limits of artistic taste, and even the museum spokesperson concluded that the images "went beyond what we expected." The museum's director responded to the governor's request by saying that the museum's guidelines would be clarified. Both support and opposition greeted the governor's action, and one commentator concluded that the risk inherent in such action was "that it elevates the status of the artist and enrages civil liberties groups."[141]

This current worry about photographs of nude children goes back to the mid-1970s when Anita Bryant and Judianne Gensen-Gerber decided that children were in special danger from pornographers and sex perverts. Distorting the threat by bogus statistics, the moral crusaders were able to get Congress to pass the first law dealing with child pornography in 1978. In the next decade the federal law was strengthened and states passed further laws. In 1984 the very receipt of child pornography was criminalized. Federal government agents became sellers of such material to interested parties who then found themselves arrested under the new law. Convictions now mounted, often the result of sting operations that brought to mind the activity of Anthony Comstock in an earlier century.[142]

When the federal government funded artists during the New Deal, some advocates hoped that this public support for art would continue into the indefinite future. The public benefit, they believed, more than outweighed the cost. Not until 1965, with the establishment of the National Endowment for the Arts (NEA) was this hope realized. The NEA's purpose was to increase public appreciation of art by supporting artists and art institutions. With an initial budget of less than three million dollars the endowment would grow to a high of almost 176 million dollars in 1992. Since that time it has declined and beginning in 1995 would hover around one hundred million dollars for the rest of the decade. With encouragement from his wife, President George W. Bush supported increases in funding with the budget increasing over 25 percent for fiscal 2006.[143] However, from its very inception, the NEA has been mired in controversy. Late in the twentieth century, attention focused on photography and performance art, two relatively small areas of NEA activity.

Almost from the outset, however, the endowment became a political target with some senators and representatives urging its disestablishment on the basis that government should not fund the arts. Others contested the endowment's definition of art, for which it tended to rely upon experts in the various fields. In the 1970s the focus was on sexually charged literature, the most notorious grant being the five thousand dollars to Erica Jong for her racy book, *Fear of Flying*. This grant incited the freshman senator from North Carolina, Jesse Helms, to bombard the NEA with demands that the director explain why he was using public money to fund a "reportedly filthy, obscene book."[144] To Helms, public monies came with strings that made the supported artists trustees of the public taste.

In 1989 the NEA's funding of the exhibitions of certain photographs captured the attention of more members of Congress. Senators Jesse Helms and Alfonse D'Amato of New York levied the first attack. Their focus was a sixty-by-forty-inch photograph by Andres Serrano of a crucifix submerged in the photographer's urine and labeled "Piss Christ." A scheduled exhibit of the photographs of Robert Mapplethorpe at the Corcoran Gallery of Art in Washington became the next target. Titled "The Perfect Moment," the exhibit was a retrospective of the work of the artist, who had recently died of AIDS. Congressman Dick Armey of Texas collected the signatures of a hundred colleagues in Congress threatening the NEA with cuts in its budget if it persisted in funding such "morally reprehensible trash."[145] Among the pictures were homoerotic and sadomasochistic images, along with a few shots of nude children. Fearing political reprisal, the Corcoran, which had received NEA support, cancelled the exhibit. The exhibit was rescued by the

Washington Project for the Arts, which saw record attendance for the show as a result of the publicity.[146]

The Serrano and Mapplethorpe controversies in October 1989 resulted in Congress reducing NEA's budget by forty-five thousand dollars, the amount involved in the awards to Serrano and the Mapplethorpe exhibit. Furthermore, Congress attached to the appropriation a prohibition on using NEA funds "to promote, disseminate, or produce material which in the judgment of [the NEA] may be considered obscene, including but not limited to depictions of sadomasochism, homoeroticism, the sexual exploitation of children, or individuals engaged in sex acts and which, when taken as a whole, do not have serious literary, artistic, political, or scientific value." This was a version of the amendment that was introduced in July by Jesse Helms. In response to the Congressional directive, the NEA required grantees to certify in writing that they would not use the granted funds in such a way as to run afoul of what Congress had prohibited. Numerous organizations and artists turned down NEA grants to protest this obscenity pledge.[147]

Bella Lewitzky and her dance company brought suit, claiming that the proviso attached to the grant was unconstitutional. They had turned down an award of seventy-two thousand dollars because of the certification requirement. Finding the pledge unconstitutionally vague, a California federal district court struck it down. Such vagueness, the court said, had a chilling effect on artistic expression. Although the government had no obligation to subsidize anyone, when it initiates a program, the court continued, it cannot violate the First and Fifth Amendments in its execution.[148]

Although the court decision had not yet been handed down, Congress was aware that the proviso regarding grant monies might not pass constitutional muster. Seeking to compromise differences, the legislative body scrapped the content restrictions. Instead, it directed the chair of the NEA in providing for review of grant applications to take into account "general standards of decency and respect for the diverse beliefs and values of the American public." In December 1990 the NEA chairperson, John Frohnmayer, said he would not reject panel-approved grants on the basis of this decency provision.[149]

The fallout from the Mapplethorpe episode had important ramifications for the Corcoran Gallery in the nation's capital. Two exhibits had to be cancelled when the artists withdrew their work in protest over the cancellation of the Mapplethorpe exhibit. The gallery attempted to atone for its decision by asking a New York collective to organize an exhibit dealing with censorship, which would include photographs by Serrano and Mapplethorpe, but their attempt failed. Noting that the Corcoran had not yet apologized for cancelling the Mapplethorpe exhibit, the New Yorkers refused. Then, in December 1989, on the eve of the board of directors' vote on whether to retain her services, Christina Orr-Cahall, the Corcoran's director and the person responsible for the Mapplethorpe decision, resigned.[150]

Another casualty was John Frohnmayer, whom President George H. W. Bush had appointed to head the NEA in July 1989 in the middle of the Serrano and Mapplethorpe brouhahas. An Oregon lawyer with respect for artistic freedom, Frohnmayer found the right wing of the Republican Party difficult to satisfy. However, he was no hero to the artistic community, which saw him as too inclined to compromise for political ends. Eventually it was an attack by Patrick Buchanan, a challenger to President Bush for the Republican nomination in 1992 that led the president to conclude that Frohnmayer was a political liability who would have to go. The NEA head was allowed to resign in 1992.[151] In the following year, he captured his experiences at the agency in the aptly titled *Leaving Town Alive: Confessions of an Arts Warrior*.[152]

The Corcoran had suffered embarrassment as a result of its cancellation of the Mapplethorpe exhibit, but Dennis Barrie, director of the Cincinnati Contemporary Arts Center, suffered the indignity of an arrest and trial when he staged the Mapplethorpe exhibit. This episode is the first recorded incident of a museum director being charged with obscenity. Eventually, a jury of eight persons acquitted him of violating the state's obscenity law.[153]

Despite episodes of local censorship, the male nude rather than the female nude has become a major subject of late twentieth-century controversy. At times male nudity has been perceived as a "vehicle for homo-erotic feeling." In seeking recognition for homosexual art, Mapplethorpe had been a leader, though his death in 1989 meant that he would miss much of the controversy that his photographs would provoke.[154] That the problem was bigger than one photographer's photos was illustrated in an exhibition of David Wojnarowicz's works on homosexuality and AIDS sponsored by Illinois State University. Although the university expected controversy and decided to stand by the New York artist, they might not have been prepared for the massive assault launched by the American Family Association (AFA) upon the exhibit. The organization sent its complaint to every member of Congress, a thousand Christian radio stations, a hundred Christian television stations, and well over a thousand church leaders and pastors. With the mailing the AFA sent pictures of small portions of the collages in the exhibit without notice that the cropped pieces were parts of larger works. Wojnarowicz said this action misrepresented his work and sued the AFA. A district court verdict in his favor required the AFA to send a letter to all the original recipients correcting the misrepresentation.[155]

Strong homophobic feelings have been joined with concerns about sexuality and aggressive feminism. Where the homophobic attitudes have generally targeted photographic exhibitions, primarily female performance artists have suffered attacks from those who are made uncomfortable by the aggressive sexuality of such performers. Perhaps the most infamous of the female performance artists were the former porn movie star Annie Sprinkle and the woman who stripped and smeared food, including chocolate, over her body, Karen Finley. When the organizations that welcomed their performances were found to have received NEA funds, questions about the NEA supporting such work simply escalated.[156]

When the NEA withdrew initially approved grants to four performance artists, including Finley, all of whose performances dealt with sexuality, the artists sued on the basis that the Congressional requirement violated the First Amendment, and, as such, could not stand. On its surface, they claimed, the decency stipulation that Congress now required was vague and not viewpoint neutral. Both the district and circuit courts agreed, but the United States Supreme Court took the case and reversed the determination. As interpreted by the NEA, the Court majority saw no merit in the attack on the provision. Unlike direct regulation, the Court said, here where government officials choose among applicants they have wide latitude to make choices without encountering any constitutional obstacle. Since neither regulation nor criminal sanctions were involved, the Court continued, the guidelines were not impermissibly vague. The majority recognized the subjectivity inherent in any such selection process. Justices Antonin Scalia and Clarence Thomas, although agreeing with the result, chided the majority for its failure to uphold broadly any restrictions that Congress chose to place on the award of public funds. Only Justice David Souter dissented, claiming the majority erred in refusing to find viewpoint discrimination in the regulations.[157]

In the wake of the Corcoran's cancellation of the Mapplethorpe exhibit, Rita Bartolo, project director for Arlington County's Bluemont Park Sculpture Project was agonizing over a commissioned set of anatomically correct, reclining nude figures. Her boss, Arlington cultural director Norma Kaplan, exclaimed "We never suspected that the male would have genitals." Worried that the sculpture would be vandalized or stolen, Bartolo chopped an inch or so off the penis, carefully saving the severed part in case the atmosphere changed and it could at some point be reattached. One of the two artists who created the figures summed up his feelings: "I feel silly in some respects arguing about an inch, but people's rights are taken away from them in small increments."[158]

At times victories for those who fought against censorship came from strange places. Take the city of Alexandria, Louisiana, where an exhibit at the Museum of Art excited a former state representative whose publicized views received support from the city council. A naked female bottom was pictured in one piece titled *Fuck Me, Fuck You*, and the other was a full-length photograph of a nude man. The museum board fought off requests for the removal of the pieces, saying that it would not engage in such censorship. In fact, the board's president, Sally Foster, lectured the untutored, saying, "the nude human body has been an acceptable subject of paintings and sculpture for centuries and could hardly be considered offensive by anyone who has ever visited a major art museum." She said that the museum respected "this adverse comment in the tradition of mutual free expression" and agreed to reexamine the museum's guidelines for future exhibitions in a "desire both to serve the community and merit its support."[159]

Nudity or partial nudity continued to attract censors. For instance, in Great Bend, Kansas, at an art show at Barton County Community College, a female sculptor saw her male torso removed from the show because it displayed genitals. Taking up the cause of gender equality, Raylene Wilkinson, the artist, noted that her two female nude sculptures remained in the show. The discriminatory action, she said, seemed to be based on a view that "a woman's body is a piece of art and a man's body isn't."[160]

When Idaho State University barred children under the age of seventeen from an art exhibit because of paintings of scantily clad women, labeling the exhibit "adult viewing material" and placing plain brown paper over the windows, the gallery saw record attendance.[161]

In the fall of 1993, at both William Patterson College in Wayne, New Jersey, and Northern Virginia Community College in Loudoun, pictures of female nudes brought protest and demands for their removal from public view. School officials, however, stood firm. In both cases they rejected any compromise, saying the right of free expression prevented such censorship.[162]

In the past censors could succeed by simply pronouncing certain images offensive, but now with greater legal protection for artistic expression, the rationale for censorship has narrowed. Censors have had most success in recent times when they can claim that offending works of art would be seen by children. When that rationale was not available, censors have found their task much more difficult. However, a relatively new approach to justifying censorship has been born of an age of political correctness with its inroads on free speech.

The attack on pornography by women's groups who feel that such sexual material objectifies and degrades women is based upon a new group sensitivity that threatens free expression.[163] Such critics demand that the public forum be sanitized. In 1991, Elizabeth Broun, the director of the National Museum of Art in Washington, D.C., decided to remove part of an exhibit in contemporary American photography. The piece was done by Sol LeWitt. It consisted of a black box with ten openings through which the viewer could peer and watch a nude woman come closer and closer. Broun concluded that it was a "degrading pornographic experience." Jock Reynolds, the exhibit organizer who hosted the Mapplethorpe exhibit after the Corcoran cancelled it, was incensed, as were many of the other participants whose work was included in the show. Eventually a compromise was worked out by which the LeWitt work remained but was introduced by two different cards affixed to the wall, one done by Broun and the other by Reynolds. In addition, viewers could write their comments in a book that was made available.[164]

In addition to opposing pornography as demeaning, some women have argued that artwork should be removed because its presence constitutes sexual harassment. For instance, some female employees at the Central Intelligence Agency found an abundance of female breasts in the paintings of Carmen Trujillo potentially harassing. The Cuban-born artist was to have been honored with the exhibit as part of Hispanic Heritage Month. The agency and the artist disagreed about the number of works deemed unacceptable, but they agreed that the exhibit should be cancelled. Trujillo, however, demanded an apology.[165] After complaints, firemen in Los Angeles County were instructed that certain publications, such as *Playboy*, were banned from all work areas, including lockers. The Los Angeles County Fire Department was staffed by 2,390 male and 11 female firefighters. A federal judge struck down the policy, leading a National Organization for Women chapter president to argue that the workplace was not "a free marketplace of ideas." After the judicial ruling, a compromise was worked out: sexually explicit materials would not be permitted in public areas, and "nonconsensual sharing" of such materials was prohibited.[166] When some female employees in California at the Mill Valley City Hall, which regularly hosted art exhibits, said that the nearly nude paintings in the present display made them uncomfortable, the city manager arranged for their removal. However, when the American Civil Liberties Union (ACLU) suggested that the city council get the city attorney to review the decision, the attorney agreed with the organization that the removal had violated the free expression right of the artists. Eventually a public forum that drew 150 persons was held, and the city council concluded that no such ban was necessary.[167] Finally, Marc Simmons found that certain women workers at the Connecticut Workers' Compensation Commission Office were oppressed and demeaned by a painting of his daughter and her friends in swimsuits and sunglasses hanging in the office reception area. For them *Girls on the Beach* became females in scanty attire. Also, artist Julie Kay Karlson was asked to remove her oil painting of a nude woman from the village hall by the assistant city manager in Yellow Springs, Ohio, because employees were complaining of sexual harassment.[168]

One might expect that an employee entering the Lesbian, Gay, Bisexual and Transgender Center at the University of Michigan at Flint would be equipped to handle a charcoal drawing that had been on the wall for two years. Titled *Hermaphrodite*, it depicted a naked female with wings and a penis. The employee concluded that the drawing created a hostile work environment, and when she protested, she won the support of school authorities.[169]

Whether the employee was disturbed by the naked female body or the penis or both was not reported, but clearly the penis remains the most censored of human parts. *Washington Times* photographer Kenneth Lambert would agree. He won first place in the colored features category of the annual contest of the White House News Photographers Association. The offending shot, entitled "Everything Old Is Nude Again," captured a woman and nude man looking at each other at the 1994 Woodstock festival. Normally a winning photo would be given to the president, displayed in the Library of Congress, published in the annual yearbook, and hung at the yearly dinner. Because the photo included the naked man's penis, it was unacceptable and was denied the honors accorded other winners.[170]

One would have thought by the mid-1990s that the controversy over arts funding would have run its course, but such was not the case. In a guest column in the *New York Times* Lynne A. Munson, who had been special assistant to Lynne V. Cheney, chairperson of the NEA from 1990 to 1992, expressed her views on NEA grants. She said that the awarding of grants was always political and that the federal government should get out of the business of supporting the arts. She summoned to her support Philip Pearlstein, the noted artist, who had written an article four years earlier in which he questioned the absence of representational art from consideration.[171] Pearlstein responded in a letter, saying that his comments did not support Munson's position. He not only indicated the value of such grants to the artists, including himself, but he also said that when, as a member of the peer review panel, he mentioned the absence of representational art he was invited to look at the rejected applications. He culled numerous applications from that pool and some of those so culled were granted awards. By the mid-1990s the NEA, to avoid controversy, decided to eliminate these individual grants.[172]

Most often artists withdraw work when objections are raised, but at times artists rebel. When the Barnwell County Museum's board members in South Carolina looked at Robert Sherer's nine paintings of male nudes, they claimed that they had been misled and locked the gallery. Sherer sued to have the paintings shown in the gallery and requested damages of ten million dollars for violation of his contract and his right of free expression. The museum's board finally agreed to a settlement that provided for a four-day showing and a cash award of thirty-five hundred dollars.[173]

When fig leafs are unavailable, perhaps potholders, doilies, and gloves will do. This was the response of the Deluxe Coffee House in Wilmington, North Carolina, when police found the latest art exhibit of nudes too revealing. State regulations covering businesses that offer alcoholic beverages had placed restrictions on such displays, and since the coffeehouse served beer and wine, it had to cover up the revealing parts.[174]

One might believe that after all the sexually explicit images that pervade popular culture today that the old masters might finally be safe. One would be wrong, however, as the action of school officials at Brigham Young University in October 1997 clearly demonstrate. They pulled four nudes from an exhibit of works by the French sculptor, Auguste Rodin, including his famous *The Kiss.* The university censors also decided not to distribute the visitor's guide to the exhibit because it contained pictures of two of the offending sculptures.[175]

Such episodes involving classic art seem to be dwindling, but such is not the case with modern art. Take the case of Roxie Thomas and Trina Nicklas in Bradenton, Florida. Over three years the two women planned an exhibit of works dealing with censorship titled Contained/Controlled. Twenty-six individuals, including visual artists, poets, and educators, contributed work that captured their personal views on, and experience with, censorship. The hope of the planners was to stimulate discussion. Four days before the show was to open, John James, chairman of the Department of Art, Humanities, Speech and Theater, expressed his objection to one of the artworks. It was a twenty-six-foot piece done by Barbara Jo Revelle, the chair of the University of Florida's art department. In the piece, Revelle had sought to present to viewers an understanding of the definition of obscenity. The provocative photos she included were integrated into a piece of contemporary art and as such had to be judged in terms of the whole work. Among the hundreds of photos the piece contained were a few of erect penises. When Thomas refused to remove the piece, James cancelled the show. The gallery director and the school's top administrator agreed with the decision. One critic assailed the decision as cowardly, noting that "if the public has the maturity to handle scandalous allegations against its president, it can deal with male genitalia in art."[176]

Conferring heroic status on Mayor Rudolph Giuliani of New York City in the wake of the terrorist attacks of September 11, 2001, tended to obscure his controversial record in office, especially his ongoing campaign against artists. Real estate interests found a ready supporter in the mayor in their attempt to prevent artists from hawking their wares on the streets of the city. Artists were regularly arrested for selling without a license, and the mayor eventually won a favorable ruling from a federal district court. Such restriction, the court said, could be imposed because art is not protected by the First Amendment. Correcting the errant district court, the Second Circuit Court of Appeals ruled that art is a form of fully protected speech. Therefore, artists could not be required to obtain a license, and the city was barred from preventing the display and sale of the art. Furthermore, the court continued, the public itself had free expression rights that had to be protected—the right to view and purchase art on the streets. Lecturing the compliant district judge and mayor, the appellate judges said: "Such myopic vision not only overlooks case law central to the First Amendment jurisprudence but fundamentally misperceives the essence of visual communication and artistic expression."[177]

A leading opponent of Giuliani, Robert Lederman, an artist and writer and a plaintiff in the second circuit case, was arrested in the nation's capital on Arts Advocacy Day in 1997 for handing out leaflets protesting Mayor Giuliani's campaign against street artists. When his case came to trial, the District of Columbia judge found the underlying law banning expressive conduct in front of the Capitol an unconstitutional restraint on speech. Lederman's legal victories were further contested, primarily in regard to Central Park. Artist protests in front of the Metropolitan Museum of Art led to further arrests. What followed was the closure of one hundred New York City streets to all vending.[178]

Victories by artists over censors are not the rule, but they do occur. In 1996 city authorities in Pasco, Washington, arranged with the Mid-Columbia Arts Council for an ongoing public exhibit of artworks in city hall. Printmaker Janette Hooper and sculptor Sharon Rupp were among the artists selected for an early exhibit. When Hooper delivered her linoleum relief prints, which pictured Adam and Eve visiting certain German landmarks, city officials balked at the nudity in the prints, saying they were too "sexual." Rupp had better luck in that her sculptures were displayed for a week before the request came for their removal. In one bronze piece entitled *To the Democrats, Republicans, and Bipartisans,* a woman is shown with her buttocks exposed. Rupp was told that the sexual nature of such pieces, coupled with their political implications, made her sculptures unacceptable. With the help of the ACLU, Hooper and Rupp responded by suing the city. Eventually they were vindicated, as the Ninth Circuit Court of Appeals ruled in 2001 that once the city had opened the public building as a forum for local art it could not "make choices based on the content of the art." In the subsequent settlement, the city agreed to pay the ACLU seventy-five thousand dollars for attorney fees and legal costs and to issue a formal apology to the artists for "censoring their artwork."[179] The ACLU was also successful in representing Daria Fand, whose nude woman on a cross was banned from an annual Honolulu Hale exhibit composed of the work of women artists. The city included the painting in the 2002 exhibit and paid the ACLU five thousand dollars for fees and costs.[180]

Such suits, however, are costly and arise most often when an interest group, such as the ACLU, embraces the cause and shoulders the costs. Furthermore, such suits require some commitment to defend free expression. One suspects that the gallery owner's initial response in Pilot Point, Texas, is much more typical. When police served notice that the painting of a nude Eve on the side of his gallery might lead to a charge of distributing harmful material to minors, the owner agreed to clothe Eve. To those persons who felt that he should have contested the threat, the owner replied: "I don't feel it's my job to jeopardize my financial stability for the constitutional rights of the citizens of Pilot Point."[181]

Wes Miller, the gallery owner, got the artist, Justine Wollaston, to cover the offending nipples with mock crime-scene tape. The tape did not survive high winds, and once again Miller complied with requests to cover Eve. Now the artist wired a bikini top made of artificial flowers across the offending breasts. By this time, the town of four thousand people had become national news over the Eve incident, and the ACLU offered aid to Miller to challenge the ban by seeking an injunction against threatened police action. Miller said he was lucky that the incident had attracted national attention: "It had First Amendment issues, a bit of religion, a bit of nudity, and then you mix in small town mentality and stir that all up with art." As legal bills mounted, the town leaders decided to agree to a settlement that would restore Eve to her natural state. Miller invited interested parties to the new unveiling, and Wollaston used wire cutters to remove the bikini top, which she whirled over her head before throwing it into the cheering crowd.[182]

In a democracy that is best understood in terms of interest-group politics, the story of Wes Miller is instructive. In weighing his options initially, he realized that a challenge to the police demand would be financially costly; only when he was offered support that would eliminate the financial burden was he willing to insist upon his rights. That rights are not immediately recognized and that challenges to inroads upon them requires money, and often a substantial amount, is simply a fact of life. Here in the community of Pilot Point the ACLU was able to call upon resources that caused town authorities to decide that the cost of covering Eve's nipples to please some residents was just too high. Freedom from the financial burden and victory, however, does not free such a challenger from other costs in a community where disapproval does not terminate with a judicial order.

The Constitution with its protection of free expression does indeed give room to artists, as well as others, to challenge prevailing social values. Many critics would agree that such a challenge is art's noblest function. Were some art not offensive it would not be performing its social role. As it performs this function, it stirs opposition, often sufficient enough to convince legislators or other government officials to take action. The ban on such action that the Constitution imposes frustrates the majority will, but then that is its purpose—to protect the individual's free expression from suppression by the majority.

With so much of the human anatomy on display in all sorts of media today, one would expect that the prudery that characterized the nineteenth century and led would-be American artists to seek instruction in Europe to have disappeared. It has not in Middletown, New York. There, popular high school art teacher, Peter Panse, ran into difficulty when he suggested to his advanced students that they take figure-drawing classes, in which naked men and women pose. That such an exercise is an integral part of traditional artistic training did not prevent school authorities from suspending Panse from his teaching job. A petition against the action garnered fifteen hundred signatures.[183]

Panse's case stirred national attention, but even more controversy was generated by what happened to a veteran elementary school teacher north of Dallas in Frisco, Texas. Sydney McGee, a popular art teacher for twenty-eight years, took fifth grade classes to the Dallas Museum of Art in April 2006. In September her principal sent her a memo saying that she had exposed the students to nude statues and paintings. She was suspended by the school board and denied a transfer to another school. School authorities denied that the action was simply taken because of the field trip, but their protests were weakened by the fact that McGee had always received superior evaluations.[184]

Although the nude human form has regularly been both the focal point of art instruction and a fertile subject of artistic production, its exhibition as art continues to stimulate the censorial urge. Making the male's sexual organs the most censored part of the human anatomy only encourages artists to do battle on that front. And, as censors since the beginning of time have discovered, their work often succeeds in publicizing the existence of the offending art, thus whetting the public's appetite for it. When coupled with constitutional protection, this counterproductive effect makes censorship less of a threat than it potentially could be.

Battles over art at the local level can be expected to continue, not only because nudity in art continues to engage the censorial urge but also because of the challenge that art regularly poses to the status quo. What has changed is the willingness of artists to fight back and a willingness of organizations to take up the cost of challenging censorship in the arts.

In the movie She Done Him Wrong *Captain Cummings (Cary Grant) asks Lady Lou (Mae West): "Haven't you ever met a man who could make you happy?"* Photo from mptv.net.

3

The Movies

Teaching the Wrong Lessons and in the Dark as Well

The Cinema, that Temple of Sex, with its Goddesses, its Guardians, and its Victims.[1] (Jean Cocteau, 1959)

The first law of censorship—and probably the only important one not inscribed on the statute books—is this: in a democracy, the more popular the art form, the greater the demands for censorship of it.[2] (Murray Schumach, 1964)

It may be that sex in the movies will be surrounded by hypocrisy till it's put there by a generation that does not equate it with sin.[3] (David Shipman, 1982)

We who made the pictures were sometimes led to wonder whether commercialized virtue might not be as unhealthy for the country as commercialized vice, while utterly lacking the latter's brighter side.[4] (William C. DeMille, 1939)

The Hays Production Code sought to ban any film that "shall infer that casual or promiscuous sex relationships are the accepted or common thing."[5] So, when Paramount Studios tested the waters in 1930 on the possibility of bringing the popular Broadway star, Mae West, and her musical, *Diamond Lil*, to the screen, the Hays Office rejected the idea. Its "vulgar dramatic situations and highly censurable dialogue" were unacceptable. What else could one expect from a performer and writer who had brought a production titled *Sex* to Broadway, and her play, *The Drag*, about homosexuality, to nearby New Jersey. Paramount shelved the idea, but as the Depression worsened in 1932 and the company reported a loss of twenty-one million dollars, it thought that Mae West might be what the financial doctor ordered. Looking for new worlds to conquer, West, however, was not awed by Hollywood. On her arrival in Los Angeles she said to reporters: "I'm not a little girl from a little town makin' good in a big town. I'm a big girl from a big town makin' good in a little town." And right she was; her platform shoes and long dresses added to her natural height of five feet, four inches. And her full figure added to the impression that she was a big woman. By the comment, of course, she meant that she could take care of herself. In many ways she personified the sexual revolution that had taken place in the 1920s. She was smart and in control, the aggressor who toyed with men, the mistress of the double entendre, who one critic said could not sing a "lullaby without making it sexy." In a small part in a movie starring George Raft, the star himself commented: "She stole everything but the camera."[6]

Paramount sought to capitalize on her box office appeal, and West insisted that the vehicle be *Diamond Lil*. The studio decided to challenge the ban on the property and began preparations for production. William H. Hays, the former postmaster general and now the movie czar, was not unsympathetic to the studio's financial plight. He convened a special board meeting that gave its approval to the project on the condition that the title be changed. It would appear as *She Done Him Wrong*, but no one was fooled. Certain elements of the plot were cleansed; the crime involved became counterfeiting, not white slavery, and with everyone's eager concurrence the film was to be a comedy, not a drama.[7]

At a time when Jean Harlow and other actresses were exposing their physical attributes in their films, Mae West was always covered from head to toe. John Wayne suggested that this modesty concealed the fact that she was really a man. However, the problem the censors had with West was not the exposure of flesh but rather what she said and how she said it.

Within three months of the release of *She Done Him Wrong*, it had garnered box office receipts of two million dollars, ten times its cost. Women loved this actress who put men in their proper place, who did what they, themselves, could not do. Cary Grant plays the disguised federal agent who becomes West's target. She asks "Why don't ya come up and see me sometime." Telling him he can be had, West responds to his query about whether she has ever found a man who could make her happy, saying, "Sure, lots of times." Some city and state censor boards banned the entire film, though many others simply cut the famed one-liners along with the lyrics from the song entitled, "A Guy What Takes His Time."[8]

Hays had to deal with the protest of those custodians of morality including the Roman Catholic Church, whose launching of the Legion of Decency is often credited to Mae West's early films.[9] He cited the critical and popular acclaim, though he also recognized that decisions here at the center of the industry were not limiting the hatchet work of the local censors. West's second success was *I'm No Angel*. Some clergymen called it "demoralizing, disgusting, suggestive and indecent," but audiences delighted in West's ribald humor. Again playing opposite Cary Grant, West announces, "When I'm good, I'm very good. But when I am bad, I'm better." Accused of relationships with many men, she replies "It's not the men in my life, but the life in my men."[10] Audiences responded enthusiastically to the humor, but for the custodians of the moral welfare such responses only confirmed how very much their crusade was needed.

The League of Decency extended its influence by lending its support to strengthening the enforcement of the Hays Production Code. West's later features would feel the brunt of the new regime, and her films would suffer as a result.[11]

When movies began to gain popular attention in the 1890s, spoken dialogue was more than a generation away. That fact mattered little, for what then seemed so challenging to the moral order was the ready availability of the moving images themselves. For instance, in 1896 many viewers congregated to watch *The Kiss*, forty-two feet of images running less than half a minute and projected on the screen by a contraption known as the Vitascope. The filmed sequence was lifted from a musical farce, *The Widow Jones*, that had been playing at New York's Bijou Theatre. Just before the final curtain, fortyish May Irwin succumbed nightly to the charms of her leading man, John C. Rice, in an embrace culminating in the kiss.[12] The stage kiss was so unexceptional that it received no notice in the *New York Times'* review of the production.[13] But when the production's stars traveled to Thomas Alva Edison's West Orange studio to film their concluding scene, *The Kiss* became the target of those self-appointed keepers of the public morals.

In the film, Rice smoothes his mustache; then Irwin backs away coyly; Rice advances and they snuggle; and then, as he caresses her cheek, Rice plants a kiss on Irwin's upper lip.[14] What bothered the would-be censors in this first screen kiss was the physical contact between man and woman captured in film for all to see. And, because of the close-up, it seemed much more real than the nightly stage kiss.

From the beginning of screened entertainment, the moralists' ire often redounded to the benefit of the box office. *The Kiss* became the most popular

Vitascope film,[15] despite, or maybe just because of, the protests of those who labeled the film filthy and immoral.[16] When the film came to Chicago, Herbert S. Stone, publisher of the *Chap Book*, a periodical aimed at the cultural elite, called it vulgar and degrading. He suggested that it was time for "police interference."[17] Sex was to be hidden from public view, not blatantly displayed in pictures that moved.

In the following year, censors focused their attention on Biograph's film of the belly dancer, Fatima.[18] May Irwin and John C. Rice had been fully dressed in characteristic Victorian garb, but Fatima wore filmy garments and moved her body in suggestive ways. In fact, her peep show dance did incur protest, and the distributor superimposed white cross-hatching across the dancer's breasts and hips. This doctoring still left her naked midriff and navel exposed.[19] However, a Fatima competitor, *Dolorita in the Passion Dance*, has the distinction of being among the first films to incur official censorship. On the boardwalk in Atlantic City, New Jersey, was a well-patronized Kinetoscope parlor that featured the filmed dance. The men waiting their turn outside had stirred the interest of a local minister, who, upon viewing the peep show, contacted the police. They convinced the establishment's owner to stop showing the film, thus marking the start of government officials deciding what was or was not appropriate to be shown on the screen.[20]

As movies became the first great mass medium, they would be caught up in the changing morality of the dawning century. Although the stage was and still is not free from would-be censors,[21] from the very beginning there was something much more disturbing about movies.[22] "Their extraordinary power to capture reality and give it representation in the most simply understandable terms has . . . convinced many persons that they have a special capacity for harm."[23] Furthermore they were created for a national market with a distribution system that limited the effects of local censorship. Unlike the stage, which attracted limited audiences and tended to segregate classes by the nature of the entertainment, motion pictures were a medium designed to attract the widest possible audience. Censors never worried about *their* own lack of control or susceptibility to undesirable influences; their concern was always directed toward those individuals or groups who were perceived to be immature or impulsive, those who would absorb the wrong lessons from this pervasive and persuasive medium. So, while the May Irwin and John C. Rice kiss was repeated nightly at the Bijou, it became potentially harmful only when it was shown again and again to audiences that might not be able to resist its suggestive appeal.

Motion pictures were christened the "democratic art," because of their accessibility to all,[24] including immigrants unfamiliar with the English language. Children were eager patrons of the nickelodeons, the makeshift, storefront theaters that, beginning in 1905, spread like wildfire throughout the country. Because of the perceived power of the image over the word, the motion picture was subjected to that most dreaded of restraints—prior censorship. As the American nation emerged from its colonial beginnings in the late eighteenth century, one of the prized rights that its people insisted on protecting was free speech, and what that meant, at the very least, was freedom from prior restraint. The imagined power of the moving image broke down what had been an American aversion to such restraint.

The drive to restrict what could be shown on the screen began in the great cities.[25] *The Great Train Robbery* of 1903 began to tap the exciting potential of the new medium, and the story film became the new standard. By 1907 the *Chicago Tribune* was ready to condemn the nickelodeons, saying that they were "ministering to the lowest passions of children" and should be suppressed for their "wholly vicious" influence. About 100,000 moviegoers daily patronized the 116 nickelodeons, 18 vaudeville houses, and 19 peep shows.[26] The *Tribune* editorial kicked off a public debate in the Windy City newspapers in the spring of 1907. While detractors of the new medium pointed to titles, such as *Old Man's Darling, Beware, My Husband Comes*, and *Gaieties of Divorce*, supporters cited *Cinderella*, and the *Passion Play*. Critics who stressed the educational value of the movies implied that, if adolescent patrons "were set on the high road to hell by the *Gaieties of Divorce*, they could be "brought back on snowshoes by the *Wonders of Canada*." Although Jane Adams, the founder of Hull House, a social settlement that ministered to the needs of recent immigrants, advocated regulation rather than suppression, the Chicago City Council decided otherwise.[27] Chicago's charter gave the city authority to "license, tax, regulate, suppress and prohibit exhibitions, shows and amusements," and the council used this authority to mandate a permit for the showing of any movie. That permit could be denied by the police chief or his delegates if they judged the movie to be "immoral or obscene."[28]

When the police chief denied a permit to two early westerns, *The James Boys*, and *Night Riders*, a number of nickelodeon operators appealed the decision to the courts. The exhibitors did not claim that their free speech rights had been denied; rather they argued that they were singled out from other amusement providers for discriminatory treatment. They also claimed that power had been unlawfully delegated and that their property interests had been invaded. Quickly disposing of the first argument by saying that all motion picture exhibitors were treated the same way, the Illinois high court then ruled on the delegation issue. Was the legislature giving to the police chief what amounted to legislative power? No, said the court, adding that "the average person of healthy and wholesome mind knows well enough what the words 'immoral' and 'obscene' mean." Finally, in regard to the invaded property interest, the court said that the plaintiffs had "no legitimate property interest in immoral or obscene commodities." In conclusion, the court ruled that Chicago authorities could use their power to secure decency and morality to head off "evil effects upon youthful spectators."[29]

Repeatedly the judgments of the Chicago chief of police or his delegates were upheld when challenged, but a federal court intervened, ruling that Chicago censors had exceeded their authority.[30] In 1914 the ordinance was amended to allow for a special permit that could be granted with the stipulation that persons under the age of twenty-one be denied admission when the movie was deemed harmful "to the minds of children." Both a federal trial and a federal appellate court interpreted the age restriction section of the Chicago ordinance to confer no authority to employ different standards in determining what was obscene or immoral. In other words, before persons under twenty-one could be excluded from a film show, the authorities had to determine that the movie was immoral or obscene using the entire public as the standard—"the old and the young, wise and foolish, learned and ignorant." Only then would the age restriction provision come into play.[31]

Although Chicago became the first city to institute a system of movie censorship by law, the bigger metropolis to the East, New York, adopted another approach in dealing with the imagined harm movies could inflict. These first attempts to control the content of movies came during the period known as the Progressive Era, when reformers had confidence that human nature could be shaped by changing the environment. Worry about the influence of the movies shown in darkened places that invited "illicit lovemaking and iniquity" was part of a larger reform concern about vice in the nation's cities. Urban businessmen and professionals saw disruptions of the family unit coming from the mingling of classes and from the evolution of a new woman growing restive with her assigned place in Victorian society. In controlling vice, reformers hoped to preserve the sexual order that the family represented.[32]

As censors were on the march in Chicago, their counterparts were equally active in New York City. *The Unwritten Law*—a movie based on a recent trial that made headlines from January to April—had been a target in Chicago and was now one in New York as well.[33] In May 1907 the Children's Society, which repeatedly saw danger in the nickelodeons and penny arcades, secured the arraignment of a theater owner for showing the movie. Members of the society said that his venue had been packed with children from ages four to fifteen enjoying the film with its scenes of a marriage ceremony, drugging, and the murder of the noted architect, Stanford White at the hands of Harry K. Thaw. The object of their mutual affection, teenager Evelyn Nesbitt, debuted in this, her first film.[34] Eventually, child advocates were able to secure a city ordinance banning children under sixteen years of age from motion picture houses, unless they were accompanied by an adult. The law was impossible to enforce, and theater owners were not about to turn away a clientele that has always been important to the profits of the movie industry.[35] In fact, theater operators often advertised age limits on attendance for the very purpose of attracting more customers.

Acting upon earlier advice given to him by the police commissioner, New York's mayor, George B. McClellan issued an order closing all five-cent movie theaters by revoking their licenses on Christmas Eve, 1908. He was challenged in court, and his decision was reversed. When he then sought their closure on Sundays unless the films they showed had educational value, he was met by inventive theater operators that had narrators point out what was being shown on the screen, such as, "these are railroad tracks."[36]

Fear of such official censorship, however, was ever present, and the producers of films conceded that some type of regulation might be acceptable. The alternative, then, to the type of censorship imposed by Chicago, was a form of self-censorship. In New York a National Board of Censorship was created, which changed its name in 1915 to the National Board of Review. Volunteer censors, both men and women, viewed the movies in the offices of the Motion Picture Patents Company. The industry financed the board and found its members in harmony with the industry's interests both in improving the quality of motion pictures and in heading off both state and federal government censorship. Although the board was criticized because of its close relationship to the industry, it did achieve a degree of influence in the city and in the nation as a whole. Its seal of approval, the industry hoped, would head off further censorship.[37]

The board's permissive attitude, especially in dealing with matters of sex, however, did not stall the censorship drive. For instance, in a five-month period in 1914, when the Chicago police chief and his delegates rejected one hundred films, the board of censorship only banned thirteen, and when the Chicago authorities asked for 928 cuts, the New York board requested only 198. New Yorkers were more worried about excessive violence and criminal conduct than they were about sex. Sexual themes in the movies were early recognized as crowd pleasers, and the New York censors had no blanket objection to films about birth control, nudity, or even prostitution. One Midwestern citizens' group complained about the board's certification of *The Little Girl Next Door*, a motion picture dealing with the world's oldest profession. Although the film ended in a traditional manner with the sinful being punished, the group felt that a thirty-day jail term was far too light a punishment. Furthermore, the group said, throughout the picture the prostitutes "were so attractive, well-dressed and apparently happy" that a dangerous lesson was being taught to youngsters.[38]

Movies were not the cause of all evil, but they became a convenient target for reformers. More than any other medium, they established direct contact with people in the audience, thereby short-circuiting church, home, school, or any other filtering agency. Increasingly they were being made not by native Protestants, as had been the case earlier, but rather by Jews who were part of the new immigration that seemed so threatening to traditional values.[39]

The films of the silent era were really quite daring. For instance, the writer and director Lois Weber made two films on birth control in 1916 and 1917. The latter one closely followed the pioneering work of Margaret Sanger, but the first film, *Where Are My Children*, was more of a sensation in that it dramatized the case for birth control. It followed the prevailing convention by having women who had abortions suffer, in one case by death and in the other by incurring her husband's condemnation and by her subsequent childlessness. The story was introduced by commentary that argued that film was a proper medium by which to carry on a public discussion of birth control and that children whose parents bring them to see the film might well profit from the information it contained.[40]

Such claims to educational value made sense to those who wondered how a woman's virtue, so greatly valued, was often so closely linked to keeping her ignorant of sexual matters. To make virtue a by-product of ignorance was to demean women. For instance, censors were adamant that pregnancy and its effect on the woman's body never be shown; in Pennsylvania a woman could not even be shown making baby clothes. When one of the state's censors was queried on such cuts, he responded: "The movies are patronized by thousands of children who believe that babies are brought by the stork; and it would be criminal to undeceive them." Scenes of "prolonged passion," defined as a yard of celluloid or thirty-six seconds, led the state censor to reach for the scissors.[41] When one exasperated screenwriter was asked by a Pennsylvania censor if he recognized that the first scene of the film under review was set in a brothel, the writer responded no, but then he added, apparently "the censors know more about brothels than I do."[42] Although an industry game developed that might be called "Getting It by the Censors," those persons who assumed the role tended to be suspicious individuals who were quite ready to pronounce any woman with tired feet a streetwalker.

Federal inquiry into the possibility of national censorship regularly occupied Congress's attention. Congress in 1912 had banned prizefight films from interstate commerce and in 1913 gave the secretary of the treasury the power to ban imported films. Apparently the latter authority was never exercised, but in 1930 the Customs Service was endowed with the power which it did exercise.[43] Although movie producers generally opposed federal regulation, the idea of some uniform standard being nationally applied was not unappealing.

Chicago's governmental censorship became an attractive model for reformers. In 1911 Pennsylvania became the first jurisdiction to institute censorship statewide; Kansas and Ohio followed in 1913; then Maryland joined the group in 1916, and finally New York, dissatisfied with the National Board of Review, passed a statewide law in 1921, essentially displacing the board.[44] Virginia followed the next year, and although Massachusetts, Florida, and Louisiana took official censorship action in subsequent years, their activity was for various reasons much less intrusive.[45] Although as many as ninety city movie censor boards existed,[46] such censorship activity was less of an obstacle to movie distributors in that the film could be found in its original state in the next city or town. For instance, residents of Memphis, which apparently gained the reputation of censoring more movies than any other city, could go across the Mississippi River to West Memphis to see the uncut version.[47]

In the second decade of the twentieth century the motion picture gained more respectability and the industry found a new home in Hollywood.[48] Motion picture theaters of grand scale and luxuriousness were being built, and with these palaces came increasing numbers of middle-class patrons. The one-reeler lasting fifteen minutes was being replaced by the multireel film.[49] In 1915 with D. W. Griffiths's *Birth of a Nation*, the story of the Civil War and Reconstruction as originally told in *The Clansman* by Thomas Dixon, the motion picture came of age. President Woodrow Wilson watched it in the White House, and members of the United States Supreme Court and the diplomatic corps were given a special showing.[50]

Less than a week after the justices had witnessed the film,[51] the members of the Court considered the constitutionality of movie censorship. The justices reviewed cases coming from federal district courts in Ohio and Kansas because of the claim that interstate commerce was being burdened by the state censorship of films. Rejecting that claim, the Court then addressed a free speech claim based upon the Ohio Constitution.[52] Often the justices have blundered when faced with the implications of new technology on the law. The decision in *Mutual Film Corporation v. Industrial Commission of Ohio* is an excellent illustration of such blundering. Justice Joseph McKenna, for the unanimous Court, devoted most of his opinion to the free speech/free press issue. He began by noting that state concern for public morals and welfare has led to regulation of motion pictures because "they may be used for evil" and "a prurient interest may be excited and appealed to. Besides, there are some things which should not have pictorial representation in public places and to all audiences." McKenna asserted that common sense and "judicial sense" concurred in rejecting the notion that movies can be equated with speech or the press. And then in words that have often been quoted he continued: "the exhibition of moving pictures is a business, pure and simple, originated and conducted for profit, . . . not to be regarded . . . as part of the press of the country, or as organs of public opinion." The justice sought to defend this conclusion by saying that movies simply portray events, ideas, and sentiments already "published and known." He realized, however, that much has been added to a simple verbal description when he concluded that the "attractiveness and manner of exhibition" of movies affords them a power that makes such governmental regulation reasonable.[53] What made this ignorance so damaging was that it came from the highest court in the land.

This unfortunate decision would hover as an ever-present threatening cloud over the movie industry for the next generation. However, had the Court accepted the argument of state incapacity and struck down the laws, the federal government surely would have gotten involved in film censorship. In fact, in the year of the Court's decision a bill was introduced in Congress that would have created a Federal Motion Picture Review Commission.[54]

Haphazard regulation of the movie industry by states and cities led to inconsistent results. For instance, the issue of white slavery attracted the attention of filmmakers as lurid hearings in Congress led to the passage of the Mann Act in 1910. Although the federal government had no power to suppress prostitution in the states, Congress used its commerce power to criminalize the transportation of women across state lines for immoral purposes. One of the biggest grossing films of its time, *Traffic in Souls* dealt with this racy subject. And although it was censored in some areas of the country, in other areas it played without interference. What was clear to movie producers was that such films attracted big audiences. From this point forward, "sexual themes became an industry staple."[55] Although New York City censors allowed audiences to be titillated by *Traffic in Souls*, they drew the line when Margaret Sanger sought to educate women with a nontitillating film titled *Birth Control*.[56]

The Great War in 1914 would end an age of American innocence.[57] Contemporary observers talked about the "repeal of reticence" or breaking the "conspiracy of silence."[58] Movies seemed to reflect that fact as the pat ending of sin being punished and virtue being rewarded was being challenged.[59] In fact, movies from 1907 to 1915 contributed to this repeal of reticence, as they reflected the search for the modern woman.[60] Furthermore, more of the feminine form was being revealed, and in Theda Bara, moviegoers had their first sex goddess, captured in the nude in *Cleopatra*. Theodosia Goodman, who took the screen name Theda Bara, made forty movies beginning in 1915 that one critic summed up as "redolent of damnation, transgression, fall from grace, profane worship and rest of the folklore and topography of heaven and hell."[61] Whether she played a vampire, as she did in her first film, or a historical woman, such as Du Barry or Cleopatra, her sexual desire was insatiable, as she used it to destroy powerful men. She, alone, seemed a threat to the social order. Furthermore, Bara was responsible for adding the word "vamp" to the English language, which "became an all too common noun and in less than a year . . . a highly active verb, transitive and intransitive."[62] She and her imitators made "screen sex fascinating to the growing middle-class audiences." However, it was Cecile B. DeMille, who provided "lessons in sexual pleasures and martial comforts" in a batch of films from 1918 to 1922, films that focused on the bathtub and the bedroom.[63] One editor in 1920 lamented that "children everywhere are receiving more 'education' in feminine anatomy . . . than adult humans formerly received in a lifetime."[64] DeMille also was able to film sexual orgies insulated by the fact that he was filming aspects of the Bible.[65]

The successor to Theda Bara, the dark-haired seductress, was the red-haired Clara Bow, the "It" girl who made sex less a foreign import than a domestic product. She seemed to be in constant motion, stirring to the rhythms of the Jazz Age. Unlike the vamp, Clara was a model for millions of young women who indeed were filling the workaday roles that the "It" girl played on the screen. Her career that began in the mid-1920s came to an end with the talkies. She had been implicated in a number of scandals, and her flat, unattractive voice worked against her survival in an age of sound.[66] Sex goddesses of the future not only had to appeal to the eyes of viewers but their ears as well.

Heterosexual women, however, were not forgotten by movie producers, as male stars bared arms, legs, and chests. When men wore tights, as did Douglas Fairbanks and John Barrymore, however, their sexual organs were so tightly bound so as to suggest their absence.[67] And when bulges appeared, so, too, did the censor's scissors.[68] Although Fairbanks and Barrymore might have caused a few hearts to flutter, those idols were eclipsed by the dark and mysterious Rudolph Valentino, who stirred many a woman's romantic fantasy.

Although the 1920s were a formative period in the creation of our modern society, contemporaries were caught up in a whirlpool of change. Movies had become a national phenomenon, and weekly attendance was estimated from fifty to one hundred million in a population of no more than 120,000,000.[69] Movies, more than radio or the automobile, were a prime target for the anxiety of those Americans who saw their values being challenged. A new woman was emerging who ill fitted the traditional role assigned to her sex. And the ratification of the women's suffrage amendment to the Constitution only seemed to stir more vigorously the caldron of change. Although books and women's fashions incurred the censors' wrath, movies remained their primary target. In 1927 about 80 percent of the major studios' film product was subject to censorship, which took effect not only through state and municipal regulation but through local exhibitors wielding the scissors as well. This activity was not only artistically disturbing, but also expensive to an industry that bore the costs.[70]

Critics of movie fare were abundant. Late in 1920 the Reverend Wilbur Fisk Crafts, superintendent of the International Reform Bureau, promised to end the menace brought by the movies by rescuing them "from the hands of the Devil and the 500 un-Christian Jews," who, Crafts believed, controlled the industry.[71] Edward A. Ross, an eminent sociologist at the University of Wisconsin, sought to explain the devastation that this new medium had caused. Although stage plays and novels contained material to awaken the sexual urges, Ross said that the young found them boring and paid them little attention. Movies, however, were a different story in that they made the inappropriate novel or stage play appealing to the young. The result was devastating, Ross added, in that it has created a generation of "sex-wise, sex-excited and sex-absorbed" youngsters who have become so obsessed with the "love chase" that they have shed the reserve of previous generations. He cited women's dress off and on the beaches, stories about sex in the magazines, "provocative dances," and the automobile as abundant evidence of the influence of movies on the younger generation. He suggested that not much "great achievement" could really be expected of young people who "gave themselves up to the pursuit of love."[72] That the sociologist had plenty of company in his complaints is reflected in the fact that over three-quarters of the state legislatures had introduced an average of three movie censorship bills. The General Federation of Women's Clubs found problems with 80 percent of the 1,765 films they previewed.[73]

Those persons seeking respectability for the movie industry officially criticized censorship but realized that without some form of self-censorship such respectability would be impossible. Prostitution and white slavery were early subjects with considerable audience appeal, as were movies dealing with sex hygiene and venereal diseases. Perhaps the most popular of the latter was *Damaged Goods*, which made the transition from the stage to screen in 1914. In 1919 eight new films of a similar variety were released, including the well-received *The Spreading Evil*. Any censoring of the films was more the result of some discomfort with the subject matter, for their morality was quite acceptable. The films "espoused morality and continence as a middle-class defense against the threat posed by the subordinate classes."[74] The government contributed to this trend with three training films for use with the armed forces; the films had particularly graphic scenes of the effect of syphilis. Apparently this surfeit of such films led to a backlash that led mainstream filmmakers to reject this subject and related others as fit objects for film production. This rejection led to what has been called the classic exploitation film. In addition to sex hygiene, sex, prostitution, abortion, birth, nudity, and drug use were common subjects. Such movies incurred the ire of local censorship boards and were often barred from the largest markets. When films were shown, the cuts local censors made left gaps in the continuity of the movie. Cheaply made, their distributors found enough theaters to show them, making the venture quite profitable. Because of a tie-in between Hollywood studios and theaters, many theaters were closed to such motion pictures. Worries about the practice being in violation of the antitrust law, however, halted film industry initiatives against the screening of such films. This type of film would survive the changes that took place in the film industry with its self-censorship and generally exist outside of its surveillance. In the late 1950s the mainstream film industry would begin to absorb the taboo topics that had been the fodder for exploitation films, thus bringing the genre to an end. Perhaps the most recognizable titles in the genre are *Birth of a Baby, Reefer Madness*, and *Mom and Dad*.[75]

Ellis Paxson Oberholtzer, head of the Pennsylvania Board of Censors and generally regarded as the most restrictive of movie censors, found such films especially troublesome. Under the banner of education, they preyed "upon the salacious tastes of the people."[76] He defended his censorial work in a book entitled *The Morals of the Movie*, which detailed what was being routinely offered by moviemakers generally. Trying to stir an apathetic public to action, Oberholtzer proclaimed that the movies had plunged us "into an abysmal morass of fornication, adultery, pandering and prostitution. The seduction of mill girls and stenographers by their employers, men living with mistresses and women consorting with men without marriage are flashed into the eyes of old and young, willy nilly, in our 'movie' houses." He scoffed at distributor claims that such movies were educational, saying that far too often "the lesson goes astray."[77]

As if parents were not concerned enough, a popular song entitled "Take Your Girlie to the Movies," gave advice to Johnny, who yearned to be alone with his girl, as follows:

Take your girlie to the movies,
If you can't make love at home. . . .
Take your lessons at the movies,
And have love scenes of your own![78]

To concerns about the darkness of the theater and the content of films was added a series of scandals that rocked Hollywood. They concerned the divorce of America's sweetheart, Mary Pickford, and her subsequent marriage to Douglas Fairbanks; wild parties in which Fatty Arbuckle, the popular film star was involved; the suicide of Pickford's sister-in-law; and finally the murder of the English director, William Desmond Taylor.[79] Further scandals involved Charlie Chaplin, Clara Bow, and Jean Harlow.[80] By the mid-1920s motion picture companies were writing morals clauses into the contracts with their stars.[81]

This constant stream of criticism could not be ignored by the moviemakers if they wanted to stay in business. In 1916 they created the National Association of the Motion Picture Industry (NAMPI) supposedly to encourage moral responsibility in films as well as to fight censorship bills in cities and states. In 1921 NAMPI issued thirteen points to guide what should not be shown on the screen: they included nudity, prostitution, illicit love affairs, prolonged displays of passionate lovemaking, and anything that made vice attractive. The penalty for violation was expulsion from NAMPI, but no one was expelled and the guidelines were more ignored than followed. When a newly passed New York censorship law threatened film's most lucrative market, studio heads realized that more than pious platitudes were necessary for their continued financial success.[82]

Fortunately, a model was provided in another entertainment field— professional baseball. Sullied by the Black Sox scandal of 1919 in which eight Chicago White Sox players had accepted bribes to throw World Series games, the owners looked for a savior. They found Judge Kenesaw Mountain Landis, who, as baseball's first and most powerful commissioner, brought integrity back to the game. Could the movie industry do the same?

The studio heads of the so-called Big 8, Columbia, Loews (later Metro-Goldwyn-Mayer [MGM]), Paramount, Radio-Keith-Orpheum (RKO), Twentieth Century Fox, United Artists, Universal, and Warner Brothers created a new trade association. The Motion Picture Producers and Distributors of America (MPPDA, changed in 1945 to Motion Picture Association of America [MPAA]) was to maintain the highest possible moral and artistic standards. The Big 8 made 90 percent of American films.[83] Studio executives sought a Landis-like figure to head the organization. They considered Herbert Hoover but settled for another member of President Warren Harding's cabinet, Postmaster General Will Hays. He had reorganized the postal service and had supervised enforcement of the federal obscenity law, the Comstock Act, which barred obscene material from the mail. Hays accepted the job late in 1921, agreeing to act as "the conscience of the industry."[84]

His first substantial challenge came with the murder of the English director, William Desmond Taylor. Police found a collection of pornographic photos of Taylor with some of Hollywood's well-known leading ladies. Rumors of frequenting gay bars and drug dealing abounded. Taylor's killer was never found, but Hays kept the lid on the explosive mix by carefully controlling the information given to an inquisitive press.[85]

Hays's political skill was also evident in heading off movie censorship in the states. Minnesota had decided against such censorship in 1921 without any help from Hays, but in that year New York had instituted it, becoming the sixth state that had written movie censorship into law. Within the next year most of the other states considered such censorship bills. Hays's initial success came when he addressed the annual convention of the General Federation of Women's Clubs. The organization had earlier passed a procensorship resolution that it now replaced with one condemning censorship.[86] To win these women to his side was significant because women had been newly enfranchised as a result of the Constitution's Nineteenth Amendment. Furthermore, women had gained control of the antiobscenity reform movement in large part because its basis, a concern for children, fell within the domestic arena over which women were traditionally assigned control.

The problem in Massachusetts was that club women and others had been influential in getting the state legislature to put before the voters a referendum on movie censorship with the hope, of course, that it would pass. The new anticensorship position of the General Federation was in conflict with the position taken by the chapters in Massachusetts in seeking the referendum. To help attract women to the anticensorship view, Hays employed Catherine Cooke Gilman, who had been so successful in persuading women in Minnesota to oppose movie censorship. Her efforts there had gained her national visibility. Hays poured three hundred thousand dollars into the Massachusetts campaign, seeking to convince both men and women voters that censorship was contrary to the American way. The state's voters were apparently convinced, for the measure failed by a count of two to one.[87]

If such successes as the one in Massachusetts were to have a lasting effect, Hays realized that the industry would have to censor itself. After starting a registry to prevent confusing duplication and to discourage sexually titillating titles, he and the major studio heads reached agreement on what subjects movies should avoid, in part by refurbishing the NAMPI guidelines. White slavery, nakedness, extended passionate love scenes, improper sex, and anything that made vice appealing were among the thirteen elements to be avoided. Movie producers agreed in 1924 to send materials that they were thinking of adapting for the screen to a public relations committee. The committee would then outline any problems the adaptation might present. In the first year of using the formula, sixty-seven properties were rejected, including Theodore Dreiser's *An American Tragedy*.[88]

Such voluntary cooperation was limited. One studio ignored the committee's recommendation and went ahead with *What Price Glory?* When the film proved to be a big hit, Hays felt that a stronger system of self-regulation was necessary. Consequently the Studio Relations Committee, published a list of thirty-seven "Don'ts and Be Carefuls" that the moviemakers were to avoid. Among the don'ts were nudity, even if only suggested, sex perversion, even if only inferred, white slavery, miscegenation, sex hygiene and disease, scenes of childbirth, and children's sex organs. Among the "be carefuls" were prostitution, rape, man and woman in bed together, first night scenes, seduction of women, excessive or lustful kissing, and even marriage itself. Producers could appeal a decision to a committee of three of their own, who not surprisingly usually sided with their fellow producer against the committee.[89]

Enforcement teeth were still missing, and, again as one might suspect, moviemakers fudged on their compliance with the "don'ts" and "be carefuls." Lavish sinning was often followed by a quick repentance at the fadeout.[90] In fact, looking at the movies of the late 1920s into the early 1930s, as sound entered and then dominated the medium, moviemakers enjoyed a freedom in dealing with sexual matters that they would not enjoy again until at least a generation later. Gloria Swanson's very popular Sadie Thompson might be a far cry from Rita Hayworth's a generation later, but even the Studio Relations Committee's tampering with Somerset Maugham's *Rain* still resulted in a film that could not have been made a decade later. As the 1920s ended, the committee was reviewing only about 20 percent of the stories that were being filmed, either before or after production.[91]

Although purists worried about what synchronized sound would do to motion pictures as an art form, movies had usually been combined with some sound, whether it be a lecturer, a person doing sound effects, a piano player, or a whole orchestra. What was new was what Thomas Alva Edison and others strove for at the birth of motion pictures—synchronized and amplified sound. The talkies arrived with *The Jazz Singer* in 1927, and by the end of the decade were solidly entrenched.[92] If censors had worried about the power of the projected image when silent, sound now made that image much more powerful and much more potentially troublesome.[93] Synchronized sound made cutting and rearranging scenes much more disruptive to the flow of the movie's narrative, and the MPPDA hoped that the introduction of the spoken word would bring the motion picture within the embrace of the free speech and free press clauses of the Constitution. Censors were not dissuaded from their task, and once again, as happened periodically, Congress was considering a federal movie censorship law. Hays saw an even greater need for the industry to act.[94]

At this precise time Hays was approached by Martin Quigley, the wealthy publisher of *Motion Picture Herald* and a devout Roman Catholic with close ties to the church hierarchy.[95] With the aid of Father Daniel Lord, a Jesuit priest, Quigley had put together a code to govern the motion picture industry. He shared it with Hays who realized its potential in creating the moral environment in which motion pictures should be made. One of the general principles of the code was that "No picture shall be produced which will lower the moral standards of those who see it." In early 1930, on the heels of the stock market crash of the preceding fall, the MPPDA accepted what became known as the Production Code. This code would outlast Hays's administration and would straightjacket the industry for a generation. The code was composed of two parts, the first a more detailed version of the "don'ts" and "be carefuls" of earlier years, and the second, specific applications containing restrictions on what could be shown on the screen. The applications imposed a bar on justifying adultery, making illicit or explicit sex attractive, sex perversion, white slavery, sexual diseases, nudity, and suggestive dances, among other things. Although crime and violence were also targets, the code and its application emphasized sex as the major concern. Eight of its twelve categories dealt with sexual matters, and the locations section singled out bedrooms for special concern.[96] Shortly thereafter, an Advertising Code was also adopted that banned nudity and "salacious postures."[97]

The acceptance of the Production Code did not immediately change things, even though Hays in 1931 got the MPPDA to make compulsory the submission of scripts to the committee.[98] An appeal process was still in place, and generally the appellant prevailed.[99] Sex sold movies, and the producers said they were only responding to the public's tastes. Flapper movies, some starring Joan Crawford, seemed to many critics to be actually setting tastes in fashion and techniques of lovemaking. And since sex sold, Hollywood injected it into all sorts of films, including historical dramas and musicals. Busby Berkeley's famous chorus girls, in scanty costumes, could tease as long as they remained unsullied. Despite the work of the Hays Office, the movies of the early 1930s were filled with sex, whether starring Constance Bennett, Loretta Young, Joan Blondell, or Barbara Stanwyck. The latter's *Baby Face* led one reviewer to write: "Three cheers for Sin! If you don't think it pays, get a load of Barbara Stanwyck as she sins her way to the top floor of Manhattan's swellest bank."[100] In fact one recent critic argued that the period from 1929 to 1934, before the strict enforcement of the code prevented "women from having fun," was the golden era for women's movies. In those films women "acted the way many of us think women only acted after 1968."[101]

Fallen women, played by the Crawfords and Stanwycks, seemed tame when compared to Mae West. In fact West is often credited with making censorship a reality in Hollywood. Mae oozed, paraded, and parodied sex. The sexual aggressiveness she projected riled critics who saw the threat that such a redefinition of womanhood posed. So, although Mae West was not single-handedly responsible for bringing effective self-censorship to the movie industry, she did figure prominently in the evidence cited for the need to put teeth into the Production Code.[102]

Will Hays did his best to emphasize the many other films that Hollywood produced that stirred no censorial passion, but one of West's films did more damage than a hundred others could balance. He also defended the movies, arguing that no casual link had been forged between what was being shown on the screen and any detrimental effect on children. The concern for children that has figured so prominently in the censorship story has always had a hollow ring. Any real concern has sufficient tangible targets, such as poverty and malnutrition, without having to speculate on possible detrimental influences caused by media exposure. What was at stake then and today in our modern culture wars was cultural power—whose views were to dominate, define, and establish the social norms.

At the time, however, social scientists were enlisted to help forge just such a link. The Payne Study and Experiment Fund paid for a study by the Motion Picture Research Council, a conservative procensorship organization, on the effects of movies upon behavior. Twelve investigations by psychologists, sociologists, and educators produced reports that were popularized in *McCall's* in 1933 and in an oft reprinted book entitled *Our Movie Made Children* by Henry James Forman. The academic studies were fairly well-balanced, but the Forman popularization stressed the negative effects.[103]

Well over a third of the movie audience, Forman summarized, were minors and fully a sixth of the estimated seventy-seven million in weekly attendance were under the age of fourteen. Over 75 percent of the films dealt with sex, love, and crime. Wilford Beaton, editor of the *Hollywood Spectator* condemned Hollywood's recent output of sex pictures, which he said were filthy things "manufactured by business men." Then alluding to the stock market crash, he added: "Virtue may have been at a premium once—but apparently it slumped along with other leading stocks."[104]

Forman agreed with the head of the MPPDA that movies taught lessons, but the critic saw the wrong lessons being taught. Citing evidence that particular ethnic and racial attitudes were changed by viewing certain motion pictures, Forman worried about the power and influence of the silver screen. In one of the studies looking at 142 movies, the researcher had found "726 scenes of aggressive love-making." Moral pollution, he warned, was no less dangerous than water pollution.[105] He drew heavily from comments of adolescents, both young men and women, who concluded that the movies had taught them much about sex and lovemaking and had in fact molded their behavior.[106] Perhaps the most quoted portion of the book dealt with what was called "sex delinquency" in which Forman quoted liberally from incarcerated young women about how films had contributed to their degradation.[107]

Such "scientific evidence" gave further credibility to the idea that the movies were potentially dangerous. Just as Roman Catholic pressure had been influential in getting the Production Code in the first place, now Catholic dissatisfaction with its toothless enforcement led to a renewed attack on the immorality of the cinema. The Synod of Bishops meeting in November 1933 formed a committee to investigate the movies, a move that led to the creation of the Legion of Decency in April 1934. Roman Catholics pledged during church services to boycott films condemned by the legion. Two years later the legion established its own film classification system.

Seeing condemned films was no less than a mortal sin. Synagogues and Protestant churches followed the Catholic lead, as their flocks took similar pledges. For instance, the Federal Council of Churches of Christ in America threatened to enlist its twenty-two million members in the legion and lobby for federal censorship as well.[108]

A recovering film industry was especially vulnerable to such boycotts, and with new federal government initiatives in all areas of life coming with the New Deal, the possibility of federal censorship legislation loomed larger than ever. Facing the united opposition of church, state, and social science, the MPPDA agreed to overhaul the enforcement mechanism to give teeth to the code. On July 1, 1934, the Studio Relations Committee and the appeal process were replaced by the Production Code Administration (PCA). Hays made Joseph I. Breen, an adviser to the old Studio Relations Committee and a prominent Catholic layman, chief of the PCA, a position he would hold, except for a brief hiatus, for the next twenty years.[109]

Before a member of the MPPDA could distribute and exhibit any film, a Seal of Approval from the PCA was required.[110] Violators were to be fined twenty-five thousand dollars. Despite the fact that fines would only be levied twice and never collected, this time the moviemakers would follow the guidelines of the Production Code and accept the censorship imposed by Breen. What had changed was the bargaining strength of the PCA.[111] Although Breen could be overturned by the New York Board of Directors, these men were not moviemakers fighting for artistic freedom but rather businessmen with their eyes fixed on the bottom line.[112] Within a few years after Breen took charge, over 98 percent of screen time in the United States was occupied by films bearing the PCA seal.[113]

Will Hays had not been the Landis-like leader moral reformers had hoped for, but in Joseph Breen they found their man. Labeled the "supreme pontiff of picture morals," he defended his role as simply the executor of a code sanctified by the experience and commitment of the movie industry.[114] He quickly became the arbiter of movie morals. Precode pictures were either drastically cut or shelved, and few moviegoers could miss the way the moral universe of the movies had changed.[115] In that universe when one sinned one had to pay for the transgression in the here and now. Not only could women not be seen in their bras and panties, but also such garments could not be seen hanging to dry with the rest of the laundry. Women's underwear was an especially troubling subject for the censors in the Hays Office. They did not want a woman rising from bed in her underwear, and they continually reminded moviemakers of the need to cover a woman's breasts.[116]

Some critics objected to the influence of the Catholic Church in limiting the creative process. Clearly, the relationship between the Hays Office and the Legion of Decency was extremely close, especially during the Breen years. Breen distrusted Jews, who seemed to control moviemaking, saying they "seem to think of nothing but money making and sexual indulgence."[117] Although the legion clearly influenced the content of films for well over twenty-five years,[118] what made Breen successful was his ability to control both the producers and the clerics.[119]

The kiss, which we have seen disturbed censors early in the history of the cinema, was once again a focus of censorial interest. One Dallas movie critic concluded that screen kisses had been shortened from four seconds to one and a half since Breen took over. His counterpart on a rival paper wondered whether sexy stars would now have to don pinafores.[120] Actually, the Hays Office would eventually set a limit of thirty seconds on a screen kiss. Alfred Hitchcock in *Notorious* made a shambles of such a time limit when the Cary Grant character, while talking to the FBI chief, is kissed by the Ingrid Bergman character for almost three minutes. Open-mouthed kissing, however, was forbidden.[121]

Themes that were not banned but that were troublesome had to have "compensating moral value." Such value could be found by having a character condemn the immoral conduct or through the suffering, punishment, or reform of the wrongdoer. To aid writers and reviewers, Joseph Breen's secretary published a handbook to outline how the code was administered in practice.[122] The Production Code drew no distinction between education and titillation. As an illustration, we can look at the PCA's denial of a golden seal to *The Birth of a Baby*. This documentary, supported by eminent medical authorities, traced a woman from the learning of her pregnancy to the emergence of the child's head from the womb. The producers hoped to get some independent theaters to show the film. When New York censors banned the film, the state commission of education concurred, saying it was "indecent, immoral, and would tend to corrupt morals." In a speech before the Virginia censorship board the mayor of Richmond seemed to agree, saying that seeing such a movie would "make the minds of the young boys . . . dwell on sex." The *New Republic* disagreed, contending that the movie was "no more an incentive to lust than a plate of lamb kidneys or a motor-car accident."[123]

Although such documentaries did stir the interest of moviemakers, ever since movies adopted a narrative style, books and plays attracted their attention. From the beginning certain stories were so problematic that they were either rejected at the proposal stage or the story was changed substantially, at times including the title as well. For instance, William Faulkner's novel *Sanctuary* became *The Story of Temple Drake*, one of the problem pictures of 1933.[124] Also, two decades passed before the musical *Pal Joey* was brought to the screen. In finally making the transition, the relationship between the former stripper who had become a society matron and her paid lover had been sanitized and camouflaged. The same thing happened to

Larry Hart's lyrics, including "Bewitched, Bothered, and Bewildered." "Vexed again. Perplexed again. Thank God I can be oversexed again," would not survive Hays Office scrutiny.[125]

The generally smooth operation that Breen ran increasingly distanced the world of film from everyday life.[126] However, he generally freed moviemakers from controversy, closed markets, and pressure from various interest groups. Although homosexuality, venereal diseases, and white slavery were banished from the screen, various other sexual themes remained if they were essential to the plot and if the wrongdoer was suitably punished. After all, sexualized romantic stories were a mainstay of the movie business. Under Breen's watchful eyes, sexual matters were often submerged and had to be rescued by the imagination of the viewer. Movies desexualized their language and subject matter. Tarzan's Jane was outfitted with a skirt, Busby Berkeley's chorus girls were now more clothed than their predecessors, Jean Harlow did not bare her breasts, and Clark Gable kept his shirt on. Studios complied with the Hays Office, as Breen's operation was popularly known, and although this self-censorship did not eliminate all state and local censorship, it satisfied many of the industry's critics.[127]

Foreign-made movies generally were not submitted for approval because they were shown in relatively few theaters to relatively few people. The most notorious of the foreign films, in fact the first one barred by United States Customs from entering the country, was revised and submitted to the Hays Office. The title was *Ecstacy* and it starred a nude Hedy Keisler, who later took the name Hedy Lamarr. It never received the golden seal.[128]

While stars such as Mae West did not survive the new era, in part because she refused to tweak her image, others did. For instance, one New York newspaper headed a review of a Jean Harlow vehicle as follows: "NEW HARLOW PICTURE HAS MORALS: 'Holdout for Matrimony' Advice to Girls in Capitol Film."[129] Harlow was credited with shifting male interest from female legs, so much on display in the 1920s, to breasts, the nipples of which were often quite visible.[130] When the erotic appeal of cleavage seemed to run its course, the sweater girl in the person of Lana Turner appeared, causing Breen to ban tight sweater shots as well.[131] Whores, shady ladies, and women of the evening did not disappear in the mid-1930s. They were not clearly identified, but audiences still could pick them out. This was not only true with the never subtle sexuality of Marlene Dietrich but also with the quiet sensuality of Greta Garbo.

The attempt in 1939 to censor *Citizen Kane*, uniformly hailed as one of the greatest of American films, did not center on sex and did not involve the Hays Office, but it is worth our attention. William Randolph Hearst, the newspaper baron, took exception to what he believed to be the fictional portrayal of him and his mistress in Orson Welles's film. His mistress, Marion Davies, the actress who Hearst could not marry because of his wife's refusal to give him a divorce, was portrayed in the film, for code purposes, as Kane's second wife. Hearst used all his resources to have the movie suppressed, and in the process gave substantial credibility to the view that the movie portrayed his life. *Variety* reported in its March 5, 1941, issue that "a lot of insiders are willing to believe that an $800,000 bonfire of prints and negatives is not impossible."[132] Threats were issued that the private lives of the involved motion picture executives would be exposed in the Hearst papers if the film was released. Despite the power of Hearst and his network of newspapers, he could not suppress the film, but it became a casualty at the box office. The same might be said for many of those persons associated with the production, including Welles himself.[133]

Unlike Hearst who could not suppress nor censor the film that troubled him, Breen could, though he did not win all his battles. The instances of successful resistance are notable because they are so few. David O. Selznick won more than he lost in his battles with Breen over the sexuality in *Gone with the Wind*. Maverick Howard Hughes, the aircraft magnate and filmmaker, in seeking to bring a new sexuality to a traditionally sexless Hollywood staple—the Western—repeatedly contended with Breen. The censor said that the script of *The Outlaw* had "two sequences suggestive of illicit sex" between the main characters, Billy the Kid and Rio. The wrestling of the two in the hayloft, he wrote, has to be shot "to avoid any questionable angles and postures," and when Rio's dress is torn, no bare skin should be shown. Rio in her nightgown should be covered with a bathrobe throughout the picture, and the utmost care must be exercised in the "scene of Billy pulling Rio down on the bed and kissing her, to avoid sex suggestiveness." Also the words "a fair exchange is no robbery" to signify that Billy had use of Rio, Doc's girl, because Doc had use of Billy's horse had to be changed. Breen suggested "tit for tat" to describe the exchange, a suggestion to which Hughes readily agreed.[134]

Three months later, Breen screened the completed film and was appalled. Nothing had been done to eliminate the intimation of an illicit sexual relationship; in fact two such relationships were inescapably suggested. The censor, however, was even more incensed by something that was not found in the script—"countless shots of Rio in which her breasts are" prominently featured. Breen told Hughes that before the picture could receive a Seal of Approval "*all* the shots of the girl's breasts where they are not fully covered must be entirely deleted from your picture."[135]

Breen had been somewhat restrained in writing to Hughes, but the next day he informed his boss, Will Hays, about "a marked tendency on the part of the studios to more and more undrape women's breasts." A Universal feature was held up because of "a shocking display of women's breasts," and a Columbia picture also because scattered throughout were "'sweater shots'—shots which emphasized women's breasts by means of close-fitting garments." Last on his hit list was *The Outlaw*, which, he said, "outdoes anything we have ever seen on the motion picture screen." He said that in his ten years of critically examining movies he had "never seen anything quite so unacceptable as the shots of the breasts of the character of Rio. . . . Throughout almost half the picture the girl's breasts, which are quite large and prominent, are shockingly emphasized and, in almost every instance, are substantially uncovered."[136]

Hughes, of course, was quite aware of what he had done. In fact, he drew upon his experience as an aeronautical engineer to construct a special bra for the then unknown Jane Russell, who played Rio. The cantilevered design thrust her breasts forward, making them quite visible. He even toyed with the idea of false nipples, since Russell's natural roundness tended to submerge hers.[137]

After blowing off steam, Breen turned to the task of making Hughes's movie acceptable, saying many of the breast shots can be cut "without seriously interfering with your story line." Reel four contained six breast shots, "two of them in our judgment quite bad." Reel seven contained a dozen "very objectionable shots." Reel eight had some salvageable shots but eight or nine were objectionable, and those in reel nine were "particularly bad." Hughes appealed the decision, and eventually Breen capitulated and granted a Seal of Approval after about thirty-five feet of such shots, or less than sixty seconds of screen time, were deleted. A late casualty, for obvious reasons, was the "tit for tat" suggestion that Breen had made when he read the original script.[138]

Breen and local censors seemed to win the first round, as Hughes postponed the release of the film for a year and a half.[139] Perhaps tired of fighting over breasts, Breen resigned his job as chief censor to accept a position as head of production for RKO Studios. Finding the administrative routine boring, in less than a year he returned to the Hays Office in May 1942.[140]

What had been unacceptable earlier was not always unacceptable now. The well-received comedy, *Miracle at Morgan's Creek*, concerned a young woman who gets drunk at a party with servicemen, returns home pregnant, convinces her boyfriend to marry her, and finally has sextuplets. The film seemed so out of kilter with the Production Code that James Agee, a prominent movie critic and writer, concluded that "the Hays office has been either hypnotized into a liberality for which it should be thanked, or has been raped in its sleep."[141]

Upon his return to the Hays Office, Breen again encountered *The Outlaw*. The Justice Department in 1938 filed suit against the movie industry because the industry's control of production, distribution, and exhibition of movies constituted an illegal trust. In a consent decree, signed in 1940, the studios ceased their acquisition of any more theaters and loosened their distribution policies. Industry lawyers also convinced Hays to loosen restrictions on exhibitors of movies by changing the Production Code to make only producers and distributors responsible for violations and leaving exhibitors free to show movies that had not been given a Seal of Approval. Hughes took advantage of this new policy and opened the film in San Francisco, and although it received poor reviews, it attracted curious viewers. Its condemnation by the Legion of Decency only made it more attractive. Without explanation Hughes again withdrew the film from circulation and did not release it again until four years later in 1946. This time the complaint was with the advertising of the film, and in April Hughes was charged with violating the Advertising Code. When he lost, he sued what was now the MPAA on charges that it violated the antitrust law. The MPAA prevailed and withdrew its Seal of Approval. Although the movie ran into local censorship and was not freed from Ohio censorship until 1954, it became a top money grosser.[142]

Another Western, *Duel in the Sun*, a David O. Selznick production, ran into trouble with the Hays Office in 1946, but that trouble seemed slight when compared with the film of the popular steamy novel *Forever Amber*. Although Darryl F. Zanuck had submitted a script that was cleared by the censors, it was not the one he used in shooting the film. Amber was a Restoration woman who used her charms and body to rise in court circles. Both movies were cut and eventually received a Seal of Approval, but the latter came close to stirring a Roman Catholic boycott. Often the threat of condemnation by the Legion of Decency was a boon to box office receipts, but the outcry against *Forever Amber* led to cuts that so tamed Amber that she lost her appeal at the box office. The project was not helped by the addition of a prologue to provide a moral lesson. The prologue said: "This is the tragic story of Amber St. Clair . . . stranger to virtue . . . fated to find the wealth and power she ruthlessly gained wither to ashes in the fires lit by passion and fed defiance of the eternal command . . . the wages of sin is death."[143]

Despite changes to please the censors, the film of James Cain's *The Postman Always Rings Twice*, led *New York Times* critic, Bosley Crowther to praise the sensitive application of the code toward the end of allowing "more truthful, adult films." Not all were in favor of such films, which some critics charged with polluting American life.[144] These critics were equally upset by new foreign films, especially those from Italy and France, which were now being submitted for approval to an often disapproving Hays Office.

In fact in late 1949 Breen complained that over half of the material submitted had to be rejected, saying it reminded him of his early days. Of course, the reason for the increase in sex and violence in films was the perceived need to distinguish the feature film from the product increasingly being made available on the home television screen.[145]

Although at times the Hays Office convinced moviemakers to make changes on the basis that local censors would butcher their work, this argument certainly did not stay the hand of state and city censorship boards. In fact, the moviemakers dealt with local censors in various ways, always keeping in mind the bottom line. New York's board in 1946 totally banned the film *Scarlet Street*, in which a prostitute uses her sexuality to ensnare a middle-aged man. The New York market was central to the success of major motion pictures, and Universal, the distributor, negotiated successfully to reverse the ban. Universal was less successful in Atlanta despite its efforts, but eventually the film was shown in both cities.[146]

Hays formally resigned his spot as head of MPAA in 1946, turning the reins over to Eric Johnson with little noticeable change. However, the retirement of Joseph Breen in 1954 was a different story. The Production Code was being severely tested; an official morality enforced by a code seemed increasingly dated and now almost un-American. Furthermore, television was mounting a challenge that the motion picture industry had never faced before.[147] Radio had only an audio dimension that hardly challenged movies, which had always emphasized the visual. Free television now provided a visual alternative.[148]

As television posed its threat to the film industry, the federal government's scrutiny of the monopolistic practices of the major studios, a concern of trustbusters for over a dozen years, reached its logical outcome in a decision by the U.S. Supreme Court in 1948.[149] The ruling severed studio control over distribution by directing Paramount Pictures to divest itself of first-run theaters. In the Paramount decision, the Court all but overturned the ruling that movies were entertainment and not protected by the free speech and free press clauses of the Constitution. "We have no doubt," it said, "that moving pictures, like newspapers and radio, are included in the press whose freedom is guaranteed by the First Amendment."[150] Over the next decade or so, the other major studios followed suit, culminating in 1959 when Metro-Goldwyn-Mayer severed its connection with Loews Theatres. With the loss of an assured market came further erosion of Production Code enforcement.[151]

The Court did suggest in the Paramount case that governmental movie censorship might be vulnerable to attack. Attacked it was when New York refused to grant a permit to Joseph Burstyn to show an Italian movie titled *The Miracle*. In the film an ignorant peasant woman is seduced by a man she takes to be St. Joseph. She subsequently bears a son, who she believes is a son of God. Although a license initially was granted to the movie despite complaints that it was "sacrilegious," a statutory ground for denying a permit, that license was rescinded when the New York State Board of Regents responded to a deluge of complaints about the film. All members of the

Supreme Court in 1952 agreed on striking down the law that permitted license denials to sacrilegious films.[152]

Overturning the *Mutual Film Corporation* decision of 1915, the justices now held "that motion pictures are a significant medium for the communication of ideas." That movies entertain and that they constitute a business, they continued, was irrelevant. Even if their effect on the young could justify some governmental control, the Court ruled, "it does not authorize substantially unbridled censorship as we have here."[153] Admonishing the state for setting its censors loose to indulge their particular religious views, the justices said: "It is not the business of government to suppress real or imagined attacks upon a particular religious doctrine, whether they appear in publications, speeches, or motion pictures."[154] The decision did not end movie censorship, but the Court in subsequent decisions placed movie censorship under the heavy burden of tightly drawn guidelines targeting only obscene films. That the Court meant what it said was demonstrated in a series of decisions in which, without opinion, it reversed movie censorship decisions in New York, Ohio, and Texas.[155]

What the Court left for future resolution was the definition of obscenity; the earlier notion that what was obscene could be determined without further help by persons of reason and good faith was now reinspected as a matter of constitutional law. In 1957 the justices addressed these matters. First, they put their stamp of approval on the proposition that to determine obscenity one must take the entire audience into account, not simply the weaker or immature members,[156] a position some lower federal courts took forty years earlier.[157] Next, they upheld both state and federal obscenity laws by placing obscenity beyond the reach of the First and Fourteenth Amendments as "utterly without redeeming social importance." The justices were forced to define obscenity to separate such material from what was protected. One could not pronounce a work obscene on the basis of isolated parts detached from the whole. Material was obscene, the justices said, by determining "whether to the average person, applying contemporary community standards, the dominant theme of the material taken as a whole appealed to the prurient interest." Prurient interest was defined as "a shameful or morbid interest in nudity, sex, or excretion." The Court was careful to distinguish sex and obscenity, saying that the former "has been a subject of absorbing interest to mankind throughout the ages; it is one of the vital problems of human interest and public concern."[158]

Applying its new definition of obscenity, the Court overturned a Chicago ban on a film depicting a woman's seduction of a boy of sixteen who then goes on to engage in sexual relations with a girl of his own age.[159] In 1959 it overturned another movie censorship decision, ruling that no theme by itself can be considered obscene. The theme in question was adultery, long a concern of the Production Code as well as New York's movie censorship law. The Supreme Court accepted the characterization of the film as one that presented adultery as desirable in certain circumstances, but then said that New York cannot censor a disfavored idea without striking "at the very heart of constitutionally protected liberty."[160] Then, in 1961, a deeply divided Court confronted the issue of whether censorship prior to exhibition was constitutional. Five members of the Court said it was, but four of their brethren took exception and were ready to strike down the type of censorship that had existed in various places since its start in Chicago in 1907. Chief Justice Earl Warren, reviewing what the Court had done to make free speech and free press meaningful rights since 1915, warned that the approval of such censorship in regard to the movies might stimulate restrictions on other media as well.[161]

That the justices had difficulty in these cases is well illustrated in a 1964 decision in which six of them agreed that the French film *The Lovers*, was not obscene. The Ohio trial judge had found that the film whetted "the sexual appetite" and stimulated "thoughtful and lustful desires."[162] Some disagreement arose on the Supreme Court as to whether the obscenity test should employ national or local standards, a matter not resolved until 1973 when the Court accepted local standards as the measuring rod.[163]

Certainly U.S. Supreme Court decisions aided the campaign to get rid of a censorship that limited screen freedom, but social change had made the Production Code and its enforcement seem anachronistic and regressive in a society that was beginning to come to terms with its own diversity. Although historians have labeled the 1950s an age of consensus, beneath the surface calm bubbled the eruption that would characterize the next decade or so.

Television had challenged the movies to provide images and dialogue that tempted viewers away from the small screen. In Breen's last years, the challenge of filmmakers to the limitations of the code increased. Often, gaining the Seal of Approval was only the first hurdle, for in a number of cases the Legion of Decency paid little heed to the seal. For instance, after changes were made to earn *A Streetcar Named Desire* the seal, the legion still condemned the film.[164] Such censorship, however, only seemed to whet the public's appetite for the controversial film, a fact that encouraged producers to tackle more sensitive subject matters.[165]

From the beginning, as we have seen, films tapped the live stage for subject matter, and in 1953 Otto Preminger brought a sex farce entitled *The Moon Is Blue* to the screen. His intention was to challenge the code, and he secured the Academy Award–winning actor, William Holden, to play the male lead. Holden was sympathetic to Preminger's aim and agreed to take his pay in terms of a percentage of ticket sales. A Hollywood newcomer, Maggie McNamara, played the frank and direct young lady who talked of seduction and virginity, words banned by the code. When Breen refused to give a seal to the picture, Preminger appealed the decision. When the board upheld Breen, the director went public and said he would release the film without the Seal of Approval. United Artists, the distributor, resigned from the MPAA, and released the film without the seal. The legion issued its condemned rating and urged boycotts of any theaters showing the film, but its campaign fizzled, as the film gained wide distribution and handsome profits at the box office. When local censors agreed with the legion, courts repeatedly overturned their decisions.[166] Eight years later, in 1961, United rejoined the organization.[167] In the same year *The Moon Is Blue* was finally granted the seal.

Breen retired in 1954 and later acknowledged that his adamant stand against the movie was a mistake.[168] His assistant, Geoffrey Shurlock, took over his former boss's job and would serve until the demise of the code in 1968.[169] Early in his new role, Shurlock was disturbed by a scene that he witnessed being filmed in *Let's Make Love*, a title that obviously would not have survived in the reign of his predecessor. In the scene Marilyn Monroe wriggled and rolled around on a bed with her costar, the French actor Yves Montand. When Marilyn asked what was wrong with the scene, Shurlock said her horizonal activity seemed to be a prelude to sexual intercourse. With her cultivated naïveté, Monroe responded that intercourse could take place just as well when the parties were standing.[170] The scene stayed in the film.

More flexible than Breen, Shurlock generally allowed more than his predecessor would have allowed. For instance, Breen had killed off the filming of a short story dealing with an unscrupulous gossip columnist in part because of a suggestion of incest and a steamy sex scene. With only minor revisions, Shurlock gave the seal to the movie titled *The Sweet Smell of Success*. The same was true with *Tea and Sympathy* and *Baby Doll*. Although the legion had more difficulty with these films, it revised its own rating system to accommodate the growing sophistication of contemporary American and foreign films.[171] *Baby Doll*, based on a story by Tennessee Williams, was one of the most controversial movies of the 1950s. The title character was dressed for almost the entire movie in a two-piece short nightgown that the picture would make a fashion success. Partial nudity was coupled with a flouting of motion picture morality with its emphasis on marriage and the home.[172]

The 1960s would not only see great changes in American filmmaking but also in American society in general. Although production money was dependent upon getting the PCA to give tentative approval to a movie script, Shurlock seemed to be quite accommodating. When imports such as *Room at the Top*, which dealt with the sexual exploits of a social climber, and *Never on Sunday*, which dealt with a happy Greek prostitute, won Academy Awards, Shurlock may not have had much choice.

Such imports seemed more true to life, and the American film industry was in danger of losing its position in the world market. Filmmakers responded to the danger. In *Splendor in the Grass* the failure of the young couple to break through sexual inhibitions is seen as an unfortunate denial of natural impulses, a far cry from the days when Breen enforced the code. And when the first two James Bond pictures caused some moral critics to complain about their blatant sexuality, Shurlock responded: "It's only a little fucking. What's all the shouting about?" Increasingly words were now being heard in theaters that had never before emerged from characters on the screen.[173]

The code was modified in 1961 to allow the depiction of what it called "sexual perversion," which included homosexuality. *Midnight Cowboy*, the story of a male hustler, was a box office success and won an Academy Award for Best Picture. Despite its success as the decade ran out, more time would pass before Hollywood embraced gay characters. Also, the movie *Lolita*, based on Vladimir Nabokov's shocking best-seller of a man in love with a twelve-year-old girl, got a Seal of Approval despite the so-called sexual perversion at the heart of the novel and film.[174]

Another PCA barrier that fell in the 1960s was nudity. On the stage the musical *Hair* had a scene in which the actors shed their clothes, and *Oh! Calcutta!* brought a new frankness to the legitimate stage with its nude scenes of sexual exploration. What followed was nudity in dance and opera as well. Movies could not be far behind. Independent films not submitted for PCA review exploited this audience interest. A former photographer, Russ Meyer, tapped this vein in a low-budget film titled *The Immoral Mr. Teas*. In the film, a man acquired the ability to peer through clothes and see women naked, most of whom were large-breasted. The film played in legitimate theaters and spawned numerous imitations, supposedly 150 in three years.[175]

Nudity escaped the strictures of the Production Code in a widely heralded film titled *The Pawnbroker*. The movie contains two scenes, one in which a woman bares her breasts and the other in which a nude woman appears in a concentration camp brothel. Shurlock, increasingly besieged by moralists who condemned the new permissiveness of the PCA, demanded that the scenes be cut. When the producer and director refused and the seal was denied, they appealed to the review board. The board voted to grant a special exemption from the code if the scenes were shortened, leaving the final decision to the PCA chief to determine if such cuts were enough. The producer agreed to cut a few more frames to gain Shurlock's approval and the seal, but such changes were not enough to satisfy the legion's concern. The condemnation was based on the nude scenes, which movie critics, and even some Protestant clerics, saw as an integral part of the powerful film. Clearly losing ground even among local parishes, the legion opened its evaluative screenings to a broader cross section of Catholics. This move resulted in a liberalizing of the legion's judgments and in a new name, the National Catholic Office of Motion Pictures (NCOMP).[176]

That the '60s had brought considerable change to American society was illustrated in a number of ways. Allen Funt, the creator of the popular television series, *Candid Camera*, decided to go for a big screen audience by taping people's reactions to an attractive naked woman in *What Do You Say to a Naked Lady?* Although the woman was not shown, the comments of those who saw her constituted a substantial discourse on nudity. A growing challenge to the code from more adult-themed movies was met with resistance that was felt not by the studios but by the owners of theaters. By 1965 censorship activity at the local level greeted 60 percent of the films. Such action included prosecutions, boycotts, arrests, confiscations, and license revocations, up ten times in the last three years.[177]

Eric Johnson, the head of MPAA since 1946, died in 1963 and the MPAA drifted for a couple of years, despite pressure for either changes in the code or for some system of classifying films in terms of age suitability. Eventually Jack Valenti, an adviser to President Lyndon Johnson and former head of an advertising and public relations firm in Houston, Texas, was chosen president of the MPAA in 1966. Valenti promised to take charge, indicating that he did not see his job as one of presiding "over a feckless Code." Age classification was attractive to many, but the industry worried about its teenage audience because it had become an even more important revenue generator in the post-television age. Valenti took over as head of the MPAA in the middle of a squabble over the film version of the Edward Albee play *Who's Afraid of Virginia Woolf*. Shurlock had refused to confer a Seal of Approval on the film because of its profanity and blatant sexual references. Valenti did not challenge the ruling, but he said the final decision would be made by the review board. The board demanded two minor cuts in the dialogue, but then, as it had done with *The Pawnbroker*, it made another special exemption. Warner Brothers, the distributor, had agreed to limit attendance to persons over the age of eighteen unless accompanied by an adult. This second special exemption was followed quickly by a third for the British film, *Alfie*, the story of a womanizer who arranges an abortion for the married woman he has impregnated. In both cases the Catholic organization NCOMP went along with the MPAA ruling, apparently inclined to support the age restriction attached to both films. The success of what came to be a trial run of age classification spurred the movement away from the code and toward a ratings system.[178]

Actually the board of directors scrapped the old, lengthy code in 1966 for a streamlined version consisting of twelve sentences. The new general wording on sex left much room for interpretation, as it prohibited "indecent or undue exposure of the human body," the justification of sin or "illicit sex relationships," "intimate sex scenes violating common decency," and "obscene speech, gestures or movements." Additionally, it urged the utmost care and restraint "in presentations dealing with sex aberrations." Furthermore, scenes were to be judged not by themselves but in their relationship to the entire film. And the PCA could attach the seal to questionable films by tacking on the phrase, "Suggested for Mature Audiences." Whether these changes could stem the sexual permissiveness that the moral critics worried about was doubtful.[179]

When MGM could not gain PCA approval for Michelangelo Antonioni's *Blow-Up* because of a sexual romp of the photographer with some teenage girls and a scene of sexual intercourse, it released the film through a subsidiary. The disapproval of both the PCA and NCOMP could not prevent the film from being a success. It was praised not only by critics but also by some Protestant churchmen. In the wake of *Blow-Up*, restrictions on sexuality were loosened further and nudity and even intimations of oral sex were not enough to deny the Seal of Approval to a batch of films. In fact, the "Suggested for Mature Audiences" label was found on more than half of all studio releases.[180]

The movie business had changed; the old autocratic studio heads, who were committed to the code as evidence of their public responsibility, had been replaced. Executives now in charge measured success by the bottom line, and they realized what moviemakers had always known—sex sells. Bare breasts and suggestions of sexual relations that had so long been the target of censors at all levels were not now uncommon sights on the large screen. However, not all taboos were vanquished. Full frontal nudity was still unusual, and the erect male penis was the exclusive preserve of the unrated hard-core films.

Meanwhile, the Supreme Court, which had been routinely reversing obscenity findings, began contending with the process of movie censorship itself. In 1965 it not only reversed a decision of the Maryland board, but it also took the censors to task for their "undue inhibition of protected expression."[181] The justices required that the censors assume the burden of proof and provide for a speedy judicial evaluation of their decision. In the wake of the Supreme Court admonition, Maryland rewrote the law, but the board of censors was repeatedly reversed for failing to carry the burden of proof.[182] In the wake of the Court's decision, Kansas, New York, Virginia, and Memphis ended movie censorship.[183] Maryland finally disbanded its state censorship board, and the few remaining local boards withered away.[184] Movies henceforth would enjoy the same protection as other means of communication, subject as all were to state and federal obscenity laws.

Valenti gradually realized that even a revised code could no longer control the industry, and his choices were either to end any self-regulation or move to a system of classifying films by age suitability. The choice seemed obvious for recent moves had tested age classification and found it workable, and to end self-regulation might well invite a new round of governmental censorship. When the United States Supreme Court in 1968 gave its approval to a variable concept of obscenity based upon age and then applied it to movie censorship,[185] Valenti had no choice but to institute an industry ratings system.

He moved quickly and put it into effect on November 1, 1968. Tacking on the streamlined Production Code of 1966 at the end, the new version said the goal was to keep the film industry "in close harmony with the mores, culture, the moral sense and change in our society." Toward this end the new ratings system sought to "encourage artistic expression by expanding creative freedom" while assuring that this freedom "remains responsible and sensitive to the standards of the larger society." Calling censorship "odious" because it preempted individual choice, the MPAA pledged to give parents the information they needed to "fulfill their responsibilities" in guiding their children.[186]

This information consisted of ratings provided by the Code and Rating Administration (CARA). They initially consisted of G for general audiences, M (changed to PG in 1972) for mature audiences including mature youths, R for restricted to people sixteen or older unless accompanied by a parent or adult guardian, and X for a complete ban on patrons under the age of sixteen (changed to seventeen in 1970). The Seal of Approval was retained and given to all motion pictures without an X rating.[187] In 1984 a PG-13 rating was created, alerting parents to the fact that the film contained material that "may be inappropriate for children under 13."[188]

Ratings at both ends of the spectrum played poorly at the box office. Well over 60 percent of films received an R rating, apparently the most profitable rating. G was to be avoided at all costs. For instance, Steven Spielberg's family film, *E.T.* avoided the G by inserting the phrase "penis breath" into the dialogue.[189] Mainline producers sought to avoid the X rating, which limited the screens available to the film and often denied it advertising in the local press.[190] What this meant of course was that the ratings system had not ended the self-censorship in the industry, for nearly half of the commercial films submitted were changed as a result of the reaction of the seven censors who constituted CARA.[191] Producers often compromised with CARA to delete the material that caused an X rating, thus allowing the motion picture to be released with an R rating.

Those filmmakers who avoided the system and produced sexually exploitive films often proudly displayed a whole string of Xs on theater marquees. They were the heirs of the stag film producers, who began work in the early decades of the twentieth century and then were displaced in the early '70s "when the feature length, legitimate, X-rated 'porno' had dramatically supplanted the silent, one-reel, illegally made and exhibited stag."[192]

Some of these generally low-budget sex exploitation films attracted wider audiences. For instance, Russ Meyer's *Vixens*, labeled "soft-core pornography" became a box office success in 1969. Hard-core films, such as *Deep Throat* and *The Devil in Miss Jones* in 1972 and 1973 respectively, almost entered the mainstream as audiences for the genre grew.[193] More money was put into the features, and production values improved. For instance, *The Opening of Misty Beethoven*, often heralded as the best of the hard-core films, had a substantial budget and was a rather lavish production, shot in locations in New York and Italy. Despite the new market, the Hollywood establishment never sought to embrace hard-core imagery, such as ejaculation (the cum or money shot), fellatio, cunnilingus, the erect penis, or penetration. A brief flirtation in the early 1970s with pictures, such as *Last Tango in Paris* with Marlon Brando, and the French film *Emmanuelle*, both rated X and both promoted as prestige or art pictures, was as close to hard core as the major studios would get. United Artists, distributors of *Last Tango in Paris*, fought local censorship attempts successfully. Columbia Pictures also backed its entry, *Emmanuelle*, and advertised its portrayal of sex as fun: "X was never like this." Despite the success of both pictures, the studios did not follow up this flirtation with X films, leaving that playing field to the hardcore producers.[194]

Those producers ran into state attempts to prevent the showing of such films by declaring such showings nuisances. The problem of proving obscenity remained, for only the showing of obscene films could be construed to constitute a nuisance. Otherwise, nuisance law could be used to suppress protected speech. Whether this type of civil action would make censorship easier remained in doubt. The United States Supreme Court cooperated to the extent of preventing federal intervention in the state proceeding until state remedies were exhausted.[195]

A batch of Supreme Court decisions in 1973 effectively eliminated competition from hard-core films. *Miller v. California* not only struck "utterly without redeeming social value" from the test for obscenity but also ruled that the community standards by which obscenity was to be judged were not national but local.[196] Although *Miller* dealt with pictorial advertisements for books, its ruling governed other media as well. Furthermore, the same majority decided that an adults-only admission policy did not immunize theater owners from prosecution for showing obscene films.[197] The final blow came with two decisions that failed to extend a 1969 precedent that protected individuals from prosecution for possessing obscene materials. If individuals could possess such materials for private use, could they not then import and transport them. The Court answered no in both instances.[198]

Even in advance of the decision in *Miller*, a New York court had banned local screenings of *Deep Throat*. Now, the Supreme Court's ruling encouraged prosecutors in jurisdictions from Baltimore to Beverly Hills to proceed against the film and its ilk. By the end of the year Hollywood had been freed from the competition of hard-core films, as only a few venues remained for their showing. For the next decade, before the VCR created a new market for the hard-core product, Hollywood had a monopoly on what was shown in the nation's theaters. As convincing evidence, the Hollywood studios reported record profits in 1974.[199]

The Court's willingness to aid the film industry in its competition with hard-core films was again evident in the year following *Miller*. Georgia had attempted to ban a studio product, *Carnal Knowledge*, which in one scene implied oral sex but had no real or simulated hard-core elements. The Court majority made clear that its willingness to accept a local standards test for obscenity did not give the states "unbridled discretion." Quoting *Miller*, the Court said "under that holding 'no one will be subject to prosecution for the sale or exposure of obscene materials unless these materials depict or describe patently offensive "hard core" sexual conduct.'"[200] Critics lamented the Court's willingness to accommodate those persons who saw too much sex in motion pictures, but Jack Valenti and the MPAA got a boost from the rulings. If a film got an R rating, it now was immunized from claims of obscenity. Censorship fights would then tend to be confined within the industry itself.[201]

Although the implementation of the new ratings system got off to a rocky start, in part because of turnover among key personnel at MPAA, gradually the kinks were worked out. In 1973 Valenti put an end to script reviews, displaced so-called professional reviewers with a panel of educated parents, and found a new head for CARA who would bring stability and continuity to the operation for the next twenty years. However, complaints about the sexual permissiveness now permitted on the big screen only increased.[202]

Relatively few CARA ratings were appealed. Two-thirds of the members of the appeals board, composed of Jack Valenti, nine studio representatives, eight representatives of the National Association of Theatre Owners and four independent members, had to vote to override the initial determination.[203] Producers generally compromised to get the more acceptable rating. However, the cuts asked for were often idiosyncratic. For instance, in a foreign film that dealt with homosexuality in a rather frank fashion, the cut was not of the scene of anal intercourse but rather of the smile on the face of the person penetrated. And in *Crimes of Passion* CARA objected to the male nudity displayed in the prints of Aubrey Beardsley hanging on the apartment wall.[204] Such subjectivity is an inseparable part of any censoring process.

Moral critics, who had influence for so long in regard to the content of motion pictures were now vigorously opposed by groups and individuals ready to fight for greater artistic freedom. Grove Press, which had fought and won some notable literary censorship battles, got into the business of film distribution with the Swedish film *I Am Curious—Yellow*. When the United States Customs Service refused to allow the movie into the country, summoning up thoughts of Hedy Lamarr's *Ecstacy*, Grove Press challenged the decision in court. When a jury upheld the Customs Service, Grove Press took the case to the Second Circuit Court of Appeals. Although granting that the film depicted "sexual intercourse under varying circumstances," contained "scenes of oral-genital activity," and was more sexually explicit than "any other film produced for general viewing," the court said the movie was not obscene, thus freeing it for distribution in the United States.[205] That decision did not mean that it would not meet local opposition, as it did in both Boston and Maryland, where it was banned.[206]

Eliminating legal obstacles did not assure the film an audience. Edward De Grazia, a professor of law who had argued on behalf of Grove Press in its censorship battles, suggested that local censorship be dealt with by hiring local lawyers to challenge decisions. The lawyers would be paid out of the receipts earned by the film in their areas. Grove Press was relieved of further financial strain by the participation of the American Civil Liberties Union in the campaign.[207]

Female nudity became quite common in mainstream films as the '80s dawned. Bo Derek was groomed for stardom by her husband John Derek by shedding her clothes in films such as *10* and *Tarzan, the Ape Man*. In the latter instance, some nude scenes were removed by order of a federal judge supposedly charged with determining the fidelity of the new version to Edgar Rice Burroughs's original story. The Dereks attempted to win support for their campaign against such censorship, but neither the studio executives nor the press seemed interested in such a fight. Bo Derek concluded that this lack of interest was the result of the film's lightweight subject matter.[208] Still much of Bo's nudity survived the judge's censorial cuts. Some critics saw nudity as detrimental to a performer's screen future, and certainly this proved true in regard to Bo Derek's film career.[209] Other critics attributed her demise to a lack of acting talent.

Bo Derek's films carried an R rating, but confusion over the X rating and how it was applied led the MPAA to abandon it in 1990. NC-17 with the same qualifications was substituted for X, thus distancing MPAA from those moviemakers who had confused some people with their eager self-application of X and multiple X ratings.[210] Critics on the left attacked the NC-17 rating. It did what government itself could not do by overriding both parental choice and existing law in forbidding attendance by those persons under the age of seventeen. One critic suggested that the MPAA's defense of preempting governmental censorship was "simply disingenuous; the MPAA has not met the enemy, but instead has given away what the enemy lacks the power to take."[211]

Both of Brian De Palma's controversial films, *Dressed to Kill* and *Body Double* were released well before NC-17 replaced X, and both of them, even after some cuts, still received the X rating. De Palma agreed to further cuts in the first of the two films that airbrushed some visible pubic hair and toned down some of the sexual violence and got his R rating. The advertisements for the film sought to capitalize on the fact that the film had been censored. Critics liked the film; some even called it funny and satirical. Protests of groups such as Women Against Pornography came after the film had raked in 250 percent of its cost. In fact, the protests of women because of the sexual violence sent the film up to number one on the list of highest grossing films. Protests by lesbians and gays also elevated films such as *Basic Instinct*, which had not charmed critics, into box office successes. De Palma's *Body Double* went further yet by graphically depicting a woman being murdered. The new De Palma film only further enraged protestors. *Film Comment* provided a medium for the contesting parties to air their views. Al Goldstein, publisher of *Screw*, summed up the protest, saying "Feminists are the new Nazis, and pornographers are their Jews."[212] Of course, the antipornography feminists did not represent the views of all feminists, many of whom were committed to defending even offensive expression. The battle, though, had moved from street protests to the printed page, which was also the case with *Fatal Attraction*, in which a woman was not willing to be discarded after a steamy affair.[213]

While restraints were generally being lessened on filmmakers, the Court in 1982 did find a new variety of unprotected sexual speech, child pornography. A bookseller was arrested in New York for violating a state law seeking to protect children under the age of sixteen by selling two films of young boys masturbating. The New York Court of Appeals found the state statute unconstitutional, but the United States Supreme Court reversed the decision and made room for this new genre of unprotected sexual speech. Most of the justices insisted that the seller must have knowledge of the product and that it lack "serious literary, artistic, political, or scientific value," but the film did not have to meet the other tests for obscenity, patent offensiveness, prurient interest, and exceeding community standards. Worry about protecting children had always been associated with film censorship, but now a new level was added. Justice Byron R. White, for the Court, echoed a Senate report when he said that recently "the exploitive use of children in the production of pornography has become a serious national problem."[214] The decision helped intensify a search for child pornographers that continues today.[215]

Why the Court had to pronounce child pornography nonprotected speech was because finding something obscene had become increasingly difficult. This difficulty also led censors to seek other ways to accomplish their purposes. Bringing sexual speech under the umbrella of the First

Amendment did not mean it was protected in all places and at all times. Time, place, and manner restrictions have often been upheld, and in 1986 the Supreme Court considered whether a city could zone adult movie theaters. City officials in Renton, Washington, prohibited such theaters within a thousand feet of a residence, church, park, or school. Although the trial court upheld the ordinance, the Ninth Circuit Court of Appeals struck it down. The court found that the ordinance did substantially curtail protected speech and that the city had not justified the intrusion.

The six-justice majority, supported by a concurrence, relied upon a 5 to 4 decision the Court made a decade earlier in regard to a Detroit ordinance.[216] It now agreed with the district court that the law was not aimed at the content of the films shown but at the secondary effects of the presence of these theaters. Those effects concerned the quality of urban life by seeking to prevent crime, promote the retail trade, and maintain property values. Finally, the majority said, Renton could rely on the experiences of Detroit and Seattle with similar ordinances.[217] Reflecting some of the shift in the political opinion that came with the election of Ronald Reagan, the Court majority clearly looked for a way to justify a limitation on speech that seemed to accommodate the temper of the times. Zoning remains a means to censor sexual speech.

Although local censorship in terms of review boards has been eliminated, local censorship has not been. Still, a particular local decision has little overall box office effect, meaning the most significant current censorship battles are fought over a film's rating. A study by the Harvard School of Public Health looked at the ratings of almost two thousand films from 1992 to 2003 and concluded that a motion picture rated R in the early '90s was rated PG-13 in the new century.[218] Despite this shift, an NC-17 rating still remains box office poison, primarily because many theaters refuse to show such films and newspapers refuse advertisements for them.[219]

Three examples of films released with a NC-17 rating are *Henry and June*, dealing with Henry Miller and his sexually liberated partners, wife June and Anaïs Nin, *Showgirls*, and David Cronenberg's *Crash*. The first was an art film with limited appeal, but the latter, with substantial advertising behind it, still faltered at the box office. Cronenberg's movie, however, won the Special Jury Prize at Cannes Film Festival in 1996. Its sex scenes were so integral to the story that cutting would not have been possible. Cronenberg blamed Ted Turner, who delayed the release of the film, for undermining its chances at the box office.[220]

The mid-1990s saw an escalation in worries about child pornography that made a remake of *Lolita* a most hazardous enterprise. Taken from the Vladimir Nabokov novel of the same name, a stepfather has a sexual relationship with his underage stepdaughter. When the film was finally made, it could not find a theatrical distributor and was picked up by the cable channel Showtime. Sex with children was a no-no in American films of the era, as the motion picture *Happiness* also confirmed. The film, which sought to humanize a pedophile, won the International Critics Prize at Cannes in 1998. The film was sold back to its producers and released unrated and uncut. Relatively few theaters were willing to run it.[221]

Sex with children is taboo, but not intercourse with an apple pie. The producer of *American Pie*, a teen comedy, said it took four trips to the rating board to get an R rating. The problem was the four thrusts into the pie; the MPAA said two were enough, and eventually the thrusts were halved.[222]

Although some moviemakers distribute controversial movies unrated, most often they compromise to obtain an R rating. Filmmakers have generally accepted the lesson that an R rating must be obtained if the product is to have a chance at the box office. This was the message received by Stanley Kubrick and Trey Parker and Matt Stone in 1999 with regard to *Eyes Wide Shut* and the animated feature *South Park: Bigger, Louder and Uncut* respectively. They made the changes, as did those in control of a puppet movie titled *Team America: World Police*. What had prompted the NC-17 was a torrid bedroom sex scene, which included simulated oral sex. The filmmakers wondered why the board had to "protect people from two puppets who love each other," while at the same time mounting no objection to a scene in which a woman puppet's head is blown off. At any rate, they cut some of the bedroom scene, and the board gave its approval with an R rating.[223]

Why the absence of genitalia did not deter the board in initially rating *Team America* may be explained by the fact that certain conventions were developed to make the ratings job easier. Director Danny DeVito thought he could get away with three "fucks" is his comedy, *Throw Mama from the Train*, but the "automatic language rule" allowed only one "fuck" and then it must be an expletive, not a verb used in a sexual context.[224]

What bothers movie censors has changed over the decades. In the 1950s they were disturbed by sexual immorality and words such as "virgin," "seduce," "rape," and "contraceptive." In the early 1960s they focused on glimpses of nude bodies, explicit sexual language, and simulated sexual acts, the latter often referred to as soft-core pornography. By the 1970s, despite some lapses, the earlier concerns looked quaint as suggestions of conventional sexual intercourse gave way to suggestions of oral sex and other sexual variations. Soft-core or adult films were assimilated by major studios and hard-core films entered not only theaters but also homes thanks to videotapes.[225] As this home market allowed filmmakers to release unrated versions of their work, moralists made video stores that had such material for rent and sale their targets in the early 1990s.[226]

Despite this alternative market, New York film critics labeled CARA "a punitive and restrictive force [that] effectively tramples the freedom of

American filmmakers." The critics were upset with the cuts made in the 1999 film *Eyes Wide Shut*, not because they were so crucial to the film but because they were indicative of the way in which art was subordinated to commercial considerations. Worried about the negative impact on creativity and the art of film, these critics noted that the purpose of the rating system certainly was not to promote art. Its aim, they said, was to ensure that the products "move freely and profitably through the vast entertainment marketplace." The unfortunate result, they concluded, was "watered-down, dumbed-down products." Los Angeles film critics agreed in a letter to Jack Valenti and the MPAA. Valenti responded by calling the critics "a small band of constant whiners."[227]

Art, in all its forms, has always relied upon patrons and has had to accommodate their wishes. With movies, the patrons are the consumers, and unless the product gets into the stream of commerce it languishes. The key to this entry is a non-NC-17 rating. From the very beginning of the rating system, its purpose was not to protect art but the film industry itself. One student of the present-day American cinema concludes that "the political and social utility of film censorship is altogether secondary to its economic function."[228]

Specific interest groups with no direct linkage to the movie industry or government have made specific movies or specific themes a matter of their concern. This activity creates publicity and informs the public about the film, but it does not alter the product. In other words, speech in the form of the unadulterated motion picture is met by other speech challenging it, thereby tossing competing views into the marketplace. Antipornography feminists publicly protested movies such as *Dressed to Kill*, contending that the portrayal of the murder of women was not erotic. Gays and lesbians have criticized movies, such as *Basic Instinct*, as homophobic. In both instances such groups have had some influence on moviemakers.[229]

For instance, the earlier invisibility of gays and lesbians in motion pictures has been replaced with sympathetic portrayals on the big screen. As evidence, consider the accolades heaped upon *Brokeback Mountain* in 2005–2006. Would a story of love between two sheepherders be popular fare was answered by patrons lining up at the box office in response to glowing reviews and best picture awards.[230] The accolades, however, did not stop the Conference of Catholic Bishops from finding the film morally offensive. Nor did it stop theater owners in Salt Lake City and Poulsbo, Washington, from canceling the movie's showing.[231]

Although such local action was limited, a documentary entitled *This Film Is Not Yet Rated*, shown at the 2006 Sundance Film Festival, used a split screen to depict similar heterosexual and homosexual activity for the purpose of illustrating how the latter has been more unsympathetically rated than the former. The documentary, which the MPAA board rated NC-17 for its "graphic sexual content," penetrated the secret workings of the ratings board. A number of independent filmmakers were interviewed, including John Waters. His 2004 film, *A Dirty Shame*, which dealt with a woman who becomes sex obsessed after a blow to her head, was rated NC-17 and amassed receipts of a little over a million dollars. His *Hairspray*, a PG film, made almost sixty-seven million.[232]

The George W. Bush administration, which has paid more than lip service to the agenda of social conservatives, has conferred with leaders of a number of organizations that have been concerned about the ready availability of pornographic motion pictures. Claiming that such movies violate exiting obscenity laws, organizations such as Citizens for Community Values (CCV), the Family Research Council, and Concerned Women for America have recently centered their attention on the availability of such films in hotel rooms. Phil Burress, the campaign's leader and head of CCV who describes himself as a former pornography addict, was successful in pressuring fifteen Ohio and Kentucky hotels to stop offering the sexually explicit movies. In the summer of 2006, however, the groups concluded that they needed government aid in their battle. In a full-page advertisement in editions of *USA Today*, they urged the Department of Justice to take legal action, specifically identifying LodgeNet and OnCommand as the suppliers of much of the targeted material. Hotel spokesmen denied that what was offered was obscene, and responded that local franchise-holders make the decision to offer such movies and that guests can readily ignore or block such offerings.[233]

For those critics who see contemporary motion pictures as too sexual, too vulgar, too unwholesome, and too destructive of family values,[234] or simply too true to life, they might pause to examine the places and times when native filmmakers conveyed only idealized or sanitized conceptions of human existence. In Stalinist Russia and Nazi Germany, wholesome films contained no vulgar language and not much sexuality; furthermore the actors were attractive, well behaved, and courteous. In a repressive society the spirit of art is submerged so that what is created bears only a superficial resemblance to the society itself. As with free speech and free press, much is suffered that many persons would prefer to avoid, but the question is always the high cost that such a purge exacts. The admonition that people should be careful or they may get what they think they want seems especially on point.

Cartoonist Mark Parisi addresses the controversy surrounding Louie, Louie *and changing standards in popular music.* Cartoon © Mark Parisi. Reprinted with permission.

4

Music and Dance

Stirring the Senses and Unleashing the Beast

The introduction of novel fashions in music is a thing to beware of as endangering the whole fabric of society, whose most important conventions are unsettled by any revolution in that quarter.[1] (Plato, c. 390 BC)

The connection between exuberance and eroticism is evidenced by the aphrodisiac effect of music and dance. . . . If it's not the wild and wicked whirl of the waltz, which is spinning our youth into its first steps on the primrose path, then it's . . . the frenetic spasmodicity of the Charleston, or the sensual attack of squealing trumpets and obscenely slithering saxophones.[2] (Raymond Durgnat, 1966)

Many popular music idols of the young now sing about rape, masturbation, incest, bondage, violence, and just plain intercourse. This "auditory pornography" . . . has become a tempting appetizer on the abundant menu of pornography . . . that is being fed to younger and younger audiences.[3] (Tipper Gore, 1987)

[T]oday's salacious lyrics are not the exception to otherwise generally respected sexual standards and community values, but a symbol of their collapse.[4] (Terence Moran, 1985)

Not only were its sensuous black roots showing, but its very name—rock 'n' roll—was slang for sexual intercourse.[5] With its raucous sounds and often simple-minded, repetitive lyrics, rock had arrived in the mid-1950s. Earlier concern about the music of the young seemed to pale in comparison to this new threat to moral standards.

In 1956 Richard Berry, a young singer born in Louisiana but raised in Los Angeles, wrote a song that told the story of a sailor in

137

a bar late at night. He is pining for the woman he left behind in the islands. The bartender who listens to the sailor's lament is honored by the song's title—"Louie Louie." Berry recorded the song with a group called the Pharaohs. It did not thunder or shatter the eardrums, as some Berry songs would; rather it was a rhythm and blues tune with a touch of cha-cha, something to dance to. It had no rock-and-roll beat, but it worked its way up the West Coast and became a regional hit. In 1959, Berry, in need of money, sold his half interest in "Louie Louie" to the publishing house that already held the other half. The $750 Berry got seemed like a good deal, given the fact that the song had all but disappeared. *Billboard* had called it a nonentity, and so it seemed to be.[6]

In early January 1964, however, the song climbed to number two on *Billboard*'s "Hot 100." In time, it would be enshrined in the Rock and Roll Hall of Fame and Museum as one of the "500 songs that shaped rock and roll." What had happened? As the song moved into the Pacific Northwest, the cha-cha rhythm was displaced by a rock beat. In 1963 two Portland groups recorded the song, the more established Raiders and the Kingsmen. The Kingsmen recording was made under rather primitive conditions with a vocalist who had to stand on his tiptoes to reach the boom mike that was picking up his voice. This version is the one that made the hall of fame. The chorus was clearly infectious and the chord changes were appealing, but the secret of its success lay in the mumbled lyrics. Was the vocalist, Jack Ely, singing dirty words? Once the rumor started it spread rapidly, and there seemed no limit to what eager listeners could hear in the vocal. The song's historian called the phenomenon "the most profound and sublime expression of rock 'n' roll's ability to create something from nothing." Some listeners played the 45 rpm record at 33 rpm, contending that the slower speed revealed the dirty words; others needed no such help in hearing the sex talk. Wasn't that "I felt my boner in her hair?"[7]

The most common set of dirty lyrics read as follows:

Chorus: Oh, Louie, Louie, oh no
Get her way down low
Oh, Louis, Louie, oh baby
Get her down low
A fine little girl a-waiting for me
She's just a girl across the way
Well I'll take her and park all alone
She's never a girl I'd lay at home.
(Chorus repeat)
At night at ten I lay her again

Fuck you, girl, Oh, all the way
Oh, my bed and I lay her there
I meet a rose in her hair
(Chorus repeat)
Okay, let's give it to them, right now!
She's got a rag on I'll move above
It won't be long she'll slip it off
I'll take her in my arms again
I'll tell her I'll never leave again
(Chorus repeat)
Get that broad out of here![8]

We are indebted to the Federal Bureau of Investigation (FBI) for preserving this version along with other variants. How did the FBI become involved? Were not these filthy words being transmitted over the air by radio disk jockeys for all to hear? And was not the national police force charged with enforcing the federal law against the interstate transportation of obscene material? So began a thirty-month investigation of the song "Louie Louie" by federal agents in six cities. The preliminary finding was that the words of the song were unintelligible no matter what speed the record was played. Although this conclusion was reached again and again in different sound laboratories, the J. Edgar Hoover FBI seemed intent upon exposing the subversive influences of rock and roll by concentrating on the alleged dirty lyrics of "Louie Louie." Apparently Hoover and his agents never got the joke that rock-and-roll enthusiasts had perpetrated; the authorities had been panicked by the creation of "something that rock 'n' roll needed: a secret as rich and ridiculous as the sounds themselves."[9]

One of the troubles with rumors is their long life. In the spring of 2005 the superintendent of schools, Paula Dowling, in Benton Harbor, Michigan, banned a middle school marching band from playing "Louie Louie" in the coming Blossomtime Festival because of its "sexually explicit lyrics." No matter that the version was strictly instrumental. Band members protested that it was too late to learn a new piece. Citing "the multiple versions of the song" and the permission of the parents, Dowling reversed her decision.[10]

Despite the failure to find dirty words in "Louie Louie," such words could be found aplenty in the ribald lyrics often grafted on to common folk tunes. Such lyrics were a part of the country's musical heritage from its colonial beginnings. In a path-breaking study Ed Cray, a journalism professor at the University of Southern California, published the choice lyrics, many of which were in danger of perishing. The survival of the words had depended upon their continued oral transmission since fear of prosecution under obscenity laws had earlier worked against their being preserved in written form. Cray organized his welter of material under five headings.[11]

His first category consists of Anglo-Irish traditional ballad tunes to which ribald lyrics were added, lyrics that went on for stanza after stanza telling a story. As an example, the innocent melody of "My Bonnie Lies over the Ocean" had the traditional lyrics replaced to become one of the nation's most well-known bawdy songs, "My God, How the Money Rolls In." The reworked version included the following stanzas:

> Grandmother makes cheap prophylactics;
> She punctures the end with a pin.
> Grandfather performs the abortions.
> My God, how the money rolls in.
>
> My sister was once a virgin;
> She didn't know how to begin.
> I showed her the tricks of the trade.
> My God, how the money rolls in.[12]

Cray's second category is an American-bred variety that was much too impatient with long stories and sought its amusement in shorter, earthy tales. The "Charlotte the Harlot" lyrics, most of which were sung to the tune of "Sweet Betsy from Pike," are examples. This particular one, however, used the melody from "Down in the Valley":

> Down in Cunt Valley where the Red River flows,
> Where cocksuckers flourish and maidenheads grow,
> That's where I met Lupe, the girl I adore,
> She's my hot-fucking, cocksucking Mexican whore.
>
> Chorus:
> She'll fuck you; she'll suck you; she'll gnaw at your nuts;
> She'll wrap her legs 'round you, and squeeze out your guts.
> She'll hug you and kiss you till you wish you could die.
> I'd rather eat Lupe than sweet cherry pie.[13]

Third is the parody, perhaps the most serviceable of all the types. For instance, the following lyrics written from the female perspective clearly indicate the original tune:

> M is for the many times you made me.
> O is for the other times you tried.
> T is for the tourist cabin weekends.

H is for the hell you raised inside.
E is for the everlasting passion.
R is for the 'reck you made of me.
Put them all together, they spell "Mother,"
And that is what you made of me.[14]

Fourth is a category Cray calls "Undergraduate Coarse," in which he places those songs that are passed on from one group of undergraduates to the next. Here Cray puts "Roll Me Over," saying it might "well be the most popular song in the American oral tradition:"

Oh, this is number one, and the fun has just begun.
Roll me over, lay me down and do it again. . . .

Oh, this is number ten, and its time to start again.
Roll me over, lay me down and do it again.

Finally, the last category is the ribald song of the foot soldier that knows no national boundaries. Cray includes here a song that probably got its start as a bawdy number associated with the Royal Naval Air Service in World War I. It was quickly picked up by soldiers of all nationalities and would also be sung by those men who served in subsequent wars. Only in 1940 was it cleaned up and copyrighted as "Bless 'em All." The following affords a taste of the ribald versions:

Fuck 'em all, fuck 'em all,
The long and the short and the tall.
Fuck all the blonde cunts and all the brunettes.
Don't be too choosey, just fuck all you gets
'Cause we're saying good-bye to them all
As back to the barracks we crawl.
You'll get no erection at short-arm inspection,
So prick up, you men, fuck 'em all.[15]

The preceding examples capture much of the range of the American bawdy song, but what made it appealing and preserved its existence was the ability of individuals to join together with others in singing words, such as cunt, fuck, cocksucker, balls, etc., that were suppressed in public discourse. In today's society the words may still jar but they are much more commonly heard, and, for that matter, in popular music. The bawdy song, as with so much that was once considered obscene, has been absorbed within today's more permissible culture.

Of course, popular music, as with so much communication in the late nineteenth century, was part an information revolution that came with the rapid industrialization of the United States and the rise of mass media. As audiences increased, costs declined. Sheet music became cheap, and the song one heard at the music store could be transported home. Although the delivery of the notes on the page necessitated a musical instrument, the piano was prevalent in a rising number of middle-class households. In the absence of a musical instrument, the words, themselves, were reminders of the tune and could easily be sung.

Although some writers date the rise of popular music much earlier, say prior to the Civil War with Stephen Foster, not until rhythmic, melodic, and harmonic changes were consolidated beginning in the 1890s did the American popular song emerge.[16] Also, music had to become transportable in a relatively cheap form before it truly could be called popular. Further contributing to the transportability of music in mass society was the recording. Whether on early cylinder or disk, the music was now captured to be released at the beck and call of a purchaser with a player. The record as a disseminator of popular songs was discovered in 1919, and quite quickly record sales outdistanced the sales of sheet music and became the new barometer of a song's popularity.[17]

Despite problems in sound reproduction that would take decades to solve, now music was even more transportable. One did not need to play an instrument to savor the music. In fact, as time passed, the piano would gradually disappear from the inventory of middle-class household goods.

Folk music existed long before popular music, and although folk music at times would become popular music, the two genres should not be confused. Popular music was distinguished from the genteel tradition of the past by publisher catalogues, more aggressive sales tactics, and the search for a hit. It was a genre that catered to a clientele that had the leisure time to seek personal enjoyment. For instance, was it a coincidence that the first million seller, "After the Ball," appeared in 1892, the same year in which Coca Cola stopped advertising itself as a patent medicine and began advertising itself as a pleasurable drink? The product no longer had to be good for you; that it was tasty and enjoyable was enough.[18]

Americans may have been slow to become consumers, having been taught for generations about thrift and the need to save for hard times, but the industrialized society at the turn of the century, which needed consumers to survive, gradually undermined that old mentality. This shift from work and self-improvement to leisure and fun unleashed new worries among those persons who saw themselves as social arbiters. What had kept the masses in check for so long was an economic structure that made work central to survival, one that superimposed structure upon individual choice, leaving little room to go astray.[19] The decline in the workweek led to popular amusements found in spectator sports, dance halls, and amusement parks. This new popular culture not only challenged high culture but also loosened restraints on the male-female relationship.

Generally, what first brought such popular music to the attention of moralists was not the lyrics but rather the changing musical styles, concern about the music's roots, and the way in which it was wedded to social dancing. Dancing emphasized the physical body in a form of "sexual display," and it figured prominently in the relationship between the sexes. Not only has dance been bound up with popular music, but it has provided "the most public setting for music as sexual expression. . . . [T]he dance crazes of the beginning of the century . . . set new norms for physical display, contact and movement."[20]

Today the waltz hardly appears to be a wicked, scandalous dance that threatens the virginity of young women, but so it was perceived in the United States in the 1880s. The dance had its beginnings in Europe a century earlier and was known as a Central European couple dance. Its music in three-quarter time was synonymous with American popular music from 1890 to 1910.[21] Its formality and caution seem more European than American, but it truly was subversive of the existing order in social dancing. Earlier social dancing was group based. Dancers were not paired off but were loose partners in a collective enterprise. Man and woman were kept at arm's length, and they danced to the authority of the caller or the dancing master in set patterns that afforded no individual choice. Such restraint tended to minimize the inherent sexuality that was part of dancing. When the waltz took direct aim on such restraint by requiring man and woman to embrace in public, thereby closing the gap between partners, social dancing would never be the same. Regimen and order had succumbed to an individuality that would henceforth characterize social dancing. Swaying and gliding, the partners established a bond separate from the other dancers. They occupied the same room but only had eyes for each other.[22] Once the waltz entered the ballroom all that followed in social dancing seemed inevitable.

One of the foremost critics of such social dancing was a former dancing master, Thomas A. Faulkner, who, in his own words served the "Evil One" before becoming a servant of Jesus Christ. Titling his work *From the Ballroom to Hell*, he blamed the ballroom or dance hall for leading women to a life of sin. He describes such a descent as follows:

> Her eyes look into his, but she sees nothing; the soft music fills the room, but she hears it not; he bends her body to and fro, but she knows it not; his hot breath, tainted with strong drink, is on her hair and cheek, his lips almost touch her forehead, yet she does not shrink; his eyes, gleaming with a fierce, intolerable lust, gloat over her, yet she does not quail. She is filled with the rapture of sin in its intensity; her spirit is inflamed with passion and lust is gratified in thought. With a last low wail the music ceases, and the dance for the night is ended, but not the evil work of the night.[23]

If the waltz with its broad steps across the dance floor required physical stamina, the two-step went even further in sapping the dancers' energy.

John Philip Sousa, the march king who supplied the music, believed "the march should make a man with a wooden leg step out."[24] The two-step was a quick marching step with skips, "done as rapidly as a couple could conveniently go forward, backward, and turn." It "elbowed into retirement the older dances that had served to express lively spirits," such as the schottische and polka, and shared center stage with the waltz from the early 1890s through the first decade of the twentieth century.[25]

As the twentieth century dawned and women were shaking loose from the confines of Victorian dress, a new type of music was emerging, one indigenous to the American scene. Called ragtime, it became a component of America's greatest contribution to the world of music—jazz. Ragtime's origins lay primarily with African Americans, and it was the music of the bordello, but the music's appeal respected no racial boundaries. Social arbiters, however, were appalled. In 1899 the *Musical Courier* editorialized: "A wave of vulgar, filthy and suggestive music has inundated the land. . . . It is artistically and morally depressing and should be suppressed by press and pulpit."[26] Using a marchlike bass line and melodic syncopation, the music left the waltz beat behind. Its two/four and four/four rhythm simplified dancing, and for one of the few times in history the new music's attraction was shared by the older generation. Syncopation stimulated not only the senses but the feet as well. Music was now given a popular beat that invited dancing, and the United States went "dance mad." The *Musical Courier* condemned the cakewalk's "obscene posturings" and "lewd gestures" and speculated upon the effect such degenerate music would have upon the young. Music publishers, quick to spot the emerging trend, now insisted that all new songs be danceable.[27]

Perhaps dance was a target because it, like sex, is so body involved. For instance, the hugging embrace and direct bodily contact that came with ragtime music challenged earlier social norms. But far more was involved, for at the core of the concern "were very real fears about social contact and social control, especially racial appropriations and transgressions of the careful boundaries of class, race and gender."[28]

The cakewalk had come from ragtime's minstrel roots, but many dances were given animal names after the creatures whose gait and manner they appropriated, such as the grizzly bear, bunny hug, lame duck, kangaroo dip, camel walk, and turkey trot. A distinguished music critic believed that such animal dances were driving out decency in American dance halls. As the turkey trot penetrated ballrooms in New York City and Newport, the dance incurred the ire of William Hearst's *New York American*, which called the dance "disgusting and indecent."[29]

As dance halls, in which sexes mixed largely without supervision, proliferated in urban America and attracted a large immigrant working-class clientele, moralists called for their regulation. The government regulation that was forthcoming was local but quite extensive. For instance, in Cleveland dance halls had to obtain a license and an inspector was appointed who supervised forty other male and two female chaperones. Despite the increase in governmental regulation, one survey in 1921 concluded that "one of America's gravest problems" was the "promiscuous public gatherings" in which dancing took place.[30]

Adding to the concern were the changes in women's fashions. In the period before the Great War, American women had bared their arms and shed Victorian dress in favor of looser, less restraining clothing. The Nineteenth Amendment had given women the vote in 1920, and in the ensuing decade they bobbed their hair, discovered cosmetics, flattened their breasts, and showed their legs by raising their hemlines to the knee.

Irving Berlin penned a song that captured the new dance craze titled "Everybody's Doing It Now." The song so enthralled eighteen-year-old Grace Williams that she sang it as she danced the turkey trot while traversing the sidewalk in front of the residence of a former justice of the peace. He and his wife were shocked and had Grace charged with disorderly conduct. Before a jury, she testified that she sang the song because she liked it and could not help dancing to its beat. Her lawyer offered to sing the song for the jury. After the judge overruled the prosecutor's objection, the lawyer sang the song. The spectators in the courtroom joined him on the chorus. Moving to the second stanza, he danced his version of the turkey trot to the delight of the applauding jury. After deliberating only five minutes, the jury found Grace Williams not guilty.[31]

Of these animal dances, only the fox trot, in a tempered version, has survived. All the dances saw couples move closer together as they engaged in rather coarse (some said lewd) movements and pranced along at a rapid pace. Although the waltz, two-step, polka, and schottische did not altogether disappear from the dance scene, the new and different dances attracted and empowered the young. For instance, the bunny hug, with its clear association with the breeding of rabbits, was banned in numerous dance halls. Blacks had their counterpart dances as well, but they did not hesitate to acknowledge their sexual nature, with names such as fanny bump, funky butt, and the slow drag. In the latter dance the partners would embrace and move to and fro in the same spot for hours.[32] Despite the casualness and distance that would characterize the dancers, the dances "symbolized the high value placed on mutual heterosexual intimacy and attraction."[33]

Another intruder into what had been the rather decorous ballroom was the tango, the first of a series of Latin dances that stirred the censorious. Boston banned the tango, and other moral arbiters sought to rein in its more sensuous versions. They preferred the restrained but stylish way that the dance was performed by Vernon and Irene Castle, the famous couple of the 1910s for whom the Castle Walk was named.[34] The Castles were "able to discipline, refine and sanitize dance movement and attendant behavior," giving the modified new dances a certain respectability.[35]

Jazz further synthesized ragtime and the blues and gave both a name and dance direction to the decade. There was the black bottom, the shimmy, the varsity drag, and above all, the Charleston, named after the city in which black dockworkers had performed it. It had exuberance, speed, and rhythm, but what made the dance so shocking to those who saw the end of civilization in its wake was the casual manner in which women flicked their knees open, thus inviting peek-a-boo glances up their thighs. The dances of the '20s began a movement away from the closed couple dances, such as the waltz, that had shocked the older generation in the 1890s. Changing partners was common, now often at the woman's initiative, and the individual dancer was much less dependent upon his or her partner.[36]

The prosperity of the 1920s was followed by the Depression of the 1930s and, if one could not afford records (one hundred million records were sold in 1927, but only six million were sold in 1932[37]), one had only to turn on the radio where the music of the day was swing. On Saturday nights stations carried live broadcasts of big bands—Harry James, Benny Goodman, Artie Shaw, Glenn Miller, etc.—performing in various parts of the country.

Dancing to the beat, which earlier had been known as the lindy, eventually emerged as jitterbugging and gained a new popularity during the '30s and '40s. Dancing became even more of an athletic contest, as the woman was often tossed through turns and supported jumps. Skirts were creeping higher, and a female dancer had to put as much thought into choosing her underwear as her skirts. Dancing seemed even more spontaneous, as fixed steps gave way to innovation.[38]

By the mid-1950s, rock and roll had burst upon the popular music scene. *American Bandstand*, with an audience that grew to twenty million, began telecasting in 1956 and became the showplace for the dances of the young. Early in its run the dances were the stroll and the creep; the former brought back a form of group dancing and the latter introduced a new casualness, a slump, into the couple's movements around the floor. The key word was "cool."[39]

The rock-and-roll era found the young separated from its predecessor generations by a sense of alienation, along with a constant need for novelty. With easy talk of sexuality and dancing in a "bump-and-grind" manner that the older generation had forgotten, young people appeared as rebels. Yet the dances were not in themselves sexy. It was the heavy beat that was condemned as stirring animalistic instincts.[40]

Lyrics seemed to be submerged in this throbbing beat, and most of rock music was played loud. There could be little conversation on the dance floor, and often the couple separated, each of the partners going his or her own way, challenging the idea that social dancing had something to do with a social relationship. The closed couple, so feared at the time of the waltz, was now fully broken up into its component parts, two individuals dancing at the same time and in the same vicinity but only very loosely together.[41]

In 1960 Chubby Checker appeared on *American Bandstand* with a song called "The Twist," which gave its name to a dance as well. Its simplicity made it very popular and not only among the young, as it became the first rock-and-roll dance to bridge the generation gap. Although the hip swiveling bothered some would-be censors, others, including many of the older generation, demonstrated once again how quickly the shock of yesterday dissipates.[42] In the twist the partners did not touch and they often seemed unconcerned with what the other was doing. And in variations, such as the loco-motion, the couple got lost in the group of eight, which mimicked the start of a steam locomotive.[43]

The 1960s were the heyday of the disco, where nonstop canned music replaced live music. In this environment dances were invented and discarded with regularity, although the jerk and frug lasted the decade. Again most of the dances separated the partners; each dancer moved to his or her own beat.[44]

In the 1970s the hustle brought the partners together again. The music, in the Latin American tradition of the tango, rumba, samba, and cha-cha, was called salsa. A smooth dance with quick footwork and a stomp, it revealed its Latin origins. Reunited couples were allowed some individuality within the dance's boundaries, but the partners, who had been separated in so much recent social dancing, were now reunited.[45]

Some of the opposition to social dancing was the result of a disapproval of certain dances or of generational differences, but the most consistent and generalized opposition has been religiously based.[46] A fairly recent episode of opposition brought religious fundamentalists into collision with claimed constitutional guarantees. The high school in Purdy, Missouri, with its less than one thousand residents, had never had a dance on school grounds. If students wanted a dance, they had to rent space elsewhere. In 1986 students held a rally to protest the ban, but the school board refused after five ministers signed a letter to the board contending that dancing led to immorality. Twenty-one students and their parents filed suit in federal court insisting that the ban was based on a religious belief in the sinfulness of dancing. The school board disagreed, but Judge Russell G. Clark of the federal district court ruled in favor of the students. In the divided community, the superintendent of schools, who argued that the school was not the place for dancing, barred alumni and students from other schools from attending the dance.[47] Two subsequent dances were held with the restrictions being eased, but that apparently ended the brief interlude of dancing in Purdy.

A three-judge panel of the Eighth Circuit Court of Appeals overturned
Judge Clark's decision, ruling that "the mere fact a governmental body takes
action that coincides with the principles or desires of a particular religious
group, however, does not transform the action into an impermissible establishment of religion."[48] A request for a rehearing by the entire court was
denied by a 5 to 4 count, the dissenters arguing against what they called "religious tyranny." Calling the decision to uphold the Purdy ban wrong, they
objected to "the unwarranted precedent created in this circuit and throughout the nation providing a devious springboard for further destruction of
the wall separating church and state."[49] The United States Supreme Court
refused to hear the case, allowing the Purdy school board to reimpose its
ban on dancing.[50]

During times of social change, "dance, with its power to arouse, has subversive potential. . . . That the instrument used for both dance and sex is the
human body has long made dance suspect or immoral in some people's
eyes."[51] Although the focus here has been on social dancing and not dance
as performance, court decisions concerning exotic or nude dancing are
worth mentioning. Ever since the Court turned its attention to protecting
free speech in the aftermath of World War I, it has broadened the First
Amendment's protective reach. Students of dance have always considered
dance a form of expression. In 1991 eight out of nine Supreme Court justices agreed but then differed on whether a particular Indiana regulation
was constitutional. It required the dancers to wear a G-string to cover their
pubic area and pasties to cover their nipples. Despite an inability to get five
members of the Court to agree on an opinion, a majority did conclude that
Indiana had a substantial governmental interest in banning public nudity
and its law was not designed to suppress the erotic message of the dance.
Justice David Souter, who provided the fifth vote, cautioned that only harmful secondary effects would justify regulation of such artistic expression.
Four justices disagreed with upholding the Indiana regulation, concluding
that the erotic message was muted by the requirements of a G-string and
pasties.[52]

Nine years later the justices still could not agree on an opinion in a nude
dancing case, but they did send the case back to the Pennsylvania court that
had declared the law unconstitutional.[53] In late 2002 the state court again decided that the ordinance under consideration was unconstitutional, this time
based upon the court's reading of the state constitution, which it interpreted
as more broadly protecting expression. In conclusion, Erie cannot pass an ordinance whose purpose is to muzzle the erotic message of the dance.[54] In the
summer of 2006, the Utah Supreme Court, by a five to four count rejected a
claim that nude dancing was protected under its state constitution's free
speech clause.[55] The result is that G-strings and pasties can come off in Erie,
Pennsylvania, but they must stay on in South Salt Lake, Utah.

Turning now from erotic dancing to erotic song lyrics, the record displaced sheet music as the barometer of popular taste late in 1920. New concern about sex in such music escalated and would continue from records to tapes to CDs to digitized music. A noted violinist speaking before the National Federation of Women's Clubs in 1913 said that contemporary popular music was depraved with its "brazenly suggestive words" playing "upon immature minds at that dangerous age." Suggestive words led to suggestive dancing, posing even more of "a menace to the social fabric."[56] To combat this menace she proposed a censorship board. Such concerns would mount in the coming years, as sales of such music added appreciably to the six-fold increase in total record sales between 1914 and 1919. By 1921 one hundred million records were being sold, making the record the number one recreational purchase of Americans.[57]

Popular music became "one of the most significant, meaningful, sought after, and defining elements of day-to-day life, of generational identity, and of personal and public memory."[58] Jazz replaced the old warhorses of classical and other popular music on the airwaves and, for the first time, "seized hold of the great mass of American young men." Its "syncopation, the phallic brashness of the saxophone and drums, the unpredictability of the improvisation" all spoke to their feelings of rebellion against Victorian culture.[59] Debate began on the subject of whether such music corrupted American values. A popular woman's magazine concluded that "Jazz Put the Sin in Syncopation."[60] Racial and class tensions, which would reemerge in the 1950s and 1980s as well, spilled over into the debate. Youthful white rebellion was married to black music. This race music, as it was sometimes called, was attacked by the custodians of middle-class white culture as an abomination. The *Ladies' Home Journal* said that it threatened civilization and raised the rate of illegitimate births.[61]

Popular music of the 1920s had built upon pre–World War I beginnings to shed the restraints of the sentimental ballad and incorporate some strange and different sounds. For instance, jazz was sometimes referred to as jungle music because of its incorporation of what were believed to be African sounds. In fact when Duke Ellington performed at the Cotton Club in the late '20s, his group was called the Jungle Band. If the summoning up of the uncivilized jungle with such musical effects was not enough to alarm those custodians of morality, the lyrics that accompanied such rhythms were. When Irving Mills put words to Ellington's "The Mooche" in 1928, protestors blamed the provocative lyrics for endangering women by increasing the number of rapes in the country.[62]

As in all areas of popular culture, would-be censors had to steep themselves in the material they sought to censor. For instance, "jelly roll" could mean the cake but to others it was a reference to a woman's genitalia. "I Ain't Gonna Give Nobody None of My Jelly Roll" was understood among the initiated to be a reference to sexual intercourse. And "Phonograph Blues" with its talk of an overplayed needle was even less subtle.[63]

Books were not the only medium being banned in Boston and elsewhere in the 1920s. Sophie Tucker's "He Hadn't Up Till Yesterday" was a favorite target. *Variety*, which listed best-selling records, refused to list certain hits that were too suggestive. When *Billboard* took over such listings, it was no more tolerant of such recordings. It condemned sexual references in lyrics and encouraged bans against jukeboxes that included such songs.[64]

Even the less risqué music reflected the changing times as the lyrics spoke more directly about sexual relationships and needs. Although "A Bird in a Gilded Cage" and "My Heart Belongs to Daddy" tell a similar story of a young woman in a relationship with a wealthy older man, the latter is far more explicit about sexual relationships than the former.[65]

In fact, the lyrics, written by Cole Porter, were considered so risqué that they were deemed unsuitable for transmission by radio. Only with the advent of radio did a concern for the words that accompanied popular music become a matter that generated much public attention. Only needing a receiver, the listener could be flooded with songs, moving without wires and without discrimination into the sanctity of the home. The unwitting listener might well be subjected to smutty words. Porter apparently agreed to having a colleague write substitute words that made the song playable to radio audiences. And with "Let's Do It," where the "it" clearly conveyed what the birds, bees, and educated fleas were doing, Porter accommodated would-be censors by adding to the title the parenthetical phrase "Let's Fall in Love."[66]

In New York City, the home of the major networks, a minister urged mothers to unite in protest against the indecent songs on the airwaves. Station and network censors, eager to head off such protests, either sanitized lyrics or banned the songs from the air. For instance, Harry Warren and Al Dubin's "Young and Healthy" from the movie of the same name was banned. A line in "I Love Louisa," that talked of choosing women for the size of their bosoms was changed to worrying about a loss of affection. And the title number from *42nd Street* now noted attractive women rather than ones who were sexually indiscreet. When a watch company wanted to use the song, "Every Little Movement Has a Meaning All Its Own," it was vetoed as being "too suggestive."[67]

Apparently even Cole's mother could not persuade the composer to change the lyrics of "Love for Sale."[68] One of Porter's most socially sensitive songs, it was written during the Depression in 1930. The lyrics tell the story of a streetwalker hawking her youthful body to those men who can afford the cost.[69] The song was from a show called *The New Yorkers* and was well accepted by the audience, but a critic from *New York World* found the song and its presentation to be "in the worst possible taste." Radio executives apparently agreed and banned the song from the airwaves, giving substance to another critic's worry that "when and if we ever get . . . censorship, I will give odds that it will frown upon such an honest thing."[70]

Custodians of the prevailing moral order called upon Congress to censor the salacious and lewd lyrics that often accompanied the music. Federal legislation regulating radio began in the early 1920s. Eventually, the Federal Communications Commission (FCC), created in 1934, was the federal government's answer to the need to bring order to chaos by regulating the limited bandwidth that was available to broadcasters. What that limited bandwidth meant was that government in the United States would now be involved in licensing, opening up the real possibility that with that licensing would come some form of censorship. Licensees were required to serve the public interest.

In fact, the FCC was prodded by members of Congress in 1935 to take action against station WJZ in New York for broadcasting a Spanish song in a program sponsored by the Mexican government. They agreed with a Catholic magazine's description of the song as "a filthy piece of unabashed pornography." Its translated lyrics, made part of the *Congressional Record*, contained the following lines:

Oh, how many nights I passed there
Beside a girl
Of well-shaped and graceful form,
Of firm and wide thighs!
. . . .
But my greatest delight
Was when she stood naked
Of her flowing garments
And, like a bending branch
Of a willow, uncovered to me
Her beauty, an unfolding rose
Which breaks its bud
And displays all its loveliness.

Moving cautiously in its early years, the FCC concluded that the lyrics did not tend to corrupt morals and were neither indecent nor obscene.[71]

Shortly after the enactment of the Communications Act of 1934, popular orchestra leaders formed a committee to evaluate songs on a weekly basis. Five orchestra leaders, Rudy Vallée, Paul Whiteman, Guy Lombardo, Richard Himber, and Abe Lyman joined together in the Committee of Five for the Betterment of Radio to place a ban on songs with sexy titles and lyrics. "Love for Sale" was at the top of their list. Apparently they became self-censors because of worry that the concern about sex on the silver screen might spill over and target radio broadcasting as well.[72] If the song's publisher refused to make suggested changes to the lyrics, that information was sent to all orchestra leaders, most of whom had agreed not to play such songs over the air. The network spokesmen indicated that they were satisfied with their internal censors but were pleased that the dance bands were now also addressing the problem. The committee acknowledged that local stations, not the networks, had been the biggest offenders.[73]

Not to be outdone, radio executives were also censoring songs. For instance, Ernest LaPrade, director of music research for the National Broadcasting System (NBC) assured the network's listeners that "to insure that their programs serve the public interest with respect to morals, ethics, and good taste, broadcasters have formulated certain policies governing program content." What this meant for aired music was that "the text of every vocal composition must be approved by a lyric editor before it may be sung on the air."[74] The result was the banning of 290 songs.[75] For instance, mother's warning was reinforced by NBC when it banned "Keep Your Skirt Down, Mary Ann." *Variety*, show business's bible, aided the effort by excluding from its lists songs with suggestive lyrics, such as the blues classic about the sexual prowess of the "Hoochie Coochie Man."[76]

Networks also received complaints about Rudy Vallee and Bing Crosby, singers known as "crooners." Some listeners said that the songs they often sang were indecent. A Roman Catholic cardinal in Boston characterized such crooning as "bleating and whining, with disgusting words, the meaning of which is a low-down source of sexual influence."[77]

The FCC was part of the New Deal regulation of American life, and it coincided with new fears in the movie industry that federal governmental censorship would displace that industry's self-regulation unless the Production Code enforcement was stepped up. Synchronized sound had captured the industry and music had become an integral part of that sound, so one might well expect that just as stage dramas and novels often ran afoul of censors as they were transformed into motion pictures, so, too, would stage music.

Cole Porter ran into difficulty with the Motion Picture Production Code when Hollywood decided to do a film, supposedly based upon his life. As with many screen biographies of musical composers, the story told had little relationship to the subject's actual life. Even if Porter had not been a homosexual addicted to fleeting encounters with younger men, the moviemakers were less interested in biographical accuracy than in telling a simple story that would give them an opportunity to present the composer's music. Except for some sexual suggestiveness in a dialogue between Porter and his wife and worry that the costumes would not fully cover women's breasts, Joseph Breen, the chief censor under the Production Code, was most upset by the composer's lyrics. Words such as "gigolo," and phrases such as "led astray" would have to go. If these changes were not made, Breen added, local censors would snip away and cause annoying skips in the soundtrack.[78] The changes were made.

If Porter felt put upon, he got off rather easy in comparison to his colleague, Lorenz Hart. Hart's sensuous lyrics for the musical *Pal Joey* helped make the property unfilmable during Joseph Breen's tenure as the movies' chief censor. By the time it was filmed, Hart was dead. Even in 1957 songs such as "Den of Iniquity" and "Bewitched, Bothered and Bewildered" could not be presented in their unexpurgated form. In "Den of Iniquity" the woman, who is keeping her man, sings about the propriety of separate bedrooms but then adds that one's for play, the other for display. The entire song was dropped from the movie, and Breen had earlier recommended that "Bewitched, Bothered and Bewildered" meet the same fate. The lyrics traced her passage from her oversexed state to her lover's bed.[79] When the movie was made, the song was retained but the lyrics were substantially shortened and sanitized. For instance, the woman laid awake alone rather than in her lover's bed. Only about a quarter of the lyrics were used at all.[80]

In the late 1930s Abner Silver and Robert Bruce in *How to Write and Sell a Hit Song* summed up the prevailing attitudes on sex. They warned would-be songwriters that "direct allusions to love-making, or the use of such words as 'necking,' 'petting' and 'passion' must be avoided. Love, in popular songs, is a beautiful and delicate emotion, and marriage is a noble institution."[81]

The show tune or Tin Pan Alley song[82] was the subject of *Billboard's* introduction of the best-selling record list in 1940. By the end of the decade the magazine had three separate lists corresponding to the three different genres of popular music. Rhythm and blues (R&B) was the music of blacks, sometimes referred to as race music. Country-western was the music of whites in rural America and in the urban working class. The remaining category, into which the work of Hart and Porter fit, was the music of the white, urban middle class. Each genre had its own performers and radio outlets. Although African American groups, such as the Ink Spots and Mills Brothers, now and then appeared in two lists, such crossovers were rare.[83]

Although the lyrics in much R&B music had to be toned down, the result was still much more sexually suggestive than lyrics in other popular music. For instance, Hank Ballard with the Moonlighters topped the R&B chart for seven weeks in 1954 with one of the many Annie songs, then titled "Work with Me Annie." Originally it was titled "Sock It to Me Annie," but even the word "work" was risqué, since it was slang for sexual intercourse. Many radio stations refused to play the Annie songs,[84] one of the most banned being "Annie Had a Baby" in which her lover complains about how the child's needs have replaced his.[85]

Network affiliates usually ran television programming without much thought, but an interesting battle between NBC and its affiliate in Detroit, WWJ-TV over music developed in the early 1950s. The local station decided that one of the songs on *The Wayne King Show*, a novelty number titled

"Sweet Violets" with double entendre lyrics, was too sexually suggestive and therefore cut the sound during the performance of the song. Emboldened by its action, the station again silenced the sound when "I Get Ideas" was performed on *Your Hit Parade.* The song, an adaptation of a 1932 tango, suggested, as censors regularly feared, that dancing would lead to the arousal of sexual feelings.[86] Critics divided over the censorship, some praising it and some condemning it. The station manager defended his decisions, saying television is not radio, "it's too powerful, too vivid, too compelling to be allowed to run loose." Apparently he or his supervisors capitulated when threatened with a loss of revenue from their network affiliation.[87]

Worry about some of the words that accompanied the lush melodies of the 1930s and 1940s and even the novelty songs would seem rather quaint as the 1950s gave birth to a dramatically new musical style. What happened in the mid-1950s could not have been anticipated. Black music, always viewed as more sexual, crossed the color line, was sung by whites, and rechristened "rock 'n' roll."[88] In July 1953 "Crying in the Chapel" by the Orioles, number one on the R&B chart showed up at spot number eleven on the pop chart. In December 1954 "Earth Angel" by the Penguins, number one on the R&B list, reached number eight on the pop chart. Then, in May 1955, "Rock around the Clock" by Bill Haley and the Comets, which would redirect motion picture music for the future, reached number one on the pop chart and number four on its R&B counterpart.[89] The song had been recorded two years earlier and made no real impression. However, when the recording was integrated into the soundtrack of the motion picture *Blackboard Jungle,* a tale of urban youth and juvenile delinquency, it became the "real opening gun in the rock revolution."[90] Teenagers jumped from their seats in theaters playing the film to dance in the aisles. Neither movie soundtracks nor popular music would ever be the same. The song became the anthem of "teenage rebellion. . . . It became the first song to have a special secret defiant meaning for teenagers only."[91]

Earlier generations had used popular music to declare their independence but now the younger generation seemed to be engaged in guerilla warfare against their elders. The new music was loud, raucous, aggressive, and sexually suggestive. The monogamous love ballad would all but disappear, as members of the young generation believed that sex was not something to sing pretty, little songs about; rather it should be dealt with honestly and erotically and not be hidden or submerged.[92] Rock-and-roll music was no less than a proclamation of youth coming of age. Sex was necessarily involved, for one came of age both sexually and in terms of popular music at about the same time. That linkage is what frightened parents who believed that the very core of sexual morality had been breached. All restraint and reticence had been lost. Rock fans seemed manic and their role models were equally strange, as the performers cultivated sexy images and laced their lyrics with matching words.

Although it may have been unprecedented for young girls to swoon as they did at the crooning of Frank Sinatra in the 1940s, he was a conventional band singer who excited his audience with his voice. His successor as a pop idol, however, was anything but traditional both in what he sang and, even more, in how he sang it. As he sang, Elvis Presley, often garbed in leather or lamé, rolled his hips and thrust his pelvis forward, movements that had previously been confined to black dance clubs. The so-called obscene movements led Ed Sullivan on his weekly Sunday television show to insist, after complaints about the singer's first two performances on the show, that Elvis be shot by the camera only above the waist.[93] Rock and roll had arrived, and although Elvis was white, he acknowledged his indebtedness to the black musicians and black music that had given birth to a whole new genre of popular music. His "Good Rockin' Tonight" was a special target of Houston, Texas, censors who sought to deny playtime and sales to the song. Indeed the lyrics talk of a young man meeting his girl behind the barn and proving that he was "a mighty, mighty, man," but in comparison to the genre from which such music was lifted the lyrics were tame indeed.[94]

Presley's records would soon scale new heights in sales, just as "After the Ball" had shattered previous sales of sheet music a few generations earlier. Elvis made the breakthrough to the third list, country-western, in February 1956, when "Heartbreak Hotel" occupied the number one spot on the pop and country-western lists and number five on the rhythm-and-blues chart. Later that same year the Presley duo of "Don't Be Cruel" and "Hound Dog" swept the number one spot on all three lists. Elvis would do it again with "Let Me Be Your Teddy Bear" in June 1957 and later in October with "Jailhouse Rock."[95] Perhaps this result was inevitable, for rock was in fact a merger of all three genres of popular music.

At first rock music seemed to subordinate the simple and repetitive lyrics to the beat of the music. From the start rock and roll was visual; it was performance oriented. The rock concert would become a staple of popular music. Would-be censors worried about the raucousness of the music and its often racy themes, but initial concern focused upon the performers themselves and the bad examples they set. Just such concern had led Ed Sullivan to censor Elvis's swiveling hips. In the next decade the Rolling Stones, although they appeared five times on his show, caused problems for Sullivan. He was, however, successful in their last appearance in getting them to change "Let's Spend the Night Together" to "Let's Spend Some Time Together."[96]

Although Sullivan asked the Rolling Stones back, he did not relax his ban on Jim Morrison of the Doors. Morrison apparently reneged on his agreement to change some lyrics in the song "Light My Fire." Perhaps the sexiest of the male sex symbols of the rock era, Morrison entered a period of decline following his arrest and conviction for indecent exposure during a concert in Miami. Although testimony differed, the jury apparently believed that he had masturbated on stage, or at the very least exposed his genitals. He served six months in jail. The conviction led to the demise of the Doors and Morrison. Radio stations stopped playing his records, worried that they would incur the wrath of the FCC. Within a year of his trial, he died in Paris at age twenty-seven, apparently of a drug overdose.[97]

Worry about rock's baleful effects began to spread as early as 1954 when Representative Ruth Thompson of Michigan introduced a bill in Congress seeking to ban certain rock records from the mails as pornographic material.[98] In the same year the Songwriter's Protective Organization and the Music Publishers' Protective Association agreed that certain R&B records containing references to sex should be censored for affronting current moral standards. Some jukebox vendors and radio deejays supported the formation of screening committees to review records. On their own initiative, some radio station managers banned songs because of their sexually suggestive lyrics, claiming that by such action they were promoting good citizenship, protecting the American way of life, and promoting good morals. Behind much of this censorship was the assumption that hearing such music would corrupt the young. Dirty music was equated with dirty postcards, and *Variety*, citing sexually explicit lyrics that it called "leer-ics" advocated self-policing by the recording industry to head off outside regulation. Not surprisingly the target of much of the protest was R&B music performed by black singers. Rock concerts also attracted censors, who worked from the assumption that rock music led to disturbances and violence among the young. In 1957 Congress again contemplated action directed toward rock music, this time considering a screening process that would be interposed before the music was sold or broadcast. Antirock sentiment was rising in the country and increasingly radio stations were removing all such music from their playlists. Deejays in Milwaukee burned two hundred records in the station's parking lot, the first of many such episodes throughout the country.[99]

What was clear, however, to an industry that had initially looked with suspicion on rock and roll was that the musical style sold records. Sales more than tripled in the decade of the 1950s, from 189 million dollars to almost six hundred million dollars.[100]

Rock music's birth in the 1950s anticipated the turbulence of the 1960s. The coming of the pill led to a sexual revolution, accompanied, of course, by music. Some optimists trumpeted the end of '50s rock, citing as evidence the disparate styles of the music that made the charts in the early '60s. They failed to notice that British groups were carrying on the tradition. These groups would soon mount a full-scale invasion of the American popular music scene.

One British group, the Beatles, with little visibility in the United States at the end of 1963, captured the top five spots on *Billboard*'s Top 100 chart in early April 1964.[101]

Although their long hair and charismatic appeal worried parents, the Beatles, compared to the groups that would follow this first British wave, looked clean-cut and well scrubbed. The Rolling Stones, who based their music on "raunchy American blues," posed a sexual threat that the Beatles had not. Coupled with sexually suggestive lyrics was the stage persona of the leader, Mick Jagger. He easily displaced Elvis Presley as "the prototype for stage sexuality."[102] Rolling Stones' songs, such as "Satisfaction (I Can't Get No)," and "Let's Spend the Night Together," were banned from radio play.[103]

In 1967 Gordon McLendon, an owner of thirteen radio stations, mounted a campaign against the "obscene" songs that came with this British invasion, suggesting that Americans follow the example of the patriots at the Boston Tea Party. At this "Wax Party" the offending British records could be dealt with as the tea had been in 1773. A group, known as the American Mothers' Committee, heeded the call and persuaded over a hundred stations, including those of the American Broadcasting System, to remove such records from their playlists.[104]

Censorious surveyors of the music scene were not only concerned with what was on the vinyl inside the cover but often with the cover itself.[105] With rock music came album art; the plain cover depicting the artist or group and providing basic information was increasingly replaced by artwork that, as with a book's dust jacket, would help sell the product. When Jimi Hendrix's album, *Electric Ladybird* was released in London, its cover contained a picture of nineteen naked women; clearly that would not do for the American version, which displaced the offending picture with concert photos. When one of the Beatles, John Lennon, and his wife, Yoko Ono, released an album titled *Two Virgins* with nude pictures of themselves, front and back, on the covers, Capitol Records refused to distribute it. An independent label released the album with a brown paper wrapper covering the naked bodies. Still, Chicago police closed a retail store in Chicago for carrying the album, and New York City officers seized thirty thousand copies. FBI director J. Edgar Hoover vowed to keep it from being imported.[106]

In these instances the showing of breasts or genitalia caused the problem, but the most explicit of these images was not placed on the cover of an album but rather included as a poster within the album's covers. The punk rock group Dead Kennedys, for their album titled *Frankenchrist*, had decided to include a poster of a surrealist painting depicting interlocking penises and vaginas that had been exhibited in a number of museums and included in a book on erotic art. Furthermore, they put a warning sticker on the album crediting the artist and acknowledging that some people might find the poster "shocking, repulsive or offensive." The sticker concluded with the remark, "Life can sometimes be that way." The group's lead singer, Jello Biafra, said the painting was "a kind of crowning statement of what the record was trying to say musically, lyrically, and visually." After a teenage girl bought the album, the assistant district attorney for Los Angeles charged Biafra and his associates under a statute prohibiting the distribution of material harmful to minors. An extensive trial ended with a hung jury. The defendants agreed not to include the poster in the record's packaging, instead allowing those who said they were at least eighteen to obtain a copy by mail.[107]

Album covers would continue to spark controversy. Jane's Addiction released an album titled *Ritual de lo Habitual* with a cover that depicted a sculpture done by one of the band members of two naked women and a man with an exposed penis. An alternative cover was made available that included the album title, the group's name, and the text of the First Amendment. A Warner Brothers executive acknowledged that the first cover did not meet "with as much resistance as we thought it would."[108]

As the 1960s turned into the 1970s, censors worried more about drugs than sex, though the two "evils" were often linked. For instance the FCC in 1971 sent telegrams to all radio stations suggesting that by playing rock music they were endangering their licenses, for the agency would have to consider at renewal time "whether continued operation of the station is in the public interest." To aid the stations the FCC listed some examples, but some worried station owners expanded the warning to cover all controversial subjects. Dissident FCC commissioner Nicholas Johnson accused his colleagues of taking such action to "harass the youth culture" and to further the administration's striving "to divert the American people's attention" from much more substantial social and political problems.[109]

Specifically the agency singled out lyrics glorifying drug use. Even John Denver's "Rocky Mountain High" came under attack. Apparently teenagers were to be kept ignorant of "The Pill," for Loretta Lynn's song of that name, touting woman's new control over the reproductive process, was refused airtime by numerous stations. Such ignorance was brought to public attention by Reverend Charles Boykin of Tallahassee, Florida, who cited popular music as the cause of teenage pregnancy. He proclaimed that a survey of one thousand unwed mothers revealed that 984 of them conceived to the strains of rock music. His bonfire that consumed copies of the "devil's music" certainly would have included, had it been recorded yet, Rod Stewart's "Tonight's the Night." The singer asks his lover to open a pathway for sexual intercourse, a segment of the lyrics that RKO radio insisted on cutting before giving the song airtime.[110]

Yale Broadcasting Company filed suit against the FCC claiming that its order warning about "drug oriented music" constituted the censorship that the agency was specifically forbidden to exercise. The District of Columbia Court of Appeals rejected the claim, saying that the FCC was simply reminding stations of their responsibilities. Chief Judge David Bazelon dissented, arguing that the order did amount to censorship. The judge said his colleagues should recognize "that the threat of legal sanction can have as much effect on the conduct of threatened parties as the sanction itself." He questioned whether the agency could ban protected speech from the airwaves on the basis of protecting children, a question the Supreme Court would shortly answer.[111]

In the late 1970s the United States Supreme Court upheld an FCC ruling that forbade airing indecent words during times when children might be listening to the radio.[112] For a decade the FCC was content if such words were not broadcast before 10 p.m. and after 6 a.m. Then, informed by critics of this so-called safe harbor that children were listening to the radio in this time period, the FCC sought to halt indecency after 10 p.m., especially in the lyrics of rock music. The U.S. Supreme Court concluded that the agency had gone too far and that it had to provide a safe harbor for the airing of indecency. Congress, in a rider to an appropriations bill, then weighed in on the side of the FCC by providing for a twenty-four-hour ban on indecency in broadcasting. When the ban was declared unconstitutional by a lower federal court, Congress again responded, this time providing for a safe harbor from 10 p.m. to 6 a.m. for public radio stations and from midnight to 6 a.m. for commercial stations that broadcast during those hours and for 10 p.m. to midnight for commercial stations that shut down during the early morning hours. The FCC specifically targeted stations that aired rock music with indecent lyrics outside of these safe harbor times. For instance, it levied fines on stations playing Prince's "Erotic City."[113]

In 1975 *Time* published an article on what it called "sex rock," citing Donna Summer's "Love to Love You Baby," which it said contained "a marathon of 22 orgasms." The following year Jesse Jackson made such lyrics a boycott target of his civil rights organization, Operation PUSH (People United to Save Humanity). He believed that radio and television were setting low moral values for the young and that the sexy songs that were such a staple of programming contributed to the high rate of teenage pregnancies. He proposed "media ethics" conferences, but only a Chicago meeting was held. Little would change for the time being, even with support from the Southern Baptist Convention and concern expressed by the National Association of Broadcasters (NAB).[114]

Popular music has always been about love and sex; what was now different was the explicitness of the lyrics. They had moved from describing thoughts or feelings to describing physical action. For instance, Olivia Newton John's song "Physical," ran into trouble. One radio station called the lyrics "too pubescent." They did suggest a horizontal mode of communication.[115] What had been shocking to earlier generations now seemed tame indeed. Instead of this fact tempering the censorial urge, it was used to buttress the need for censorship at a time when all reticence had seemed to disappear.

By the middle of the 1970s, country music had moved successfully into the popular mainstream, to the dismay of many early aficionados and performers. For instance, old-timers such as Grandpa Jones and Cindy Walker deplored the appearance of what they called "skin songs" in the genre. They had in mind a certain sensuousness that had crept into country music with such songs as "Behind Closed Doors," "Help Me Make It Through the Night," "Sexy Lady," and "Ruby, Don't Take Your Love to Town."[116]

Despite the fact that country songs often dealt with sexuality in rather frank terms, generally they were not targeted by censors. Country music never posed the threat many critics found in rock and later rap music. Its audience traditionally had been patriotic and politically and socially conservative, posing little challenge to the status quo that the audiences for other popular music regularly mounted. Frank Zappa, a musician fighting the introduction of a ratings system for albums, at one point argued that such a system would "have the effect of protectionist legislation for the country music industry."[117]

The decade of the 1980s brought the music video into the popular music mainstream, at times in the most imaginative ways. Visual presentations of songs went back to the 1930s when they were shown as shorts in theaters, but the genre had all but disappeared. When it was reborn it bore only a passing resemblance to its ancestor; these new visual interpretations of songs were costly productions in themselves, a far cry from the filming of a standing vocalist singing into a microphone. MTV, a cable channel that began broadcasting on August 1, 1981, provided the perfect vehicle for this new wedding of moving images to music and lyrics. It brought rock and roll to television, pretty much retaining the radio format of playing songs in succession, and then repeating the most popular ones. Deejays would become veejays.[118]

Success, of course, depended upon the new venture's ability to enter the major markets by winning both cable operators and advertisers. Both goals could only be achieved by creating demand for what the new channel offered. Labeling this audience, "cable brats," the campaign said that they had grown up with both music and television and now MTV had merged the two: "rock and roll wasn't enough for them—now they want their MTV." The latter words became the slogan, as youngsters were urged to demand this new viewing opportunity. A little over a year after its inception MTV cracked the New York City and Los Angeles markets and gained the attention of the national press. In March 1983 two productions by Michael Jackson raised the artistic level of the music video and assured its widespread acceptance. MTV had become "a full-fledged cultural phenomenon." A poll of high school students found that 85 percent of those whose homes were wired for cable watched MTV.[119]

Such national attention was accompanied by the lamentations of moral arbiters. When the "We Want Our MTV" advertising campaign had just gotten underway, authorities at a mental hospital in Connecticut quickly concluded that MTV viewing was detrimental to their patients' well-being. That criticism would grow in the days to follow. At first the critics were concerned parents worried about social decency, the same type that fretted over Elvis's swaying hips or Cyndi Lauper's "Girls Just Want to Have Fun." As MTV's influence grew, parents were joined by others who questioned whether the young might be adversely affected by this new contagion. C. Everett Koop, the nation's surgeon general, speculated that slightly clad women and violence, ingredients that seemed in abundance in the music video, could not sustain healthy relationships between men and women. Ted Turner, the founder of CNN, took every opportunity to lambaste MTV. Spokesman for the cable channel responded that they worked within the same restrictions on nudity and language that governed the major networks.[120]

Indeed, MTV does have its internal censors. As with all such operations, the observer finds little consistency in their work. To fend off criticism, the channel ran some videos only late at night. One such video presentation was of Cher's "If I Could Turn Back Time," in which the singer's tattooed rear end appeared in a leather thong. It still attracted the attention of some Texarkana residents. Although the censors had had no trouble with women's breasts and behinds gyrating, they ruled out showing condoms or mentioning the word prophylactic. They also barred depictions of homosexual and lesbian contact.[121]

As a cable channel, MTV and system operators had to fight local attempts to eliminate it from the service provided or add it only as a paid channel. They were not always successful. In Weymouth, Massachusetts, a petition drive calling MTV "decadent, morally degrading, and evil," succeeded in denying residents access to the channel. Offer of a channel blocker with which the individual subscriber could block reception of MTV was rejected. Such a compromise, however, was accepted in Texarkana, although only forty of the twenty-two thousand subscribers took advantage of the offer. Furthermore, MTV won some big battles. When Tele-Community Antenna (TCA), which had some 420,000 subscribers in Texas, Mississippi, and Arkansas, dropped the "borderline pornographic" channel from its service, orchestrated protest by MTV brought it back in two weeks. Then, when Sammons Communications, which operated fifty-five cable systems in nineteen states, wanted to make MTV a paid-for-service, the channel operators refused, worried about losing advertising revenue. Sammons then dropped MTV from its offerings, but, responding to customer protest, it restored the channel just four months later.[122]

Just as Michael Jackson's lavishly produced videos tended to subordinate the song to the spectacle, Madonna's videos, no matter what the song, were about SEX. She was the hit of the first MTV Music Video Awards show in September 1984. While perched as a bride atop a giant wedding cake, she sang "Like a Virgin," the title song of her new album. Music videos created Madonna, the singer and pop culture icon. Girls as young as eight were proud to be Madonna wanna-bes, and one New York disk jockey suggested that MTV had become a sexy *Sesame Street* teaching all the wrong values.[123]

In the late 1980s and early 1990s, Madonna pushed the envelope of what could be shown on television, and her popularity only increased. "Express Yourself" was done for video with a number of sexy scenes, and "Vogue" presented Madonna in a see-through blouse, made acceptable only by the fact that her nipples were covered. When Madonna, however, made a video of "Justify My Love," which depicted what she said were her sexual fantasies, MTV drew the line. The fantasies included group sex, gay and lesbian foreplay, and nudity. Censorship, critics cried, and MTV's action became a news story. Eventually the eagerly awaited video was shown on the American Broadcasting Company's *Nightline* in early December 1990. This second-highest rated installment of the program clearly violated the network strictures against nudity, but, then, Madonna and MTV had become news, not merely entertainment.[124]

The Reagan years also gave support to cultural conservatives who saw much that they disliked in the permissive society, including the sexually explicit lyrics of some songs. The censorial attempts of the 1950s that were revived in the mid-1970s would now bear fruit. Prince had recorded an album called *Dirty Mind* and eagerly capitalized on the fuss made over his sexually explicit lyrics and androgynous persona. His big breakthrough came with the double-album *1999*, which would remain on *Billboard* charts for three years. In October 1983 Rick Alley and his children in Cincinnati, Ohio, were attracted to the title tune. Allen apparently was unaware of the artist's reputation and the simple fact that the song was a tribute to partying now, regardless of the consequences. If the beat overcame the lyrics in certain songs, that was not the case with "Let's Pretend We're Married." The lyrics made clear that the purpose of the pretense was to enjoy a night of sexual bliss without guilt.[125]

Such lyrics, Alley concluded, were not only unfit for his children's ears but they did not conform to the printed lyrics that had been included with the album. When he brought his concern to the *Cincinnati Inquirer*, he found other parents with similar complaints. A reporter suggested that Alley seek the support of the PTA at his children's elementary school. Ultimately nineteen other local PTAs joined in a petition delivered at the annual meeting in Las Vegas asking the national organization to take up the cause. Alley's story won the support of the delegates who vowed to use the clout of the five and a half million strong organization to advance the campaign. In June 1984 the convention adopted a resolution calling for accurate lyrics to accompany albums and a ratings system to alert buyers to the appearance of "profanity, sex, violence, or vulgarity" in the album's lyrics. When the president of the national organization sent copies of the resolution to twenty-nine record companies, she suggested a ratings system similar to that in use for motion pictures. A spokesman for the Recording Industry Association of America (RIAA) rejected the analogy, saying that each year there were only four hundred motion pictures but twenty-five thousand songs. Furthermore, he likened the proposal to censorship, saying it "would open a Pandora's box of unpleasant possibilities." For the record companies, only a Warner Brothers executive responded, saying that his company would never put such ratings stickers on their products, adding that "one of the functions of rock 'n' roll is to annoy parents."[126]

Before 1984 ended, however, the PTA initiative that began with a concerned parent would gain independent support from other parents, also stirred to action by Prince's lyrics. One new concerned parent was Tipper Gore, the wife of Senator Albert Gore of Tennessee. She had purchased Prince's best-selling soundtrack album entitled *Purple Rain* for her eleven-year-old daughter. As they listened to it, they heard the song "Darling Nikki," which began with an encounter with the young woman of the title as she masturbated in the lobby of a hotel.

When Tipper Gore's younger children, six and eight, asked her about videos on MTV, she decided to watch some of the fare. She was appalled by the graphic sex and violence that flooded the tube.[127]

Susan Baker, the wife of the secretary of the treasury and mother of eight children, along with other women, most of whom were the wives of government officials, shared Gore's concern about such lyrics. Of twenty original members of the organization they would form, seventeen were married to powerful politicians. One writer noted that fully half of them "are married to 10% of the Senate."[128] Aside from Prince's "Darling Nikki," the Washington wives cited Sheena Easton's "Sugar Walls," and Judas Priest's "Eat Me Alive." They established a nonprofit organization, named it the Parents' Music Resource Center (PMRC), and installed it in headquarters provided by the socially conservative Adolph Coors Foundation. Clearly this activity at the seat of the national government posed more of a potential threat than did the National PTA's resolution. Almost four hundred people showed up at a meeting in Washington, D.C., on May 15, 1985. Despite invitations, no representative of the recording industry attended the meeting. However, the National Association of Broadcasters (NAB) was represented, and a letter from its president, Eddie Fritts, was read indicating that he shared the group's concerns.[129]

A few weeks later Fritts wrote to the heads of the major record companies asking that recordings made available to broadcasters be accompanied by the lyrics of the songs to enable broadcasters to make responsible decisions about giving the albums airtime. Record industry spokesmen were not especially receptive to the idea. A mole in the recording industry, whose identity Tipper Gore promised to keep secret, advised PMRC on how to proceed: Deal only with Stan Gortikov, the president of the RIAA, which represented all the major recording companies, and give him no choice. In the meantime, the PMRC was advised to publicize its cause. It worked to make its concerns national, and it sought some solution that would also be acceptable to the PTA. The ratings system that the PTA had sought was rejected by Gortikov as being too costly.[130]

Concerned with "a sexuality that is graphic and explicit," the PMRC made no distinction between women as victims or women in control, thus conveying the impression that "sex is bad." Susan Baker said it was Madonna's "Like a Virgin" that led her to help launch the PMRC, and another founding member, Pam Howar, said the singer was teaching girls "how to be porn queens in heat."[131]

More than 150 newspaper and magazine editorials expressed support for the PMRC. A guest editorial in *Newsweek* written by a female chorale singer complained about "orgasmic moans and howls" and "tasteless, graphic and gratuitous sexuality saturating the airwaves and filtering into our homes." David Gergen, a newspaper columnist and former White House press secretary, joined in condemning the "filth," saying the difference between sex in earlier songs and sex in today's music was akin to swimsuit models in *Sports Illustrated* being compared to the centerfold in *Hustler*. William Raspberry, a columnist for the *Washington Post*, said the PMRC was fully justified in its attempt to protect children from such degeneracy. The PMRC had energized the media and had found a sympathetic audience.[132]

Nowhere in the PMRC's initial agenda was there a request for a warning label. What the Washington wives wanted was the printing of lyrics on the album covers, the keeping of sexually explicit covers under the counters of record stores, and a ratings system for both records and concerts that was similar to that used in the motion picture industry. They were also interested in imposing some limitation on the conduct of performers on stage, and in establishing an industry/citizen board that would exert pressure on broadcasters not to air "questionable talent."[133]

Repeatedly accused of censorship, the PMRC denied the charge, saying its purpose was to inform, not limit, consumer choice. Artistic free speech, Tipper Gore said, should no more be sacrificed than should the right of parents to protect their children from harm. She insisted that the group sought only truth-in-packaging. It left to the industry, not government and not concerned citizens, the responsibility for determining what was or was not "musical pornography." This responsibility was properly placed, Gore continued, for the industry sustained itself largely through the purchases of children. The PMRC campaign had been misrepresented, she concluded, by those persons seeking to escape "corporate responsibility for the impact their products may have on young people."[134]

Zappa emerged as the industry's most visible spokesman. Citing the First Amendment, he derided the PMRC's campaign as an "ill-conceived housewife hobby project." He said it was "based on a hodge-podge of fundamentalist frogwash and illogical conclusions." He drafted a letter to President Ronald Reagan in which he said that legislators who made bad law were far more dangerous than songwriters who celebrated sexuality.[135]

In September 1985 the PMRC joined with the PTA to form a coalition to force the recording industry to take responsibility by instituting a rating system based on the lyrics contained in the album. The industry, however, resisted the establishment of a uniform standard. A Senate hearing on the matter, held on September 19, 1985, seemed to turn the tide. The committee chair, Senator John Danforth of Missouri, denied that Congress was considering any legislation dealing with rock lyrics. His colleague, Senator Ernest Hollings of Florida, seemed to disagree, saying that there was a pressing need to "rescue the tender young ears of this nation from this—this ROCK PORN."[136]

Actually the hearing rescued from oblivion some "of the vilest rock lyrics ever penned" and put them "straight into the minds of millions of innocents."[137] Tipper Gore sought examples of the worst lyrics, but the result, as is so often the case, was to thrust into the public spotlight material that in all likelihood would never have seen much exposure at all. In this way censors become purveyors of the very material that they wish to purge. This is why those who seek to push the envelope of the permissible need the censor to call attention to their work.

After the hearing, both sides now saw room for compromise, though Gortikov feared that concession here "will somehow constitute . . . censorship." What apparently made the RIAA amenable was less the threat of federal regulation than the hope that Congress would protect the industry from what it called piracy. Would-be customers were using tape recorders with blank tapes to deprive the industry of revenue; to compensate the industry a home audio recording bill was introduced in Congress that would place a tax on tape recorders and blank tapes. Since such a bill would eventually have to gain the approval of the Senate Judiciary Committee, the RIAA did not wish to alienate its members with a rigid stand on the warning issue. The committee was headed by Senator Strom Thurmond of South Carolina, whose wife was a supporter of the PMRC. In fact, the agreement on labeling came only two days after a hearing was held on the proposed piracy legislation, one of whose sponsors was Senator Albert Gore, Tipper's husband.[138]

The compromise was a warning label that would have the words "Explicit Lyrics: Parental Advisory" placed on the album. Compliance, however, was voluntary and each record company would decide what albums should carry the warning. Another option, one chosen by MCA Records, was to make the lyrics visible to a would-be buyer. Cassettes, which, at the time, were the leading seller in recorded music, carried a label referring the interested party to the record for the lyrics. The PMRC, RIAA, and PTA jointly announced the agreement on November 1, 1985, at the National Press Club in Washington, D.C. The parties agreed to cease further agitation and assess the plan's success in a year.[139]

A group called the Musical Majority, which was formed to challenge the PMRC, urged companies to follow the lead of MCA Records and use the visible lyrics option, because it posed less of a threat to artistic expression. The American Civil Liberties Union was less sanguine, feeling that free speech had been unfortunately compromised by the agreement.[140] Part of the fear in the popular music business was that the warning label would spawn further censorship because the albums that carried it would become pariahs. If certain outlets refused to carry such albums, they would not only be less available to children but also to adults. Censors regularly used the child in need of protection as the stalking horse for a much more widespread censorship. If the retail market was not sufficiently intimidated by public pressure then perhaps local enforcement officials could threaten prosecution, in effect criminalizing albums with warning stickers.[141] Although some of the offending artists of the past, such as Prince and Judas Priest, released new albums in 1986, none bore a warning sticker. In fact, the first album to carry the sticker was one by a rather obscure French singer who sang in his native tongue.[142]

Industry inaction caused the PMRC and Tipper Gore to continue their campaign. By early 1986 a dozen states, Arizona, Delaware, Florida, Illinois, Iowa, Kansas, Maryland, Missouri, New Mexico, Oklahoma, Pennsylvania, and Virginia were considering legislation either to ban or restrict sales of albums with warning labels. A PMRC mailing had energized a Maryland state legislator to get the lower house to pass proposed legislation making the sale of labeled records to persons under the age of eighteen a crime. Only after opposition mobilized did it stall in the state senate. In 1987 Tipper Gore, with substantial fanfare, published her book entitled *Raising PG Kids in an X-Rated Society*.[143]

Almost five years would pass before a universal sticker regularly appeared on recordings. In the interim each record company determined when stickers were necessary. CBS Music sought to avoid the sticker by encouraging artists to change offensive wording. Zappa, the outspoken opponent of labeling, made his own idiosyncratic statement by having a warning label placed upon his album, *Jazz from Hell*, comprised wholly of instrumental selections.[144]

When rap music revived the controversy over sexually objectionable lyrics, there was talk about federal legislation to enforce the 1985 agreement. Finally, the National Association of Record Manufacturers (NARA) pressured the RIAA to issue the universal warning sticker that the agreement had called for. So did the PMRC, which revived its campaign by focusing on the repeated failure of the record companies to warn customers about the lyrics in the albums. The RIAA could hold out no longer, and in March 1990 the universal black and white sticker carrying the words "Explicit Lyrics— Parental Advisory" made its appearance. The general policy outline required either printed lyrics or the sticker when the content related "to explicit sex, explicit violence, or explicit substance abuse." Albums with the sticker began to appear in substantial numbers. Restrictions on sales of such recordings were instituted by various chain stores, and some store managers were told to remove albums with the warning sticker if they disturbed customers. Wal-Mart announced it would not carry such albums, and some record companies responded by having the artists clean up their lyrics for sale at such major retailers. Proudly, the PMRC pointed to statistics that showed that in 1985 only 22 percent of adults found ratings of record albums desirable, but in 1991 the figure was 53 percent.[145]

More sweeping legislative initiatives in states were slowed by the new sticker standard, but local and state proposals to ban the sale of such material to minors proliferated. As time passed, many critics believed that more specific standards were necessary to achieve consensus among the record companies. Some company executives, however, saw the sticker as good public relations in indicating acceptance of industry accountability, while others milked the sticker for additional record sales.[146]

An observer might have erroneously concluded that rock and roll had racially integrated popular music, but such was not the case. Although Michael Jackson seemed to break the color barrier, whites appropriated elements of black music for themselves and covered the songs of black artists. For instance, Pat Boone recorded over sixty songs done originally by black rhythm-and-blues artists, often cleaning up the lyrics in the process. Motown Records, in the forefront of the rhythm-and-blues boom of 1960s and the leading seller of records, was indeed a black corporation with black performers. Critics, however, would say that these blacks were accepted because they adopted white ways. Performances were restrained, and songs were about romance not sex. How one carried oneself, what one wore, and how one spoke counted as much as musical talent. Not only was black music co-opted but so also were black performers.[147] Further evidence came from the disco craze of the 1970s. Reverend Jesse Jackson railed against such music, saying such songs as "Shake Your Booty" and "Let's Make a Baby" encouraged promiscuity. Although black vocal music did dominate the dance clubs, it came in the form of heavily orchestrated arrangements that "had

little to do with spontaneity, improvisation, and participatory re-creation—
the traditional hallmarks of black expressive culture."[148]

That all dramatically changed in the 1990s when rap, black music
wrapped in black culture, invaded the field of popular music. Born on the
city streets in the South Bronx in the mid-1970s, rap or hip-hop had all the
"traditional hallmarks of black expressive culture." In the mid-1980s *Run-
D.M.C.*, the title of the album and of the group, became the first rap album
to sell a million copies. In the early 1990s, however, rap recordings outsold
rock, and by 1992 almost three-quarters of the purchasers of rap offerings
were white. One critic wrote that "whenever white teenagers bring home
music created by black musicians, trouble is close behind."[149]

Although much of the outrage came from the graphic violence and sexism captured in what was known as hard-core or "gansta" rap, raunchy sex
was not far behind. In fact 2 Live Crew's *As Nasty As They Wanna Be* with
over eighty references to oral sex and songs titled "Me So Horny," "Dirty
Nursery Rhymes," and "The Fuck Shop," provided inviting targets for censors. In fact, censors kept such songs in the public eye for much longer than
the music itself merited. Furthermore, they helped create a growing white
audience for the group. Jack Thompson, a Florida attorney, made 2 Live
Crew and its album a personal crusade. He enlisted the Broward County
sheriff in a campaign that eventually reached the courts. 2 Live Crew sought
a ruling that its work was protected under the First Amendment, but the federal district court declared the recording obscene, and, as such, outside the
protection of the free speech clause. A retailer of the album became the first
person convicted of selling obscene music.[150]

The Florida prosecution called further attention to the album. Community pressure and the recent notoriety led retailers to refuse to stock the album, and The Record Bar, a Southern chain, would not even carry the
cleansed version of the album titled *As Clean As They Wanna Be*. Florida, Indiana, Ohio, Pennsylvania, Tennessee, and Wisconsin passed legislation
that labeled *As Nasty As They Wanna Be* obscene.[151] Eventually the Eleventh
Circuit Court of Appeals reversed the district court's ruling that the album
was obscene.[152] By the time that the United States Supreme Court turned
away an appeal, 2 Live Crew had largely faded from public view. One critic
saw the whole campaign as racially motivated, "fueled in large part by the
black male phallic paranoia."[153]

Henry Louis Gates Jr., a noted African American scholar, argued that "the
very large question of obscenity and the First Amendment cannot even be
addressed until . . . [critics] become literate in the vernacular traditions of
African-Americans." Testifying on behalf of 2 Live Crew, he said that their
blatant sexism was a parody, part of a oral cultural tradition of rhythmic
teasing in which lewd behavior was used to make a point.[154] 2 Live Crew
and other macho rap groups were eventually answered by female rappers,

such as Salt-N-Pepa, Mc Lyte, Yo-Yo, and Nikki D, asserting their own sexuality. Critics who had lambasted the misogyny of the macho rappers were hardly content with the blatancy of the female rappers, who saw women not as victims but as sexual aggressors.[155]

Hip-hop not only captured the popular music scene by the early 1990s, but it continues in modified form to be an integral part of that scene today. Brian Turner, the president of Priority Records, contends that it is today's rock and roll. He cites the evolution of the genre as going from rap to a joining together of rap and heavy metal rock all the way to the demise of rap in hip-hop pop, "a fusion of hip-hop beats with romantic 1970s R&B rock vocals and gospel-influenced harmonies."[156] In fact *Newsweek* called this evolution of rap to hip-hop pop no less than a move from "raunch to romance."[157] The magazine was referring to groups such as the Spice Girls, Lauryn Hill and the Fugees, the Backstreet Boys, and 'N Sync.

Despite this return to romance with its greater reticence, would-be censors were not at a loss for targets. Early in the new century, the FCC sought to provide greater guidance on the indecency standard by summing up past findings. Saying that indecency must be judged in context, the agency then listed what it considered significant factors: "[T]he *explicitness or graphic nature* of the description or depiction of sexual or execratory organs or activities; *whether the material appears to pander or is used to titillate, or whether the material appears to have been presented for its shock value.*"[158]

As it further defined indecency, the FCC specifically targeted music. It fined a Chicago station for playing the song "Kiddie Porn" and a Miami station for numbers such as "Walk with an Erection" and "Penis Envy." In the latter case the lyrics were more political than sexual. The song concludes with a tribute to the economic and political power of a penis. As the century was waning, the noncommercial station of the New York State University at Cortland, New York, was fined for playing "Yodeling in the Valley" with its explicit lyrics dealing with sodomy and sexual organs. As the new century dawned, a reconstituted agency seemed even more intent on ridding the airwaves of indecent music. Stations in Miami and Los Angeles felt the wrath of the FCC for playing songs with sexually explicit lyrics, such as "Uterus Guy" and "You Suck."[159] The *New York Times* music critic said such songs "suggest only that sexuality is pleasurable or funny." He then added: "The thought that such messages can be squelched by the government is more distasteful than an off-color joke."[160]

Rap music, of course, provided a new panorama of indecency. The FCC fined KKMG in Colorado Springs for playing an expurgated version of Eminem's "The Real Slim Shady." Even with the deletions of expletives, the agency found the references to sex organs and their functions, to masturbation, and to bestiality offensive. Citadel Broadcasting, which owned the station, defended the song for its comments on social justice and hypocrisy.

Hilary Rosen, president and CEO of the RIAA said that the action taken on the basis that the lyrics were suggestive constituted the very "idea-based censorship" that the FCC had been forbidden to exercise. Upon reconsideration, the FCC backed down and did not fine KKMG.[161] The Eminem case revealed another problem with censorship, and that is the censor's inability to draw the distinctions that must be made to avoid placing a heavy hand on artistic creation. In the Eminem situation the language was essential to convey the message for the language itself was an essential component of the message.

This point can be further illustrated in the case of female rapper and performance artist, Sarah Jones. Station KBOO in Portland, Oregon, was fined the same amount as the Colorado Springs station, seven thousand dollars, for airing Jones's "Your Revolution." The lyrics, the spokesman for the station said, constitute a "feminist attack on male attempts to equate political 'revolution' with promiscuous sex." In no uncertain terms Jones challenged such a linkage and placed her body off limits. As she paraphrased lyrics from other rap songs, her intent was to condemn the female degradation that characterized much of the genre. That the lyrics contain a clear political component is difficult to ignore. But in issuing the Notice of Apparent Liability for Forfeiture (NAL), the FCC rejected merit, social commentary, and popularity as factors that should preclude a finding of indecency. It concluded that the song was indecent because "the sexual references appear to be designed to pander and shock and are patently offensive."[162]

In response to the action against the station, Jones filed suit against the FCC for violating her First Amendment rights. She received support from People for the American Way, an organization established in 1981 whose announced purpose was to seek legal and social justice. She challenged what she saw as "a double standard that victimizes certain voices."[163] Twenty-one months after the song had been purged from the airwaves, the FCC recanted, exonerated the song and rescinded the fine. The sexual references were now deemed not graphic enough to warrant punishment. Taking so long to come to the conclusion, Tony Mauro of *USA Today* claimed, was "a constitutional offense of the highest order." He concluded that the FCC, with "the astonishing ability to chill the expression of almost any vocal artist by fiat," had "picked the wrong target: a talented woman whose message goes against the sexually abusive content of many of the songs of the male rappers." If the commissioners at the FCC found the message difficult to decipher, that was not true of girls who were "spellbound" as Jones continued to perform the song before high school audiences around the country. And in the brief filed contesting the fine, she argued that hip-hop was a "beautiful and creative art form" in which the disturbing elements often associated with it could be best answered "with something more sophisticated and meaningful."[164]

When the FCC proceeds against a station for playing a song, the effect has a reverberating and inhibiting effect throughout the broadcast industry. The song is banned from playlists, not only at the station under fire but at all stations. This is the type of chilling effect that the First Amendment's protection of speech is designed to prevent but one that continues to take place with the preemptive acts of the FCC.

Congressional hearings have continued into the twenty-first century with critics of the record industry calling for a much more stringent and more closely monitored ratings system. The very fact that the hearings continue carries the implied threat that the federal government will take action should the industry not regulate itself better. Responding to such criticism, the RIAA in October 2000 issued new guidelines for the affixing of the warning label, along with the requirement that the label be used both in print and online advertisements. In February 2001 the Federal Trade Commission (FTC) issued a report that said that the guidelines were not being implemented. Rosen agreed and said the industry would have to do better. He did, however, take exception to the charge that the industry was targeting children with inappropriate products and did state his opposition to any attempt on the part of government to censor creative expression. The rating system was designed to provide information so that parents could supervise their children's exposure to certain records. Rosen objected to what had been a rather common criticism of the warning label—that it did not provide enough information. He said that the demand for uniform ratings across the spectrum of movies, television, CDs, and video, computer and Internet games made no sense because each medium was different. The concern over lyrics, he insisted, made recordings more like books, which carried no warning at all. He suggested that parents accept the fact that the First Amendment precludes governmental censorship and make use of a parental media guide available on the Internet.[165] In 2002 BMG Music Group released Lady May's *May Day* with an enhanced sticker that carried additional warnings about language and sexual content.

Proposals for greater regulation of music were regularly introduced in local and state lawmaking bodies. What emerged from the legislative hopper often ran into First Amendment difficulties. Although regulations were usually couched in terms of keeping certain products out of the hands of children, more often than not the reach was too broad, having the practical effect of limiting the speech protected by both the First and Fourteenth Amendments of the Constitution. The state of Washington passed a law prohibiting the sale of "erotic music" to minors, a ban that inadvertently ensnared much classical music. The Pennsylvania, Georgia, and North Dakota legislatures considered bills to ban retailers from selling labeled products to minors. Tennessee considered a measure to impose upon the state's Department of Children's Services the task of screening music, video games, and movies for their appropriateness.[166]

Even President Bill Clinton, who had substantial political support from the entertainment industries in his two successful campaigns for the presidency, lent his support to an across-the-board universal ratings system in January 2000. He said the various ratings systems were confusing to parents. The major concern was violence rather than sex; however at times the two subjects were linked.[167]

What also attracted the attention of censors were the concerts that were so much a part of rock-and-roll music. Legislators in South Carolina and Michigan sought to have these rock concerts carry ratings as movies did. Local regulations and prohibitions were enacted to regulate these concerts, including where they could be held and who could be admitted.[168]

One of the problems with censorship is that it too often sweeps up the good with the bad, for the easiest way to handle complaints is to eliminate what motivated them. A case in point is a parental complaint about a song played on a school bus. In Mishawaka, Indiana, students being transported to school were entertained by the latest music. Shaggy, a rap-reggae artist, was singing "It Wasn't Me," from the album titled *Hotshot*. The lyrics described sexual intercourse on a counter, on a sofa, in the shower, and finally on the floor of the bathroom. The school district's response to the complaint was to ban all music from the buses.[169]

Shaggy's *Hotshot* carried no warning sticker and the offending song had received considerable airplay, but another rap artist, the white Eminem, regularly found his albums carrying the warning sticker. And well they should, said Lynne Cheney, the wife of the then Republican candidate for vice president, who called Eminem's albums "shameful."[170] Of all the albums bearing warning stickers, his offerings were indeed advertised and often sold by chain stores. The reason was obvious, as his 2002 release *The Eminem Show* so clearly demonstrated. In its first full week of availability, 1.3 million copies were sold, making it the number one album in the country.[171]

The rapper's success illustrates a problem that plagues censors in all areas, leading them often to seek the total banishment of the offending material. Despite the music industry's resistance to the warning label, some artists and their promoters realized quite early that the sticker might well pave the way to increased sales and profits. It calls attention to the product and increases its attractiveness. The forbidden has always had special appeal, going back, at the very least, to the Garden of Eden.

Eminem, whose given name is Marshall Bruce Mathers III, has posed problems from the start of his recording career, but that was not the case with the rock legend, Bruce Springsteen. His 2005 album *Devils and Dust*, which quickly climbed the charts, was his first to carry a warning sticker. Furthermore, Starbucks, that ubiquitous coffee chain that is evolving into a substantial distributor of CDs, refused to stock Springsteen's album. The problem, represented by the sticker, was a song called "Reno." It involved an encounter with a prostitute and anal sex.[172]

Also in 2005 another popular singer, country-western star Willie Nelson, after years of performing the song in selected concerts, finally recorded "Cowboys Are Frequently, Secretly (Fond of Each Other)." With words proclaiming that a lady lurked in every cowboy, the song took direct aim at the stereotypical image of rugged maleness. Nelson felt the time was right, especially with the accolades heaped upon the motion picture, *Brokeback Mountain*, which dealt with the romance of two male sheepherders. The song first aired on Valentine's Day 2006 on satellite radio, beyond the reach of the FCC.[173]

Perhaps the best way to end the survey of censorship in this area is to look at the present controversy engendered by two recent developments in the area of music and dance. The first has been called the rave culture. Disco may have died in the United States in the late 1970s but it survived in European clubs in the form of all-night dance parties. These events featured disc jockeys who blended electronic music styles, such as techno, trance, and jungle, into a pounding beat, emphasized by the ubiquitous drum machine or "beat box." The Deejays became celebrities, in many cases more notable than the artists whose music they played. By the early 1990s rave parties were part of the music scene in the metropolitan areas of the United States. From the very beginning of these raves, drugs, especially one popularly called Ecstasy, seemed to be a part of the culture. At the turn of the twenty-first century, raves had left their hip, urban settings and branched out to include all areas of the country where teenagers were in abundance. Drug use in turn led to some open sexual activity in what were called "chill rooms." The Department of Justice became so concerned that it put out a special bulletin on the dance and music phenomenon, emphasizing, of course, its association with drugs.[174]

Promoters complained that this federal linkage was an attempt to crush a vibrant music culture and was designed to provide leverage for censorship. On December 2, 1999, the National Institute on Drug Abuse launched the "Club Drug Campaign" with a budget of fifty-four million dollars. It said the problem was electronic dance music. Calling such profiling of a musical genre unconstitutional, the Electronic Music Defense & Education Fund (EM:DEF) was founded. When music promoters and a concert hall manager were arrested by the Drug Enforcement Administration (DEA) for staging a rave, such fears were realized. The indictment rested upon a federal "crack house" law[175] that, for conviction, did not require any proof that the promoters or managers provided drugs, assisted anyone in procuring drugs, or had any relationship at all to drugs. Eventually, because of the cost of a trial, a compromise settlement was worked out in which some defendants pled guilty. They agreed to pay a one hundred thousand dollar fine and institute certain limitations in staging such dances, including enforcing a minimum age of eighteen for attendees. The government also banned, as drug paraphernalia, glow sticks, masks, and chill rooms. Later in 2001, after a five-year investigation, the federal government prosecuted a club in Panama City Beach, Florida, under the same law. It took the jury only a little over an hour to find the defendants not guilty.[176]

This setback did not discourage the DEA and government censors. Congress continued to legislate in regard to rave clubs. The Ecstasy Prevention Act sought through financial incentives to get local and state governments to take action against raves.[177] More recently in 2003, Congress passed and the president signed the Illicit Drug Anti-Proliferation Act, the RAVE Act, that increased individual and corporate penalties for drug use taking place on the premises of a business. New sanctions provided for fines of five hundred thousand dollars and two million dollars for an individual and corporation respectively, up to twenty years in prison, and finally forfeiture of the business assets.[178] The basic law that was designed to reach crack houses has now been expanded to allow DEA officers to target musical and cultural events, just as the RICO Act had been broadened beyond its initial purpose to reach purveyors of obscene materials. The danger, of course, is that a legitimate purpose, such as the prosecution of drug dealers, is used to justify suppressing "music and lifestyles disliked by the political establishment."[179] In April 2005 the government took some credit for what was reported to be a decrease in the use of Ecstasy.[180] Opposing such efforts on the part of government leaves one open to the charge of condoning drug use, but EM:DEF and other organizations and individuals are not pro-drug but anticensorship.

The second recent development in social dancing that has attracted censors is a form of dance called "freaking." Given birth by MTV in its hip-hop videos, it was described in the ban imposed by Montgomery High School authorities in Santa Rosa, California, as follows:

> Dancing styles that involve intimate touching of the breasts or genitals or that simulate sexual activity are not allowed; when dancing back to front all dancers must remain upright—no sexual squatting or sexual bending is allowed, i.e. no hands on the dance floor with your buttocks facing or touching your dance partner.

One scholar, noting that all social dancing was sexy and that "[e]very generation finds its successors' dances to be improprieties," saw little "difference between frontal body rubbing and one person rubbing a backside against a front side." Principal Charles Salter at Aliso Niguel High School in Aliso Viejo, California, heartily disagreed. He was so shocked by a September 2006 dance at the school that he captured it on tape and showed the video to hundreds of parents. He then banned all future dances, as did Principal Patricia Law in Windsor High School north of Santa Rosa, until a plan to stop freaking had been crafted.[181] By the new year, Aliso Niguel had developed a plan that led Salter to lift the ban.[182]

Freaking was not limited to California; it was a national phenomenon. Speaking for the National Association of Secondary School Principals in Reston, Virginia, Shana Kemp said freaking had generated an especially high number of recent calls. Nor was such dancing confined to high schools, for preteens soon emulated older children. School authorities in a middle school in Sunland, California, troubled by the dancing, cancelled an annual holiday dance. Convinced that at least part of the problem was that the students were ignorant of other forms of social dancing and the music that accompanied them, one teacher gained support for the hiring of a dance instructor. The vice principal agreed that encouraging more modest dances was a better approach than banning dances or ordering students not to dance. He was somewhat disappointed when only fifty students showed up for the extracurricular activity. In February 2007 dance instruction became a regular school activity for twelve to fifteen students, twice a week. Vice principal Adams hoped that future school dances would provide a variety of musical styles, rather than rely solely on the hip-hop genre that had spawned freaking. As might be expected, student reaction ranged across the spectrum from opposition to skepticism to a willingness to learn new steps.[183]

Of course, the difficulty for those adults who see a moral responsibility to supervise the young is that disapproval and even outrage is what the young expect. Music and now dance as well are an inevitable part of the process of coming of age, a search that by its very nature necessitates a break away from the norm or the acceptable. To go back to the waltz and then up to the present, one cannot ignore how consistently yesterday's rebellion becomes today's status quo. Just as rock music excited the censorial urge despite the long tradition of the bawdy song and the prevalence of sexual allusions in other musical genres, so, also, have raves and freaking. Perhaps humankind is sentenced to unending generational conflict. Assuming that a censorial role for parents over their children is the most acceptable form of censorship, then the hope is that parents pick their battles carefully by distinguishing what is passing nonsense and what is worth the fight, thus giving their children the room to grow.

Janet Jackson and Justin Timberlake in Houston, Texas, during the halftime show at Super-bowl XXXVIII on February 1, 2004, shortly after the "wardrobe malfunction." AP Images/ David Phillip.

5

Home Invaders

Radio, Television, and the Internet

[E]ach communications revolution has been met with bewilderment, confusion, and doubt by people who saw the evil but not the good.[1] (Jonathan Wallace and Mark Mangan, 1996)

Ironically, because sex has been a human preoccupation since time began . . . , new technology which is designed to inform, educate, enlighten and entertain is bound to find it looming large as a matter of interest.[2] (James L. Lynch, 1996)

[I]f television and radio can pose as an instrumentality, under the guise of art, to permeate salaciousness and obscenity throughout the fabric of our society, then a serious mistake will surely be made.[3] (Senator Joseph O. Pastore, 1971)

[I]f we are not willing to eliminate books and libraries because they may contain "dangerous" ideas, why would we attempt to keep young people from the Internet and the World Wide Web? What is needed is not censorship but powerful and thoughtful dialogue focusing on inquiry and the development of personal judgment. Only then will tomorrow's adults be prepared to deal with the difficult decisions that will face them in the 21st century.[4] (Kay E. Vangergrift, 2006)

Although Super Bowl XXXVIII on February 1, 2004, did not lack the drama of some of its predecessors, it had to share the headlines the next day with the furor caused by the halftime show. That show, produced by MTV, featured Janet Jackson and Justin Timberlake. What caused the furor was an incident at the end of their song, "Rock Your Body," in which Timberlake, singing "Gonna have you naked by the end of this song," ripped off the right cup of the leather bustier Jackson was wearing. This "wardrobe malfunction," as the episode was initially explained, resulted in baring Jackson's right breast. Her naked breast, however, was not unadorned. Piercing the nipple and encircling it was a silver sunburst; however it hid neither the nipple nor the ampleness of her breast.[5] This portion of the performance lasted only three seconds before Jackson covered her breasts with crossed arms, but that interval was long enough. As a writer for the *San Diego Union-Tribune* put it, Timberlake's yank exposed "the breast that launched a whole new chapter in our country's culture wars."[6]

Indeed the whole halftime show by MTV was seen by some critics as exhibiting bad taste with sex-laced lyrics and sexual gyrations, but such criticism would have sparked little interest without the baring of the jewelry-bedecked breast. With current TV programming filled with jiggling breasts, partial nudity, and sexually explicit dialogue, one might well wonder why the quick shot of an exposed breast unleashed such a firestorm. What it gave to the critics of sexually permissive TV was a wedge to exploit. First of all, there was the audience of over 143 million including many children, watching the telecast. This worry about children and unconsenting adults now provides the only acceptable rationale for censoring such images. In this case, the worry about children may seem paradoxical, for the first part of the female anatomy with which so many become quite familiar is the nurturing breast. Second, while the roundness and ampleness of breasts are acceptable images, nipples are not. Not much was made of Jackson's nipple adornment; the problem was the avenue of nourishment, the nipple, whether pierced and surrounded by metal or not.

At any rate, this little episode, quickly labeled "Nipplegate," had big repercussions. Columbia Broadcasting Company (CBS), the network that televised the game, the National Football League, and even MTV quickly apologized. CBS promised that, in various ways, including time-delay telecasts, an unwitting public would never again be exposed to such indecency.[7] A year later when Super Bowl XXXIX was played, the halftime show featured Paul McCartney; two years later for Super Bowl XL, the featured group was the Rolling Stones. Few informed observers could miss the irony of calling upon such performers to bring decorum to the halftime shows. At the height of their popularity, these same performers were perceived as threats to establishment values.

In response to the outcry over the Jackson affair, the Federal Communications Commission (FCC), the airwaves policing agency, became involved. Michael K. Powell, its chairman, could hardly avoid responding to the more than two hundred thousand complaints the agency received in the ten days following the Timberlake-Jackson moment.[8] The American Family Association encouraged filing complaints, and the Parents Television Council made the process easy by putting a form on the Internet that could be filled out and dispatched with a minimum of effort.[9]

In fact, the Super Bowl incident resulted in groups demanding more censorship contesting with other groups that fought any censorship. For instance, for the millions who missed the revealing of Jackson's breast, it was made available in both stills and motion picture format on the Internet.[10] Aaron Schatz, who had tracked Internet searches since 1999, said the search for photos of the breast-baring incident set a new record. He added: "It's the sort of thing that makes us look like a nation of prudes and jackasses that we would go trampling over each other in a stampede to get a look at Janet Jackson's nipple."[11] Politicians in Congress, always quick to jump on a bandwagon, expressed their outrage and began considering bills to raise the fine on an indecent broadcast incident to as much as five hundred thousand dollars.[12]

Often accused of being inconsistent in its enforcement of the indecency ban in broadcasting, the FCC now took action. It had already come under fire when its law enforcement division cleared the use of the word "fucking" in a Golden Globes Award telecast in 2003. The rationale was that the word was used as an adjective rather than as a verb.[13] Saying it had now received 540,000 complaints about the breast-baring incident, the FCC in September 2004 levied a fine of $550,000 on CBS, $27,500 for each of the twenty TV stations it owned. One commissioner complained that the fine was much too low, but a First Amendment scholar said that "one fleeting incident does not rise to the level of offensiveness that ought to empower the government to engage in such a punitive action."[14] Now energized, the FCC, which in 2003 had levied fines of less than five hundred thousand dollars, would in 2004 levy fines totaling eight million covering both radio and television incidents.[15]

TV and radio station operators responded to the new FCC activity by installing digital-delay systems that would give them the opportunity to delete audio and video snippets that might run afoul of the reinvigorated ban on indecency.[16]

This breast-baring episode is instructive in how it impacted all electronic media. It began with a fleeting moment on a network telecast that would be preserved on the playpen called the Internet, which, in turn, was used to funnel complaints to the governing agency, the FCC. The federal agency then stepped up its enforcement of the indecency provisions in its regulations against not only television but radio broadcasts as well. From its inception, the federal government has been a censor of the electronic media in a way that would clearly be barred were the media nonelectronic. In addition, the electronic media has had other censors as well.

RADIO: THE VOCAL INTRUDER

Radio was the first electronic visitor to the home, and as a medium of entertainment, it was born in the business-oriented decade of the 1920s—a fact that explains how it would evolve in the United States. In contrast to England where radio became a government monopoly, the medium in the United States was left to private development. From the Radio Act of 1912 to the Radio Act of 1927, which finally brought some order to the chaos of a limited and crowded bandwidth, a persistent concern was the possibility of government censorship. A new regard for the First Amendment's protection of free speech and press had come out of the First World War. In four radio conferences held in the 1920s, the constant refrain was that the airwaves were the property of the American people and should be used to further the public interest.[17] Clearly with the limited bandwidth some regulation was necessary, but who was to regulate radio and under what standards? The question was answered by the Radio Act of 1927, which placed in an independent commission, the Federal Radio Commission (FRC), the authority to allocate frequencies and to extend and renew licenses. Section 29 of the act barred the broadcast of "obscene, indecent, or profane language." Congressional concern, however, led to the inclusion of a provision specifically prohibiting the agency from engaging in censorship.[18] The Federal Communications Act of 1934 carried over most of the provisions of the 1927 legislation and rechristened the regulatory body the Federal Communications Commission (FCC).

Less than a quarter of American households had radio receivers in 1927, but seven years later the number approached two-thirds. Radios had come down in price and the cost of programming was born by advertisers. In the early 1920s advertisers were hesitant to use the medium, worried about offending listeners. By the end of the decade, however, advertising agencies and sponsors not only provided the economic foundation for American radio but also for over 50 percent of network programming.[19] Such economic facts meant that advertisers would have considerable influence in determining the content of what was broadcast.

The fact that radio would be a visitor into the home was both a boon and a bane to those who sought for radio broadcasts the same protection that was granted to printed and oral speech. It was a boon in the sense that the home was recognized as protected space in which government had no place. This protection is what concerned the lawmakers who insisted that the regulatory agency not engage in censorship. It was a bane in regard to the fact that the transmission could be heard by all, regardless of age or in some cases personal choice. Although a receiver had to be turned on, once it was, all within its range could listen. This simple fact led to the statutory provision barring "obscene, indecent, or profane language." Obviously such a ban involved some censorship.[20]

Early radio recognized cultural and class differences, but that would change with the rise of networks. The National Broadcasting Company (NBC) and CBS controlled nearly all the high-powered stations. Their programming consisted of entertainment in the form of comedy and variety shows, soap operas, westerns, detective shows, and sports. Such programming was designed to capture a national audience and in part to create a national culture.[21] In this quest, the networks sought to avoid controversy.

Although the FRC and later the FCC, were forbidden to interfere "with the right of free speech by means of radio communication," the need for stations to apply for license renewal every three years and satisfy the commission that they were serving the public interest imposed restrictions that were not imposed on other media. What more devastating exercise of censorship authority could be imagined than shutting down the vehicle of communication, which was why the censorship issue was never much below the surface. Early on, the commission interpreted the public interest requirement to consist of the right of the listener to receive clear and uninterrupted signals. However, the FRC did warn stations that "it was not in the public interest to use radio for personal controversy, slanderous attacks on individuals, or the exploitation of the personal views and business of the licensee."[22] John Brinkley of KFKB in Kansas and Norman Baker of KTNT in Iowa were denied renewal of their licenses not for medical quackery but for promoting their own economic interests to the detriment of the public interest. In response, both men established stations in Mexico.[23]

Reverend Robert Shuler and KGEF in Los Angeles, established by a grant from a parishioner to air Shuler's sermons and comments, posed a more substantial problem for regulators.[24] Shuler denounced the Roman Catholic Church, Jews, government agencies, courts, and civic and governmental officials. Shuler was amazed when Morris Ernst, the lawyer for the American Civil Liberties Union (ACLU) came to his defense, arguing that the FRC did not have the power to silence stations with which it did not agree. The ACLU saw this episode as one in which the commission was seeking to use its authority to suppress a minority viewpoint.[25] Shuler had a host of other supporters as well, but one critic dismissed them, saying they "were delighted to have their imaginations stimulated with ideas of sexual and other vices at the same time that they were emphatically assured of their own superior righteousness."[26] The FRC denied Shuler a license renewal on grounds that he was disserving the public interest, a decision that was upheld by the court of appeals.[27]

Even though claims of indecency and vulgar language were made against Brinkley, Baker, and Schuler, the FRC seemed hesitant to deny renewal on those grounds. That was not true in the case of William Schaeffer and KVEP. Schaeffer was the owner of the station that aired the diatribes of a candidate for office against his opponent both before and after the election. Robert Duncan accused his opponent, Franklin Korell, of being "a sissified Sodomite," who practiced "the vices that caused the destruction of Sodom and Gomorrah." He added that his opponent had slept with a man convicted on a morals charge and called upon all "natural men" to turn Korell out of office. Holding Schaeffer responsible for these broadcasts, the FRC decided not to renew his license. Saying that the First Amendment does not protect indecent language, the FRC concluded that "the right of freedom from censorship thereby becomes a qualified right subject to such reasonable control by the Commission as would be consistent with the primary consideration of the public welfare." Schaeffer could not afford to appeal the decision, but Duncan, who had been convicted for using obscene, indecent, and profane language over the air and sentenced to six months in jail and a five hundred dollar fine, did.[28] The Ninth Circuit Court of Appeals found in Duncan's language "no tendency to excite libidinous thoughts," but upheld the conviction on grounds that some of the cited language had indeed been profane.[29]

Worried about violating the ban on censorship, the federal commissioners relied upon the broadcasters themselves to safeguard the American home from inappropriate material. In 1928 the National Association of Broadcasters (NAB) adopted its first code of ethics, which sought, among other things, to purge the airwaves of indecent programs. Apparently American broadcasters took this obligation seriously, especially with the threat of nonrenewal of their licenses always on the horizon. When the FRC received complaints about objectionable song lyrics, sexually suggestive dialogue, or discussions about birth control, it directed the complainant to the network, the station, or the sponsor of the program. However, the FRC did regularly say that it would take such complaints into account when licenses had to be renewed.[30] NBC, a heavyweight in the industry, took the occasion to ban two hundred songs from its airwaves because of their lyrics.[31] *Variety*, the entertainment weekly, noted in 1930 that since all persons concerned understood the requirements of the medium, "radio programs offer the cleanest, nicest, and strictest of all entertainment."[32] Such a conclusion was possible because radio, the first electronic visitor to the home, was censored or threatened with censorship at so many levels. For instance, the vaudeville comedian had no intermediary between himself and his audience. When he took to the airwaves, however, he faced a host of such intermediaries, including writers, sponsors, advertising agencies, the network, its affiliates, and finally the FRC or the FCC. All these intermediaries had an interest in not offending the audience and therefore were either real or potential censors.

Obscene, indecent, and lewd words were banned from the airwaves, and sex, of course, was a taboo subject. The American Birth Control League was especially disturbed about its inability to get its message on the air. When the National Broadcasting System refused to carry the organization's convention, the league, joined by the ACLU, protested to the network's Advisory Council. The ACLU argued that stations were obligated to carry both sides of a contentious issue, but the FRC said it could not interfere in a matter between the organizations and the network. NBC's Advisory Council rejected the request saying that the public was not yet demanding a discussion on the matter. The argument that public interest necessitated discussion of controversial issues made little headway. As a contemporary radio critic said, "for all practical purposes, radio in America is business-owned, business-administered and business-censored."[33]

The ACLU considered the possibility of censorship enough of a problem to form the National Council on Freedom from Censorship in 1931. It sought to limit the right of radio stations to censor speakers and to curtail censorship by the FRC with regard to license renewal. The way to accomplish these ends, it believed, was to have Congress reign in the meaning of public interest by restricting it to technical matters. When provisions were all bundled together in the Communications Act of 1934 creating the FCC and housing all communications under the new commission, little was done to clarify public interest along the lines that the ACLU had suggested.[34]

In the early 1930s radio began to attract vaudevillians who had not before been subject to censorship. Beginning with Eddie Cantor, the networks were worried about ethnic comedians. For instance, an NBC memo cited the presence in the medium of theater writers and comics, saying that it was "imperative that from this date on no remarks of a questionable nature be permitted." "Radio," the memo continued, "got its great start by giving clean, wholesome entertainment . . . and we must stop material in bad taste."[35]

With the FCC, sponsors, and broadcast censors at work, the problem was less sex than sin, vulgarity, and dissident political views.[36] For instance, censors at the network levied a ban on nudist skits and jokes. Fred Allen and Eddie Cantor were affected, but so was Gracie Allen of Burns and Allen, who offered the comment that nudism helped a girl get a lot of things off her chest. NBC issued the following standing order: "Obscene or off-color songs or jokes, oaths, sacrilegious expressions, and all other language of doubtful propriety must be eliminated."[37] After all, the FRC and its successor, the FCC, were not only worried about indecency but also profanity. That worry about disturbing the faithful is well illustrated in Mae West's appearance on the *Chase & Sandborn Radio Hour* with Edgar Bergen, the ventriloquist, and his dummy, Charlie McCarthy. Bergen's act was a relatively sophisticated nightclub act that some worried would not be suitable for radio. From its inception in 1937, however, it was among NBC's most popular evening shows.

Mae West, with announcer, Don Ameche, did a ten-minute sketch about Adam and Eve. NBC received over a thousand letters protesting the show, and the advertising agency for *Chase & Sandborn* apologized for any offense that may have been caused. Although the script had passed the network censors, with Mae West it was always a matter of *how* the words were said. The sketch involved a "lazy and lukewarm" Adam and his bored wife, Eve, trapped in the Garden of Eden with a long-term lease. Eve finds that the lease can be broken if they eat the forbidden fruit. When a snake comes along, Eve sees her chance, for the snake can squeeze through the fence around the apple tree. Eve asks the snake to get her an apple, saying, "I feel like doin' a *big* apple." As the snake is squeezing through the fence to get the forbidden fruit, West, feigning the breathlessness of an orgasm, says, "There! There! Now you're through." The snake gets the apple, Eve makes applesauce of it, and Adam joins Eve in eating it. One paradise is lost, but another is found in sex, as they embrace and join together in the "Original Kiss." Whether the protesters did not like the twist the author put on the biblical story or that the program was aired on Sunday or simply the sexual suggestiveness is difficult to say. One of the letters NBC received was from the chairman of the FCC who demanded to see a transcript, calling the skit "a serious offense against the proprieties and a rather low form of entertainment."[38]

What works against sexual suggestiveness as a full explanation is the fact that dialogue between the dummy, Charlie, and Mae was much more sexually tinged than were the lines in the skit. When Charlie questions whether Mae could find a man to love, she predictably responds "Sure . . . lotsa times." And when she asks Charlie, the reputed Casanova, who she describes as "all wood and a yard long," whether he worries that she will do him wrong or do him right, he says he needs time to think about that. Mae responds, "I like a man what takes his . . . time! Why doncha come up home with me now honey? I'll let you play in my . . . woodpile." Mae finally brushes off Charlie, saying, "No man walks out on me—they might carry them out, but they never walk out."[39]

At any rate, the FCC formally censured NBC and its fifty-nine affiliates and warned that the incident would be considered when licenses came up for renewal. The FCC added: "A clear recognition of the social, civic and moral responsibility for the effect upon listeners of all classes and ages requires [banning] . . . features that are suggestive, vulgar, immoral or of such other character as may be offensive to the great mass of right-thinking, clean-minded American citizens."[40]

Despite or perhaps because of the stern words from the FCC, the popularity of the show did not suffer. It would continue into the mid-1950s with new sponsors and a new name, but with a sassy Charlie still calling attention to the pulchritude of women guests. Mae West, however, was effectively barred from the airwaves, NBC censoring even the mention of her name on the air. Noting that forty million people had listened to the broadcast, she wondered why, if they found the broadcast so offensive, they did not turn it off, or why they were home and not in church.[41]

The episode did convince stations to pay more attention to their censoring responsibilities. Sally Rand, the fan dancer and burlesque star, ran into this heightened sensitivity when she agreed to appear on the program *For Men Only*. She said she would prepare her own material—material that had been tested before women's clubs and chambers of commerce. The ad agency rejected her script, prepared one of its own, which she, in turn, rejected. They finally agreed on a third version that was still too racy for the program's sponsor. The three parties agreed on a fourth version that, then, was rejected by the station censor. A fifth version was prepared by the broadcast station and, before three broadcasting executives and a lawyer in the control room, who apparently were ready to pull the plug should she deviate from the text, Rand delivered the scripted lines.[42]

In the late 1930s the head censor at NBC was Janet MacRorie. She and her six assistants were charged with inspecting some ninety scripts a day. The writers often challenged "The Old Maid on the Fourth Floor." When in doubt, MacRorie tried out the lines on either page boys or elevator operators, who, she contended, have heard everything. With the Mae West episode in mind, writers tried to sneak Adam and Eve into their scripts, but MacRorie expanded the ban on West to include Adam and Eve as well. She realized that reading the words might not capture the way a line could be delivered, and apparently she had learned from an episode with Bea Lillie to be extra cautious with her scripts.[43]

Other targets of MacRorie were gay humor and ad-libbing, subjects that would also concern television censors in the future. Some of NBC's best-known comedians—George Burns and Gracie Allen, Jack Benny, and Bob Hope—she said, made jokes about "effeminate gentlemen and sex-perverted characters." She directed that all "female gentlemen" jokes be excised. In regard to ad-libs, content not included in the scripts, Eddie Cantor, George Burns, and Fred Allen often got into trouble. In the case of Fred Allen, one of the censors assigned to his show complained of "cases where particularly dirty jokes were made out of seemingly innocent ones."[44]

Of course, reading live from scripts did not ensure against what we have come to call bloopers. Announcers were chosen not only for their melodious voices but also for their ability to read scripts without making verbal mistakes. Still, the best of them could misspeak. One of the classic instances involved the usually word-perfect Ben Grauer. In 1942 when war was loosening customary social restraints, he said, "Go to the Plaza Theater, where the feature is *The Vanishing Virgin* . . . er, I mean *Virginian.*"[45] Apparently the FCC did not make threats about licenses as a result of such one-time flubs.

Not only were licenses at stake but there was also the constant threat of governmental action should self-censorship fail. Self-censorship, however, could be quite heavy-handed. When in 1937 General Hugh S. Johnson wanted to do his weekly commentary on venereal disease, the network refused.[46] And when a speaker in a program produced by a medical association wanted to call attention to the social problem of syphilis, the CBS censor asked the speaker to avoid the word. When the speaker refused, he was denied airtime. A network executive explained that broadcasts were heard by many different groups of people and "must at no time whatever be offensive to any of them by any established standard whatsoever."[47] When the networks and the NAB set up policies to implement this goal, much bland programming resulted.[48] Yet, the major target of radio censors was not sex, a primary concern of the movie censors at the time, but rather certain political views, expressions of support for labor, and comments reflecting religious prejudice. During World War II, the government established an Office of Censorship that provided guidelines that the stations conscientiously followed, but again the problem was neither sex nor sin but rather fear of compromising the two-front war effort.[49]

In the postwar world, radio would be confronted by television, the new medium that added pictures to the sound. Advertisers gradually switched to television.[50] The disparity in advertising dollars between the two mediums would grow with each succeeding year. Some of radio's most popular shows shifted to the new medium. Radio was becoming increasingly local, as television followed radio's earlier path of network consolidation. Only in the latter years of the twentieth century, when ownership limitations were lifted, would radio stations be combined once again into large organizations that would feed programming to local units.

Despite the heightened appeal of television, much censorial concern would continue to be focused on radio broadcasts. As radio became more local, station owners discovered the disk jockey, a glib talker who could fill in the gaps between segments of recorded music. In fact, music would become increasingly the fare of radio, especially FM radio with its improved fidelity. This reliance on disk jockeys beginning in the 1940s was cheap, but it also put a certain premium on talk, which would offend some people and become a target of the FCC.

In 1959–1960 the FCC considered the nonrenewal of licenses in Denver and in Kingstree, South Carolina. In both instances the station owner pleaded ignorance of the sexually suggestive talk of the radio personality and fired the offending party. With a promise of increased supervision and acceptance of a cease and desist order, the FCC overrode the decision of its Broadcast Bureau in regard to the Denver station and renewed the license. The South Carolina owner might have benefited from a similar leniency, but he was trapped by a hearing examiner's findings that he knew what his employee was saying on the air and that he had sought to mislead the FCC by falsifying information. He appealed on free speech grounds, but the appellate court ignored the claim and upheld the nonrenewal because of the misrepresentations of the owner.[51]

The FCC began to levy fines on stations at least as early as 1961, but the first fine imposed for violating the indecency standard was imposed on a Philadelphia station in 1970 that aired an interview with the Grateful Dead's Jerry Garcia. The musician's responses were laced with words such as "fuckin'" and "shit."[52] Apparently the FCC was attempting to get some judicial clarification on whether it could distinguish indecency from obscenity, but the low fine hardly invited a judicial contest.[53]

Earlier attacks on song lyrics came as a result of the suggestiveness of the language, but the FCC seemed as intently focused on particular words. In fact, Lorenzo W. Milan, the founder of KRAB-FM, a community radio station that ran afoul of the FCC, argued that the "smarmy sniggering" of certain talk show hosts was "the real obscenity of American communications." When such a complaint was received, the FCC sent out a request for the station to respond. KRAB had received a number of such letters, and when license renewal time came, the FCC said it would only renew the station's license for one year. KRAB challenged the decision, which was based upon five instances of language judged to be indecent, obscene, or profane. In one case a black minister had talked of castrating experiences at the university and "pimps that freak you off," and in another broadcast six or so obscene words dotted the forty-six minute presentation. After three days of hearings, the FCC examiner concluded that the station had acted responsibly and judged its programming overall as "outstanding and meritorious." It was granted a renewal for the regular three-year term.[54]

In reflecting later on the episode Milam said, "I think that the fucks and shits and motherfuckers are indeed the language of the people—their real language, pure and unrestrained. . . . I am damned if I think that the government can or will even try to tell me what the language of certain citizens is or should be." The hearing examiner seemed to agree that the context controlled, when he denied that "an immutable, time resistant glossary" could be compiled that would definitely settle what words could not be broadcast.[55]

Comedian George Carlin disagreed in a twelve-minute monologue entitled "Filthy Words" in which he identified seven words that "you couldn't
say on the public . . . airwaves." Shit, piss, fuck, cunt, cocksucker, mother-
fucker, and tits comprised the list. His monologue was recorded in a theater
before a live audience and later broadcast by a New York station owned by
Pacifica Foundation.[56]

Pacifica Foundation stations were noncommercial and innovative. The
foundation's first station and the first noncommercial station, KPFA in San
Francisco, is credited with the "first truly gay radio broadcast" when in 1956
Allen Ginsberg read his poem "Howl" on the air.[57] In 1971 the FCC defended
the foundation against the attempt of certain senators to force the agency to
censure the foundation. Commissioner Kenneth A. Cox, who spoke for the
majority of the commission, praised Pacifica for offering "a range of service
to the community that is all too often lacking on commercial stations,"
which often "operate under the assumption that no one should be offended." In performing its recognized public service, he continued, Pacifica
was "bound to tread on the sensibilities of some people."[58]

Broadcast at 2 p.m. in October 1973 by Pacifica's New York station, the
Carlin monologue provoked a complaint from a father who, with his fifteen-
year-old son, had heard the broadcast. Finding the broadcast indecent, the
FCC issued an order that it lodged in Pacifica's licensing file to be considered
with any further complaints. Pacifica challenged the action on grounds that
the absence of prurient interest, one of the elements necessary in proving obscenity, prevented such a finding and that the FCC so broadly interpreted indecency that it encompassed much that was constitutionally protected. Essentially Pacifica was seeking judicial approval for its position that indecency
was too vague a term and had to be interpreted as a synonym for obscenity.
The court of appeals in a split decision agreed with Pacifica, but the Supreme
Court reversed. Justice John Paul Stevens, for the Court, said that the anticensorship provision in the enabling legislation banned prior restraint but
did not prevent the FCC from reviewing completed broadcasts. He added
that indecency was a separate standard, which did not require a finding of
prurient interest.[59] Those persons, including the regulators at the FCC, who
hoped that the Court would define indecency as it had obscenity, were disappointed when the majority indicated that each situation would have to be
judged in its own context.

Stevens then sought to justify the distinction between the treatment of
speech on the radio and oral or printed speech. First, he said the individual's right to be free of "patently offensive, indecent speech" in the home
"plainly outweighs the First Amendment rights of an intruder." Second, he
continued, "broadcasting is uniquely accessible to children, even those too
young to read." Such reasons, the justice concluded, "justify special treat-

ment of indecent broadcasting."[60] All three dissenters, Justices Potter Stewart, William J. Brennan Jr., and Thurgood Marshall, would have ruled that Congress had intended indecency to meet the test of obscenity. Brennan and Marshall saw the FCC exercising the very censorship that was prohibited by its enabling statute.

The Court was careful to narrow the reach of the indecency provision and to limit the opinion's precedential value. It seemed to say that such words might not be actionable were they broadcast when children generally would not be listening.[61] For almost a decade following the *Pacifica* decision, the FCC limited its concern to broadcasts before 10 p.m. that contained words similar to those found in the Carlin monologue. However, with the political swing to the Right bolstered by social conservatives who wanted something done about the sexually permissive society, the FCC responded. It now defined indecency as "exposure of children to language that describes in terms patently offensive as measured by contemporary standards for the broadcast media, sexual or excretory activities and organs."[62] In 1987 the agency fined three stations for indecent programming after 10 p.m. and then sought to narrow what was called the "safe harbor" by delaying the start of the period to midnight. The DC Circuit Court of Appeals upheld the indecency definition but struck down the FCC's attempt to further limit the safe harbor. Subsequent wrangling led Congress to eliminate any safe harbor for indecent programming. When the FCC sought to implement the new rule, the DC Circuit Court struck down the twenty-four-hour ban. Finally in 1995, the entire circuit court upheld a 6 a.m. to 10 p.m. prohibition on indecent programs.[63]

As Congress, the FCC, and their opponents were arguing over the width of the safe harbor, the FCC continued to send out warning letters concerning indecent broadcasts and to levy fines. The popularity of the program or its acceptability to the vast majority of its listeners was no defense, as the FCC continued to emphasize its concern for children. Much of the activity dealt with talk about sexual activity, whether it be intercourse, fellatio, cunnilingus, or masturbation.[64]

Vulgar words are part of the normal speech of many people, but in certain settings their use is designed to shock others as part of an exhibitionism that characterizes some of the practitioners of talk radio. Although talk radio, that is radio in which there is a host and audience participation, can be traced back to the very beginnings of commercial radio, the trend from music to talk began seriously in the 1960s. By mid-decade, over two-thirds of all radio stations had some such programs, raging from standard interviews, to call-in and advice shows. Insult shows were also born in this permissive decade, and the best or worst example was *The Joe Pyne Show*, originating in Los Angeles and eventually syndicated to 165 stations. More and more the talk show revolved around the personality of the host. By the end of the century, there were twenty-five hundred talk/news stations and the National Association of Talk Show Hosts had three hundred members.[65]

Stations in the 1970s deliberately sought women listeners, and *Feminine Forum* with radio personality Bill Balance, launched by KGBS in Los Angeles in 1970, provided a model. Such shows were aimed at young females who were willing to talk about their sexual relationships. Topics such as "Who first turned you on?" And "What place do you like to do it best?" set the day's discussion. The format caught on and soon about fifty stations had such a program. What was initially called "topless radio" was born. Clearly the frank and unfiltered sex talk affronted some persons who either deliberately or inadvertently tuned in the broadcasts.[66] One of the copycats was one bearing almost the same program name, *Femme Forum*, broadcast by WGLD in Chicago. Here the host, Marianne Moore, drew out her callers on oral sex. She found a woman who took the boredom out of a long drive by performing fellatio on the driver, another who touted the virtue of spreading peanut butter on her lover's sexual organs, and one who cited her mate's worries as her teeth encircled his penis.[67]

Whether such shows were perverse or healthy was a subject of much discussion, but some members of Congress were as irate as those individuals who complained to the FCC. They all suggested that the FCC take some strong action. Chairman Dean Burch of the FCC in late March 1973 agreed that something had to be done to rid the airwaves of "the prurient trash that is the stock-in-trade of the sex-oriented radio talk show."[68] The FCC asked WGLD to respond to complaints about its obscene broadcasts. Denying any redeeming social value in the station's *Femme Forum*, the FCC said that the "titillating, pandering exploitation of sexual materials" certainly qualified as "broadcast obscenity." WGLD's parent company, Sonderling Broadcasting, was fined the maximum of two thousand dollars and invited to take the case to court to determine the authority of the FCC. Sonderling simply paid the fine and promised to ban sexual subjects from the program.[69] The Chicago chapter of the ACLU and a group called Illinois Citizens Committee for Broadcasting did, however, appeal the decision. Agreeing with the FCC's determination that the broadcasts were obscene, the District of Columbia Circuit Court of Appeals said that "the repeated and explicit descriptions of the techniques of oral sex" were clearly intended to titillate.[70]

The NAB condemned such programming, and the result of the condemnation, the FCC action, and the court ruling was to end topless radio after its brief life of a little over two years. Worry about their licenses led the stations to surrender. One of the FCC commissioners, Nicholas Johnson, argued against fining Sonderling because it amounted to the censorship that the commission was forbidden to exercise, but his was a lonely voice.[71]

When Ronald Reagan came to Washington in 1981, his administration sought to serve two masters, corporate America, which wanted government deregulation, and socially conservative America, which wanted to enlist government to curb the blatant sexuality so visible in society. When it came to the airwaves, the two interests were in conflict. For instance, when social conservatives said broadcasting companies should be penalized for the smut they put out on the airwaves either by denying them renewal of their licenses or barring them from expanding their station holdings, the deregulators argued that such penalties would be far too harsh.[72]

If the winners in the battle against topless radio had hoped to cleanse radio of sex talk permanently, they were to be disappointed. A decade later listeners would encounter the "shock jocks of raunchy radio," of whom Howard Stern was the most notorious.[73] He began his career in broadcasting in the mid-1980s in Philadelphia, moved to New York, and syndicated his program in 1991.[74] The fines the FCC levied on the stations carrying his broadcasts only seemed to give Stern more publicity and enlarge his national reputation and audience.

One might be inclined to believe that the indecency charge is only levied against the worst of the programs, but this conclusion neglects the fact that the airwaves are discriminated against in terms of free speech protection. For instance when KSD-FM read an article on the air that had appeared in *Playboy* about the sexual relationship of Jessica Hahn and Reverend Jim Bakker, the station was fined. Although the major news outlets reported on the appearance of nude photographs of the first black Miss America that had appeared in *Penthouse*, when they were discussed on WLUP-FM in Chicago, the station was fined. And Howard Stern's material, which had attracted FCC's fines totaling over a million dollars, went unmolested when it appeared in book form. Stern's *Private Parts*, the book involved, sold over a million copies within two weeks of its release.[75]

The Janet Jackson Super Bowl episode had stirred the FCC to action, as fines increased sixteen-fold in 2004.[76] Clear Channel Communications agreed to pay 1.8 million dollars in a consent decree in June 2004 that covered a number of indecency complaints against its radio stations. It was fined $755,000 for the broadcasts of a Florida disk jockey, Todd Clem, known as "Bubba the Love Sponge" for his sexually explicit talk about oral sex, masturbation, and intercourse. The 1.8 million dollars was in addition to this earlier incident and covered the actions of Howard Stern. In fact, the largest prior monetary amount paid for an indecency violation came in 1995 and covered a number of years of the Stern show. Now Clear Channel indicated its conversion by dropping the controversial show in April, after the FCC levied a $495,000 fine over a twenty-minute segment Stern did on anal sex.[77] Although Viacom, CBS's parent company, continued to challenge the fine imposed on CBS for the Timberlake-Jackson incident, it agreed in November to pay the FCC 3.5 million dollars. This amount covered other indecency complaints, including those involving the raunchy Stern, who had been employed by Infinity Broadcasting, another unit of Viacom.[78]

Saying he was "tired of the censorship," Stern announced in October 2004 that he would move his show to satellite radio on January 1, 2006, when his contract with Infinity came to an end.[79] Despite the trouble Stern caused Infinity, his show had generated about five hundred million dollars in earnings. He was regarded as "one of the best pitchmen in the world of media." With Stern's twelve million listeners, Sirius Satellite Radio, the smaller of the two companies in this new medium, was betting that this new deal would finally make the corporation profitable.[80] Stern had control of the eighteen-to-forty-nine male demographic, but how many of his listeners would shell out the new subscription costs was initially unclear.[81] Sirius figured if only a million of Stern's Sirius listeners paid the thirteen-dollar monthly charge to get satellite programming, that sum would cover the five-hundred-million-dollar cost of producing the show.[82] Before the show even switched to Sirius, Stern was awarded 225 million dollars in stock because of a five-fold increase in Sirius subscribers.[83] By January 2007, almost three years after Stern agreed to terms with Sirius, subscriptions had increased from seven hundred thousand to more than six million. In the year that Stern broadcast on satellite radio, the growth reached 82 percent. As a result, Stern and his agent were granted additional stock in Sirius, valued at close to eighty-three million dollars.[84] With the new wealth of course came freedom from the reach of the FCC. How transformational the whole Stern business will be for satellite radio is left for the future to determine.[85] However, FM was belittled in the 1960s before it became dominant in radio broadcasting, and cable programming was demeaned until it began winning broadcasting awards. With substantial time devoted to commercials on both AM and FM, the lure of commercial-free radio may be greater than the skeptics believe.

Where success is found, others follow and many shock jocks can be found in local markets. Some of these persons are syndicated, but few approach the visibility of Stern and Don Imus, once his most obvious rival. As the new century dawned, newcomers Opie (Gregg Hughes) and Anthony (Anthony Cumia), using language that Stern said he could not, became the highest-rated afternoon talk show in New York City, with Stern's morning show still leading all others. They staged whipped cream bikini contests and rated mothers as sex objects, but they were best known for their invitation to women to flash their breasts while driving on Wednesdays. The fact that listeners were "outraged, shocked and amused" led Infinity Broadcasting, which had paid substantial fines in regard to the Stern show, to syndicate Opie and Anthony. But, as is often the case, the duo crossed the line when they set up and broadcast a couple having sex in St. Patrick's Cathedral. As Opie and Anthony soon found out, no mixture remains more volatile in American society than sex and religion. For three days the number of critics grew. WNEW, the originator of the show, fired the duo and Infinity cancelled the show's syndication.[86] Opie and Anthony were subsequently employed by XM Satellite Radio, the competitor of Sirius Satellite, the new home of Howard Stern. Viacom, the company that owns WNEW, eventually agreed to pay a record 3.5 million dollar fine to the FCC, a settlement that included the St. Patrick's incident and some Stern violations as well.[87]

The problem with radio broadcasts from the FCC's perspective had always been words, phrases, and what they suggested. Instrumental music was never censored, though lyrics were.[88] If sound had caused the regulatory agency such trouble, what would happen when that sound was accompanied by moving pictures?

TELEVISION: THE VISUAL INTRUDER WITH SOUND

With motion pictures, the moving images came first, followed only later by synchronized sound, but with radio and television the sequence was reversed. The new combination of sound and picture, however, convinced censors that the threat to the social order was greater than ever before. As with radio stations, television stations were licensed by the federal government and commanded to serve the public interest by the FCC, meaning that the infant industry would have far less freedom than the press enjoyed.

Commercial television began before World War II, and one of the first recorded instances of censorship occurred shortly after NBC, after a wartime lapse of two and a half years, resumed studio programming in 1944. Eddie Cantor, one of the first radio stars to appear on television, was singing a song with Nora Martin entitled "We're Having a Baby, My Baby and Me." The sound was cut off on the basis that the lyrics were too suggestive. And when Cantor did the hula, the cameraman was told to blur the camera's focus.[89] Song lyrics would continue to bother the censors, but the hula would not.

Only in the postwar period did television begin to blossom. By 1948 Americans wanted TV receivers.[90] A number of new shows generated interest, no one more than the *Texaco Star Theater* with comedian Milton Berle (Uncle Miltie), who cleaned up his nightclub act to make it work in the new medium. His outlandish costumes and slapstick routines made good use of the visual medium. The same year also saw the start of the *Toast of the Town* with columnist Ed Sullivan as the host of this variety hour that would in the 1950s present Elvis Presley and in the 1960s the Beatles to the show's large audience.[91] Another radio star, Arthur Godfrey, had a variety show on the tube from early 1949 well into 1959. His reputation and down-home style was such that, despite some bawdy stories and sexually tinged jokes, he never felt the wrath of censors.[92]

The medium's first hit comedy was *I Love Lucy* with Lucille Ball and her husband, Desi Arnaz. On the first episode of *I Love Lucy*, Lucy alluded to sex when she complained that "since we said 'I do,' there are many things we don't." Apparently sometimes they did, for Lucille became pregnant. Despite opposition, the Arnazes insisted that Lucille's real-life pregnancy not be disguised on the show. They won, but the word "pregnant" was banned. Lucille and Lucy were "expecting," and the first show dealing with her condition was labeled "Lucy Is Enceinte." Apparently the French word meaning "with child" was acceptable.[93]

In 1951 when *I Love Lucy* premiered, the television industry began coast to coast broadcasting and the NAB issued a code of ethics to internally govern the new commercial medium. A review board was charged with reviewing all programming, an impossible task that meant that, although the board could set standards and hear complaints, meaningful surveillance would have to be entrusted to the stations and networks. Initially, as with radio, advertisers had considerable influence on programming. What sponsors wanted was the largest audience possible, certainly not controversy that might diminish the audience and rub off on the product. This influence was reduced in favor of network control in the 1960s.[94] Each of the three networks had their own ethical codes enforced by a department of standards and practice, and internal censors would have considerable power over the next thirty years.[95]

The initial television code of the NAB said that programs were "to foster and promote the commonly accepted moral, social, and ethical values of American life." Among other things, the code banned obscenity and cautioned against both costumes and camera angles that emphasized certain anatomical details, meaning of course a woman's breasts. Some observers questioned whether such self-censorship was desirable, but the precedent had been set with radio and the extension to another home invader seemed all but inevitable. Although the fear of government regulation was ever present, some critics believed that self-censorship would be even more restrictive.[96]

This self-censorship had little of the repressive effect such a scheme had on motion pictures, but there a system of enforcement had been set-up in the 1930s that had proved quite effective. By the late 1970s and early 1980s the code for television was outmoded, and the NAB responded by dropping the code in 1982. In 1990, it issued a Statement of Principles of Radio and Television Broadcasting that essentially left the matter of censorship to the broadcasters themselves. The NAB did suggest caution in regard to sexually oriented material, but it now cited the First Amendment as protecting the individual choices the association now encouraged.[97]

As Janet MacRorie supervised radio censorship at NBC, Stockton Helffrich in the period of 1948 to 1960 presided over television censorship at the network, heading what was euphemistically called the Continuity Acceptance Department. How he handled what came out on the network with regard to the publications of Alfred Kinsey on the sexuality of the human male and female in 1948 and 1953 respectively provides a glimpse of his approach to his task. Despite the flaws in his sampling technique, Kinsey publicized a world of sexual experience at odds with traditional and widely espoused views. Helffrich had had trouble with a new offering, *The Arrow Show* with comedian Phil Silvers. One of his offenses involved joking about homosexuality, something regularly blue-penciled. Now he tried to get away with a joke involving the first Kinsey report. A couple that had been patiently waiting for a table at a restaurant inquired of the maître d', just "what are a man and woman to do?" He responded, "how should I know, my name's Ginsburg not Kinsey." The joke was deleted, as were all such comedic references.[98] The reports could be tastefully discussed but not made the butt of jokes. After all, sex was serious and sensitive business.

To illustrate the difference, a story of a married woman's infidelity that enraged her son and required her husband's sensitive interference, was broadcast on *The Armstrong Circle Theatre*. Despite viewer protest that the show was "depraved and immoral," Helffrich brushed off his critics, saying they preferred illusion to "dramatic fare pointing up . . . facts about ourselves." However, when it came time to make some theater classics suitable for home viewing, he did not hesitate to sanitize the story. In Luigi Pirandello's *Six Characters in Search of an Author*, incest and prostitution are among the subjects treated. Not only were words changed but whole scenes as well; how much of the author's message was left is debatable.[99]

Squelching the stereotype that censors are prudes, Helffrich, when he left his post, provided a list of subjects that television should tackle in the future, either dramatically or in discussion format. In time, programmers would tackle just about all of them, including premarital sexual relations, unwed mothers, and birth control. He said, "you cannot at one and the same time in any medium of artistic expression hope to capture the intelligent without exposing the innocent to considerations alleged to be better understood by adults."[100]

During his tenure, however, Helffrich spent considerable time and effort dealing with women's breasts on the tube. Clothing styles emphasized the breast, and buxom women were no less than "bombshells." Women who appeared on the screen in commercial television's early days, such as Faye Emerson and Ilka Chase, were often dressed in gowns with considerable décolletage. This "social obsession with the female bust shown (or implied) on the nation's home screens quickly made bosoms the hyper-sexualized locus of negotiation for postwar network censorship."[101]

Early complaints about sex on television, as the first television code indicated, dealt with décolletage. Arkansas congressman Ezekiel Candler
Gathers held hearings in the House of Representatives on television and
morality and achieved some success in raising the plunging necklines of
buxom women who appeared on television. In fact, the hearing scared CBS
to the extent that it banned the word "sex." One of the early TV personali-
ties was a twenty-three-year-old woman, Virginia Ruth Egnor, with the stage
name of Dagmar, whose forty-inch bust magnified her appeal. In this era of
live TV, accidents did happen and now and then a stray breast did escape
from confinement. Furthermore, too tight sweaters that made nipples visible were also subjects of constant worry.[102]

Although Dagmar and the show on which she appeared, *Broadway Open
House* with comedian Jerry Lester, did not long survive, it attracted a considerable degree of attention in Boston. The general manager of WHDH-TV
expressed concern over Dagmar's ample bosom and the burlesquelike humor of the show. Roman Catholic archbishop Richard J. Cushing found the
station morally deficient for showing Dagmar. Congressman Thomas Lane,
agreeing with the many complaints he received, supported a Federal Censorship Board to put an end to "the primitive sate of nudism" on view.[103]
NBC responded by establishing a cleavage control policy by placing a censor in the control room during live broadcasts. The network president sent
letters to all those persons who appeared on NBC shows. Even a shot of
nude mannequins was not acceptable.[104]

One final area of some concern during Helffrich's tenure was the televis-
ing of modern dance. Here the censor tended to brush away complaints as
the result of a lack of exposure on the part of those who found the dances
"too lurid" or "pornographic and revolting." These were responses to the
dances of Ruth Mata and Eugene Hari, who appeared regularly on *Your
Show of Shows.* One of Helffrich's subordinates reported on their first appearance on the program. He said, "the female dancer in a sinuous routine,
fell back on the stage with her legs spread apart and the pursuing male
dancer fell upon her." When a mother complained that a male dancer's
tights were "too revealing," Helffrich replied that the contours were only average. Apparently when the contours were still only average in a routine in
which comedian Jack Carter was dressed in tight long johns, the censor
found the exhibition "pornographic."[105]

Prime-time TV was the target of censors, and late-night discussion shows,
such as *Open Mind,* and daytime soaps that dealt with sexual matters more directly generally escaped their attention. So also did the commercial that aired
to promote Clairol hair color, beginning in 1956. Showing an attractive
blonde, the commercial provocatively asked "Does she or doesn't she?"[106]

As the 1950s were succeeded by the more sexually permissive 1960s, television's censors moved away from a focus on words that were taboo and

dealt more substantially with content. Still, not until 1986 in a *Cagney & Lacey* show was the word "condom" used.[107] As one who was involved as the lead censor at the American Broadcasting Company (ABC), Alfred R. Schneider, said, "year by year, program by program, in comedy and drama, television programming ventured into more and more controversial and sensitive subjects in the arena of sex." Despite "protracted negotiations about the actual presentation," many controversial projects were eventually made available to the viewing public.[108]

Television programming continued to attract the attention of Congress. The first hearings, held in the House of Representatives in 1952, focused on immorality and offensiveness, along with violence, crime, and corruption. Three years later, the Senate held hearings on the long-term effects of exposure to television violence. It would be a rare Congress that did not hold such hearings, and although violence seemed to be the major issue, it was often linked with sex. For instance in 2004, the Senate held hearings designed to inquire into how children could be protected from indecent and violent programming. Senator John McCain from Arizona suggested that cable companies give subscribers the option to select the channels they receive.[109] At times the hearings over the half century led to legislation, but more often they were reminders to the TV industry to monitor programming.

Threats of regulation often produced results, but critics would argue that the long congressional campaign against sex and violence on television has had little effect on programming decisions. Dr. Marvin Heller, professor of psychiatry and codirector of the Unit of Law and Psychiatry at Temple University, was hired by the television industry to develop criteria for evaluating television programs. He correctly predicted that less violence in programming, which did occur in the 1960s, would lead to an "increased emphasis on sex."[110]

One contribution to filling this gap was the movie industry, which was in the process of being freed from the restraints of the Hayes Code. Movie moguls initially saw free television as a deadly competitor and only slowly came to realize that it was a medium that could add profit to the move industry's bottom line. Only slowly were major motion pictures released for television and then for quite a while only those made before 1949. The truce came in September 1961 when NBC, to kick off its *Saturday Night at the Movies* obtained *How to Marry a Millionaire* with Marilyn Monroe, Lauren Bacall, and Betty Grable, a 1953 release. By 1970 as many as nine recently released movies were available to viewers on the networks each week.[111]

What was being shown in theaters, with the demise of the Hayes Code in 1968 and the introduction of the ratings system, provided problems for network censors. Alfred R. Schneider, the head censor at ABC estimated that television ran five to ten years behind motion pictures in regard to the treatment of sex. However, he was sensitive to the need to change with the times and relax past standards.[112] He informed affiliates of his view that "topical program treatments dealing with interpersonal relationships, if presented in a thoughtful, concerned and non-exploitive manner . . . are proper television fare." ABC had just purchased *Midnight Cowboy*, *Klute*, *The Graduate*, and *The Last Picture Show*, a quartet of films that challenged the censors. In regard to the last of the lot, Schneider told concerned station managers that "thirty-two scenes were edited, nudity was eliminated, and the looping and/or deletion and redubbing of thirty-seven words had been accomplished." It was telecast with the disclaimer, "this film deals with mature subject matter. Parental judgment and discretion are advised." Over two decades later broadcasters would implement a rating system incorporating this caution.[113]

Schneider found the now friendly movie industry at first quite accommodating in that from 1971 to 1979 he and his staff, after the edits they suggested, had succeeded in getting the Motion Picture Association of America (MPAA) to change the ratings on such edited motion pictures from R to PG. This process, however, came to a halt when MPAA refused to reconsider its initial rating of *Looking for Mr. Goodbar*, saying that the organization refused to become a censor.[114]

By 1979 cable television was beginning to make inroads on network programming, leading the networks to revisit their censoring operations. Actually the stimulus was Woody Allen who refused to bend to the censor's wishes, as he rejected all attempts to edit his Academy Award–winning *Annie Hall*. "Penis," "masturbation," and "humping" were taboo words, as was the reference to oral sex contained in the remark: "I'm starting to get some feeling back in my jaw." Schneider finally decided that with unedited films running on cable he would take the chance and pass the unedited version. Again a warning ran before the film. Only one station and three and a half minutes of advertising were lost.[115]

In addition to theatrical features, television was supplied with made-for-television movies beginning in the mid-1960s. By 1987 the made-for-TV product was outstripping theatrical releases three to one.[116] What made this development especially significant was the fact that the TV movie would become the vehicle for introducing hitherto taboo sexual subjects to the television audience.

For instance, in 1972 a project dealing with homosexuality was turned down by NBC but picked up by ABC. The TV movie titled *That Certain Summer* concerned the relationship between a father and his teenage son as it was affected by the father's decision to leave his wife to live with the man he loved. In dialogue the father confesses that he does not know if it is a sickness that can be cured, but then he adds, "but, it's the only way I can live."[117] Two years later, *A Case of Rape* presented viewers with realistic portrayals of not one rape but two. Censors balked, but Elizabeth Montgomery, the star, threatened to quit the movie if the scene was deleted. She won.[118] Rape posed a special problem in that it joined sex with violence. In the same year NBC telecast *Born Innocent* dealing with girls in a reform school. The leading actress, Linda Blair, played a character who was accosted in the shower room and sodomized with a mop handle. Originally vetoed by the director of broadcast standards, as the censor at NBC was titled, the television movie was eventually made and even hailed internally at the network as showing youngsters the wisdom of refraining from conduct that would land them in reform school. The movie brought together those who felt that TV had too much sex with those who felt that it had too much violence and seemed to strengthen the case for some form of censorship.[119]

The made-for-TV movie, however, continued to flourish. It explored prostitution, lesbian parenting, single woman sexuality, and feminism, among other hot topics. Then in 1984 ABC aired *Something about Amelia*, which dealt with the most forbidden of topics, father-daughter incest. The warning the program carried minced no words, saying the presentation dealt "with incest and its painful consequences." It recommended family viewing, but advised parental discretion. The program carried a toll-free number for those seeking assistance about such matters.[120] Two years later *Second Serve* was aired; it dealt with a transsexual tennis pro.[121] The most ambitious movie ever developed directly for TV was the thirty-hour miniseries *War and Remembrance* adapted from the novel by Herman Wouk in 1988. In dealing with the Holocaust, the movie presented problems for the censors. In one scene involving frontal nudity, the censor found it so integral to the story that no changes were made. In another scene where oral sex was the price for saving her child, Jane Seymour, who played the part with convincing realism, ran afoul of the censors. A cut and a more distant shot of the scene satisfied the censor. Then in 1990 the TV movie *Unspeakable Acts* dealt in a frank and forthright way with child molestation and abuse. The movie centered around two doctors, man and wife, interviewing victims, whose comments, as one might expect, included talk of penises and vaginas.[122]

If even child abuse was an acceptable subject for TV viewing, one might wonder why the subject of homosexuality still encountered problems. Perhaps the Mapplethorpe controversy over homoerotic pictures had a chilling effect. At any rate, PBS television stations throughout the nation refused to run *Tongues Untied*, a film by Marlon Riggs that dealt with homosexuality.[123]

Since motion picture executives had not only made peace with TV but also had come to realize that TV provided an important market for their product, one might expect that they would have had the foresight to embrace the videocassette recorder (VCR). On the contrary, they were heavy contributors to television fare and fought the new device as a threat to their copyrighted products. Narrowly, the United States Supreme Court ruled that the manufacturers of VCRs by selling their product to consumers who taped programs for viewing later were not guilty of contributory infringement. The majority of justices reasoned that such time-shifting would not lessen the potential market for the copyrighted products.[124] The decision spurred the sales of VCRs.

In the early 1980s when VCRs were first catching on, a popular view was that a person bought one to watch dirty pictures. This suspicion was not without some foundation. One can make a convincing case that pornography deserves credit for advancing new technologies, such as the VCR, by providing a market for buyers willing to pay the high costs extracted from early adopters of new technology. A study of videotape sales found that in the late '70s, X-rated movies constituted over 50 percent of the sales of all prerecorded videotapes. With the spread of the technology and declining prices, that percentage would drop by the mid-1980s as the VCR began to entice other kinds of customers.[125] While only 4 percent of American homes had a VCR in 1982, almost 60 percent did by 1988, a span of only six years.[126]

The VCR spawned the creation of businesses renting videocassettes for enjoyment at home. In 1987 during the Senate confirmation hearing on Robert Bork's nomination to the U.S. Supreme Court, a reporter for a weekly District of Columbia paper obtained the rental records of the nominee. He then drew a profile of the judge based upon the 146 films he and his family had rented from the store.[127] The disclosure was given little public notice, and the nomination failed for other reasons. Congress, however, did take notice, passing the Video Privacy Protection Act of 1988.[128] It banned the disclosure of personal rental information except under warrant or court order and provided for a civil remedy of no less than twenty-five hundred dollars. Video stores had to destroy rental records one year after an account was terminated, and nothing in the federal act precluded states from providing greater protection for renters of videos. Three years later when another Supreme Court nominee, Clarence Thomas, was answering a charge of sexual harassment before the Senate Judiciary Committee, what might have been a more spicy rental record was sheltered from public view.

Although the motion picture industry contributed to the sexual content of television fare, so also did other programming. The racy world of daytime soap operas was brought to nighttime TV by ABC in 1964 when *Peyton Place*, based on Grace Metalious's novel of the same name, aired. The viewing public approved and made it a top ten hit in the 1964–1965 season. Apparently viewers were not affronted by the extramarital affairs that fueled the show's five seasons. Nor were they scandalized by the real-life affair between the young star of the show, Mia Farrow, and Frank Sinatra. Times indeed were changing, though too slowly for some.

Daytime soap operas, so-called because they were sponsored by soap companies including Proctor & Gamble, were always laced with sex, going back to their beginning in radio. In fact, some critics have called the programs "pornography for women." Yet they did not really disturb either the sponsors or network censors. Their continued focus was on nighttime programming.

Beginning with *That Girl* starring Marlo Thomas in 1966 and continuing with the more popular *Mary Tyler Moore Show* in 1970, television now portrayed the single career woman. Neither woman was dealt with as a sexual being, but television was now reflecting new realities in American society. TV had previously portrayed women within the family unit as the prime domestic. Now released to find her own way, the single woman series reflected some of the real world in which traditional roles were under revision.

In 1965 when the situation comedy *I Dream of Jeannie* premiered, the network censor barred the showing of Barbara Eden's navel in her genie costume. Only a couple of decades later on a reunion show was Eden's navel made visible to the viewing public. Women's navels, however, were a regular feature on *Rowan & Martin's Laugh-In* by the end of the 1960s.[129] At the same time, the Smothers Brothers were challenging the censors at CBS, which had required the screening of their shows by affiliates to determine whether those stations wanted to run the program. Much of the concern was over political commentary but problems arose as to sex as well. In fact, just before the show was abruptly cancelled by CBS, one of the contentious issues was a monologue by comedian David Steinberg that contained double entendre lines in the retelling of the biblical account of Jonah and the whale. For instance in his rendition, Steinberg said, "then the Gentiles grabbed the Jew by his Old Testament."[130]

One way to break barriers in depicting real life on television was to stress the medium's educational function. In 1961, Newton N. Minnow, then head of the FCC, surveyed television programming and pronounced it a "vast wasteland."[131] As with radio, optimists had hoped that the new electronic media would undertake the task of educating the American public. However, the decision with radio and then with television to have advertisers bear the cost of programming inevitably subordinated education to entertainment. The trick then was to put education in an entertainment box. This is precisely what MGM Television tried to do by publicizing the campaign against venereal diseases in a two-part program that began on *Mr. Novak*, a series set in a high school, and *Dr. Kildare*, a popular medical offering. The story concerned a seventeen-year-old contracting syphilis after sexual contact with three young women. Public concern about venereal diseases had inspired the venture, but censors found the theme of teenage sex inappropriate for family viewing. The two-part show never aired.[132]

By the early 1970s the climate had changed. *Marcus Welby, M.D.* dealt with pregnancy, abortion, homosexuality, and pedophilia. In January 1971 the situation comedy *All in the Family* first aired with the highly prejudiced working-class Archie Bunker as its lead character. ABC Television passed on the pilot because of its sexual content.[133] CBS, however, proved more adventurous as it picked up the series and ran it for the next twenty years. The first episode contained many of Archie's racist epithets, but what seemed even more disturbing was the implication of midmorning sex between Archie's daughter and son-in-law. Norman Lear insisted on keeping the scene intact. The opening show in the second season introduced temporary impotence into the mix, and again Lear won.[134] One of the offshoots of the series was *Maud*, which in 1972 ran an episode dealing with the forty-seven-year-old title character deciding to have an abortion.[135]

By mid-decade Congress was again threatening to regulate television programming. To head off threatened legislation, Richard E. Wiley, the head of the FCC, met with network executives in late 1974 to see what self-regulation they were willing to impose. Eventually CBS responded by proposing an amendment to the NAB Television Code that would set aside the first hour of network programming for family viewing. Should a program contain material not suitable for children, parents would be alerted by an on-air warning. By the summer of 1975, the new family hour was in place.[136]

What followed was a new level of scrutiny on situation comedies in which sex had been a staple. Their writers quickly ran afoul of network censors. A review of the story lines for the popular series *M*A*S*H* led the censor to question plots dealing with venereal disease, impotence, and adultery. A CBS censor concluded that abortion, birth control, prostitution, and even pregnancy would have to be banished from the family hour. The vagueness of the new standard tended to lead censors to very different conclusions. After a battle over a program in which a mother fretted over whether her daughter had lost her virginity, one critic assessed the outcome as follows: "As a test case, it seemed to prove that CBS would permit some discussion of premarital sex, but perhaps only if a few key writers threatened to resign and, even then, only if there really wasn't any sex at all."[137] *Newsweek* summarized its view of family hour programming by saying that "the new policy is akin to separating the dross from the gold—and then throwing away the gold."[138]

The Writers Guild decided to bring suit against the networks and the FCC. Clearly the family hour requirement had censored ideas, but the tie to government action would have to be established to establish a free speech violation. The case was assigned to a sympathetic judge, Warren J. Ferguson, who refused to dismiss the action. After testimony and affidavits, the judge suggested that the parties settle the case. When that could not be done, he responded in November 1976 with an extensive opinion that concluded that the family hour would never have been instituted had there not been "fear of federal regulation." Therefore, the judge continued, "the adoption of the Family Viewing Policy by each of the networks constituted a violation of the First Amendment."[139] He further warned the FCC that it was not authorized to "use the licensing process to prevent programming which it regards as offensive."[140]

Some critics noted the irony of the networks' new position. Having long contended that they should be as free from government interference as were the print media, they now were uncomfortable with the judicial blessing placed on their long-argued First Amendment claim. A CBS spokesman called the decision "a dangerous precedent." The judge's ruling had left the networks free to continue the family hour as long as they did it individually and not in concert with the NAB or the FCC. All three networks indicated that they would retain the hour. What this announcement meant in practice was quite different than what the networks seemed to promise. For instance, one study concluded that in the 1976–1977 season violent incidents in the hour had doubled, and references to sex had not disappeared.[141] By 1983–1984, the family hour had faded away.[142]

Since network television was provided at no cost to viewers because of corporate sponsorship, those persons seeking to censor what the networks made available inevitably were led to pressuring advertisers. The National Citizens Committee for Broadcasting (NCCB) headed by a former FCC commissioner Nicholas Johnson had been successful in convincing advertisers to limit their support of violent police shows.[143] Since violence on television had been reduced, television programmers now filled the gap with sex. In fact, the debate about the acceptability of pressuring advertisers focused on a program called *Soap*, an evening satire on the standard afternoon fare of soap operas. One ABC editor described the program as "a further innovation in the comedic/dramatic form of presenting a larger-than-life frank treatment of controversial and adult themes." As an example of such themes, he listed "pre-marital sex, adultery, impotence, homosexuality, transvestism, [and] transsexualism."[144]

Soap became the "year's lightening rod for controversy." ABC explained to its affiliates that it decided to air the show because it was "an exceptionally entertaining program." The network promised to avoid salacious material, but then said that "any program that spoofs and satirizes contemporary matters and mores" cannot "avoid controversy or appeal to every viewer."[145] One reason for the special concern were the thirty-two thousand letters, all but nine railing against the show, that ABC had received prior to the first episode's airing in 1977. One religious critic rhetorically asked who "besides the churches is going to stand against the effort of television to tear down our moral values and make all of us into mere consumers?"[146] Although the show contained the first homosexual character in a prime-time series, pressure that began before the show aired increasingly resulted in toning down the final product. Its scripts were so tamed that in 1978 ABC dropped the parental discretion warning.[147]

Such issue-oriented situation comedies were not the only targets of censors. *Charlie's Angels*, which debuted in the fall of 1976, led critics to bemoan the depravity and declining moral standards of television. *Charlie's* three female detectives led some critics to use alternative titles for the series, such as "tits and ass" and "jiggle TV." As the head network censor remembered the show, he recalled a weekly tradition of long distance phone calls and recurrent battles.[148] The following year *Three's Company* debuted. It dealt with one man and two women living together and thrived on sexual innuendoes. ABC's head censor in reviewing the script for the show's premiere considered it an extended dirty joke, two-thirds of which he found unacceptable. He got changes but the result was still salacious. However, it would soon become one of television's most highly rated programs.[149]

The Parent Teacher Association (PTA), which had earlier made television violence a target, now concluded that "sex is not an appropriate or acceptable substitute for violence." Sears, Roebuck, which earlier had responded to the campaign against television violence by pulling its ads from certain programs, now agreed to do the same with "immoral" shows as well. Threatened picketing of its stores by the National Federation of Decency helped spur the latter decision.[150]

Actually the late 1970s saw a rather dramatic rise in the sexual content of television programming, almost a decade after the code restrictions were lifted on the movie industry.[151] TV had moved from condemning extramarital sex and weighing participants down with guilt and remorse to situations where there was "lots of sex, very little remorse." One critic contended that television programming reflected liberal values that were out of step with the nation's increasing conservatism.[152]

This is an interesting observation, which suggests that as social conservatives sought to enshrine their values by going to the polls and electing representatives who seemed to share their views, the entertainment industry was winning the values battle. Conservative groups saw control of the political process as the way to achieve their collective goal, but limits are imposed on governmental control by the constitutional order. In addition to such constraints, Americans often speak one way and act another. They condemn sexual explicitness on television, yet they continue to respond to its call. In the final analysis, TV viewers may be influenced by the decisions of media conglomerates and advertising to want sexual programming or they, as curious human beings, may come to the same conclusion for themselves, but either way the result was more sex, not less, in television programming. If viewers were opting for cable, they found even often more explicit sex. Certainly television had become the nation's leading sex educator, and this conclusion led to increased concern about what lessons were being taught.

For some moral critics of the medium, more threatening than the loose sexual morals of heterosexuals played out on the small screen was television's willingness to give to what they called deviant sex its seal of approval. One of these critics said the conclusion one would draw from TV's interest in such behavior was that "homosexuality is more frequent than the common cold."[153] The prostitute was not ostracized, and adultery and premarital sex were simply presented as facts of life. Television programming seemed to be furthering such immorality by being sympathetic and tolerant. Unquestionably, such programming did break down barriers and in so doing increase social acceptance of what the critics condemned.[154]

Television always had its critics and the sexual content of shows had been one of their targets, but the conservative social and political swing introduced by the Reagan administration gave such critics a more prominent platform. In June 1981 *Newsweek* reported that over 130 interest groups were engaged in trying to affect the content of television programming. Reverends Donald Wildmon and Jerry Falwell sought to combine forces and force the networks to rid the airwaves of morally objectionable material. The Coalition for Better Television (CBTV) that emerged from the meeting claimed almost four hundred civic and religious groups. It threatened boycotts of sponsors that advertised on the objectionable shows. *Newsweek* in reviewing the fall schedule of shows noted the absence of controversial shows, and ABC confessed that some sponsors were pulling their support from risqué shows. However, the network challenged CBTV's assumption that the organization spoke for the American public, saying its own study of fourteen hundred adults confirmed the network's argument that its standards were simply reflective of prevailing attitudes in society. Other challengers to the CBTV cried censorship and promised a war of rival organizations, led by Norman Lear's People for the American Way. A vice president for Proctor & Gamble, TV's largest advertiser, said that the industry does not enter "this debate with clean hands" and that Wildmon does indeed "have a point."[155]

If, however, CBTV, as many organizations before and since, thought it had found the answer to regulating TV content, it was wrong. As *Newsweek* concluded, the arbiters in the final analysis are not pressure groups but the marketplace itself.[156] Apparently enough sponsors decided that when the views of organizations such as CBTV are in conflict with Nielsen ratings, which register what the viewers want to see, the latter, not the former, determines where the advertising dollar will go.

Still, the pressure on advertisers became the most viable if not only avenue for censorship when, in the deregulatory mood of the late 1970s and 1980s, the Justice Department took aim on the NAB. In 1982 a three-year-old suit against the NAB on antitrust grounds was settled, resulting in the demise of the Radio and Television codes. That left each network completely free to develop and enforce its own standards on programming.[157] Hour-long nighttime soaps, such as *Dallas* and *Dynasty*, which chronicled the sexual adventures of the rich, became standard fare during the 1980s.

Although police shows were a staple of early TV, the 1980s began a new trend by making the dramas sexually provocative. *Miami Vice*, which began in the mid-1980s, had all the vices, including sexual varieties, presented in stylish form. NBC, which had been mired in third place among the networks, had a big success with *Hill Street Blues*, which ran from 1981 to 1987. Unlike some of the popular situation comedies, this new breed of police show won the plaudits of critics. The show flirted with nudity but generally backed away from showing it. However, it dealt quite realistically with sexual relationships among both the regular cast members and in its story lines. Barbara Babcock as Grace Gardner was as sexually aggressive a female character as TV viewers had ever seen.[158] Then, beginning in 1993, came *NYPD Blue*, with language and nudity that often took attention away from its well-crafted plots. In fact, even before the premiere aired, Reverend Donald Wildmon and his latest group of television monitors had put pressure on the show's advertisers.[159]

Cable was still more daring than the networks. For instance, Showtime's *A New Day in Eden* showed nude and topless women, along with lesbian love scenes. Network programming talked about all sorts of sexual subjects; cable programming just showed more of it.[160] However, cable did push the networks to abandon "the decades of self-censorship that kept television relatively bland and noncontroversial" for much of its early history.[161]

ABC, CBS, and NBC had more than cable to worry about when a new network, Fox, surfaced in 1986. The following year Fox hit pay dirt with *Married . . . with Children*, a raunchy show filled with sexual situations that inspired a boycott. The applied pressure had little effect as the show lasted ten years, constantly pushing the frontiers of what was permissible on television.[162]

ABC eventually responded with *Thirtysomething*, which portrayed the problems of young parents and their "sexual yearnings, frustration and fatigue." ABC's head censor allowed a scene of coitus interruptus, one of a diaphram dropping on the floor, and one of two men in bed together, but not one of two men kissing.[163] Near the turn of the century, that remaining barrier would fall as both Fox's *That '70s Show* and NBC's *Will & Grace*, the show in which a gay man and straight woman share an apartment, each depicted such an encounter.[164]

No Fox show would have greater longevity than *The Simpsons*, which first aired in 1989. It traced the trials and tribulations of a family unlike any television had seen before. That the members were cartoon characters seemed to afford the writers greater freedom.[165] A recent sexual foray saw Homer Simpson, the title character, take advantage of a local ordinance designed to encourage tourism by conducting a series of gay marriages.[166]

Even when a show was about nothing, as NBC's *Seinfeld* claimed to be when it premiered in 1990, viewers quickly discovered that what it really was about was sex. Sexual plotlines often involved Elaine. In one episode a saxophone player fails his audition after performing oral sex on her. In another episode, Elaine withholds sex from her boyfriend in the belief that it would sharpen his intellect and bolster his test performance only to be dumped.[167] And in one episode all four of the principals embark upon a contest to see who could go the longest without masturbating. Although the word itself is not used, viewers can hardly miss what the contest involves.[168] The sexual situations in the show were limited only by the writers' imaginations.

In 1991 Reverend Wildmon and his American Family Association tallied more than ten thousand sexual incidents shown by the networks, most of which involved unmarried partners.[169] In fact, if you believed TV, married folks had little sex, if any at all.[170] When researchers compared what was shown on network television a decade earlier with what was shown in 1989, there was no dramatic difference, though sexual intercourse was discretely shown in the latter year when it had been left to suggestion in the former.[171]

What especially bothered the Planned Parenthood Federation of America was that a study it commissioned confirmed its view that the results of irresponsible sex were not being conveyed. For instance, while twenty-seven sexual references were made in each hour of nighttime network TV, it took ten hours to find one reference to sexually transmitted diseases, and fifty hours to find a reference to birth control. The organization urged the networks "to balance their overly romanticized and unrealistic portrayals of sex with messages about responsibility."[172]

The 1990s had arrived and not much in regard to sexual depiction would be left unexplored by the networks. When Ted Baehr of the Atlanta Christian Film and Television Commission sought to resurrect the old movie Production Code to regulate film and television, he was ridiculed by the media. Even the support he expected from the Roman Catholic Archdiocese of Los Angeles was denied.[173] Again it was Fox that challenged the boundaries of sex on TV with the show *Flying Blind*, which clearly directed the viewers' imagination with scripts that were infused with a "steamy sensuality."[174] The show would last only a season, but NBC's answer to Fox, *Friends*, which premiered in 1994 and dealt with six bright young people in their twenties, lasted a decade. It would come to be rated by the Center for Media and Public Affairs as "prime time's most sex-heavy show."[175]

In 1994 *Entertainment Weekly* suggested that television had entered the "Gay '90s," in reference to the way in which the medium was incorporating

lesbians and homosexuals into its nighttime programming.[176] Actually, between 1990 and 1992 the issue was in doubt as advertisers refused to sponsor a number of episodes, including ones in *Lifestories*, *Thirtysomething*, and
Quantum Leap because of their gay content. The conclusion was that such
programs were not only controversial but that they lost money. The Gay &
Lesbian Alliance Against Defamation (GLAAD) mounted a counteroffen-
sive that began to pay dividends as early as 1992. Over the following years
network executives and advertisers as well realized that gay material would
spice up bland offerings and become attractive to viewers.[177]

A few episodes in the period from 1993 to 1997 helped gay material
maintain a not undesired controversial edge. The first was perhaps the most
groundbreaking because teenage sex had always been presented on television as heterosexual. In 1993 an episode of the dramatic series *Picket Fences*
dealt with two teenage girls experiencing same-sex attraction. The scene
consisted of two kisses, a tentative, experimental one followed by a passionate one. CBS officials, worried about public reaction, ordered that the
second kiss be reshot in the dark. In the next season ABC executives were
wary of an episode of the show *Roseanne* in which the lead character, played
by Roseanne Barr, planted a kiss on a woman. To show how times were
changing, when their initial decision not to air the show was overcome, the
show, now advertised as the "lesbian kiss" episode, attracted thirty million
viewers. In 1997 the leading character in the situation comedy *Ellen* came
out of the closet. Over forty-two million viewers watched the episode. Ellen
DeGeneres, the actress playing the show's Ellen, also took the opportunity
to acknowledge her lesbian identity. The programs had indeed attracted
controversy, but they attracted sponsors and viewers too. Clearly the 1990s
welcomed gays into network programming, though critics noticed a certain
ambivalence in the fare as it mixed "homophobic stereotypes with gay-
affirming narratives." For those persons so long excluded from television
programming, the increase in TV visibility "was no doubt moving, affirming, frustrating, entertaining, and insulting."[178]

If the sexual content of network programming was not explicit enough or
the nudity partially covered, the viewer could turn to cable programming.
The exploits of four single women, given the most appropriate title *Sex and
the City*, developed for HBO in 1998 dealt quite explicitly with the sexual
adventures of single women. It would establish a new benchmark for cable
television, being the first cable show to win an Emmy, in this case for Outstanding Comedy Series in 2001.[179] When the series came to an end in
2005, slightly cropped reruns became available without additional cost to
cable subscribers on WTBS.

In the same year that saw the birth of *Sex and the City*, worries about entertainment that contained intimations of oral sex took a backseat to the
revelation of the real life drama of President Bill Clinton's graphically de-

tailed sexual relationship with Monica Lewinsky. One British critic saw the episode as instructive, contending that "scandal is the dominant form through which 'deviant' sexual practices are circulated in the mainstream media." She attributed this fact to the influence of Puritanism, where sin had to be exposed so that it could then be condemned. Through such media events, she continued, "the boundaries of acceptable sexual behavior are continually renegotiated."[180] How deviant oral sex was in the 1990s can be disputed, but certainly its treatment as news of the highest order gave it a prominence that caused *Newsweek* to provide advice to parents when their children asked about oral sex. The news weekly did not advise parents to lie and confirm that oral sex was talk about sex, but rather stonewall it by foregoing the educational moment and avoiding any details.[181] Talk about a blow job on entertainment television was still blue-penciled, but the term "fellatio" could be substituted.[182]

Concern about sexual material unsuitable for children, however, only grew more insistent, and in the Telecommunications Act of 1996 Congress provided that all television sets manufactured after 1998 would have to include a V-chip, a device to block programs with a certain rating. If the industry did not come up with a ratings system within a year, the FCC was authorized to impose one. By the end of the year, the television industry came up with an age-based system with six ratings: TV-Y, suitable for all children; TV-Y7, suitable for children over the age of seven; G, for a general audience, including all children; TV-PG, program contains material that is unsuitable for young children; TV-14, program contains material unsuitable for children under age fourteen; and TV-MA, adult programming that might not be suitable for children under seventeen. Continued complaints about television fare and threats of further congressional action forced the industry to supplement the latter three ratings with S for explicit sex, V for graphic violence, and L for vulgar language.[183]

The ratings system, so long fought by the industry, had the actual effect of increasing the sexual content of network programming. One study saw a 42-percent increase in prime-time sexual content from the 1996 to the 1998 season. The Parents Television Council (PTC) compared 1989 and 1999 and found that sexual content had tripled over the decade. From approximately one reference an hour, the total now stood at three and a half. Kinky sex and homosexual references grew substantially, and oral sex, absent in 1989, was now found twenty times. PTC especially lamented the fact that the shows spent so little time dealing with sexual responsibility and the consequences of sexual intercourse.[184]

No medium's content has been more thoroughly investigated than television programming, and increasingly that content has been scrutinized for sexual references.[185] In considering programming from late afternoon through prime time, the Kaiser Family Foundation researchers surveying the

2000–2001 season found few programs that were completely devoid of sexual content.[186] Their report on the following season noted that, over four years, sexual intercourse, either strongly implied or depicted, had doubled in network shows. Kaiser's primary interest had been in public health and the foundation now took some solace in the more frequent references to safe sex, noting that such references had almost doubled and were now found in almost half of the shows with sexual content.[187]

In late 2001 a CBS show illustrated the blurry line between commercials and entertainment as far as sex was concerned. In the *Victoria's Secret Fashion Show Special* viewers got exactly what was advertised—shapely young women in revealing lingerie. FTC commissioner Michael J. Copps, responding to the barrage of e-mail the agency got as a result of the program, said that it "collapsed" the computer servers and signaled the need for "a reexamination of the FCC indecency standard."[188]

Certainly youngsters learned about sex from television, and what disturbed some observers was what they learned. One such critic summed up the medium's "most powerful lesson," which was "that everyone's having more of it than you are" with more attractive partners than you will ever meet. Remembering sex education in school as something that never answered the question of "why anyone would find it pleasurable," he said TV's version may be no more sexy, especially with a new emphasis on sexually transmitted diseases, defective condoms, and the like.[189] To add to the worry of those concerned about what sexual lessons television was teaching, Rand Corporation and University of California researchers concluded that children from twelve to seventeen who watch three or more hours of television a day are twice as likely to have sexual intercourse or some other type of genital contact than those who watch less. Furthermore, such excess viewing, they said, advances the sexual age of children by almost three years.[190]

In a time when the dissection of corpses ruled nighttime television and *Law and Order* spinoffs continued, a revival of the nighttime soap opera became the surprise hit of the 2004 season. *Desperate Housewives* is funny and filled with sex, but it also bites as social satire. ABC took a chance on the show and found its first real hit in some time. When some advertisers pulled their ads because of talk that the show was too sexually explicit, more viewers wanted to see what the fuss was all about.[191] ABC decided to parlay this interest in an introduction to *Monday Night Football* on November 15, 2004. The Philadelphia Eagles were playing the Dallas Cowboys. The introductory skit featured Eagle star Terrell Owens and Nicolette Sheridan, the sexually aggressive Edie of *Housewives*. Attired only in a towel, she overcomes the reluctance of the football player to fulfill her needs by finally dropping her towel. Only her bare back was shown, but the suggestive dialog and suggestion of complete nudity stirred considerable discussion and complaint. Was the skit indecent? The FCC acknowledged that it was "titil-lating," but "not graphic or explicit enough to be indecent."[192]

Ever since the Janet Jackson halftime show, Congress had been stirring with new concern over cracking down on sex on television. Representative Fred Upton of Michigan had initiated new legislation to allow the FCC to raise its fine for indecency to $500,000 from its present $32,500 for stations and $11,000 for performers. Furthermore, the bill authorized a license rev-ocation after a third offense and gave the FCC 180 days in which to deter-mine if broadcasters had indeed committed an indecency offense. The House of Representatives quickly passed the bill in 2004, but it stalled in the Senate. Initially the National Religious Broadcasters (NRB) endorsed the bill, but its leaders worried that the breadth of the restrictions might im-pact religious programming. Such worries finally led the NRB to oppose the legislation.[193]

Congress is actually bombarded with conflicting messages on sexual con-tent from rival interest groups and with the fact that the shows eliciting complaints are often popular with the viewing audience. President George W. Bush's appointment of Commissioner Kevin J. Martin to head the FCC in 2005 was perceived as an attempt to crack down on indecent program-ming.[194] In the wake of the Janet Jackson affair, a chill was felt by television station managers and programmers, who became worried about curse words and glimpses of bare flesh, uncertain about what would now be con-sidered indecent. Critics wondered whether the crusaders against sex on TV were protecting only children or whether they were seeking to censor what adults watched as well.

In March 2006 the FCC, now under Martin's leadership, rejected CBS's appeal of the $550,000 fine against twenty of the network's stations for air-ing Janet Jackson's exposed breast in the 2004 Super Bowl halftime show and found an additional reason to penalize CBS. The new problem was found in the December 31, 2004, episode of *Without a Trace*, which in-cluded "at least three shots depicting intercourse, two between couples and one 'group sex' shot," all involving teenagers. Although the program aired in the Eastern time zone after 10 p.m. and therefore beyond the indecency ban that the FCC now enforces from 6 a.m. to 10 p.m., 111 CBS stations and affiliates, apparently in other time zones, showed the program earlier. With a maximum fine of $32,500 per station and affiliate and 111 in-stances, the total came to $3,607,500. Vowing to fight the new levy, CBS said the program bore the TV-14 rating with an additional warning to par-ents to supervise their teenage children's viewing of it. Clearly the worry about an increased crackdown on television programming in light of the Jackson affair has not been unfounded.[195]

Chairman Martin, a member of the FCC since 2001, said that there were three hundred thousand complaints from 2002 to 2005 about what was being shown on TV. The recent indecency fines, the first under his administration, he said, indicated that he shared the concern the complaints expressed. Social conservatives praised the new chairman's actions, and one observer concluded that such action by the FCC could not take place without strong public and congressional support.[196]

Such support was also evident when the Senate passed a bill to increase indecency fines. Long a supporter, the House quickly agreed, and President George W. Bush signed the changes into law on June 15, 2006. The legislation was purged of any other new restrictive measures, but it did raise the maximum fine for a single instance of indecency tenfold to $325,000 with a total cap of three million dollars on any single act.[197]

Some of the activity in Congress also tried to reach the world of cable, where the FCC has no content jurisdiction.[198] When Congress sought to require cable providers to include local broadcast channels in their service in 1992, the Supreme Court instructed the legislators that their control over broadcasting did not extend to cable.[199] In the Communications Decency Act of 1996, however, Congress sought to regulate cable by requiring channels with sexually oriented programming to either direct their programming to the safe harbor late night hours or filter out all signal bleed. Such bleeding often resulted in nude images or sexually explicit words or sounds finding their way to the screens of nonsubscribers. Congress received complaints about the unwanted receipt of "orgiastic moans and groans." This protest gave the provision in the 1996 legislation the nickname of "the *When Harry Met Sally* law."[200] It was so-named after the scene in the movie when Meg Ryan responded to Billy Crystal's challenge by faking an orgasm in a delicatessen, leading one envious woman to order whatever it was that Meg was eating. The members of the Supreme Court did not disagree with Congress on the need to respond to the situation, but the bare majority saw less restrictive alternatives to accomplishing the congressional goal. It found the daytime broadcasting ban of such content far too sweeping and suggested that targeted blocking in response to individual requests would be much less an imposition on free speech.[201]

FCC's chairman Martin urged cable operators to give parents more options in regard to choosing what cable channels come into their homes. Some industry executives complained that such à la carte channel availability would drive up costs and eventually make fewer channels available. The two leaders in cable, Comcast and Time Warner, however, indicated that they would make "family choice" tiers available to their subscribers. This response seemed to satisfy those members of Congress who were considering how to handle parental complaints about indecent programs on cable channels. Senate Commerce Committee chairman Ted Stevens of Alaska suggested that his colleagues wait to see if the "family choice" packages solve the problem.[202]

In an April 2005 survey conducted by the Pew Research Center for the People and the Press, responders saw greater danger in government restrictions on the entertainment industries than in the industries' production of harmful content. A majority held viewers, not the suppliers, of sexually oriented programming responsible. Also, the responders overwhelmingly held parents responsible for shielding children from such objectionable material. The best way to reduce sex in the media, the poll revealed, was by public boycott. Six years earlier a similar poll had placed television and the Internet in a tie for causing the greatest concern, but the Internet was well ahead now with television falling into a tie with music lyrics.[203]

That the Internet has moved to center stage in public concern over sexual content is not surprising given the unregulated world it inhabits, and to this medium we now turn.

THE INTERNET: THE OFTEN SILENT INTRUDER

With radio and television, the focus was on the receiving devices, which should mean that the spotlight here should be placed on the personal computer, the means by which the Internet is accessed. But the computer is such an all-in-one tool that a focus placed on content inevitably leads one to the Internet. The history of the Internet goes back to 1969 when a project sponsored by the federal government, to ensure communication in the event of a nuclear attack, launched what then was called ARPANET. It was a complex system connecting computers at major institutions of higher learning and was used by computer experts, scientists, engineers, and librarians. Commercial use was initially barred, but independent commercial networks began to develop that could bypass the government-funded backbone. All government sponsorship of that backbone ended in May 1995 and the global highway was open for commercial traffic.[204]

What enabled that traffic to grow so rapidly was first, the development and acceptance of the personal computer and second, the graphical interface with search engines that made a welter of material retrievable. Introduced in the mid-1970s, the personal computer grew in appeal. The introduction of the first graphical interface in 1993 quickly followed by Netscape and then later Microsoft's Explorer made the personal computer all the more attractive by supplying wide-ranging access to the multiplying resources of the Internet. Sales showed steady growth, and by 2005, two-thirds of American households contained a personal computer.[205] Public libraries supplied access to the Internet for those who did not have a computer at home.[206] In a positive fashion Congress noticed this rapidly developing form of electronic communication by passing new legislation. The law prohibited the disclosure of the contents of electronic mail and insulated providers of the service from governmental inquiry except when the requirements of the Fourth Amendment's protection against unreasonable searches and seizures were met.[207]

One of the things that made the Internet fascinating but threatening to custodians of the social order was its unpoliced nature. At a time when media conglomerates were getting bigger and the cost of access to traditional media was becoming prohibitive, here was a truly cheap medium. A real marketplace of ideas could be established, as anyone could publish. Cyberspace was quickly filled with competing voices, creating a postmodern Tower of Babel.

As with the VCR, consumers of pornography were attracted to the new technology.[208] One analyst for the Institute for the Future, a Silicon Valley organization, saw the relationship as follows: "Porn is to new media formats what acne is to teenagers. It's just a part of the process of growing up."[209] Even before the Internet, consenting participants communicating on bulletin boards had discovered cybersex. The French government, which had sponsored Minitel in 1983 as an alternative to phone directories, soon found that sexual messages accounted for up to half of the early traffic. That percentage would decline as other services began to exploit the network. Still in 1994, four of the ten most popular bulletin boards were sexually oriented and had almost two million correspondents. Time and space had been conquered as "improved graphics and higher transmission speeds . . . moved cyberporn from the secretive habit of the few to the enjoyment of the many."[210] What is more, passive consumers became active producers, as amateurs have utilized the Internet to compete with professionals, at times offering themselves to viewers for free.

The young have always been quick to catch on to new technology and parents soon found their children not only playing video games but also finding and exploring the many sexually explicit sites that proliferated on the Internet. Furthermore, graphical interfaces came with the ability to instantly communicate with strangers in what were called chat rooms. Here one could not only be anonymous but could also create an entirely different identity to engage others in conversation. A twelve-year-old girl could become an eighteen-year-old, and a sixty-year-old pedophile could become a star high school quarterback. The potential dangers here were real, and they led to an increased concern for the welfare of children and a crackdown on child pornography.[211]

With such real and pressing concerns came a renewed demand for censorship. The Internet was filled not only with nudity but sexual images that left no arena of sexual contact unexplored. How could it be made safe for children? As we have seen, the first stage in such a battle is to call upon government to do its duty and purge the offending medium of objectionable material. However by the time this new threat was perceived late in the twentieth century, the protection of free speech had widened considerably. Furthermore, the regulatory target occupied cyberspace where national borders mean nothing and anarchy reigns. So from the outset would-be censors were faced with substantial hurdles. Legislators, however, have a difficult time rejecting the desires of powerful constituent groups, who similarly resist being told that they cannot get what they want.

Additionally, the religious right had been working for years to get politicians elected to office who would do more than give lip service to a cultural agenda that saw the wide circulation of sexually explicit as a threat to the nation. Entertainment and commerce were hawking disturbing values that had to be suppressed. House Speaker Newt Gingrich made the midterm election of 1994 a referendum on what he called the Contract with America, and the Christian Coalition supplemented his economic and political program with a Contract with the American Family. In that supplement, item number ten was a proposal to regulate the Internet to protect children from sex in cyberspace. Bruce Taylor, a former federal prosecutor of obscenity cases and now executive director of the National Law Center for Children sought to translate the call into action by helping draft legislation that would accomplish the goal. He found Nebraska senator James J. Exon, a conservative Democrat, quite eager to introduce the bill.[212] It failed to pass in 1994 but after the results of the 1994 election, its prospects brightened. Republicans gained control of both houses of Congress and the religious right felt that the party owed it for its political support.[213]

Thus began a campaign to get this part of the agenda enacted into law, a campaign that would exemplify what could and what could not be done in regard to winning a battle in the culture war. Even the Senate chaplain, Dr. Lloyd John Ogilvie, got into the fray. He opened the June 12, 1995, session with a prayer that concluded with an appeal to God to "guide the senators as they consider ways of controlling the pollution of computer communications" to protect "the minds of our children and the future moral strength of our nation." When Senator Exon reread the prayer, Senator Patrick Leahy of Vermont, who was opposed to cyberspace regulation, suggested that the chaplain stay out of the debate and pay more attention to crafting his morning prayers.[214]

Supporters in the Senate liberally quoted from a yet unreleased study that *Time* would make into a dramatic and shocking cover story[215] and that the *Georgetown Law Journal* would publish in full.[216] From the standpoint of those seeking to censor cyberspace, the results were just too good to be true. The study, which had come out of Carnegie Mellon University, claimed that 83.5 percent of all digital images found in Usenet (the Internet's early name) newsgroups were pornographic. And the pornography ranged widely from hard-core heterosexual sex through every kinky variety known to man, woman, or beast.[217] Senator Charles Grassley of Iowa inserted the *Time* story into the *Congressional Record*.[218] Other sources including ABC's *Nightline* ran with the story, and soon it was being touted as "the Carnegie

Mellon study" and cited by individuals such as Ralph Reed, executive director of the Christian Coalition. However, less than three weeks after the magazine published the article, it was being referred to as "the *Time* Magazine Cyberhoax of 1995."[219]

Actually, the people at *Time* had been hoodwinked by Martin Rimm, "The Barnum of Cyberporn."[220] In an effort to scoop the journalistic world, the magazine had failed to verify the research study. Three weeks after the article's publication, *Time* responded to the welter of criticism that the article had generated by all but repudiating its findings and the credibility of Rimm. *Time* conceded that the very medium it criticized for its pornographic content was responsible for bringing facts to light that undermined the study. Donna Hoffman, one of two associate professors at Vanderbilt University whose assault on the study was massive, had been contacted by *Time* prior to the original story. She had warned the people at *Time* about problems with the statistics, but they ignored her. Now, however, they cited the criticism of Hoffman and her colleague at Vanderbilt, Thomas Novak, as "the most telling assault" on the study. What Rimm had done was conflate paid sites and public access sites, leading to the misleading 83.5-percent finding. To illustrate the effect of this error, Hoffman and Novak concluded that "pornographic files represent less than one-half of 1% of all messages posted on the Internet." Furthermore, Internet postings filled in details about Rimm. He was an undergraduate at Carnegie Mellon who did the study as a course exercise. He had a history of conducting suspect surveys. He also had self-published two books, one a series of stories about Atlantic City's casinos entitled *An American Playground* and the other, *The Pornographer's Handbook: How to Exploit Women, Dupe Men & Make Lots of Money*. *Time*'s mea culpa concluded by saying that "It would be a shame . . . if the damaging flaws" of the study obscured "the larger and more important debate about hard-core porn on the Internet." Fairness & Accuracy in Reporting responded: "Perhaps. But it would be an even bigger shame if concern about Internet porn were to obscure the perversion of journalism by the country's most powerful newsmagazine."[221]

Such repudiation of the Rimm study did little to slow the momentum of those representatives of the people who were intent upon using law to pursue the availability of pornography on the Internet and thus save America's young people from sex in its myriad forms. Exon had been aided by Republican senators Daniel R. Coats of Indiana and Grassley, who obligingly gave voice to the views of the Christian Right, buttressed by dubious statistics.[222] The horrors of what could easily be accessed on the Internet had to be exaggerated and the legislative process would have to be manipulated, but legislation referred to as the Communications Decency Act (CDA) was finally signed into law as Title V of the Telecommunications Reform Act of 1996.[223]

The act sought to protect children by criminalizing the knowing sending of indecent or obscene messages and those dealing with "sexual or excretory activities or organs" in patently offensive terms to any person under the age of eighteen. Newt Gingrich opposed the legislation on grounds that such vague language clearly would not survive constitutional scrutiny.[224] Separate suits challenging these provisions were quickly filed by the ALCU and the American Library Association. Both organizations and their supporters contended that the standards were too vague and that the conduct the statute criminalized was protected by the First Amendment. The suits were combined in *ACLU v. Reno* and were heard by a three-judge district court that agreed, thus confirming the Speaker of the House's prediction.

An important threshold question was how would the courts view the Internet? Would it be afforded the broad protection of speech and the press or would it be grouped with broadcasting, which originally because of the limits of the bandwidth, was afforded less protection than print? The district court's opinion traced the history of the Internet and revealed a sensitive understanding of the new technology in listing 123 findings of fact. Each of the three judges agreed with the result but wrote separately. Judge Stewart Dalzell's opinion agreed that the Internet had democratized communication, saying that it "has achieved, and continues to achieve, the most participatory marketplace of mass speech that this country—and indeed the world—has yet seen." Since the Internet "is a far more speech-enhancing medium than print, the village green, or the mails," it "deserves the broadest possible protection from government-imposed, content-based regulation." Any regulation, such as the CDA, the judge concluded, "no matter how benign the purpose, could burn the global village to roast the pig."[225]

Appealing the decision, the government perhaps hoped that the Supreme Court would confront this new technology with the same blindness with which it had confronted new technologies in the past. In 1915 motion pictures were declared to be entertainment and as such entitled to no protection under the free speech clause of the First Amendment.[226] In 1928 wiretapping by the federal government did not violate the Fourth Amendment's protection against unreasonable search and seizures because there was no physical intrusion of the individual's living space.[227] And in 1965 television cameras were banned from the courtroom because they violated the defendant's due process rights.[228]

An additional factor that would affect the appellate decision was the precedent the Court put on the books in 1989 when it invalidated a 1988 addition to the Communications Act of 1934. Worried about a growing commercial trade in phone sex and its accessibility to children, Congress sought to ban indecent and obscene messages so communicated. Although seven members of the Court had no trouble with the ban on obscene messages, all the justices agreed that the ban on indecent messages could not survive. The majority concluded that the denial to adults of indecent communications went further than "necessary to limit the access of minors."[229]

As the Court now looked at the attempt to regulate indecency on the Internet, it could neither escape the findings of fact spread on the record by the district court, nor could it overlook its own First Amendment precedents. Two members of the Court, Justice Sandra Day O'Connor and Chief Justice William Rehnquist were willing to save part of the statute as it applied to communications between an adult and a child, but even they acknowledged the unconstitutional burden its breadth placed upon adult communication. Justice John Paul Stevens wrote for the majority and paid tribute to the lower court's work by quoting liberally from its findings. Finding no reason to deny the Internet the full force of First Amendment protection, he concluded that "the CDA effectively suppresses a large amount of speech that adults have a constitutional right to receive and to address to one another."[230]

Another piece of 1996 legislation, the Child Pornography Prevention Act (CPPA), sought to expand the ban on child pornography to cover "any visual depiction, including any photograph, film, video, picture . . . or computer-generated image" that purports to show "a minor engaging in sexually explicit conduct." The law also defined child pornography to include any such image that was "advertised, promoted, presented, described, or distributed in such a manner that conveys the impression" of a child "engaging in sexually explicit conduct."[231]

If such pictures must be produced to satisfy the sexual desires of some people, is it not better that the children be virtual rather than real? Those legislators who were quite ready to erase any distinction between real and virtual children apparently were seeking to erase pedophilia. The movement of the lower federal courts to a more restrictive view on the circulation of sexually explicit materials, the result of the appointment of more socially conservative judges, can be seen in the course of litigation on the CPPA. In challenging the "appears to be" and "coveys the impression" provisions, only the Ninth Circuit Court of Appeals found the provisions overly broad and unconstitutionally vague. The First, Fourth, Fifth, and Eleventh Circuits disagreed, finding no constitutional defect in the statute.[232]

However, the Supreme Court sided with the Ninth Circuit. Justice Anthony M. Kennedy, for the six-person majority, said the provisions before the Court were overly broad because they snare materials that are not obscene and that are not produced by the exploitation of actual children. "Government," Kennedy said, "may not prohibit speech on the ground that it may encourage pedophiles to engage in illegal conduct." Protected speech, he continued, may not be suppressed for the purpose of banning unprotected speech. Justices Sandra Day O'Connor and Chief Justice William Rehnquist agreed that the law was too broadly drawn, but they did suggest that it might be permissible to draw adult only zones in cyberspace.[233]

Since the Supreme Court's invalidation of legislation did not forbid all regulation of the Internet, Congress decided to try again. In October 1998 the Child Online Protection Act (COPA) was tacked on to legislation dealing with the budget. It sought to sanction operators of online commercial sites for making sexually explicit materials available to children younger than seventeen. The operators would have to establish proof of age before delivering the material. Although more narrowly and carefully drawn than the CDA, the ACLU and other opponents said the law would lead to excessive self-censorship and deprive adults of material that they should be able to receive. A preliminary injunction against the act's enforcement was granted by the district court, approved by the Third Circuit Court of Appeals, and finally upheld by the Supreme Court in June 2004.[234]

In passing upon the injunction the Supreme Court, speaking through Justice Kennedy agreed with the appellees. "Content-based prohibitions, enforced by severe criminal penalties," Kennedy began, "have the constant potential to be a repressive force in the lives and thoughts of a free people."[235] The district court had granted the injunction on the basis that there were ways that were less restrictive of free speech to accomplish what COPA and its predecessor the CDA had sought to do. What the court had in mind was blocking or filtering technology that could be used without denying adults access to such sexual materials. The Supreme Court agreed and noted that in the years since COPA was enacted, technology had advanced to the point of making such filters better able to accomplish Congress's purpose—the protection of children from the sexual content available on the Internet. Filters would give parents the ability to monitor their children's viewing. The Court gave short shrift to the government's argument that it could not mandate their use, citing its recent decision that upheld the use of governmental incentives for schools and libraries to employ them.

The Court was referring to another piece of congressional legislation, the Children's Internet Protection Act.[236] In an effort to help public libraries and schools provide their patrons and students with access to the Internet, the federal government provided financial assistance through a couple of programs. Congress now conditioned such assistance on the installation of filters to block access to pornographic images and to other material that would be harmful to children. The American Library Association (ALA) challenged the regulation, contending that filters tend to block useful and constitutionally protected information. Justice David Souter in dissent agreed with the ALA, but the Court majority did not.[237]

To illustrate the ALA's point, if the letters "sex" were to be filtered out of communications, then the user could not receive, for instance, information about the sextant, the North Carolina lithographer Donald Sexauer, or Essex County in New Jersey. Libraries, the ALA insisted, were intended to be places of inclusion not exclusion. The ALA said that filters were intended for the home market, not public institutions such as libraries. As with V-chips in television sets, parents, the proper censors, should decide what electronic communications their children could receive.[238]

Another suggestion called for the rating of websites. Such self-administered ratings have freed the movie industry, television, and even the producers of recorded music from threats of governmental control. In each of these cases, despite the differences in the three areas, the ratings are administered by a relatively small number of persons providing at least some semblance of consistency. In the global world of the Internet where sites can be easily created there would be an infinite number of persons applying their own rating standards. No one would want to rely on such ratings.

How, then, can children be protected? We can start by asking, what are we seeking to protect children from? Although empirical evidence that children are harmed by exposure to sexually explicit material is lacking, the belief in some type of connection is tenaciously held. Certainly we want to protect children from predators, but laws exist that deal with such conduct. Furthermore, predators cannot be filtered out or eliminated by governmental censorship. In a society where the routes to governmental censorship have progressively been closed by an insistence on protecting speech and adult access, the only avenue that censors can travel is one seeking to protect children. The standards employed to determine a harmful influence, however, "are relative, culturally driven, and often employed rhetorically for political ends that may have little to do with any objective showing of harm to youth."[239] Notice, also, how poorly the talk of family values squares with the fact that most child sexual abuse occurs within the bosom of the family.

That the Internet has attracted federal lawmakers should occasion no surprise. That they have been so unsuccessful, however, might. This outcome is the result of a number of factors. Usually the courts are asked to confront new technology too early, before it can be fully comprehended. In the CDA cases, the judges almost instinctively saw the Internet as akin to print media, not to the other media in which some content regulation had been accepted. Second, First Amendment jurisprudence has developed greatly in the past century, and it presents a substantial hurdle to those who seek to restrict access to information. Finally, the Internet is part of a global community and as such tends to be resistant to national controls. This form of communication, coming as it did as the older channels of communication were being closed, was a democratic godsend. With just about anyone able to publish and reach out to others on the planet, the custodians of the old world were alarmed, just as they were when cheap written and pictorial material fell into the hands of the masses.

We can expect other attempts to control the chaos of cyberspace, but even a Supreme Court that is changing must contend with strong First Amendment precedent. Notice that only when Congress tied its regulation to its spending power in the Children's Internet Protection Act did the Court reject a free speech claim.

Epilogue

[T]he struggle between expression and authority is unending. The instinct to suppress discomforting ideas is rooted deep in human nature.[1] (Arthur Schlesinger Jr., 1984)

Theatre, art, literature, cinema, press, posters, and window displays must be cleansed of all manifestations of our rotting world and placed in the service of a moral, political, and cultural idea. Public life must be freed from the stifling perfume of our modern erotism.[2] (Adolf Hitler, 1927)

Part of the puritanical materialistic, technological basis of our culture requires us to de-emphasize and restrict sexual activity so that one can devote his energy to work. . . . The idea that pleasure could be an end in itself is so startling and so threatening to the structure of our society that the mere possibility is denied.[3] (Philip Slater, 1976)

Suppressing sexual fantasies—or insisting on politically correct ones—is bad politics, bad feminism, and a bad idea.[4] (Marjorie Heins, 1998)

From the very beginning of attempts to regulate sexually explicit material, censors were motivated by the belief that certain people should be protected from exposure to it either for their own, or for society's, well-being. Such people at times included children, women, the lower classes, foreigners, the weak, the impressionable, and those controlled by their emotions. As class, gender, racial, and ethnic biases were exposed and overcome, the only group that remained was children. The one remaining rationale for such censorship—the protection of children—has reconfigured the battlefield on which supporters and opponents clash. This situation is the result of social change, individual empowerment, and new interpretations of the law and of the Constitution.

All three of these elements are connected. With the mass of new immigrants in the late nineteenth and early twentieth centuries came greater diversity and challenge to what was viewed as a preexisting social consensus. This period is often referred to as the Progressive Era, a time of reform. Reformers believed that there was little that could not be reshaped by their efforts. Certainly the industrial society that had been created had to be addressed in a substantial way, but reformers believed that they could change morals as well. Attempts to regulate individual morality, however, tended to be resisted, whether the issue was Prohibition or access to sexual information. That resistance led to the involvement of the judiciary. In the post–World War I era, the United States Supreme Court began giving serious attention to claims of individuals that their rights were being invaded by government. This attention, in effect, empowered individuals by giving them a hearing, and, in many instances, redress as well. The Court's first focus was on the free speech and free press clauses of the First Amendment, which, in 1925, were held to be binding on the states as well. By the time the Court addressed sexual speech in 1957, it had built up considerable precedent in interpreting these key clauses of the First Amendment. With regard to sexual speech, the Court also had numerous decisions of the lower federal and state courts to aid it in its consideration. Because of its then recent decisions on racial segregation in the public schools and on the rights of political dissenters, the justices were not about to add to the legion of critics by freeing all sexual speech from government regulation. The result was a ruling that upheld both state and federal obscenity laws by characterizing obscenity as unprotected speech. Since obscenity possessed all the characteristics of speech, the Court was forced to distinguish protected sexual speech from the unprotected variety. Wrestling with this task, it produced a definition that freed much sexually explicit material from regulation. The Court would tinker with the definition but the gates had been opened.

Sexual material was increasingly fed into the public square by various producers. Whether these producers shaped or responded to public taste, the result was the same. As the country turned more conservative beginning in the late 1970s and early 1980s, the values in the public square seemed to be out of kilter with this shift in political sentiment. Nowhere did this seem more evident than in the presence of much sexually explicit material in the public arena. Social conservatives believed that they could win a battle of values by gaining political power through the election of representatives who seemed to share their views. What they found out was that control of the political process was more effective in distributing favors and benefits than in changing existing values. As social conservatives, with an agenda that included not only curtailing the availability of much sexually explicit material but also banning gay marriage and stripping the constitutional protection from abortion, were making substantial political gains, the entertainment industries, as they always had, were winning the values battle. When laws were passed to advance the agenda of the social conservatives, the legislation encountered the limits placed on government by the constitutional order.

Attempts of governments to restrict the availability of much sexually explicit material were usually struck down by the courts because they interfered with constitutionally protected adult access. Once the Supreme Court recognized an individual right to receive such material, with the exception of material that could be found to be obscene, the only path left to restriction was limited to protecting children. Rhetoric alone was not enough, and neither was a relationship between the regulation and child protection, for the regulation must not substantially limit adult access and availability. Although the belief that children are harmed by exposure to such material is tenaciously held, the asserted need to protect children is sometimes a stalking horse for greater censorship. Standards employed to determine a harmful influence tend to be "relative, culturally driven, and often employed rhetorically for political ends that may have little to do with any objective showing of harm to youth."[5]

Furthermore, censors often make no distinction between the five-year-old and the fifteen-year-old. As any social observer can attest, teenagers do not need television or the Internet to stir their sexual interest. Recognizing how in the twentieth-century adolescence has become "a prolonged period of immaturity, incompetence, and cultural separation," one critic has suggested that teenagers be "treated as adults and allowed to participate in economic, political, intellectual, and even sexual aspects of life." Instead of condoning or encouraging irresponsibility, such treatment, she suggests, may well make adolescents more responsible.[6]

Radio and television programming has become a battlefield upon which censors and free speech advocates clash because the looser standard of indecency governs. The need to bring order to the airwaves led Congress to create a federal agency to oversee the task. Despite an insistence by Congress that the agency created not engage in censorship, the FCC was charged with determining whether the licensees served the public interest and with cleansing the air of not only obscene speech but indecent speech as well. As we have seen, early in the story, obscenity and indecency were treated as synonyms. Whether, when the Supreme Court defined obscenity, it thereby defined indecency as well was unclear. Not until the 1970s did the Court answer the question. Its answer left the FCC free to establish its own definition, and the agency has proceeded to leave the matter vague and judge each instance in terms of its context. The justification for this lesser standard by which sexual speech can be censored by law is that the electronic media are visitors to the home and the programming can be heard and/or viewed inadvertently by unconsenting adults and children.

Even with the FCC's special authority to sanction indecency, however, when that agency sought to cleanse the airwaves completely of indecency by eliminating any safe harbor for such broadcasts, the courts struck down the regulation. Adults have a constitutional right to receive indecent material and the electronic provider cannot deny them this right in an effort to protect children.

An alternative justification for suppression of sexually explicit material was mounted in the 1980s by law professor Catharine MacKinnon and writer Andrea Dworkin. They contended that sexually explicit writing and images were not only degrading but also coercive, and as such, a major contributor to the oppression of women in American society. Even if pornography does not incite sexual harassment or violence, they said, it inevitably contributes to it.[7] In an age in which political correctness often challenges free speech, the argument they mounted was familiar—words and images themselves constitute discriminatory and harmful action.[8] Antipornography feminists, however, believe that pornography limits the potential of women. McKinnon drafted a model ordinance that sought to put the coercion of the law behind her ideas. It was adopted by the Minneapolis City Council, but the mayor vetoed it in the belief that it was unconstitutional because it restrained speech. When the council tried again, the mayor vetoed the revised version as well.[9]

Although the views of McKinnon and Dworkin have been challenged by feminists who embrace female sexuality as a step toward greater freedom for women, the pair have found support from other quarters. Culture wars, at times, produce strange bedfellows, perhaps none stranger than these two feminists and their newfound friends on the religious right. After some other abortive attempts to write their views into law,[10] such a coalition did succeed in Indianapolis, Indiana, in the Orwellian year of 1984. The American Booksellers Association (ABA) led the charge in contesting the constitutionality of the ordinance. Anticensorship feminists filed a supporting brief, contending that the censorship of words and images, far from aiding women, would have a tendency to stymie their quest for independence.[11] The reader by now is well aware of how censorship in the late nineteenth and early twentieth century operated to deny knowledge to women about their own bodies.

In the ordinance, pornography was defined as "the graphic sexually explicit subordination of women, whether in pictures or words." The law then listed instances of such subordination. Its violation was to be handled as any other instance of impermissible discrimination. The standards for judging obscenity—prurient interest, patent offensiveness, violation of the standards of the community, and an absence of literary, artistic, political, or social value—were all ignored. Speech referring to women as equals, no matter how sexually explicit, was acceptable; speech about women as sexually submissive was unlawful. District Judge Sarah Evans Barker had little difficulty in striking down the ordinance, for attempts to criminalize speech because it is politically incorrect have met with consistent rejection by the federal courts. However, she took the opportunity to instruct the ordinance's supporters on the value of free speech:

> It ought to be remembered by . . . all . . . who would support such a legislative initiative that, in terms of altering sociological patterns, much as alteration may be desirable, free speech, rather than being an enemy, is a long-tested and worthy ally. To deny free speech in order to engineer social change in the name of a greater good for one sector of our society erodes the freedoms of all and, as such, threatens tyranny and injustice for those subjected to the rule of such law.[12]

City authorities sought review of the decision, and the court of appeals agreed with the proponents of the ordinance that pornography was "a systematic practice of exploitation and subordination based on sex which differentially harms women" in their quest for equal rights in the society. However, the court continued, this conclusion only demonstrated "the power of pornography as speech," which, whether insidious or not, is protected by the Constitution. "Any other answer leaves the government in control of all the institutions of culture, the great censor and director of which thoughts are good for us." The court reminded the ordinance's proponents that the way to change what they find undesirable in the culture is not by suppression but by more speech. Such free public discussion, the court maintained, has always been the ally of change. Finally, to the request that the court carve out portions of the ordinance that survive a claim of unconstitutionality, the court said that it could find no "sensible way to repair the defect" without appropriating legislative power.[13] Without opinion, the Supreme Court simply affirmed the court of appeals decision.[14]

One of the provisions of the MacKinnon-Dworkin draft ordinance would have given victims of sexual assault the right to sue the pornographers whose material was found to have provoked an assailant's attack. Enlisting law to serve the agenda of the censor with potentially large monetary verdicts would so chill sexual speech that it would be driven from the public square. One might imagine that congressmen would have a greater regard for the First Amendment's protection of free speech than many of their constituents, but nothing comes with the office that ensures that result. In fact, some members of Congress in 1991 and 1992 tried to get their colleagues to support a Pornography Victims Compensation Act. The proposed legislation sought the same end as the provision in the Indianapolis ordinance—making unlimited damages available to victims who could make the case that pornography led the criminal to commit the act.[15]

The use of the law, however, is a two-edged sword in that there are now well-grooved paths of constitutional interpretation that frustrate censors. At times they believe that changing the judges will produce decisions that conform to their demands. To assume that there is no difference between politicians responding to constituents and judges responding to constitutional claims is to fail to understand the constraints of the judicial role. Federal judges and some state judges have life tenure, specifically to free them from popular reprisals. Most judges follow precedent, because such consistency serves an important ordering function both in law and in the diverse society. Despite repeated accusations, judges do not define themselves as policy makers whose job it is to write either their own or the majority's wishes into the law.

Still, as we have seen, censors do not have to invoke the law to secure their ends, especially within a capitalistic society where the market tends to be a significant regulator of content. For instance, in the early days of commercial radio and television, successful pressure was placed on advertisers to withdraw their sponsorship of objectionable shows. Times have changed and recently such pressure has proved less effective. That does not mean that corporate America is playing no substantial role in censoring speech, but its interests are not in censoring *sexual* speech.[16] In fact, by making sexually explicit material generally available, entertainment corporations tend to be a target of censors. In addition, the market for sexually charged programming has grown. If the marketplace is to be the determiner of public taste and acceptance, then certainly the ranting about such programming is doomed to fail. Politicians, however, are sensitive to their constituents' wishes, and proposals to censor continue to echo in legislative halls.

Such prodding or threats from the outside often lead to some form of self-censorship. In the area of motion pictures, self-censorship first came in the form of a code that was imposed upon filmmakers who wanted access to a controlled market. When that code was challenged in the 1960s, it was replaced by a ratings system. Both forms of self-censorship have succeeded not only in heading off government regulation, but also in protecting the industry from competition.

Critics wondered why such a rating system could not be applied to recorded music and television as well. Labels or ratings, long resisted by broadcasters and music producers, have grudgingly been accepted. They are self-administered, but unlike the movie industry with its centralized system, differing standards are employed by each producer. Such labels do, however, represent a compromise in an era where law is no longer the eager ally of the censor.

Despite the continuing suppression of obscene speech, clearly there is much, some would say too much, sexually explicit material available in the public marketplace. One social critic, Rochelle Gurstein, laments what she calls the repeal of reticence. She writes: "Obscenity was successfully regulated because there was a broad consensus about indecency, rooted in the old standards of the reticent sensibility." Nineteenth-century judges, she said, shared this attitude, and their "decisions drew attention to the way obscenity corrupted private morality and 'polluted' the public atmosphere." As later judges privatized obscenity, Gurstein continued, they contributed to "the deterioration of the public sphere, the coarsening of standards of taste and judgment, or the waning of the sense of shame."[17]

The consensus Gurstein saw was based on a deference to the taste of others, something that could not indefinitely survive in a society with a much longer and much stronger tradition of dissent. Religious and political dissenters settled the British colonies on the North American continent, and such challenges to authority would forever characterize the people called Americans. For instance, worries that new immigrants from Eastern and Southern Europe would bring changes to American society were on target, but the basic principles upon which the conglomerate society had been built would not change. In fact, those principles would serve the new immigrants perhaps even better than those groups that now expressed concern. Diversity and pluralism have become contemporary catchwords, but that diversity was ensured from the American society's very beginnings.

A second factor undermining that earlier consensus is a tendency of Americans to band together to achieve their goals.[18] In a society where interest-group politics has become the norm, this need to seek change or protection through interest groups has become only stronger over time. The story told here has illustrated the importance of interest groups on both sides of the struggle.

Gurstein's indictment of contemporary American society has a nostalgic feel to it—a yearning for a time when ignorance was preferred over knowledge, when freedom was limited by those who imposed their values upon others, and when the legal system was far less responsive to a need to protect individual rights. Critics, such as Gurstein, are captivated by the idea of a national community, but a homogeneous community cannot be constructed from a nation of diverse peoples. From its very beginnings the United States has been a nation that ensures its continued diversity by placing a premium on free speech and individual development and growth.[19] New judicial readings of what was obscene were the inevitable result of courts responding to individual claims that constitutional rights had been violated.

Any hope for an American community rests not on imposing one's views on others but on recognizing that any community in the United States must rest upon a foundation of respect for the diversity of its peoples and their rights. Contemporary society takes away neither reticence nor an ability to criticize and lead by example; it does, however place limits upon one's ability to limit the discretion of others. In placing the freedom to choose where it belongs—with the individual—the nation best realizes the liberty that is at its heart. In a society where speech is free, controversy will inevitably arise. Instead of seeking to suppress it, Americans should embrace it. A society that strives to avoid offense may make people more comfortable, but it can only be purchased with a substantial sacrifice of individual freedom.

Although interpretations of the First Amendment's prohibition on abridging speech have freed most speech and even expressive conduct from prosecution, certain types of sexual speech remain beyond its protective wing. Obscenity laws are still on the books, making sex the one subject that in certain expressive forms remains beyond the protection of the First Amendment. Obscene materials are prevented from entering the country and are banned from the mails and from interstate commerce.[20] Forty-three of the fifty states currently have legislation proscribing obscenity.[21] Furthermore, Morality in Media Inc., an organization founded in 1962 to "combat obscenity and uphold decency standards," provides individuals with online forms to report possible violations of the law and public officials with legal resources.[22]

This situation is unlikely to change for several reasons. First, the United States Supreme Court has shown no inclination to reconsider its 1957 decisions outlawing obscenity. In fact in 1973, by accepting local standards of judgment rather than a national one, it accommodated some censorship. Furthermore, changes in the Court's membership have created a bench less committed to protecting individual rights. Second, society will always have people who, for various reasons, feel the need to protect other persons or the social order itself. Third, sex censorship stems from the fact that human beings are both fascinated and repulsed by sex. The fascination has led to the omnipresence of sex in the marketplace, in advertising, and in the media generally. The repulsion and worry is continually evidenced in the repeated complaints and threats about the excessive presence of sex in the public arena. Finally, censors inevitably draw attention to the material they attack, giving it a visibility that, in turn, spurs its further creation, thus creating a symbiotic relationship. At one time censorship proceeded with limited public notice. That is not the case today. Censorship incidents now generate publicity and are quickly brought to the attention of concerned individuals and groups ready to do battle. The Internet's content has made it a target of censors, but its communications reach has aided greatly in publicizing censorship incidents and mobilizing support.[23] The fact that battles are waged, however, does not necessarily envision victory, meaning that sexual speech may well constitute an unconquerable frontier.

Endnotes

INTRODUCTION

1. Marjorie Heins, *Sex, Sin, and Blasphemy: A Guide to America's Censorship Wars*, rev. ed. (New York: New Press, 1998), xxxi–xxxii.

2. Peter Blecha, *Taboo Tunes: A History of Banned Bands & Censored Songs* (San Francisco: Backbeat Books, 2004), vii.

3. Horace M. Kallen, *Indecency and the Seven Arts, and Other Adventures of a Pragmatist in Aesthetics* (New York: Horace Liveright, 1930), 39.

4. John Heidenry, *What Wild Ecstasy: The Rise and the Fall of the Sexual Revolution* (New York: Simon & Schuster, 1997), 11.

5. Robert Friedman, ed., *The Life Millennium: The 100 Most Important Events & People of the Past 1,000 Years* (Boston: Bullfinch Press, 1998), 166.

6. Garth Jowett, *Film: The Democratic Art* (Boston: Little, Brown, 1976), 11–12.

7. "If the Age of Faith adopted the index of heresy, the Age of Divine Right the index of treason, it was inevitable for the Age of Democracy to adopt the index of sex." Morris L. Ernst and William Seagle, *To the Pure. . . . A Study of Obscenity and the Censor* (London: Jonathon Cape, 1929), 163.

8. Marcia Pally, *Sex & Sensibility: Reflections on Forbidden Mirrors and the Will to Censor* (Hopewell, N.J.: Ecco, 1994), 14.

CHAPTER ONE

1. Theodore Schroeder, *"Obscene" Literature and Constitutional Law: A Forensic Defense of the Freedom of the Press* (New York: privately printed, 1911; repr., Union, N.J.: Lawbook Exchange, 2002), 81.

2. Morris L. Ernst and William Seagle, *To the Pure. . . . A Study of Obscenity and the Censor* (London: Jonathan Cape, 1929), 145.

3. Radio commentator, H. V. Kaltenborn at the 1930 American Booksellers' Association convention, quoted in Paul S. Boyer, *Purity in Print: Book Censorship in America from the Gilded Age to the Computer Age*, 2nd ed. (Madison: University of Wisconsin Press, 2002), 135.

4. Jimmy J. Walker, state senator and later mayor of New York City, quoted in Herbert Mitgang, *Once Upon a Time in New York: Jimmy Walker, Franklin Roosevelt, and the Last Great Battle of the Jazz Age* (New York: Free Press, 2000), 59.

5. Boyer, *Purity in Print*, 118, 154. The following treatment of the Clean Books episode in New York is drawn from pages 99–127.

6. Boyer, *Purity in Print*, 99.

7. "The Worst Bill Yet," *New York Times*, 18 April 1923.

8. Boyer, *Purity in Print*, 107.

9. Boyer, *Purity in Print*, 118.

10. Boyer, *Purity in Print*, 119–23.

11. Ernst and Seagle, *To the Pure*, 152.

12. The *Index* would continue to 1966.

13. For instance, see James A. Monroe, *Hellfire Nation: The Politics of Sin in American History* (New Haven, Conn.: Yale University Press, 2003).

14. Dawn B. Sova, *Banned Books: Literature Suppressed on Sexual Grounds* (New York: Facts on File, 1998), 82–83.

15. Helen Lefkowitz Horowitz, *Rereading Sex: Battles over Sexual Knowledge and Suppression in Nineteenth-Century America* (New York: Knopf, 2002), 19–23. Horowitz's book traces the change from conduct to text over the course of the century.

16. A June 25, 1745, letter was suppressed by nineteenth-century compilers of Franklin's work but now is commonly included even in one-volume collections. For instance, see Walter Isaacson, ed., *A Benjamin Franklin Reader* (New York: Simon & Schuster, 2003), 124–26.

17. Olga G. and Edwin P. Hoyt, *Censorship in America* (New York: Seabury, 1970), 102–3.

18. Nicholas J. Karolides, Margaret Bald, and Dawn B. Sova, *100 Banned Books: Censorship Histories of World Literature* (New York: Checkmark Books, 1999), 284–85.

19. In colonial Massachusetts in 1711, a law was passed dealing with immorality in which one of the delineated crimes consisted of "composing, writing, printing or publishing of any filthy, obscene or profane Song, Pamphlet, Libel or Mock-Sermon, in Imitation or in mimicking of Preaching, or any other Part of divine worship." Although the preface to the act talked of the tendency of such material to "corrupt the Mind" and "lead to all Manner of Impieties and Debaucheries," this act did not seek to punish obscenity per se but rather blasphemy, a rather common offence in colonial America. Samuel Kneeland and Timothy Green, *Acts and the Laws of His Majesty's Province of the Massachusetts-Bay in New England* (Boston: Kneeland & Green, 1742), 183–86.

20. Morris L. Ernst and Alan U. Schwartz, *The Search for the Obscene* (New York: Macmillan, 1964), 15–16.

21. Karolides, Bald, and Sova, *100 Banned Books*, 402.

22. Karolides, Bald, and Sova, *100 Banned Books*, 386–88.

23. Noel Perrin, *Dr. Bowdler's Legacy: A History of Expurgated Books in England and America* (New York: Atheneum, 1969), 165.

24. Perrin, *Dr. Bowdler's Legacy*, 181–83.

25. Perrin, *Dr. Bowdler's Legacy*, 18–20, 160; and Comstock Act, 17 Stat. 599 (1873).

26. James C. N. Paul and Murray L. Schwartz, *Federal Censorship: Obscenity in the Mail* (New York: Free Press of Glencoe, 1961), 18–24, 29–30.

27. Act of February 8, 1897, ch. 172, 29 Stat. 512.

28. Joseph W. Slade, *Pornography in America: A Reference Handbook* (Santa Barbara, Calif.: ABC-CLIO, 2000), 66–71.

29. Heywood C. Broun and Margaret Leech, *Anthony Comstock: Roundsman of the Lord* (New York: Albert and Charles Boni, 1927), 16.

30. Walter Kendrick, *The Secret Museum: Pornography in Modern Culture* (Berkeley: University of California Press, 1996), 129.

31. Broun and Leech, *Anthony Comstock*, 83–93. The authors spell Haines with a "y" instead of an "i."

32. Alec Craig, *Supressed Books: A History of the Conception of Literary Obscenity* (Cleveland, Ohio: World Publishing, 1963), 44–45, 128.

33. See Margaret A. Blanchard and John E. Semonche, "Anthony Comstock and His Adversaries: The Mixed Legacy of this Battle for Free Speech," *Communication Law & Policy*, 11 (Fall 2006): 317–66.

34. Felice Flanery Lewis, *Literature, Obscenity & Law* (Carbondale: Southern Illinois University Press, 1976), 12.

35. Anthony Comstock, *Traps for the Young*, ed. Robert Bremner (Cambridge, Mass.: Belknap, 1967), 179.

36. Lewis, *Literature, Obscenity & Law*, 18–20.

37. Lewis, *Literature, Obscenity & Law*, 6–8.

38. *In re Worthingon Co.*, 30 N.Y.S. 361, 362, 363 (1894).

39. *St. Hubert Guild*, 118 N.Y.S. 582, 586 (1909).

40. Ex parte *Jackson*, 96 U.S. 727, 736 (1878).

41. *Swearingen v. United States*, 161 U.S. 446, 451 (1896).

42. *Rosen v. United States*, 161 U.S. 29 (1896).

43. Lewis, *Literature, Obscenity & Law*, 44–45.

44. Quoted in Lewis, *Literature, Obscenity & Law*, 47, 48.

45. Lewis, *Literature, Obscenity & Law*, 51.

46. "D'Annunzio at Asbury Park," *New York Times*, 24 July 1897.

47. In addition to the matters dealt with, an obscenity prosecution involving a production of George Bernard Shaw's play, *Mrs. Warren's Profession*, was also unsuccessful (Lewis, *Literature, Obscenity, & Law*, 54–57).

48. Lewis, *Literature, Obscenity, & Law*, 59.

49. *Commonwealth v. Buckley*, 86 N.E. 910, 911–12 (1909).

50. Elinor Glyn would go on to Hollywood and write screenplays, including the motion picture, *It*, which made Clara Bow a national sex symbol. Lewis, *Literature, Obscenity & Law*, 61.

51. Quoted in Lewis, *Literature, Obscenity & Law*, 65. In pages 46–72, the author provides a good sample of the offensive passages found in the books that were the subjects of obscenity prosecutions in the period before the United States entered the First World War.

52. *United States v. Kennerley*, 209 F. 119, 120, 121 (1913).

53. Boyer, *Purity in Print*, 20.

54. Lewis, *Literature, Obscenity & Law*, 67–68, 71.

55. Lewis, *Literature, Obscenity & Law*, 68–69.

56. Boyer, *Purity in Print*, 68–71.

57. *Halsey v. New York Society for the Suppression of Vice*, 136 N.E. 219, 220 (1922).

58. Lewis, *Literature, Obscenity & Law*, 41–42.

59. Boyer, *Purity in Print*, 71.

60. Boyer, *Purity in Print*, 73.

61. Guy Holt, ed., *Jurgen and the Law* (New York: Robert M. McBride, 1923), 9–11.

62. James Branch Cabell, *Jurgen: A Comedy of Justice* (New York: Robert M. McBride, 1919), 154.

63. Cabell, *Jurgen: A Comedy of Justice*, 125.

64. Padraic Colum and Margaret Freeman Cabell, eds., *Between Friends: Letters of James Branch Cabell and Others* (New York: Harcourt, Brace & World, 1962), 108, 121.

65. Emergency Committee, *Jurgen and the Censor* (New York: private printing, 1920), 15–19.

66. Emergency Committee, *Jurgen and the Censor*, 37–39, 47.

67. Holt, *Jurgen and the Law*, 57–68.

68. Holt, *Jurgen and the Law*, 74.

69. Boyer, *Purity in Print*, 78–81, 82, 83–85.

70. Sova, *Banned Books*, 85.

71. Boyer, *Purity in Print*, 86–87, 88–91.

72. Boyer, *Purity in Print*, 96–99.

73. Boyer, *Purity in Print*, 123–27, 134–43, 143–45.

74. Jay A. Gertzman, *Bookleggers and Smuthounds: The Trade in Erotica, 1920–1940* (Philadelphia: University of Pennsylvania Press, 1999), 150; and Bernard Guilbert Guerney, letter to the editor, *Publishers Weekly*, 8 April 1933, 1212.

75. Gertzman, *Bookleggers and Smuthounds*, 1.

76. Boyer, *Purity in Print*, 168–71.

77. Boyer, *Purity in Print*, 175–81.

78. Boyer, *Purity in Print*, 196–200.

79. Boyer, *Purity in Print*, 185–86, 192–94; and *Commonwealth v. Friede*, 171 N.E. 472 (1930). See also Karl Schriftgiesser, "Boston Stays Pure," *New Republic* 8 (May 1929): 327–29.

80. Boyer, *Purity in Print*, 190–92, 201–5.

81. Paul and Schwartz, *Federal Censorship*, 56. The proposal sought to add to the ban on obscene materials, literature "advocating treason, insurrection, or forcible resistance to any law," or threatening to "inflict bodily harm upon any person."

82. Boyer, *Purity in Print*, 212–21.

83. Paul and Schwartz, *Federal Censorship*, 59.

84. Paul and Schwartz, *Federal Censorship*, 60.

85. Boyer, *Purity in Print*, 239–40.

86. "Enemies of Society," *New Republic* 58 (May 8, 1929): 319; and Mary Ware Dennett, "What Mrs. Dennett Wrote," in Boyer, *Purity in Print*, 329–32.

87. Boyer, *Purity in Print*, 241.

88. *United States v. Dennett*, 39 F. 2d. 564, 568, 569 (1930).

89. Boyer, *Purity in Print*, 242–43.

90. *Near v. Minnesota*, 283 U.S. 697 (1931). The full story of the case is told in Fred W. Friendly, *Minnesota Rag: The Dramatic Story of the Landmark Supreme Court Case That Gave New Meaning to Freedom of the Press* (New York: Random House, 1981).

91. Boyer, *Purity in Print*, 237.

92. *United States v. One Obscene Book Entitled "Married Love,"* 48 F. 2d 821, 823, 824 (1931).

93. *United States v. One Book Entitled "Contraception,"* 51 F. 2d 525, 528 (1931).

94. Boyer, *Purity in Print*, 247–51.

95. *United States v. One Book Called "Ulysses,"* 5 F. Supp. 182, 183, 184, 185 (1933).

96. *United States v. One Book Called "Ulysses,"* 72 F. 2d 705, 706, 707, 711 (1934).

97. *United States v. Levine*, 83 F. 2d 156 (1936).

98. Boyer, *Purity in Print*, 237–38, 243.

99. Kendrick, *Secret Museum*, 178.

100. Emmanuel Cooper, *The Sexual Perspective: Homosexuality and Art in the Last 100 Years in the West*, 2nd ed. (New York: Routledge, 1994), 183.

101. Quoted in James Playsted Wood, *Magazines in the United States*, 3rd ed. (New York: Ronald Press, 1971), 94.

102. Joanne Meyerowitz, "Women, Cheesecake, and Borderline Material: Responses to Girlie Pictures in the Mid–Twentieth Century United States, " in Kathleen Kennedy and Sharon Ullman, eds., *Sexual Borderlands: Constructing an American Sexual Past* (Columbus: Ohio State University Press, 2003), 321–23.

103. Theodore Peterson, *Magazines in the Twentieth Century*, 2nd ed. (Urbana: University of Illinois Press, 1964), 376.

104. Peterson, *Magazines*, 376–78. *See also*, Olga G. and Edwin P. Hoyt, *Censorship in America* (New York: Seabury Press, 1970), 38–39.

105. Mark Gabor, *The Pin-up: A Modest History* (New York: Universe Books, 1972), 76–77.

106. Fowler, *Unmailable*, 161, 167–68.

107. *Hannegan v. Esquire, Inc.*, 327 U.S. 146, 149 (1946). If the postmaster general was sustained and *Esquire* was required to use fourth-class rates, its mailing costs would have been prohibitive, increasing by approximately five hundred thousand dollars. Theodore Peterson, *Magazines in the Twentieth Century*, 2nd ed. (Urbana: University of Illinois Press, 1964), 280.

108. James R. Petersen, *The Century of Sex: Playboy's History of the Sexual Revolution, 1900–1999* (New York: Grove Press, 1999), 173.

109. *Hannegan v. Esquire, Inc.*, 327 U.S. 146, 149, 150 (1946).

110. *Hannegan v. Esquire, Inc.*, 151, 158.

111. Boyer, *Purity in Print*, 262–69.

112. Petersen, *Century of Sex*, 169–72.

113. *Commonwealth v. Isenstadt*, 62 N.E. 2d 840 (1945).

114. Ernst and Schwartz, *Censorship*, 118–20; and *Attorney General v. Book Named "Forever Amber,"* 81 N.E. 2d 663 (1948).

115. Lewis, *Literature, Obscenity & Law*, 120–21; and *People v. Viking Press, Inc.,* 147 N.Y. Misc. 813, 814, 815 (1933).

116. *Attorney General v. Book Named "God's Little Acre,"* 93 N.E. 2d 819, 821 (1950). See also, Sova, *Banned Books*, 65–67 for a fuller treatment of the book's censorship history.

117. *Commonwealth v. Gordon*, 66 Pa. D. & C. 101, 110, 118, 138 (1949).

118. Fowler, *Unmailable*, 169–72.

119. Fowler, *Unmailable*, 173–75.

120. Peterson, *Magazines*, 378.

121. Gabor, *Pin-up*, 78.

122. For instance, a survey of censorship of erotic magazines, including *Playboy, Penthouse, Hustler*, and *Oui*, from mid-1973 through 1978, found almost all of the attempts directed at newsstands. See Jerald Nelson, "Erotic Magazines and the Law," in Peter Gellaty, *Sex Magazines in the Library Collection: A Scholarly Study of Sex in Serials and Periodicals* (New York: Haworth Press, 1981), 57. For attempts to cleanse libraries of such periodicals in approximately the same time period see Bruce A. Shuman and Karen Dalziel Tallman, "Sex Magazines: Problems of Acquisition, Retention, Display, and Defense in Public and Academic Libraries," in Gellaty, *Sex Magazines in the Library Collection*, 27–46.

123. Peterson, *Magazines*, 318.

124. "U.S. Court Upsets Ban on 'Playboy,'" *New York Times*, 31 October 1958.

125. *Doubleday & Co., Inc. v. New York*, 335 U.S. 848 (1948). For a fuller treatment of this prosecution and others involving the book, see Sova, *Banned Books*, 126–28.

126. The Supreme Court had made the First Amendment's free speech and free press clauses binding on the states in *Gitlow v. New York*, 268 U.S. 652 (1925).

127. *Butler v. Michigan*, 352 U.S. 380 (1957).

128. *United States v. Roth*, 237 F. 2d 796, 802 (1956).

129. *Roth v. United States*, 354 U.S. 476, 487, 489, 496 (1957).

130. *Roth v. United States* at 488, 489.

131. *Roth v. United States* at 513.

132. For instance, see *Sunshine Book Co. v. Summerfield*, 355 U.S. 372 (1958) and *One, Inc. v. Olesen*, 355 U.S. 371 (1958).

133. *Smith v. California*, 361 U.S. 147 (1959).

134. *Bantam Books, Inc. v. Sullivan*, 372 U.S. 58, 72 (1963).

135. D. H. Lawrence, *Lady Chatterley's Lover* (New York: Modern Library, 2001), 189.

136. For a detailed account of this case, along with some others, by the lawyer hired by Grove Press, see Charles Rembar, *The End of Obscenity: The Trials of Lady Chatterley, Tropic of Cancer, and Fanny Hill* (New York: Random House, 1968).

137. *Grove Press, Inc. v. Christenberry*, 175 F. Supp. 488, 499, 502, 503 (1959).

138. *Grove Press, Inc. v. Christenberry*, 276 F. 2d 433, 439 (1960).

139. Alec Craig, *Suppressed Books: A History of the Conception of Literary Obscenity* (Cleveland, Ohio: World Publishing, 1963), 152.

140. E. R. Hutchinson, *Tropic of Cancer on Trial: A Case History of Censorship* (New York: Grove Press, 1968), 91.

141. *Grove Press, Inc., v. Gerstein*, 378 U.S. 577 (1964).

142. Hutchinson, *Tropic of Cancer*, 91.

143. For the different views of women on such images, see Joanne Meyerowitz, "Women, Cheesecake, and Borderline Material" in Kennedy and Ullman, eds., *Sexual Borderlands*, 320–45.

144. Fowler, *Unmailable*, 175–76. See *Manual Enterprises, Inc. v. Day, Postmaster General*, 370 U.S. 478 (1962) in which the Court issued an opinion dealing with homosexual periodicals.

145. "Magazines: Two Definitions of Obscenity," *Time*, 21 June 1963, 44; "Publisher Gets Jury Trial on Nude Picture Charges," *New York Times*, 26 June 1963; and "Playboy Jury Deadlocked," *New York Times*, 8 December 1963.

146. Lewis, *Literature, Obscenity & Law*, 213; and *Attorney General v. A Book Named "Naked Lunch,"* 218 N.E. 2d 571 (1966).

147. *Kingsley International Corp. v. Regents of University of New York*, 360 U.S. 684 (1959).

148. *Manual Enterprises, Inc. v. Day*, 370 U.S. 478, 486 (1962).

149. *Jacobellis v. Ohio*, 378 U.S. 184 (1964).

150. Lewis, *Literature, Obscenity & Law*, 217–18.

151. Brief for Citizens for Decent Literature as Amicus Curiae, 67.

152. *A Book Named "John Cleland's Memoirs of a Woman of Pleasure" v. Attorney General*, 383 U.S. 413, 419 (1966).

153. *Ginzburg v. United States*, 383 U.S. 463 (1966). See also John E. Semonche, "Definitional and Contextual Obscenity: The Supreme Court's New and Disturbing Accommodation," *UCLA Law Review* 13 (August 1966): 1173–1213.

154. *Ginsberg v. New York*, 390 U.S. 629, 633 (1968).

155. Marjorie Heins, *Not in Front of the Children: "Indecency," Censorship, and the Innocence of Youth* (New York: Hill and Wang, 2001), 122.

156. Lewis, *Literature, Obscenity & Law*, 192–95.

157. *Redrup v. New York*, 386 U.S. 767 (1967).

158. Lewis, *Literature, Obscenity & Law*, 196–97. As examples, see *Aday v. United States*, 388 U.S. 447 (1967); *Corinth Publications, Inc. v. Wesberry*, 388 U.S. 448 (1967); and *Rosenbloom v. Virginia*, 388 U.S. 450 (1967).

159. Paul Siegel, *Communication Law in America* (Boston: Allyn and Bacon, 2002), 421. The provisions are sections 3008 and 3010 respectively of Title 39 of the U.S. Code.

160. *Rowan v. United States Post Office*, 397 U.S. 728, 736–37 (1970).

161. "Be It 'Nude' or an 'Orgy,' Concern Won't Print It," *New York Times*, 21 June 1973.

162. Robert Atkins, "A Censorship Time Line," *Art Journal* 50 (Autumn, 1991): 36. Both this issue and the Winter 1991 issue are devoted to censorship, and both issues contain numerous pictures.

163. *Caught Looking: Feminism, Pornography & Censorship* (East Haven, Conn.: LongRiver Books, 1992), 27, 28, 29.

164. Boyer, *Purity in Print*, 292.

165. *Miller v. California*, 413 U.S. 15, 24, 37 (1973).

166. *Kaplan v. California*, 413 U.S. 115, 116–17 (1973).

167. *Paris Adult Theatre I v. Slaton*, 413 U.S. 49, 57, 60, 68 (1973).

168. *Paris Adult Theatre I v. Slaton* at 113.

169. Richard Bolton, ed., *Culture Wars: Documents from the Recent Controversies in the Arts* (New York: New Press, 1992), 338.

170. William E. Brigman, "Politics and the Pornography Wars," *Wide Angle* 3 (July, 1997): 160–61; and *Pryba v. United States*, 900 F. 2d 748 (1990).

171. *Pryba v. United States*, 498 U.S. 924 (1990).

172. Philip D. Harvey, *The Government vs. Erotica: The Siege of Adam & Eve* (Amherst, N.Y.: Prometheus Books, 2001), 209, 253–60.

173. An offense may be "prosecuted in any district from, through, or into which such commerce, mail matter, or imported object or person moves" 18 U.S.C. § 3237 (1988).

174. Heins in *Not in Front of the Children* does offer an opposing view but it is couched more in terms of the absence of evidence of harm caused by the exposure to such material and the promotion of intellectual growth than in an acceptance of children as sexual beings, which is at the heart of Levine's work.

175. Judith Levine, *Harmful to Minors: The Perils of Protecting Children from Sex* (Minneapolis, Minn.: University of Minneapolis Press, 2002), 224–25. In a paperback edition published in August 2003 by Thunder's Mouth Press, Levine contributes an afterword that details some of the controversy generated by the publication of the hardcover.

176. John Habich, "Controversy Turns to Victory for 'U' Press," *Star Tribune* (Minneapolis, Minn.), 29 April 2003.

177. National Defense Authorization Act for Fiscal Year 1997, Pub. L. 104–201, sec. 343, § 2489a, 110 Stat. 2489, 2490 (1996).

178. "Pentagon Acts to Remove Sexually Explicit Materials from On-Base Stores," *St. Louis Post-Dispatch*, 25 September 1998.

179. *General Media Communications, Inc. v. Cohen*, 131 F. 3d 273 (1998).

180. *PMG International Division, LLC v. Cohen*, 57 F. Supp. 2d 916 (1999); and *PMG International Division v. Rumsfeld*, 303 F. 3d 1163 (2002).

181. For a sample of books challenged and the success of the censors, see Sova, *Banned Books*, 11–12, 24–27, 48–49, 51–54, 72–73, 155–57, 189–91. Defenses of challenged books can be found in Nicholas J. Karolides, Lee Burress, and John M. Kean, eds., *Censored Books: Critical Viewpoints* (Metuchen, N.J.: Scarecrow Press, 1993) and in Nicholas J. Karolides, *Censored Books: Critical Viewpoints, 1985–2000* (Lanham, Md.: Scarecrow Press, 2002).

182. Mark West, *Trust Your Children: Voices against Censorship in Children's Literature*, 2nd ed. (New York: Neal-Schuman, 1997), viii. This book has interviews with a number of authors of such literature.

183. Since 1952 the ALA has published the *Newsletter on Intellectual Freedom* that keeps track of attempts to remove materials from schools and public libraries. In addition the ALA sponsors a Banned Books Week in late September and compiles lists of banned books. The *Newsletter* began as a thrice yearly publication, quickly became a quarterly, and then in 1963 became the bimonthly publication it is today.

184. American Library Association, "The 100 Most Frequently Challenged Books of 1990–2000," www.ala.org/ala/oif/bannedbooksweek/bbwlinks/100mostfrequently.htm.

185. American Library Association, "The 100 Most Frequently Challenged Books of 1990–2000."

186. Some of the titles with the objections levied are described in Nancy Kravitz, *Censorship and the School Media Center* (Westport, Conn.: Libraries Unlimited, 2002), 79–80.

187. For coverage of this book and its censorship, see Sova, *Banned Books*, 51–53.

188. Edward Wyatt, "Literary Prize for Judy Blume, Confidante to Teenagers," *New York Times*, 15 September 2004.

189. *Newsletter on Intellectual Freedom* 54 (May 2005): 97.

190. Hillel Italie, "Book Ban Threats Decrease," *News & Observer* (Raleigh, N.C.), 30 August 2006.

191. The film of the story under the same name became the surprise motion picture hit of 2005–2006, garnering several best picture awards.

192. *Newsletter on Intellectual Freedom* 55 (January 2006): 37.

193. American Civil Liberties Union of Texas, "Free People Read Freely: An Annual Report on Banned and Challenged Books in Texas, 2003–2004, www .bannedbooks.info. The report contains brief synopses of the books and the reasons for the challenges.

194. For a look at the textbook controversies, see Joan DelFattore, *What Johnny Shouldn't Read: Textbook Censorship in America* (New Haven, Conn.: Yale University Press, 1992).

195. *Board of Education v. Pico*, 457 U.S. 853, 859 (1982).

196. William J. Brennan Jr. to Chief (Warren E. Burger), 22 June 1982, Brennan Papers, Manuscript Division, Library of Congress, Washington, D.C.

197. *Sund v. Witchita Falls*, 121 F. Supp. 2d 530, 541, 547 (2000).

CHAPTER TWO

1. George N. Gordon, *Erotic Communications: Studies in Sex, Sin and Censorship* (New York: Hastings House, 1980), 33–34.

2. Kent Willis of the Virginia chapter of the ACLU, *Richmond Times-Dispatch*, 19 May 2000.

3. Anthony Comstock, *Morals vs. Art* (New York: Ogilvie, 1887), 11.

4. John Frohnmayer, *Leaving Town Alive: Confessions of an Arts Warrior* (Boston: Houghton Mifflin, 1993), 6. These words were included in the remarks he made to his staff upon his firing as the head of the National Endowment of the Arts in 1992.

5. Craig Hines, "Keeping Abreast of Ashcroft's Prudery," *Houston Chronicle*, 3 February 2002, Outlook sec.; and Shirley Reiff Howarth, *C. Paul Jennewein, Sculptor* (Tampa, Fla.: Tampa Museum, 1980), 83.

6. Howarth, *C. Paul Jennewein, Sculptor*, 111–17.

7. Jennifer Harper, "Press Keeps Abreast as Justice Curtains Naked Statues," *Washington Times*, 29 January 2002.

8. Maureen Dowd, "A Blue Burka for Justice," *New York Times*, 30 January 2002.

9. Timothy J. Burger, "E-Mails Bare Coverup," *Daily News* (N.Y.), 17 July 2002.

10. After Ashcroft was succeeded as attorney general by Alberto Gonzales in 2005, the drapes were removed. Dan Eggen, "Sculpted Bodies and a Strip Act at Justice Dept.," *Washington Post*, 25 June 2005.

11. Helen W. Henderson, *The Pennsylvania Academy of the Fine Arts and Other Collections of Philadelphia* (L. C. Page & Co., 1911), 3.

12. Jane Clapp, *Art Censorship: A Chronology of Proscribed and Prescribed Art* (Metuchen, N.J.: Scarecrow Press, 1972), 106–7. This descriptive listing of incidents of censorship over the years is invaluable to anyone interested in researching the subject.

13. Morris L. Ernst and Alan U. Schwartz, *Censorship: The Search for the Obscene* (New York: Macmillan, 1964), 11–15.

14. Justice Potter Stewart, in *Jacobellis v. Ohio*, 378 U.S. 184, 197, believed that obscenity was limited to hard-core pornography, which, he said, he could not further define but then he added that "I know it when I see it."

15. This story is well told and illustrated in William H. Gerdts, *The Great American Nude: A History in Art* (New York: Praeger, 1978).

16. Ernst and Schwartz, *Censorship*, 18–20.

17. *United States v. Three Cases of Toys*, 28 F. Cas. 112 (S.D.N.Y., 1943) (No. 16499).

18. James C. N. Paul and Murray L. Swartz, *Federal Censorship: Obscenity in the Mail* (New York: Free Press of Glencoe, 1961), 17.

19. Wayne E. Fuller, *Morality and the Mail in Nineteenth-Century America* (Urbana: University of Illinois Press, 2003), 227–28.

20. Clapp, *Art Censorship*, 131–32.

21. Oliver W. Larkin, *Art and Life in America*, rev. & enl. ed. (New York: Holt, Rinehart and Winston, 1960), 181–83.

22. Larkin, *Art and Life in America*, 180–81.

23. Gerard Silk, "Uneasy Pieces: Controversial Works in the History of Art, 1830–1950," *Art Journal* 51 (Spring 1992): 23.

24. Fuller, *Morality and the Mail*, 98–101; and Harold L. Nelson and Dwight L. Teeter Jr., *Law of Mass Communications: Freedom and Control of Print and Broadcast Media* (Mineola, N.Y.: Foundation Press, 1969), 327. The Supreme Court case is *A Book Named "John Cleland's Memoirs of a Woman of Pleasure" v. Attorney General of Massachusetts*, 383 U.S. 413 (1966).

25. Paul and Swartz, *Federal Censorship*, 17–18, 251, 254–55.

26. Act of March 3, 1865, ch. 89, sec. 16, 13 Stat. 507.

27. Anthony Comstock, *Traps for the Young*, ed. Robert Bremner (Cambridge: Belknap, 1967), x–xiv. Comstock's role in securing the legislation and his position is told in Fuller, *Morality and the Mail*, 103–9. See also the legislation itself, Act of March 3, 1873, ch. 258, 17 Stat. 598.

28. Act of July 12, 1876, ch. 186, 19 Stat. 90.

29. Paul and Schwartz, *Federal Censorship*, 27–30.

30. Ex parte *Jackson*, 96 U.S. 727, 736 (1878).

31. Timothy J. Gilfoyle, *City of Eros: New York City, Prostitution, and the Commercialization of Sex, 1790–1920* (New York: Norton, 1992), 186–87, 196.

32. Heywood Broun and Margaret Leech, *Anthony Comstock: Roundsman of the Lord* (New York: Albert & Charles Boni, 1927), 153. For a treatment of how Comstock and his crusade fit into the tangled web of sexual conversation in the nineteenth century, see Helen Lefkowitz Horowitz, *Rereading Sex: Battles over Sexual Knowledge and Suppression in Nineteenth-Century America* (New York: Knopf, 2002).

33. *People v. Muller*, 96 N.Y. 408, 413 (1884).

34. Comstock, *Morals vs. Art*, 25.

35. Clapp, *Art Censorship*, 150, 153.

36. Clapp, *Art Censorship*, 159–60, 161–62.

37. Comstock, *Morals vs. Art*, 9, 10.

38. The amended statute is quoted in *Grimm v. United States*, 156 U.S. 604, 605 (1895).

39. Nicola Beisel, *Imperiled Innocents: Anthony Comstock and Family Reproduction in Victorian America* (Princeton, N.J.: Princeton University Press, 1997), 128–31, 142–43, 144–45.

40. *Rosen v. United States*, 161 U.S. 29 (1896).

41. *Grimm v. United States*, 156 U.S. 604 (1895).

42. Clapp, *Art Censorship*, 170, 171.

43. Broun and Leech, *Anthony Comstock*, 216–19, 238.

44. Leo Markun, *Mrs. Grundy: A History of Four Centuries of Morals Intended to Illuminate Present Problems in Great Britain and the United States* (New York: D. Appleton, 1930), 621.

45. Clapp, *Art Censorship*, 187–89.

46. Clapp, *Art Censorship*, 192–94.

47. Clapp, *Art Censorship*, 191–92, 194–95.

48. Tariff Act of October 3, 1913, ch. 16, 38. Stat. 114, 165.

49. "Nation-wide Fight on All Censorship," *New York Times*, 17 December 1923.

50. Comstock, *Traps for the Young*, xxvii.

51. "Finds Indecency Flaunting as Art," *New York Times*, 12 February 1922; and "Obscene Art Sends Covington to Prison," *New York Times*, 9 May 1922.

52. Clapp, *Art Censorship*, 214, 217–18, 231, 235–36, 261–62.

53. Jay A. Gertzman, *Bookleggers and Smuthounds: The Trade in Erotica, 1920–1940* (Philadelphia: University of Pennsylvania Press, 1999), 154–57. An illustration from the book is included.

54. Gertzman, *Bookleggers and Smuthounds*, 145–218.

55. Clapp, *Art Censorship*, 226.

56. Tariff Act of 1930, sec. 305, 46 Stat. 590, 688.

57. Clapp, *Art Censorship*, 234, 236, 240.

58. Tariff of 1913, Free List, par. 652, 38 Stat. 114, 165.

59. "Brancusi Bronzes Defended by Cubist," *New York Times*, 27 February 1927; and *Brancusi v. United States: The Historic Trial, 1928* (Paris: Adam Biro, 1999), 115. This book, translated from the French, except for the preface and the afterword, is simply a reproduction of the testimony and opinion in the case.

60. Clapp, *Art Censorship*, 221–22.

61. Robert Myron and Abner Sundell, *Art in America* (New York: Crowell-Collier Press, 1968), 67–68; and Steven C. Dubin, *Bureaucratizing the Muse: Public Funds and the Cultural Worker* (Chicago: University of Chicago Press, 1987), 162–63.

62. Don Whitehead, *Border Guard: The Story of the United States Customs Service* (New York: McGraw-Hill, 1963), 236–37, 239–40.

63. Paul Blanchard, *The Right to Read: The Battle against Censorship* (Boston: Beacon, 1955), 46–47.

64. See Huntington Cairns, "Freedom of Expression in Literature," *Annals of the American Academy of Political and Social Science* 200 (November 1938): 76–94.

65. Clapp, *Art Censorship*, 263, 265.

66. *Parmelee v. United States*, 113 F. 2d 729, 737 (1940).

67. "President Praises U.S. Art Freedom," *New York Times*, 11 May 1939.

68. Clapp, *Art Censorship*, 256, 260.

69. Clapp, *Art Censorship*, 267–68

70. Clapp, *Art Censorship*, 271–72, 273.

71. Clapp, *Art Censorship*, 378. The mural is pictured on the website of Hillyer Art Library at www.smith.edu/libraries/libs/hillyer/mural.htm. The artist's statement about the piece, from which the first quote in the paragraph above is taken, is at www.smith.edu/libraries/libs/hillyer/rtstmnt.htm. The fresco was returned to Smith College in 2003 and mounted in a large atrium between the Fine Arts Center and a building housing the Department of Art.

72. See John D'Emilio and Estelle B. Freedman, *Intimate Matters: A History of Sexuality in America*, 2nd ed. (Chicago: University of Chicago Press, 1997), 288–90, picture no. 60; and Maria Elena Buszek, *Pin-Up Girls: Feminism, Sexuality, Popular Culture* (Durham, N.C.: Duke University Press, 2006), 185–231.

73. See Francine Carraro, "Seeing Red: The Dallas Museum in the McCarthy Era," in *Suspended License: Censorship and the Visual Arts*, ed. Elizabeth C. Childs (Seattle: University of Washington Press, 1997), 235–58.

74. Clapp, *Art Censorship*, 281–83.

75. "Museums Demand Freedom for Arts," *New York Times*, 28 March 1950.

76. Janet Cleves, "Modern Heresy," *Catholic World* 165 (April 1947): 79–80.

77. "Pope Condemns Art in Abstract Forms," *New York Times*, 6 September 1950.

78. Paul and Schwartz, *Federal Censorship*, 108, 280. Some observers credit the speedy acceptance of digital cameras to the desire of photographers to take the type of pictures that neither Kodak nor other developers would print.

79. "Postal Ban Falters: U.S. Won't Press Fight to Keep Nude Study from Mails, *New York Times*, 5 October 1959.

80. Peyton Boswell, "Banned in Boston, Ltd.," *Art Digest* 21 (December 1, 1946): 3.

81. "Life in Massachusetts," *Newsletter on Intellectual Freedom* 5 (December 1956): 1.

82. Clapp, *Art Censorship*, 286–88.

83. "Pittsfield Bars Breughel Painting," *New York Times*, 2 December 1951.

84. David Dempsey, "Books and Men: The Revolution in Books," *Atlantic Monthly* 191 (January 1953): 76.

85. Clapp, *Art Censorship*, 304, 308–9.

86. *Roth v. United States*, 354 U.S. 476, 489 (1957).

87. Anthony Lewis, "'Who Sees It' Held Test of Obscenity," *New York Times*, 3 January 1958.

88. Clapp, *Art Censorship*, 322–23.

89. Thomas Buchsteiner and Otto Letze, eds., *Tom Wesselman* (New York: Distributed Art Publishers, 1996), 11. This volume, based on an exhibition, reproduces a range of the artist's work.

90. Eric Fischl, *Eric Fischl, 1970–2000* (New York: Monacelli Press, 2000), 16. One of Fischl's paintings, showing a naked woman on a bed with her legs spread and a young boy viewing her as he puts his hand into her purse, is reprinted as a

frontispiece. For a selection of David Salle's work, see Janet Kardon, *David Salle* (Philadelphia: Institute of Contemporary Art, University of Pennsylvania, 1986).

91. Fischl, *Eric Fischl*, 337.

92. Fischl, *Eric Fischl*, 340–41.

93. Ben A. Franklin, "Anatomic Paintings Taken Off Walls at State Department," *New York Times*, 14 October 1965.

94. Gerald Silk, "Censorship and Controversy in the Career of Edward Kienholz," in *Suspended License*, 259–98.

95. John Canaday, *Culture Gulch: Notes on Art and Its Public in the 1960s* (New York: Farrar, Straus & Giroux, 1969), 34.

96. D. J. R. Bruckner, "Art Censors Bluster in the Windy City," *Los Angeles Times*, 12 March 1970, Calendar 39.

97. Clapp, *Art Censorship*, 354, 355, 358.

98. "A Sign of Changing Times: Coast Statue Sheds Fig Leaf," *New York Times*, 20 July 1969.

99. William Wilson, "Obscenity Charge Dropped," *Los Angeles Times*, 25 October 1970, Calendar, 60.

100. *Griswold v. Connecticut*, 381 U.S. 479 (1964).

101. *Stanley v. Georgia*, 354 U.S. 557, 566 (1969).

102. Clapp, *Art Censorship*, 375, 381.

103. "Parts of U.S. Law on Obscenity Voided," *Los Angeles Times*, 29 January 1970.

104. "U.S. Court Voids Ban on Obscene Matter," *New York Times*, 9 June 1970.

105. *United States v. Thirty-Seven Photographs*, 402 U.S. 363, 388 (1971).

106. *United States v. Reidel*, 402 U.S. 351 (1971).

107. Jules Witcover, "The Secret Study of Sex: Battle behind Scenes," *Los Angeles Times*, 23 March 1970.

108. "Of Note," *American Libraries* 1 (July/August 1970): 635.

109. "Report on Pornography 'Rigged,' Inquiry Told," *Los Angeles Times*, 12 August 1970.

110. "Obscenity Study Unit Accused of Relying on Incompetent Staff," *Los Angeles Times*, 21 August 1970.

111. "Pornography Report Barred by Injunction," *Los Angeles Times*, 10 September 1970.

112. Don Irwin," Report on Pornography Issued Amid Dissent," *Los Angeles Times*, 1 October 1970.

113. "Senate Repudiates Pornography Report," *Los Angeles Times*, 14 October 1970.

114. "Nixon Repudiates U.S. Commission's Obscenity Report," *Los Angeles Times*, 25 October 1970.

115. "Obscenity Study Edition Brings Indictments," *Library Journal* 96 (April 15, 1971): 1312.

116. Richard Bolton, ed., *Culture Wars: Documents from the Recent Controversies in the Arts* (New York: New Press, 1992), 337, 339.

117. Amelia Jones, ed., *Sexual Politics: Judy Chicago's Dinner Party in Feminist Art History* (Los Angeles: University of California Press, 1996), 10. This volume contains a number of essays that detail the way in which the *Dinner Party* has been viewed over time.

118. Steven C. Dubin, *Arresting Images: Impolitic Art and Uncivil Actions* (New York: Routledge, 1992), 128–31.

119. Elizabeth A. Sackler, ed., *Judy Chicago* (New York: Watson-Guptill, 2002), 5. See also, *Newsletter on Intellectual Freedom* 39 (November 1990): 213–15.

120. Lawrence Alloway, "Art," *Nation* 218 (April 20, 1974): 510.

121. *Newsletter on Intellectual Freedom* 22 (September 1973): 116.

122. Dennis Adrian, "In Evanston, a Fuss over Nudes," *Chicago Daily News*, 6 June 1974.

123. *Newsletter on Intellectual Freedom* 23 (November 1974): 155–56.

124. "John Hancock Says No to Anatomy Photos," *Washington Post*, 6 June 1977.

125. "Americana: Private Showing," *Time* 111(May 29, 1978), 27.

126. *Newsletter on Intellectual Freedom* 28 (May 1979): 60.

127. Kyra Belán, "Male Nudes Still Draw Hostility in Art World," *New Directions for Women* 9 (November/December 1980): 7.

128. Alyce Mahon, *Eroticism & Art* (New York: Oxford University Press, 2005), 228.

129. *Newsletter on Intellectual Freedom* 30 (January 1981): 46.

130. "Picasso Etching Saved from Fire," *New York Times*, 1 August 1987.

131. Beauvais Lyons, "Artistic Freedom and the University," *Art Journal* 50 (Winter 1991): 80.

132. *Newsletter on Intellectual Freedom* 30 (July 1981): 96.

133. *Newsletter on Intellectual Freedom* 30 (July 1981): 96.

134. *Newsletter on Intellectual Freedom* 37 (May 1988): 101.

135. *Newsletter on Intellectual Freedom* 38 (May 1989): 83.

136. *Newsletter on Intellectual Freedom* 38 (November 1989): 222.

137. Katherine Bishop, "Photos of Nude Children Spark Obscenity Debate," *New York Times*, 23 July 1990.

138. *Newsletter on Intellectual Freedom* 39 (September 1990): 173–74; and *Newsletter on Intellectual Freedom* 41 (January 1992): 23–24. In 1996 the three books of his photographs that Sturges published became the focus of an attack stimulated by Operation Rescue founder Randall Terry. Sturges's photos of nude children and teenagers were the cause of the demonstrations (*Newsletter on Intellectual Freedom* 46 [November 1997]: 164). Barnes and Noble bookstores continued to be the target of protest, and the company was indicted on child pornography charges in Montgomery Alabama, one of the offending titles being a Sturges book. The photographer notes that the indictment had the effect of causing a run on the books, including his, causing him to remark, "It is a reliable irony that when people seek to repress things, they wind up promoting them" (*Newsletter on Intellectual Freedom* 47 [May 1998]: 65–67).

139. Svetlana Mintcheva, "Protection or Politics? The Use and Abuse of Children," in *Censoring Culture: Contemporary Threats to Free Expression*, ed. Robert Atkins and Svetlana Mintcheva (New York: New Press, 2006), 172.

140. Marian Rubin, Jacqueline Livingston, Marilyn Zimmerman, and Betsy Schneider, "'Not a Pretty Picture': Four Photographers Tell Their Personal Stories about Child 'Pornography' and Censorship," in Atkins and Mintcheva, *Censoring Culture*, 212–27.

141. Michael Hardy and Bill Kelway, "Gilmore Scolds Museum: He Demands Guidelines after Unsigned Letter Complains about Mann's 'Disturbing' Photos," *Richmond Times Dispatch*, 19 May 2000.

142. Lawrence A. Stanley, "Art and 'Perversion': Censoring Images of Nude Children," *Art Journal* 50 (Winter 1991): 22–23. For a more extended treatment, see Lawrence A. Stanley, "The Child Porn Myth," *Cardozo Arts and Entertainment Law Journal* 7 (1989): 295–358.

143. The budget figures are at www.nea.gov/about/Facts/AppropriationsHistory .html.

144. Dubin, *Arresting Images*, 282–83; and Joseph Wesley Zeigler, *Arts in Crisis: The National Endowment for the Arts versus America* (Chicago: A Cappella Books, 1994), 29. Zeigler deals with a number of interesting questions involving public funding of the arts and demonstrates how funding of individual artists has been a small part of the NEA budget.

145. Bolton, *Culture Wars*, 106–8. The book contains a full documentary record of the controversy from 1989 to 1991, along with a chronology dealing with censorship from 1962 to 1990.

146. Steven C. Dubin, "The Trials of Robert Mapplethorpe," in Childs, *Suspended License*, 371–72.

147. Bolton, *Culture Wars*, 121, 346–48, 349, 353–57.

148. *Bella Lewitsky Dance Foundation v. Frohnmayer*, 754 F. Supp. 744 (C.D. California 1991).

149. Bolton, *Culture Wars*, 358–62; and *National Endowment for the Arts v. Finley*, 524 U.S. 569 (1998)

150. Bolton, *Culture Wars*, 347, 349.

151. Steven C. Dubin, *Arresting Images*, 284–86.

152. John Frohnmayer, *Leaving Town Alive: Confessions of an Arts Warrior* (Boston: Houghton Mifflin, 1993), 6.

153. Patti Hartigan, "Mapplethorpe's 'Chilling Effect': A Year Later, the Battle Goes On," *Boston Globe*, 6 October 1991. See also Dubin, "Trials of Robert Mapplethorpe," 374–79.

154. Edward Lucie-Smith, *Sexuality in Western Art* (New York: Thames and Hudson, 1991), 266.

155. Lyons, "Artistic Freedom and the University," 79–80.

156. Some of the episodes in which these concerns surfaced are covered in Dubin, *Arresting Images*, 125–96.

157. *National Endowment for the Arts v. Finley*, 524 U.S. 569 (1998).

158. Michael Welzenback, "An Inch of Prevention: Fearing Protests, Officials Alter Nude Sculpture," *Washington Post*, 4 July 1989.

159. *Newsletter on Intellectual Freedom* 42 (January 1993): 30–31.

160. *Newsletter on Intellectual Freedom* 42 (March 1993): 46–47.

161. "Idaho State U. Accused of Censoring Local Artists," *Chronicle of Higher Education* 39 (March 10, 1933): A5.

162. *Newsletter on Intellectual Freedom* 44 (January 1995): 26.

163. For a brief treatment of this matter, see the epilogue. For a more extensive review, see Donald Alexander Downs, *The New Politics of Pornography* (Chicago: University of Chicago Press, 1989).

164. Dubin, *Arresting Images*, 310–11.

165. Ruth Sinai, "Artist Accuses CIA of Censoring Her Work," *Sun* (Baltimore, Md.), 1 October 1993.

166. *Newsletter on Intellectual Freedom* 43 (March 1994): 68, 160, 203.

167. *Newsletter on Intellectual Freedom* 45 (May 1996): 106; *Newsletter on Intellectual Freedom* 45 (July 1996): 136; and *Newsletter on Intellectual Freedom* 45 (September 1996): 170–71.

168. *Newsletter on Intellectual Freedom* 46 (January 1997): 15 and *Newsletter on Intellectual Freedom* 48 (May 1999): 72.

169. *Newsletter on Intellectual Freedom* 55 (January 2006): 15.

170. *Newsletter on Intellectual Freedom* 44 (May 1995): 75.

171. Lynne A. Munson, "Art by Committee," *New York Times*, 21 September 1995.

172. Philip Pearlstein, "Continue Arts Grants," *New York Times*, 27 September 1995.

173. *Newsletter on Intellectual Freedom* 44 (July 1995): 118 and Newsletter on Intellectual Freedom 45 (March 1996): 61.

174. *Newsletter on Intellectual Freedom* 45 (May 1996): 107.

175. *Newsletter on Intellectual Freedom*, 47 (January 1998): 10, 17.

176. Robyn E. Blumner, "The Public Can Handle It," *St. Petersburg Times*, 1 February 1998.

177. *Bery v. City of New York*, 97 F. 3d 689, 695 (1996).

178. This story can be pieced together following the relevant descriptive links at www.theroc.org/roc-news/entertain.htm.

179. *Newsletter on Intellectual Freedom* 52 (May 2003): 122.

180. *Newsletter on Intellectual Freedom* 51 (May 2002): 137.

181. *Newsletter on Intellectual Freedom* 52 (September 2003): 183.

182. *Newsletter on Intellectual Freedom* 55 (March 2006): 99–100. A picture of the controversial mural can be found at www.ncac.org/art/20050111~TX-Pilot_Point~No_Nudes_Allowed_in_Texas.cfm.

183. The full story is provided at www.artrenewal.org/articles/2006/Peter_Panse/case1.asp.

184. Ralph Blumenthal, "Museum Field Trip Deemed Too Revealing," *New York Times*, 30 September 2006.

CHAPTER THREE

1. Jean Cocteau as quoted on the title page of Alexander Walker, *Celluloid Sacrifice: Aspects of Sex in the Movies* (New York: Hawthorn Books, 1966).

2. Murray Schumach, *The Face on the Cutting Room Floor: The Story of Movie and Television Censorship* (New York: Morrow, 1964), 3.

3. David Shipman, *The Story of the Cinema: An Illustrated History*, vol. 1 (London: Hodder and Stoughton, 1982), 155.

4. William C. DeMille, *Hollywood Saga* (New York: Dutton, 1939), 252.

5. Gerald Gardner, *The Censorship Papers: Movie Censorship Letters from the Hays Office, 1934–1968* (New York: Dodd, Mead, 1987), 209.

6. Gregory D. Black, *Hollywood Censored: Morality Codes, Catholics, and the Movies* (Cambridge, England: Cambridge University Press, 1994), 72–75.

7. Black, *Hollywood Censored*, 74.

8. Black, *Hollywood Censored*, 75–77, 78, 80.

9. The actual story is more complex, but West's films were a factor. See Mary-beth Hamilton, *When I'm Bad, I'm Better: Mae West, Sex, and American Entertainment* (New York: HarperCollins, 1995), 194–95; and Ramano Curry, *Too Much of a Good Thing: Mae West as Cultural Icon* (Minneapolis: University of Minnesota Press, 1996), 25–26.

10. Black, *Hollywood Censored*, 78–80.

11. Frank Miller, *Censored Hollywood: Sex, Sin, & Violence on the Screen* (Atlanta: Turner Publishing, 1994), 95–100.

12. *New York World*, 26 April 1896.

13. "Home-Made Comic Plays: May Irwin in McNally's New Farce," *New York Times*, 17 September 1895.

14. *New York World*, April 26, 1896.

15. John L. Fell, ed., *Film before Griffith* (Berkeley: University of California Press, 1983), 26.

16. Ruth A. Inglis, *Freedom of the Movies* (Chicago: University of Chicago Press, 1947), 2; and Kenneth Macgowan, *Behind the Screen: The History and Techniques of the Motion Picture* (New York: Delacorte Press, 1965), 95.

17. Terry Ramsaye, *A Million and One Nights: A History of the Motion Picture* (New York: Simon & Schuster, 1926), 258–60.

18. Shipman, *Story of the Cinema*, 19.

19. The before and after images are on view in Michael Milner, *Sex on Celluloid* (New York: Macfadden Books, 1964), 161.

20. Michael Leach, *I Know It When I See It: Pornography, Violence and Public Sensitivity* (Philadelphia: Westminster Press, 1975), 33; and Ramsaye, *Million and One Nights*, 296. For even earlier censorship of kinetoscope films, see Gordon Hendricks, *The Kinetoscope: America's First Commercially Successful Motion Picture Exhibitor* (New York: Beginnings of American Film, 1966), 77–78.

21. See John H. Houchin, *Censorship of the American Theatre in the Twentieth Century* (Cambridge: Cambridge University Press, 2003).

22. The distinction was not always made. For instance, in New York City a stage presentation of *Orange Blossoms* that involved a discrete undressing of a woman in preparation for her wedding night led to an indictment of the theater owner for "maintaining a public nuisance." The court condemned the scene's suggestion of indecency, saying that with an immoral suggestion "the more that is left to imagination the more subtle and seductive the influence" (*People v. Doris*, 14 App. Div. 117, 119 [1st Dept., 1897]). Some writers have mistakenly identified the medium in this case as a movie. For instance, see Garth Jowett, *Film: The Democratic Art* (Boston: Little, Brown, 1976), 109.

23. Richard S. Randall, *Censorship of the Movies: The Social and Political Control of a Mass Medium* (Madison: University of Wisconsin Press, 1968), 3.

24. Jowett, *Film*, 98–100. See also, "The Drama of the People," *Independent*, September 29, 1910, reprinted in Gerald Mast, ed., *The Movies in Our Midst: Documents in the Cultural History of Film in America* (Chicago: University of Chicago Press, 1982), 56–58.

25. Only later would we come to associate film censorship with more rural and provincial attitudes rather than the cosmopolitan views we now associate with urban life.

26. Ramsaye, *Million and One Nights*, 473, 474. Vaudeville houses used films to entertain the audience between acts.

27. Ramsaye, *Million and One Nights*, 474–75.

28. *Block v. Chicago*, 239 Ill. 251, 258, 87 N.E. 1011, 1014 (1909).

29. *Block v. Chicago* at 1015, 1016. See also, Randall, *Censorship of the Movies*, 11–12.

30. Ira H. Carmen, *Movies, Censorship and the Law* (Ann Arbor: University of Michigan Press, 1966), 189.

31. *Fox Film Corp. v. Chicago*, 247 F. 231 (1917), *affirmed* 251 F. 883, 884 (1918).

32. Lary May, *Screening Out the Past: The Birth of Mass Culture and the Motion Picture Industry* (New York: Oxford University Press, 1980), 44–46. See also, Nicola Beisel, *Imperiled Innocents: Anthony Comstock and Family Reproduction in Victorian America* (Princeton, N.J.: Princeton University Press, 1997), 3–7, 199–204.

33. Richard Abel, *The Red Rooster Scare: Making Cinema American, 1900–1910* (Berkeley: University of California Press, 1999), 97–98. See also Lee Grieveson, *Policing Cinema: Movies and Censorship in Early-Twentieth-Century America* (Berkeley: University of California Press, 2004), 37–77. The movie title itself indicated sympathy for Thaw, who a jury found not guilty by reason of insanity.

34. Ramsaye, *Million and One Nights*, 475. Another movie, *Escape from the Asylum*, also dealt with the episode and was credited and discredited for engendering sympathy for Thaw and illustrating the persuasive power of the new medium (Jowett, *Film*, 64).

35. Ramsaye, *Million and One Nights*, 113.

36. Ramsaye, *Million and One Nights*, 477–79.

37. The story of the national board is told in Charles Matthew Feldman, *The National Board of Censorship (Review) of Motion Pictures, 1909–1922* (New York: Arno Press, 1977). See also Matthew Bernstein, ed., *Controlling Hollywood: Censorship and Regulation in the Studio Era* (New Brunswick, N.J.: Rutgers University Press, 1999), 41–59.

38. Frank Walsh, *Sin and Censorship: The Catholic Church and the Motion Picture Industry* (New Haven, Conn.: Yale University Press, 1996), 8–9.

39. Bernstein, *Controlling Hollywood*, 18–21.

40. For a treatment of this episode, see Annette Kuhn, *Cinema, Censorship and Sexuality, 1909–1925* (London: Routledge, 1988), 28–37; and Kevin Brownlow, *Behind the Mask of Innocence* (New York: Knopf, 1990), 50–55.

41. Marcia Pally, *Sex & Sensibility: Reflections on Forbidden Mirrors and the Will to Censor* (Hopewell, N.J.: Ecco, 1994), 132.

42. Quoted in Browlow, *Beyond the Mask*, 9, 11.

43. Randall, *Censorship of the Movies*, 13.

44. Ramsaye, *Million and One Nights*, 481–82.

45. For a detailed treatment of how censorship operated in New York, Maryland, Virginia, Kansas, and the cities of Chicago, Detroit, Memphis, and Atlanta, see Ira H. Carmen, *Movies, Censorship, and the Law* (Ann Arbor: University of Michigan Press, 1966), 125–224.

46. Jack Vizzard, *See No Evil: Life Inside a Hollywood Censor* (New York: Simon & Schuster, 1970), 37.

47. Schumach, *The Face on the Cutting Room Floor*, 203.

48. See May, *Screening Out the Past*, 167–99, for this transition of the industry west.

49. See David Robinson, *From Peep Show to Palace: The Birth of American Film* (New York: Columbia University Press, 1996); and May, *Screening Out the Past*, 147–66.

50. Ramsaye, *Million and One Nights*, 641.

51. Frank Miller, *Censored Hollywood*, 26.

52. When in 1925 (*Gitlow v. New York*, 268 U.S. 652) and in 1931 (*Near v. Minnesota*, 283 U.S. 697) respectively the Court would rule that the free speech and free press provisions of the First Amendment were now binding on the states, what that protection meant in regard to motion pictures had already been decided.

53. *Mutual Film Corporation v. Industrial Commission of Ohio*, 236 U.S. 230, 242, 244 (1915).

54. Ruth Inglis, *Freedom of the Movies* (Chicago: University of Chicago Press, 1947), 75.

55. Jowett, *Film*, 63.

56. Miller, *Censored Hollywood*, 27.

57. See Henry Farnham May, *The End of American Innocence: A Study of the First Years of Our Own Time* (New York: Knopf, 1959).

58. Quoted in Janet Staiger, *Bad Women: Regulating Sexuality in Early American Cinema* (Minneapolis: University of Minnesota Press, 1995), 3.

59. Jowett, *Film*, 62–65.

60. Staiger, *Bad Women*.

61. Walker, *Celluloid Sacrifice*, 25.

62. Ramsaye, *Million and One Nights*, 704.

63. Walker, *Celluloid Sacrifice*, 25, 28.

64. Quoted in William H. Short, *A Generation of Motion Pictures: A Review of Social Values in Recreational Films* (New York: National Committee for Study of Social Value in Motion Pictures, 1928), 31.

65. Gardner, *Censorship Papers*, 80–82.

66. Walker, *Celluloid Sacrifice*, 35–40.

67. David Shipman, *Caught in the Act: Sex and Eroticism in the Movies* (London: Elm Tree Books, 1985), 20.

68. See Morris L. Ernst and Pare Lorentz, *Censored: The Private Life of the Movie* (New York: Jonathan Cape and Harrison Smith, 1930), 30.

69. Short, *Generation of Motion Pictures*, 75–77.

70. Ruth Vasey, *The World according to Hollywood, 1918–1939* (Madison: University of Wisconsin Press, 1997), 64–66.

71. Ramsaye, *Million and One Nights*, 482–83.

72. Ross is quoted in Short, *Generation of Motion Pictures*, 212–15. For summaries of other studies assessing the sexual effect of movies on adolescents, see Joel Spring, *Images of American Life: A History of Ideological Management in Schools, Movies, Radio, and Television* (Albany: State University of New York Press, 1992), 67–72.

73. James R. Petersen, *The Century of Sex: Playboy's History of the Sexual Revolution, 1900–1999* (New York: Grove Press, 1999), 100.

74. Eric Shaefer, *"BOLD! DARING! SHOCKING! TRUE!" A History of Exploitation Films, 1919–1959* (Durham, N.C.: Duke University Press, 1999), 27.

75. Shaefer, *"BOLD!"* 1–164.

76. Shaefer, *"BOLD!"* 140.

77. Quoted in Mast, *Movies in Our Midst*, 195, 199.

78. The song's lyrics are by Edgar Leslie and Bert Kalmar and the music by Pete Wending. The music along with the printed lyrics can be found at www.goldensilents .com/girliemovies.

79. Ramsaye, *Million and One Nights*, 804–8; and Miller, *Censored Hollywood*, 23.

80. Schumach, *Face on the Cutting Room Floor*, 30–33. Schumach also surveys the other scandals as well on pages 22–30.

81. Brownlow, *Behind the Mask*, 17.

82. Miller, *Censored Hollywood*, 27–28; and see Inglis, *Freedom of the Movies*, 83–84, where the points are listed.

83. Spring, *Images of American Life*, 50.

84. Miller, *Censored Hollywood*, 29.

85. Miller, *Censored Hollywood*, 29, 32–33.

86. Leigh Ann Wheeler, *Against Obscenity: Reform and the Politics of Womanhood in America, 1873–1935* (Baltimore: Johns Hopkins University Press, 2004), 62–67.

87. Wheeler, *Against Obscenity*, 67–71.

88. Miller, *Censored Hollywood*, 36–9.

89. Miller, *Censored Hollywood*, 39–41.

90. In both eras there was censorship, but in the precode era there was often a disjointedness between the bulk of the movie and the morally redeeming ending. See Lea Jacobs, *The Wages of Sin: Censorship and the Fallen Woman Film, 1928–1942* (Madison: University of Wisconsin Press, 1991).

91. Miller, *Censored Hollywood*, 47.

92. Shipman, *The Story of Cinema*, traces well the move from the silents to the talkies, 200–221.

93. See Donald Crafton, *The Talkies: American Cinema's Transition to Sound, 1926–1931*, vol. 4, *History of the American Cinema*, ed. Charles Harpole (New York: Scribner, 1997), 445–79.

94. Vasey, *World according to Hollywood*, 75–79.

95. Quigley continued for quite a while to exercise influence over the content of movies through the Legion of Decency. When Quigley's influence with the legion declined, he switched sides and found employment with some moviemakers. In that capacity he challenged the censors at the PCA and argued against their demands for cuts. See Vizzard, *See No Evil*, 190–298.

96. Miller, *Censored Hollywood*, 50–51. See also, Raymond Moley, *The Hays Office* (Indianapolis, Ind.: Bobbs-Merrill, 1945) and Vasey, *World according to Hollywood*, for treatments of the evolution of the code and its operation.

97. Inglis, *Freedom of the Movies*, 145.

98. Miller, *Censored Hollywood*, 53.

99. The first film to lose an appeal was *Tarzan and His Mate*. Mark A. Vieira, *Sin in Soft Focus: Pre-Code Hollywood* (New York: Abrams, 1999), 188.

100. Miller, *Censored Hollywood*, 62–68; and for a listing of what have been called precode movies along with a generous sampling of stills from the films, see Vieira, *Sin in Soft Focus*. Many of these films were cut during the code era; now many have been restored to their original form and are available on video.

101. Mick Lasalle, *Complicated Women: Sex and Power in Pre-Code Hollywood* (New York: St. Martin's, 2000), 1.

102. Marybeth Hamilton, *When I'm Bad, I'm Better: Mae West, Sex, and American Entertainment* (New York: HarperCollins, 1995), 194–95. *She Done Him Wrong* and *I'm No Angel* were withdrawn from circulation, and they would not be seen again until the late 1960s.

103. Henry James Forman, *Our Movie Made Children* (New York: Macmillan, 1933). For a discussion of the research, see Robert Sklar, *Movie-Made America: A Cultural History of American Movies*, rev. & updated (New York: Vintage, 1994), 135–39, and Garth S. Jowett, Ian C. Jarvie, and Kathryn H. Fuller, *Children and the Movies: Media Influence and the Payne Fund Controversy* (New York: Cambridge University Press, 1996), xv–121. The latter book not only traces the gestation of the project and the reception it received, but it also includes unpublished material from the Payne studies.

104. Forman, *Our Movie Made Children*, 13, 18, 29, 50, 51.

105. Forman, *Our Movie Made Children*, 125, 137, 140.

106. See Herbert Blumer, *Movies and Conduct* (New York: Macmillan, 1933) from which Forman took his information.

107. Forman, *Our Movie Made Children*, 141–78, 214–32.

108. Miller, *Censored Hollywood*, 79, 82. For studies of the influence of the Catholic Church on the film industry, see Frank Walsh, *Sin and Censorship*; Gregory D. Black, *The Catholic Crusade against the Movies, 1940–1975* (Cambridge: Cambridge University Press, 1997); and James M. Skinner, *The Cross and the Cinema: The Legion of Decency and the National Catholic Office for Motion Pictures* (Westport, Conn.: Praeger, 1993).

109. Thomas Doherty, *Pre-Code Hollywood: Sex, Immorality, and Insurrection in American Cinema, 1930–1934* (New York: Columbia University Press, 1999), 8–9. For an inside look at Breen both as a person and as a censor, see the delightful memoir by a colleague who joined the PCA in 1944, Vizzard, *See No Evil*.

110. The PCA was financed by fees the film's producers paid.

111. See Bernstein, *Controlling Hollywood*, 87–101, for a discussion of how negotiation limited the effect of censorship.

112. Miller, *Censored Hollywood*, 82, 83, 272.

113. Martin Quigley, *Decency in Motion Pictures* (New York: Macmillan, 1937), 79–80. Quigley also reprints the entire Production Code (pages 52–70), as does Doherty, *Pre-Code Hollywood*, 347–67.

114. Quigley, *Decency in Motion Pictures*, 330.

115. Doherty, *Pre-Code Hollywood*, 331.

116. Gardner, *Censorship Papers*, 94, 104, 106, 109–10.

117. Thomas Schatz, *Boom and Bust: The American Cinema in the 1940s*, vol. 6, *History of the American Cinema*, ed. Charles Harpole (New York: Scribner, 1997), 265.

118. Black, *Catholic Crusade*.

119. Black, *Hollywood Censored*, 298–99.

120. Walsh, *Sin and Censorship*, 110.

121. Gardner, *Censorship Papers*, 86, 163. But see Vizzard (*See No Evil*, 113), where one of the PCA censors argues that the Hays Office never imposed any time limit on kisses.

122. Olga J. Martin, *Hollywood's Movie Commandments: A Handbook for Motion Picture Writers and Reviewers* (New York: H. W. Wilson, 1937), 98–100.

123. Martin, *Hollywood's Movie Commandments*, 154–55.

124. See Vizzard (*See No Evil*, 40–42), where the author suggests that this adaptation might have influenced the strengthening of the code's enforcement.

125. Gardner, *Censorship Papers*, 16–19.

126. For instance, very few films were rejected: 14 of 1,748 in 1935 and 9 of 1,427 in 1937, but usually only 2 or 3. Inglis (*Freedom of the Movies*, 144) also provides specific examples of how the process worked. See also Gardner, *Censorship Papers*, 155–71, in which the author traces the problems faced by some of the most prominent features of those years.

127. Doherty, *Pre-Code Hollywood*, 337–38, 342.

128. Miller, *Censored Hollywood*, 102–3.

129. Miller, *Censored Hollywood*, 94, 100.

130. Jeremy Pascall and Clyde Jeavons, *A Pictorial History of Sex in the Movies* (London: Hamlyn, 1975), 58.

131. Pascall and Jeavons, *A Pictorial History*, 95, 98.

132. Quoted in Harlan Lebo, *Citizen Kane: The Fiftieth Anniversary Album* (New York: Doubleday, 1990), 133. The controversy is detailed in Pascall and Jeavons, *A Pictorial History*, 133–80.

133. The story of the battle over the film and the aftermath is well told in John Evangelist Walsh, *Walking Shadows: Orson Welles, William Randolph Hearst, and Citizen Kane* (Madison: University of Wisconsin Press, 2004).

134. Miller, *Censored Hollywood*, 114–17; and Gardner, *Censorship Papers*, 27–28.

135. Gardner, *Censorship Papers*, 28.

136. Gardner, *Censorship Papers*, 28–29; and Miller, *Censored Hollywood*, 118–19.

137. Pascall and Jeavons, *Pictorial History*, 93. This source has the most extensive discussion of Hughes's campaign to emphasize Russell's breasts.

138. Gardner, *Censorship Papers*, 29–30.

139. The way in which Hughes used that year to build up interest in the picture is described in Tony Thomas, *Howard Hughes in Hollywood* (Secaucus, N.J.: Citadel Press, 1985), 85–88.

140. Gardner, *Censorship Papers*, 119–21.

141. James Agee, *Agee on Film* (New York: McDowell, Obolensky, 1958), 1, 74.

142. Miller, *Censored Hollywood*, 126–29.

143. Miller, *Censored Hollywood*, 129–33. See also the detailed treatment of the Catholic Church's role in regard to *The Outlaw, Duel in the Sun*, and *Forever Amber* in Black, *Catholic Crusade*, 31–65.

144. Miller, *Censored Hollywood*, 136–37.

145. Schatz, *Boom and Bust*, 323.

146. Bernstein, *Controlling Hollywood*, 157–85.

147. Doherty, *Pre-Code Hollywood*, 342–43.

148. Attendance that stood near or at ninety million in the 1942–1948 period fell to half that amount by 1953. John Belton, *American Cinema/American Culture* (New York: McGraw-Hill, 1994), 257.

149. The story is well told in Jowett, *Film*, 275–81, 344–56.

150. *United States v. Paramount Pictures, Inc.*, 334 U.S. 131, 166 (1948).

151. Miller, *Censored Hollywood*, 147–48.

152. *Joseph Burstyn, Inc. v. Wilson*, 343 U.S. 495 (1952).

153. *Joseph Burstyn, Inc. v. Wilson* at 501, 502.

154. *Joseph Burstyn, Inc. v. Wilson* at 505.

155. *Commercial Pictures Corp. v. Regents of New York*, 305 N.Y. 336, 114 N.E. 2d 561, 113 NY.S. 2d 502 (1953), *rev'd*, 346 U.S. 587 (1954); *Superior Films, Inc. v. Department of Education*, 159 Ohio St. 315, 112 N.E. 2d 311 (1953), *rev'd*, 346 U.S. 587 (1954); and *Gelling v. State*, 157 Tex. Crim. 516, 247 S.W. 2d 95, *rev'd*, 343 U.S. 960 (1952).

156. *Butler v. Michigan*, 352 U.S. 380 (1957).

157. *Fox Film Corp. v. Chicago*, 247 F. 231 (1917), *affirmed* 251 F. 883, 884 (1918).

158. *Roth v. United States*, 354 U.S. 476, 484, 487, 489 (1957). The companion case, dealing with state obscenity law is *Alberts v. California*, 354 U.S. 476 (1957).

159. *Times Film Corp. v. City of Chicago*, 244 F. 2d 148 (7th Cir.), *rev'd*, 355 U.S. 35 (1957).

160. *Kingsley Int'l Pictures Corp. v. Regents of New York*, 360 U.S. 684, 688 (1959).

161. *Times Film Corp. v. Chicago*, 365 U.S. 43 (1961).

162. Quoted from the record by Randall, *Censorship of the Movies*, 63.

163. *Jacobellis v. Ohio*, 378 U.S. 184 (1964). The decision in favor of local vs. national standards came in *Miller v. California*, 413 U.S. 15 (1973).

164. Miller, *Censored Hollywood*, 153–58.

165. Black, *Catholic Crusade*, 125.

166. Black, *Catholic Crusade*, 120–28. In time even Breen admitted that he had made a mistake with *The Moon Is Blue* (162–63).

167. Vizzard, *See No Evil*, 157.

168. Miller, *Censored Hollywood*, 162–63, 166. He was awarded an Oscar by the industry that he had been both serving and combating for twenty years. Vizzard, *See No Evil*, 166.

169. For an inside look at Shurlock's administration, see Vizzard, *See No Evil*, 159–348. Shurlock, who began his assumption of the reins with the suggestion that the PCA go out of business and leave the responsibility for enforcing the code to the moviemakers themselves, gradually loosened restraints and presided over the diminishing influence of the PCA.

170. Schumach, *Face on the Cutting Room Floor*, 215.

171. Miller, *Censored Hollywood*, 166–78, 180–81.

172. See Lewis, *Hollywood v. Hard Core: How the Struggle over Censorship Saved the Modern Film Industry* (New York: New York University Press, 2000), 119–26 for a discussion of problems with this feature.

173. Miller, *Censored Hollywood*, 182–86.

174. Miller, *Censored Hollywood*, 190–93.

175. Miller, *Censored Hollywood*, 196–97

176. Miller, *Censored Hollywood*, 197–99. NCOMP lingered on until the official abandonment of its role as an evaluator of the propriety of motion pictures in 1980. Black, *Catholic Crusade*, 239.

177. Lewis, *Hollywood v. Hard Core*, 413.

178. Miller, *Censored Hollywood*, 199–204.

179. Miller, *Censored Hollywood*, 204–5.

180. Miller, *Censored Hollywood*, 205–8.

181. *Freedman v. Maryland*, 380 U.S. 51 (1965).

182. *Hewitt v. Maryland State Bd. of Censors*, 241 Md. A283, 216 A. 2d 557 (1966); *Dunn v. Maryland State Bd. of Censors*, 240 Md. 249, 213 A. 2d 751 (1965); *Trans-Lux Distributing Corp. v. Maryland State Bd. of Censors*, 240 Md. 98, 213 A. 2d 235 (1965).

183. Randall, *Censorship of the Movies*, 46.

184. Miller, *Censored Hollywood*, 213. Maryland's board was disbanded in 1981.

185. *Ginsberg v. United States*, 390 U.S. 629 (1968); and *Interstate Circuit, Inc. v. Dallas*, 390 U.S. 676 (1968). In the latter case, the Court struck down the Dallas ordinance imposing an age restriction upon certain movies because of the vagueness of the standards employed, but the majority implied that a more tightly drawn ordinance protecting minors would pass constitutional muster. Dallas redrafted its ordinance, and did not disband its rating board until 1993. Miller, *Hollywood Censored*, 268.

186. Stephen Farber, *The Movie Rating Game* (Washington, D.C.: Public Affairs Press, 1972), 112. Farber, who served on the ratings board as its youngest member for six months, traces its early operation and expresses concern that the ratings process inhibited creativity in film.

187. This material was published by the MPAA in a brochure explaining the ratings system, much of which is reproduced in Farber, *The Movie Rating Game*, 112–15.

188. Miller, *Censored Hollywood*, 239.

189. Pally, *Sex & Sensibility*, 137.

190. Miller, *Censored Hollywood*, 222–23.

191. Thomas A. Atkins, ed., *Sexuality in the Movies* (Bloomington, Ind.: Indiana University Press, 1975), 76–81. The author of this section of the book, Evelyn Renold, served on the ratings board early in its history as an intern and provides an interesting account of its functioning with suggestions for its revamping on pages 76–97.

192. Linda Williams, *Hard Core: Power, Pleasure, and the "Frenzy of the Visible,"* enl. ed. (Berkeley: University of California Press, 1999), 58.

193. Miller, *Censored Hollywood*, 222, 229–30. For a study of the history of *Deep Throat* and its legal battles, see Richard Smith, *Getting into Deep Throat* (Chicago: Playboy Press, 1973).

194. Lewis, *Hollywood v. Hard Core*, 223–29.

195. *Huffman v. Pursue, Ltd.*, 420 U.S. 592 (1975). The Court reached the same conclusion in *Sendak v. Nihiser, dba Movieland Drive-In Theater*, 423 U.S. 976 (1975), a case involving the showing of *Deep Throat*, among other films.

196. *Miller v. California*, 413 U.S. 15, 37 (1973).

197. *Paris Adult Theatre I v. Slaton*, 413 U.S. 49 (1973).

198. *United States v. 12 200-Ft. Reels of Super 8mm Film, et al.*, 413 U.S. 123 (1973); and *United States v. Orito*, 413 U.S. 139 (1973).

199. Lewis, *Hollywood v. Hard Core*, 263–66.

200. *Jenkins v. Georgia*, 418 U.S. 153, 160 (1974).

201. Lewis, *Hollywood v. Hard Core*, 273.

202. Miller, *Censored Hollywood*, 217–18.

203. Miller, *Censored Hollywood*, 134.

204. Miller, *Censored Hollywood*, 139–40.

205. *United States v. A Motion Picture Film Entitled* I Am Curious—Yellow, 404 F. 2d 196, 198 (1968).

206. Olga G. and Edwin P. Hoyt, *Censorship in America* (New York: Seabury, 1970), 61–62.

207. Edward De Grazia and Roger K. Newman, *Banned Films: Movies, Censors & The First Amendment* (New York: R. R. Bowker, 1982), 125.

208. Bo Derek with Mark Seal, *Riding Lessons: Everything That Matters in Life I Learned from Horses* (New York: HarperCollins, 2002), 153–57.

209. See Douglas Brode, *Sinema: Erotic Adventures in Film* (New York: Citadel Press, 2002), 62–63. Brode's book surveys the subject and provides illustrations.

210. Miller, *Hollywood Censored*, 245. Since X was not a copyrighted rating, as were the others, it could be appropriated without any difficulty.

211. Pally, *Sex & Sensibility*, 137–38.

212. Lewis, *Hollywood v. Hard Core*, 276–83.

213. Charles Lyons, "The Paradox of Protest: American Film, 1980–1992," in *Movie Censorship and American Culture*, ed. Francis G. Couvares (Washington, D.C.: Smithsonian Institution Press, 1996), 284.

214. *New York v. Ferber*, 458 U.S. 747, 749 (1982).

215. See chapter 2 for instances of photographers taking pictures of nude children, at times their own, and then running into difficulty with local and national authorities.

216. *Young v. American Mini Theatres, Inc.*, 427 U.S. 50 (1976).

217. *Renton v. Playtime Theatres, Inc.*, 475 U.S. 41 (1986).

218. *Newsletter on Intellectual Freedom* 53 (September 2004): 174.

219. Marjorie Heins, *Sex, Sin, and Blasphemy: A Guide to America's Censorship Wars* (New York: New Press, 1993), 57–59.

220. Lewis, *Hollywood v. Hard Core*, 296–97, 286–88.

221. Lewis, *Hollywood v. Hard Core*, 293–96, 290–91.

222. Lewis, *Hollywood v. Hard Core*, 284.

223. Anne Thompson, "Puppet Love: A Comedy with Strings Attached," *Washington Post*, 10 October 2004.

224. Pally, *Sex & Sensibility*, 129–31.

225. For a treatment of the ratings system in terms of how it worked to give major studios access to the adult film marketplace, see Bernstein, *Controlling Hollywood*, 238–63.

226. For a number of instances of this type of threat, see Heins, *Sex, Sin, and Blasphemy*, 61–68.

227. Jon Lewis, *Hollywood v. Hard Core*, 1–3.

228. Lewis, *Hollywood v. Hard Core*, 6.

229. For instances of such pressure group activity and some recognition of its success in the ongoing culture war, see Charles Lyons, *The New Censors: Movies and the Culture Wars* (Philadelphia: Temple University Press, 1997). Consider the accolades heaped upon *Brokeback Mountain* in 2005–2006 as an illustration of how things have changed.

230. Mark Rahner, "Howdy, Pardner!; Think *Brokeback* Was Groundbreaking?" *Seattle Times*, 23 January 2006. The author argues that homosexual relationships

have long been implied in westerns. See also, Wyatt Buchanan and Steven Winn, "*Brokeback* Tells a Story Gays Know All Too Well," (*San Francisco Chronicle*, 9 December 2005), for a treatment of the cultural importance of the film.

231. Adam Harvey, "Town Not Big Enough for Gay Cowboy Heath," *Daily Telegraph* (Sidney, Australia), 10 January 2006, Local, 7.

232. Ron Dicker, "Dirty Secrets," *Baltimore Sun*, 25 January 2006.

233. David Crary, "Activists Target Hotel Room Porn," *Herald-Sun* (Durham, N.C.), 23 August 2006.

234. For such a critic, see Michael Medved, *Hollywood vs. America: Popular Culture and the War on Traditional Values* (New York: Zondervan, 1992).

CHAPTER FOUR

1. Plato, *The Republic*, trans. Francis MacDonald Cornford (New York: Oxford University Press, 1945), 115.

2. Raymond Durgnat, *Eros in the Cinema* (London: Calder and Boyars, 1966), 13.

3. Tipper Gore, *Raising PG Kids in an X-Rated Society* (Nashville, Tenn.: Abington Press, 1987), 82.

4. Terence Moran, "Sounds of Sex, Why Daddy Took the T-bird Away," *The New Republic* 193 (12 August 1985): 16.

5. Geneva Smitherman, *Black Talk: Words and Phrases from the Hood to the Amen Corner*, rev. ed. (Boston: Houghton Mifflin, 2000), 248.

6. Dave Marsh, *Louie Louie* (New York: Hyperion, 1993), 16–41.

7. Marsh, *Louie Louie*, 42, 81–103.

8. Marsh, *Louie Louie*, 120.

9. Marsh, *Louie Louie*, 114–17.

10. Monifa Thomas, "Louie, Louie Ban Reversed for School Band," *Chicago Sun-Times*, 6 May 2005.

11. Ed Cray, *The Erotic Muse: American Bawdy Songs*, 2nd ed. (Urbana: University of Illinois Press, 1992).

12. Cray, *The Erotic Muse*, 1, 107–8.

13. Cray, *The Erotic Muse*, 137, 162, 169–70.

14. Cray, *The Erotic Muse*, 269, 276.

15. Cray, *The Erotic Muse*, 377, 386–88.

16. Alec Wilder, *American Popular Song: The Great Innovators, 1900–1950* (New York: Oxford University Press, 1990), 3.

17. Charles Hamm, *Yesterdays: Popular Song in America* (New York: Norton, 1979), 336–37.

18. Ian Whitcomb, *After the Ball: Pop Music from Rag to Rock* (New York: Simon & Schuster, 1972), 6–7.

19. One critic explains the persistence of the censorial urge as follows: "Part of the puritanical materialistic, technological basis of our culture requires us to de-emphasize and restrict sexual activity so that one can devote his energy to work. . . . The idea that pleasure could be an end in itself is so startling and so threatening to the structure of our society that the mere possibility is denied." Philip Slater, *Pursuit of Loneliness: American Culture at the Breaking Point*, rev. ed. (New York: Beacon, 1976), 67.

20. Lawrence Grossberg, *Dancing in Spite of Myself: Essays on Popular Culture* (Durham, N.C.: Duke University Press, 1997), 87; and Simon Frith, *Sound Effects: Youth, Leisure, and the Politics of Rock* (London: Constable, 1981), 244.

21. Nicholas E. Tawa, *The Way to Tin Pan Alley: American Popular Song, 1866–1910* (New York: Schirmer Books, 1990), 175–76.

22. Don McDonagh, *Dance Fever* (New York: Random House, 1979), 2–3, 11.

23. Excerpt from Faulkner's book reprinted in Maureen Needham, ed. *I See America Dancing: Selected Readings, 1685–2000* (Urbana: University of Illinois Press, 2002), 116.

24. Peter Buckman, *Let's Dance: Social, Ballroom & Folk Dancing* (London: Paddington Press, 1978), 152–53.

25. Mark Sullivan, *Our Times: The United States, 1900–1925*, vol. 4 (New York: Scribner, 1932), 227–29, 240–41.

26. "Degenerate Music," *Musical Courier* 39 (13 September 1899), quoted in Donald Clarke, *The Rise and Fall of Popular Music* (New York: St. Martin's, 1995), 413.

27. Sigmund Spaeth, *A History of Popular Music in America* (New York: Random House, 1948), 369–70.

28. Susan C. Cook, "Passionless Dancing and Passionate Reform: Respectability, Modernism, and the Social Dancing of Irene and Vernon Castle," in *Passion of Music and Dance: Body, Gender and Sexuality*, ed. William Washabaugh (Oxford, England: Berg, 1998), 139.

29. Sullivan, *Our Times*, 254.

30. Ann Wagner, *Adversaries of Dance: From Puritans to the Present* (Urbana: University of Illinois Press, 1997), 299, 304–5.

31. Sullivan, *Our Times*, 252, 256–58.

32. Peter Buckman, *Let's Dance*, 166–67.

33. Lewis A. Erenberg, *Steppin' Out: New York Nightlife and the Transformation of American Culture, 1890–1930* (Westport, Conn.: Greenwood Press, 1981), 154.

34. McDonagh, *Dance Fever*, 28–29.

35. Cook, "Passionless Dancing," 147.

36. Buckman, *Let's Dance*, 179–82.

37. Buckman, *Let's Dance*, 187.

38. McDonagh, *Dance Fever*, 57–58.

39. McDonagh, *Dance Fever*, 82–83.

40. Buckman, *Let's Dance*, 207–11.

41. McDonagh, *Dance Fever*, 90.

42. Buckman, *Let's Dance*, 213–15.

43. McDonagh, *Dance Fever*, 94.

44. McDonagh, *Dance Fever*, 94–95.

45. McDonagh, *Dance Fever*, 108–9, 116–19.

46. See Wagner, *Adversaries of Dance*. In appendices, 407–22, Wagner lists adversaries, most of whom are mentioned in her text, with a little biographical information.

47. William Robbins, "Ozarks School to Hold Dance at Last," *New York Times*, 10 December 1988.

48. *Clayton v. Place*, 884 F. 2d 376, 380 (1989).

49. *Clayton v. Place*, 889 F. 2d 192, 195, 197 (1989).

50. *Clayton v. Place*, 494 U.S. 1081 (1990).

51. Judith Lynne Hanna, "Dance under the Censorship Watch," *Journal of Arts Management, Law and Society* 31 (Winter 2002): 305.

52. *Barnes v. Glen Theatre, Inc.*, 501 U.S. 560 (1991).

53. *City of Erie v. Pap's A.M., tdba "Kandyland,"* 529 U.S. 277 (2000).

54. *Pap's A.M., tdba Kandyland v. City of Erie*, 812 A. 2d. 591 (2002).

55. *American Bush v. City of South Salt Lake*, 140 P. 3d 1235 (2006).

56. Quoted in Reebee Garofalo, *Rockin' Out: Popular Music in the USA* (Boston: Allyn and Bacon, 1997), 14.

57. Garofalo, *Rockin' Out*, 15; and Susan J. Douglas, *Listening In: Radio and the American Imagination from Amos 'n Andy and Edward R. Morrow to Wolfman Jack and Howard Stern* (New York: Times Books, 1999), 84.

58. Douglas, *Listening In*, 83.

59. Douglas, *Listening In*, 95–96.

60. Robert Walser, ed., *Keeping Time: Readings in Jazz History* (New York: Oxford University Press, 1999), 32–36.

61. Douglas, *Listening In*, 91.

62. Nuzum, *Parental Advisory*, 150.

63. Peter Blecha, *Taboo Tunes: A History of Banned Bands & Censored Songs* (San Francisco: Backbeat Books, 2004), 89.

64. Blecha, *Taboo Tunes*, 91, 92.

65. The lyrics can be found in Lehman Engel, *Their Words Are Music: The Great Theatre Lyricists and Their Lyrics* (New York: Crown, 1975), 19.

66. Alec Wilder, *American Popular Song: The Great Innovators, 1900–1950* (New York: Oxford University Press, 1990), 225, 229.

67. Louise M. Benjamin, *Freedom of the Air and the Public Interest: First Amendment Rights in Broadcasting to 1935* (Carbondale: Southern Illinois University Press, 2001), 142–44.

68. William McBrien, *Cole Porter: A Biography* (New York: Knopf, 1998), 192.

69. For the lyrics, see Engel, *Their Words Are Music*, 23.

70. Charles Schwartz, *Cole Porter: A Biography* (New York: Dial Press, 1977), 116–17.

71. Robert L. Hilliard and Michael C. Keith, *Dirty Discourse: Sex and Indecency in American Radio* (Ames: Iowa State University Press, 2003), 102–3.

72. Thomas A. DeLong, *The Mighty Music Box: The Golden Age of Musical Radio* (Los Angeles: Amber Crest Books, 1980), 228–29.

73. "Song Censorship for Radio Begun," *New York Times*, 15 August 1934; "Radio Heads Laud Song Censorship," *New York Times*, 16 August 1934; and "Networks 'Clean' Song 'Censors' Say," *New York Times*, 23 August 1934.

74. Ernest LaPrade, *Broadcasting Music* (New York: Rinehart, 1947), 35.

75. Douglas, *Listening In*, 92.

76. Eric Nuzum, *Parental Advisory: Music Censorship in America* (New York: HarperCollins, 2001), 150.

77. Robert J. Pondillo, "Censorship in a 'Golden Age': Postwar Television and America's First Network Censor—NBC's Stockton Helffrich," (PhD diss., University of Wisconsin-Madison, 2003), 110.

78. McBrien, *Cole Porter*, 296.

79. The lyrics of both songs are in Engel, *Their Words Are Music*, 38–39.

80. For the censorship story, see Gerald Gardner, *The Censorship Papers: Movie Censorship Letters from the Hays Office, 1934 to 1968* (New York: Dodd, Mead, 1987), 16–19.

81. Quoted in Dave Harker, *One for the Money: Politics and the Popular Song* (London: Hutchinson, 1980), 38.

82. New York became the center of the popular music publishing business in the 1890s when the publishers moved their offices to or near Union Square, which was dubbed "Tin Pan Alley." Eventually this nickname became both a shorthand reference to the entire popular-song industry and to the type of song they published and marketed. See Charles Hamm, *Yesterdays: Popular Song in America* (New York: Norton, 1979), 284–87, 323–25.

83. Hamm, *Yesterdays*, 404–6.

84. Serene Dominic, "Annie Had a Co-Worker: Hank Ballard brought Rock 'n' Sex Out of the Dark Ages and into the Hall of Fame," *Phoenix New Times*, 11 May 1995, www.phoenixnewtimes.com/Issues/1995-05-11/music/sidebar3.html.

85. "Annie Had a Baby" is on a CD titled *Freedom Sings* put out by the First Amendment Center at Vanderbilt University. It is part of a project highlighting banned music over the nation's history that has been performed as a multimedia show on various college campuses and in cities throughout the United States.

86. Bob Pondillo, "You Can't Sing That on TV!" *Television Quarterly* 33 (Spring 2003): 62–66.

87. Pondillo, "Censorship," 285, 287.

88. This story is told in David Ewen, *All the Years of American Popular Music* (Englewood Cliffs, N.J., 1977), 552–55.

89. Hamm, *Yesterdays*, 407.

90. Ewen, *All the Years*, 554.

91. Lillian Roxon, *Rock Encyclopedia* (New York, 1969), 216.

92. R. Serge Denisoff and Richard A. Peterson, eds., *The Sounds of Social Change* (Chicago, 1972), 194–95.

93. The reaction to Presley is detailed in David P. Szatmary, *Rockin' in Time: A Social History of Rock-and-Roll*, 4th ed. (Upper Saddle River, N.J.: Prentice Hall, 2000), 45–51.

94. The CD titled *Freedom Rings* published by the First Amendment Center contains an introduction that talks of the Houston ban as well as a rendition of the song itself.

95. Hamm, *Yesterdays*, 407.

96. Marie Korpe, ed., *Shoot the Singer! Music Censorship Today* (London: Zed Books, 2004), 177.

97. Rodger Streitmatter, *Sex Sells! The Media's Journey from Repression to Obsession* (Cambridge, Mass.: Westview Press, 2004), 43–56.

98. Nuzum, *Parental Advisory*, 214.

99. Nuzum, *Parental Advisory*, 216–19, 221–22. See also Linda Martin and Kerry Segrave, *ANTI-ROCK: The Opposition to Rock 'n' Roll* (Hamden, Conn.: Archon Books, 1988), 3–58.

100. Szatmary, *Rockin' in Time*, 54.

101. Hamm, *Yesterdays*, 416–24.

102. Roxon, *Rock Encyclopedia*, 422–23.

103. Nuzum, *Parental Advisory*, 225, 227–28.

104. Nuzum, *Parental Advisory*, 229.

105. For a pictorial survey of covers that don't make the marketplace, click on "Banned album covers" at www.vh1.com/shows/series/movies-that-rock/warning.

106. Nuzum, *Parental Advisory*, 70–71, 73–74.

107. Nuzum, *Parental Advisory*, 76–77, 255–59. The whole story is well told in David Kennedy, "Frankenchrist versus the State: The New Right, Rock Music and the Case of Jello Biafra," *Journal of Popular Culture* 24 (Summer 1990): 131–48.

108. Nuzum, *Parental Advisory*, 273–74.

109. Marjorie Heins, *Not in Front of the Children: "Indecency," Censorship, and the Innocence of Youth* (New York: Hill and Wang, 2001), 95–96.

110. Nuzum, *Parental Advisory*, 236, 238, 239–40.

111. *Yale Broadcasting Co. v. FCC*, 478 F. 2d 594, 605 (1973).

112. *FCC v. Pacifica Foundation*, 438 U.S. 726 (1978). This ruling is treated in detail in chapter 5.

113. Sandra Davidson, "Stern Stuff: Here Comes the FCC," in *Bleep! Censoring Rock and Rap Music*, ed. Betty Houchin Winfield and Sandra Davidson (Westport, Conn.: Greenwood Press, 1999), 52–57.

114. "Sex Rock," *Time* 106 (29 December 1975): 39; and Martin and Segrave, *ANTI-ROCK*, 251–56.

115. Nuzum, *Parental Advisory*, 159; and Martin and Segrave, *ANTI-ROCK*, 257.

116. Bill C. Malone, *Country Music USA*, rev. ed. (Austin: University of Texas Press, 1985), 369–79.

117. Quoted in Garofalo, *Rockin' Out*, 429.

118. The evolution of both the music video and MTV, a cable channel devoted to the genre, is well told in Tom McGrath, *MTV: The Making of a Revolution* (Philadelphia: Running Press, 1996). For an anecdotal and pictorial history of the channel see Jacob Hoye, *MTV: Uncensored* (New York: Pocket Books, 2001).

119. McGrath, *MTV*, 80–81, 100–101, 104; and Nuzum, *Parental Advisory*, 87.

120. McGrath, *MTV*, 81, 113–15.

121. Nuzum, *Parental Advisory*, 91–96.

122. Nuzum, *Parental Advisory*, 88–91.

123. McGrath, *MTV*, 127–28; and Gore, *Raising PG Kids*, 35–36.

124. Nuzum, *Parental Advisory*, 188–90.

125. Nuzum, *Parental Advisory*, 17.

126. Martin and Segrave, *ANTI-ROCK*, 291–92; and Nuzum, *Parental Advisory*, 17–18.

127. Gore, *Raising PG Kids*, 17–18.

128. Martin and Segrave, *ANTI-ROCK*, 292.

129. Martin and Segrave, *ANTI-ROCK*, 292; Nuzum, *Parental Advisory*, 19; and Gore, *Raising PG Kids*, 18–20.

130. Gore, *Raising PG Kids*, 20–25. Gortikov was presented with fifteen songs that the PMRC found objectionable. They are listed in Nuzum, *Parental Advisory*, 20–21.

131. Garofalo, *Rockin' Out*, 433.

132. Nuzum, *Parental Advisory*, 20; and Martin and Segrave, *ANTI-ROCK*, 293–98.

133. Nuzum, *Parental Advisory*, 22.

134. Gore, *Raising PG Kids*, 27–29, 26–27.

135. Quoted in "Frank Zappa: American Composer—Online Documentary," at www.zappa.com.

136. Martin and Segrave, *ANTI-ROCK*, 298–302.

137. Blecha, *Taboo Tunes*, 110.

138. Garofalo, *Rockin' Out*, 429; Martin and Segrave, *ANTI-ROCK*, 303; and Nuzum, *Parental Advisory*, 34.

139. Nuzum, *Parental Advisory*, 33–34.

140. Martin and Segrave, *ANTI-ROCK*, 304, 307.

141. See Garofalo, *Rockin' Out*, 429–30 for such examples.

142. Martin and Segrave, *ANTI-ROCK*, 309.

143. Nuzum, *Parental Advisory*, 34–35; and Martin and Segrave, *ANTI-ROCK*, 309–12.

144. Nuzum, *Parental Advisory*, 253. Nuzum (254–55) says that the label was placed on the album by a record retailer, Meyer Music Markets, but the author has been informed by Zappa followers that it was the performer's idea.

145. Nuzum, *Parental Advisory*, 34, 38–40, 42. Tipper Gore resigned from PMRC when her husband became vice president in 1993.

146. Nuzum, *Parental Advisory*, 42–43. Instances of such legislative activity and the concern about concerts of popular groups are documented in Nuzum, *Parental Advisory*, 267–302.

147. Nuzum, *Parental Advisory*, 100–107. See also Craig Werner, *A Change Is Gonna Come: Music, Race & the Soul of America* (New York: Plume Book, 1999), 15–27; and Gerald Early, *One Nation under a Groove: Motown and American Culture* (Hopewell, N.J.: Ecco, 1995), 4, in which Motown is credited with being an important force in the black community in that "it helped to crystallize the formation of . . . a black public and black public taste that was taken seriously as an expression of a general aesthetic among a broad class of Americans."

148. Nuzum, *Parental Advisory*, 240; and Brian Dorsey, *Spirituality, Sensuality, Literality: Blues, Jazz, and Rap as Music and Poetry* (Vienna, Austria: Braumüller, 2000), 332.

149. Nuzum, *Parental Advisory*, 100, 109.

150. Nuzum, *Parental Advisory*, 268–70. A record store owner in Alexandria, Alabama, was convicted in 1988 in municipal court of having sold an earlier 2 Live Crew album, but he demanded a jury trial, and that trial resulted in his acquittal. Nuzum, *Parental Advisory*, 261–62.

151. Nuzum, *Parental Advisory*, 271, 272.

152. *Luke Records, Inc. v. Navarro*, 960 F. 2d 134 (1992).

153. Nuzum, *Parental Advisory*, 271; and Dorsey, *Spirituality, Sensuality, Literality*, 392.

154. Henry Louis Gates Jr., letter to the editor, *New York Times*, 19 June 1990; and David Kastin, *I Hear America Singing: An Introduction to Popular Music* (Upper Saddle River, N.J.: Prentice Hall, 2002), 340.

155. Kastin, *I Hear America Singing*, 343. See also Tricia Rose, *Black Noise: Rap Music and Black Culture in Contemporary America* (Hanover, N.H.: Wesleyan University Press, 1994), 146–82.

156. Szatmary, *Rockin' in Time*, 316, 320.

157. Allison Samuels, "From Raunch to Romance," *Newsweek*, 6 April 1998, 68.

158. Quoted in Hilliard and Keith, *Dirty Discourse*, 54.

159. Quoted in Hilliard and Keith, *Dirty Discourse*, 110–11. The lyrics of Penis Envy and the latter two songs, can be found in Hilliard and Keith, *Dirty Discourse*, 123–24, 135–36.

160. Jon Pareles, "Outlaw Rock: More Skirmishes on the Censorship Front," *New York Times*, 10 December 1989.

161. Hilliard and Keith, *Dirty Discourse*, 111–13. An appendix in *Dirty Discourse* (261–67) contains the full text of the FCC's Notice of Apparent Liability for Forfeiture plus the lyrics of the song.

162. Hilliard and Keith, *Dirty Discourse*, 111, 257. An appendix in *Dirty Discourse* (255–60) contains the full text of the NAL plus the lyrics of the song.

163. Hilliard and Keith, *Dirty Discourse*, 111.

164. Tony Mauro, "FCC Muffles Artist's Message," *USA Today*, 24 February 2003.

165. Statement of Hilary Rosen before the Senate Committee on Government Affairs, 25 July 2001, www.senate.gov/~gov_affairs/072501_rosen.htm.

166. Nuzum, *Parental Advisory*, 277, 280, 293, 302. One can keep up-to-date on legislative initiatives in this area at www.theroc.org/updates/legislat.htm.

167. "President Clinton on State of Union," *New York Times*, 28 January 2000.

168. See Nuzum, *Parental Advisory*, 283, 286, 290, 292, 294, 297, 298–99, 303.

169. Click on "Banned Songs: A History" at www.vh1.com/shows/series/movies_that_rock/warning.

170. Nuzum, *Parental Advisory*, 304.

171. "Who's Who: Faces in the News," *Herald-Sun* (Durham, N.C.), 6 June 2002.

172. "Boss Too Hot for Starbucks," *Daily News* (New York), 5 May 2005.

173. "Willie Nelson Offers Gay Cowboy Song," *News & Observer* (Raleigh, N.C.), 16 February 2006.

174. "Raves," National Drug Intelligence Center Information Bulletin, Department of Justice, April 2001, no. 2001-L0424-004.

175. 21 U.S.C. § 856 (1986).

176. www.emdef.org/aboutemdef.html and www.emdef.org/laws_and_cases.html.

177. www.alchemind.org/DLL/sb1208_index.htm; and "Lawmakers Targeting Raves to Curb Teen Use of Ecstacy," *Herald-Sun* (Durham, N.C.), 30 July 2002.

178. Neva Chonin, "Congress Acts Out against Club Culture," *San Francisco Chronicle*, 27 April 2003, Sunday Datebook, 35.

179. www.drugpolicy.org/communities/raveact.

180. Donna Leinwand, "Fewer High Schoolers Use Ecstasy, Study Finds," *USA Today*, 22 April 2005.

181. Seema Mehta, "The State; Too Close to Dirty for the Dance; Some Educators Ban 'Freaking' at School Function. Relax, Others Say—It's Just Flirting," *Los Angeles Times*, home ed., 17 October 2006, A1.

182. Seema Metha and Ashley Powers, "Kids Can Dance, Not 'Freak': Aliso Niguel Principal Rescinds Ban on Dances, but Students and Parents Must Sign a Lengthy Contract of Behavior Rules," *Los Angeles Times*, home ed., 30 November 2006, B3.

183. Tony Barboza, "Getting 'Freaky' Middle School Students Into a New Groove: One Campus Is Tackling the Salacious Dancing Problem by Teaching Youths Other Moves," *Los Angeles Times*, home ed., 18 December 2006, B4.

CHAPTER FIVE

1. Jonathan Wallace and Mark Mangan, *Sex, Laws, and Cyberspace* (New York: Henry Holt, 1996), 231.

2. James L. Lynch, *Cyberethics: Managing the Morality of Multimedia* (England: Rushmere Wynne, 1996), 195.

3. The Rhode Island senator is quoted in Jeff Land, *Active Radio: Pacifica's Brash Experiment* (Minneapolis: University of Minnesota Press, 1999), 104.

4. Kay E. Vandergrift, "Censorship, the Internet, Intellectual Freedom, and Youth," www.scils.rutgers.edu/~kvander/censorship.html.

5. Frank Ahrens and Lisa de Moraes, "FCC Is Investigating Super Bowl Show; Halftime Performance Faces Indecency Standards Test," *Washington Post*, 3 February 2004.

6. Karla Peterson, "We Now Return to Our Regularly Scheduled Sleaze," *San Diego Union-Tribune*, 29 March 2004.

7. Bill Carter and Richard Sandomir, "Pro Football: Halftime-Show Fallout Includes F.C.C. Inquiry," *New York Times*, 3 February 2004.

8. Mark Jurkowitz, "Curses! The Clampdown Fed Up with Indecency on Television, Washington Begins to Fight Back," *Boston Globe*, 12 February 2004.

9. "PTC Action Alert," www.parentstv.org/ptc/superbowl/main.asp.

10. "Janet Jackson Breast," www.Staticusers.net/janet-jackson-superbowl-breast.

11. Will Evans, "Jackson's Flesh Flash the Net's Hottest Topic," *Sacramento Bee*, 4 February 2004.

12. Frank Ahrens, "House Raises Penalties for Airing Indecency," *Washington Post*," 17 February 2005.

13. C. W. Nevius, "FCC Inquiry, Uproar over Super Bowl Halftime Peepshow," *San Francisco Chronicle*, 3 February 2004.

14. Geraldine Fabrikant, "CBS Fined over Super Bowl Halftime Incident," *New York Times*, 23 September 2004. In March 2006, the FCC rejected the CBS's appeal and upheld the fine. "Keeping It Clean," *New York Times*, 16 March 2006.

15. Stephen Labaton, "Knowing Indecency Wherever He Sees It," *New York Times*, 28 March 2005.

16. One such installation is discussed in David Rani, "Keeping #**!! Off the Airwaves," *News & Observer* (Raleigh, N.C.), 22 July 2006.

17. Louise M. Benjamin, *Freedom of the Air and the Public Interest: First Amendment Rights in Broadcasting to 1935* (Carbondale: Southern Illinois University Press, 2001), 8–31.

18. Benjamin, *Freedom of the Air*, 71.

19. Paul Starr, *The Creation of the Media: Political Origins of Modern Communications* (New York: Basic Books, 2004), 354–55. For a treatment of failed reform attempts to decommercialize radio, see Robert W. McChesney, *Telecommunications,*

Mass Media, and Democracy: The Battle for the Control of U.S. Broadcasting, 1928–1935 (New York: Oxford University Press, 1993).

20. For an argument that broadcast speech should not be treated any differently than written speech, see Matthew L. Spitzer, *Seven Dirty Words and Six Other Stories: Controlling the Content of Print and Broadcast* (New Haven, Conn.: Yale University Press, 1986).

21. Paul Starr, *The Creation of the Media*, 367–68. For more comment on radio "broadcasting as an authoritarian and paternalistic agent of national unity," see William Boddy, *New Media and Popular Imagination: Launching Radio, Television, and Digital Media in the United States* (New York: Oxford University Press, 2004), 18–19.

22. Benjamin, *Freedom of the Air*, 89.

23. Benjamin, *Freedom of the Air*, 89–97.

24. See Lucas A. Powe Jr., *American Broadcasting and the First Amendment* (Berkeley: University of California Press, 1987), 13–18.

25. Benjamin, *Freedom of the Air*, 97–106.

26. Benjamin, *Freedom of the Air*, 98.

27. *Trinity Methodist Church, South v. FRC*, 62 F. 2d 850 (1932).

28. Benjamin, *Freedom of the Air*, 123, 124, 127.

29. *Duncan v. United States*, 48 F. 2d 128, 132 (1931).

30. Benjamin, *Freedom of the Air*, 135–37.

31. Dave Harker, *One for the Money: Politics and the Popular Song* (London: Hutchinson, 1980), 38.

32. Quoted in Alfred Balk, *The Rise of Radio, from Marconi through the Golden Age* (Jefferson, N.C.: McFarland, 2006), 65.

33. Benjamin, *Freedom of the Air*, 158–66.

34. Benjamin, *Freedom of the Air*, 192–202.

35. Susan Smulyan, *Selling Radio: The Commercialization of American Broadcasting, 1920–1934* (Washington, D.C.: Smithsonian Institution Press, 1994), 120.

36. For instance, there is far more in Benjamin, *Freedom of the Air* dealing with censorship of political and religious material than there is dealing with sex.

37. See Robert L. Hilliard and Michael C. Keith, *Dirty Discourse: Sex and Indecency in American Radio* (Ames: Iowa State Press, 2003), 141, 142.

38. Emily Wortis Leider, *Becoming Mae West* (New York: Farrar Straus & Giroux, 1997), 339–41.

39. T. E. McLeod, "Charlie's Big Night or, Charlie McCarthy, Mae West, and the Edge of Propriety," http://members.tripod.com/m.te/bhs/915993.html. The "yard long" bit is quoted from Leider, *Becoming Mae West*, 339.

40. "Mae West Script Brings Sharp Rebuke from FCC," *New York Times*, 15 January 1938.

41. Leider, *Becoming Mae West*, 340–42.

42. McClellan Patten, "Radio Gets the Jitters," *American Magazine* 127 (March 1939): 42–43.

43. Patten, "Radio Gets the Jitters," 164–65.

44. Robert J. Pondillo, "Censorship in a 'Golden Age': Postwar Television and America's First Network Censor—NBC's Stockton Helffrich," (PhD diss., University of Wisconsin-Madison, 2003), 111, 126–27.

45. Quoted in Balk, *Rise of Radio*, 249.

46. J. Fred MacDonald, *Don't Touch That Dial! Radio Programming in American Life, 1920–1960* (Chicago: Nelson-Hall, 1979), 105.

47. Summers, *Radio Censorship*, 129.

48. The policies are contained in Summers, *Radio Censorship*, 139–52. Examples of the programming can be found in Lloyd Morris, *Not So Long Ago* (New York: Random House, 1949), 452–93.

49. Robert H. Hilliard and Michael C. Keith, *The Broadcast Century and Beyond: A Biography of American Broadcasting*, 4th ed. (Burlington, Mass.: Focal Press, 2005), 97–98.

50. Editors of *Broadcasting* Magazine, *The First Fifty Years of Broadcasting: The Running Story of the Fifth Estate* (Washington, D.C.: Broadcasting Publications, 1982), 119.

51. Powe, *American Broadcasting*, 166–69.

52. Marvin R. Bensman, *Broadcast Regulation: Selected Cases and Decisions*, 2nd ed. (Lanham, Md.: University Press of America, 1985); and Hilliard and Keith, *Dirty Discourse*, 17.

53. William B. Ray, *FCC: The Ups and Downs of Radio-TV Regulation* (Ames: Iowa State University Press, 1990), 73–75.

54. Lorenzo W. Milam, *Sex and Broadcasting: A Handbook on Starting a Radio Station for the Community*, 3rd ed. (Los Gatos, Calif., 1975), 77, 304, 313, 327. The entire decision of the hearing examiner is in *Sex and Broadcasting*, 305–27.

55. Milam, *Sex and Broadcasting*, 77, 326.

56. *FCC v. Pacifica Foundation*, 438 U.S. 751, 726 (1978). The full monologue is provided as an appendix to the Court decision. *Pacifica* in 1949, with KPFA in Berkeley, California, was the first organization that was not an educational institution to receive a license to operate a noncommercial community station. It went on to establish stations in Los Angeles, New York, Washington, D.C., and Houston, seeking to present alternate programming to the commercial outlets. Lawrence Soley, *Free Radio: Electronic Civil Disobedience* (Boulder, Colo.: Westview Press, 1999), 40–41.

57. Phylis A. Johnson and Michael C. Keith, *Queer Airwaves: The Story of Gay and Lesbian Broadcasting* (Armonk, N.Y.: Sharpe, 2001), 27–28. In the mid-1990s the FCC warned the station that the poem could no longer be read on the air, an indication of the shifting political environment (*Queer Airwaves*, 9).

58. Jeff Land, *Active Radio: Pacifica's Brash Experiment* (Minneapolis: University of Minnesota Press, 1999), 104–5.

59. *FCC v. Pacifica Foundation*, 438 U.S. 726 (1978).

60. *FCC v. Pacifica Foundation* at 748, 749.

61. This was the reading given to *Pacifica* when the Court in *Sable Communications v. FCC*, 492 U.S. 115, 127 (1989), in dealing with "dial-a-porn" ruled that indecent telephone transmissions were constitutionally protected.

62. Don R. Pember, *Mass Media Law*, 1997 ed. (Dubuque, Iowa: Brown & Benchmark, 1997), 552.

63. Pember, *Mass Media Law*, 552–55.

64. For a sampling of what attracted the attention of the FCC in its search for indecency on the airwaves, see Jeremy H. Lipschultz, *Broadcast Indecency: F.C.C. Regulation and the First Amendment* (Boston: Focal Press, 1997), 32–38, 113–27.

65. Gini Graham Scott, *Can We Talk? The Power and Influence of Talk Shows* (New York: Insight Books, 1996), 31–44. The larger stations were mainly involved for the format costs about three times what a largely music format did (*Can We Talk?* 41, 57).

66. Hilliard and Keith, *Dirty Discourse*, 67–68.

67. Hilliard and Keith, *Dirty Discourse*, 69–70.

68. John C. Carlin, "The Rise and Fall of Topless Radio," *Journal of Communication* 26 (Winter 1976): 31.

69. Hilliard and Keith, *Dirty Discourse*, 72–74.

70. *Illinois Citizens' Committee for Broadcasting v. FCC*, 515 F. 2d 397, 404 (1975).

71. Hilliard and Keith, *Dirty Discourse*, 72–74.

72. Edmund L. Andrews, "F.C.C. Torn over Howard Stern Case," *New York Times*, 27 November 1992.

73. Hilliard and Keith, *Dirty Discourse*, 75.

74. For a brief history of Stern's career, see Scott, *Can We Talk?* 75–83.

75. Thomas G. Krattenmaker and Lucas A. Powe Jr., *Regulating Broadcast Programming* (Cambridge: MIT Press, 1994), 113–14.

76. Stephen Labaton, "Knowing Indecency Wherever He Sees It," *New York Times*, 28 March 2005.

77. Jacques Steinberg, "Clear Channel Is Said to Settle Accusations of Indecency," *New York Times*, 9 June 2004. For a sample of the talk that generated complaints against "Bubba the Love Sponge," see Hilliard and Keith, 124, 128, 130–31.

78. Frank Ahrens, "Viacom Settles Outstanding FCC Fines," *Washington Post*, 24 November 2004.

79. Joanne Ostrow, "What Price Freedom in Radio?" *Denver Post*, 10 October 2004.

80. Bill Carter and Nat Ives, "Where Some See Just a Shock Jock, Sirius Sees a Top Pitchman," *New York Times*, 11 October 2004.

81. One research company, Bridge Ratings, attributed almost seven hundred thousand Sirius subscribers in the fourth quarter of 2005 to Stern. Ben Sisario, "Howard Stern Embarks on World Conquest Via Satellite," *New York Times*, 10 January 2006.

82. Ostrow, "What Price Freedom in Radio?"

83. Eric A. Taub, "As His Sirius Show Begins, Radio Ponders the Stern Effect," *New York Times*, 9 January 2006,.

84. Alana Semuels, "Sirius Gives Stern, Agent $83-Million Stock Bonus," *Los Angeles Times*, 10 January 2007.

85. Neither Sirius nor its competitor, XM Satellite, has yet turned a profit.

86. Hilliard and Keith, *Dirty Discourse*, 89–91.

87. Frank Ahrens, "Viacom Settles Outstanding Fines," *Washington Post*, 24 November 2004.

88. For a treatment of the censorship of music on radio, see chapter 4.

89. Harry Castleman and Walter J. Podrazik, *Watching TV: Six Decades of American Television*, 2nd ed. (Syracuse, N.Y.: Syracuse University Press, 2003), 14.

90. Peter B. Orlik, *The Electronic Media: An Introduction to the Profession*, 2nd ed. (Ames: Iowa State University Press, 1997), 290–91.

91. Robert L. Hilliard and Michael C. Keith, *The Broadcast Century and Beyond: A Biography of American Broadcasting*, 4th ed. (Burlington, Mass.: Focal Press, 2005), 116.

92. Castleman and Podrazik, *Watching TV*, 47.

93. Louis Chunovic, *One Foot on the Floor: The Curious Evolution of Sex on Television from* I Love Lucy *to* South Park (New York: TV Books, 2000), 33–34.

94. Chunovic, *One Foot on the Floor*, 24–25.

95. Val E. Limburg, *Electronic Media Ethics* (Boston: Focal Press, 1994), 91–93; and Chunovic, *One Foot on the Floor*, 25.

96. "Censorship—Private Brand," *Business Week*, 24 November 1951, 130.

97. Limburg, *Electronic Media Ethics*, 57–59.

98. Pondillo, "Censorship," 375–76.

99. Pondillo, "Censorship," 380–81, 381–83.

100. Pondillo, "Censorship," 589–90.

101. Pondillo, "Censorship," 396.

102. Chunovic, *One Foot on the Floor*, 27–30.

103. Pondillo, "Censorship," 398.

104. Pondillo, "Censorship," 399–400.

105. Pondillo, "Censorship," 404–7.

106. Chunovic, *One Foot on the Floor*, 39–43.

107. Parents Television Council, "TV Timeline," www.parentstv.org/PTC/facts/tvtimeline.asp.

108. Alfred R. Schneider, *The Gatekeeper: My Thirty Years as a TV Censor* (Syracuse, N.Y.: Syracuse University Press, 2001), 4. For thirty years, Schneider was head censor at ABC Television Network.

109. See Nancy Signorielli, *Violence in the Media: A Reference Handbook* (Santa Barbara, Calif.: ABC-CLIO, 2005), 3–15. A chronology listing the various hearings can be found on pages 75–91.

110. Schneider, *Gatekeeper*, 29.

111. Tim Brooks and Earle Marsh, *The Complete Directory to Prime Time Network and Cable TV Shows, 1946–Present*, 7th ed. (New York: Ballantine, 1999), 686–87.

112. Schneider, *Gatekeeper*, 28, 30.

113. Schneider, *Gatekeeper*, 30, 31–32.

114. Schneider, *Gatekeeper*, 50–54.

115. Schneider, *Gatekeeper*, 48–49.

116. Brooks and Marsh, *Complete Directory*, 687–88.

117. Schneider, *Gatekeeper*, 33.

118. *A Case of Rape* (1974), www.imdb.com/title/tt0071286.

119. Geoffrey Cowan, *See No Evil: The Backstage Battle over Sex and Violence on Television* (New York: Simon & Schuster, 1979), 66–79. See also Castleman and Podrazik, *Watching TV*, 253–54.

120. Schneider, *Gatekeeper*, 42, 57–58. The movie won an Emmy for best TV movie of the year.

121. See www.imdb.com/title/tt0091913.

122. Schneider, *Gatekeeper*, 45, 70–71.

123. Patti Hartigan, "Mapplethorpe's 'Chilling Effect:' A Year Later, Battle Goes On," *Boston Globe*, 6 October 1991.

124. *Sony Corporation of America v. Universal City Studios, Inc.*, 464 U.S. 417 (1984).

125. Jonathon Coopersmith, "The Role of the Pornographic Industry in the Development of Videotape and the Internet," in *Women and Technology: Historical, Societal,*

and Professional Perspectives: Proceedings of the 1999 International Symposium on Technology and Society, 29–31 July 1999, New Brunswick, New Jersey, by IEEE (Piscataway, N.J.: Institute of Electrical and Electronic Engineers, 1999), 175–77.

126. "The History of Film and Television," 1988, http://high-techproductions .com/history.htm.

127. Michael deCourcy Hinds, "Personal but Not Confidential: A New Debate over Privacy," *New York Times,* 27 February 1988.

128. Pub. L. 100–618, 112 Stat. 3195 (1988).

129. Chunovic, *One Foot on the Floor,* 56–57.

130. Castleman and Podrazik, *Watching TV,* 202–3.

131. Editors of *Broadcasting, The First 50 Years of Broadcasting: The Running Story of the Fifth Estate* (Washington, D.C.: Broadcast Publications, 1982), 154–55. Both a 1961 speech and one surveying the scene thirty years later are reprinted in Newton N. Minow and Craig L. LaMay, *Abandoned in the Wasteland: Children, Television, and the First Amendment* (New York: Hill and Wang, 1995), 185–207.

132. Chunovic, *One Foot on the Floor,* 48–49.

133. Schneider, *Gatekeeper,* 30, 95, 104. For some coverage of episodes dealing with sex, see Chunovic, *One Foot on the Floor,* 61–65.

134. Cowan, *See No Evil,* 25–31.

135. Cowan, *See No Evil,* 71–72.

136. Cowan, *See No Evil,* 89–93, 108–15.

137. Cowan, *See No Evil,* 116–41.

138. Harry F. Walters and Martin Kasindorf, "TV's Fall Season," *Newsweek,* 8 September 1975, 44, 45.

139. Cowan, *See No Evil,* 230. The suit is fully covered on pages 158–230.

140. *Writers Guild of America, West, Inc. v. F.C.C.,* 423 F. Supp. 1064, 1155 (1976).

141. Cowan, *See No Evil,* 242, 243, 246.

142. Schneider, *Gatekeeper,* 114.

143. Cowan, *See No Evil,* 246–50. As FCC commissioner, Johnson had protested certain FCC decisions as censorship, but he had no objection to using marketplace pressure to affect the content of shows.

144. Cowan, *See No Evil,* 263.

145. Schneider, *Gatekeeper,* 36–40.

146. Brooks and Marsh, *Complete Directory,* 939, 940.

147. Cowan, *See No Evil,* 262–66. See also Castleman and Podrazik, *Watching TV,* 268–70.

148. Schneider, *Gatekeeper,* 35.

149. Cowan, *See No Evil,* 290.

150. Cowan, *See No Evil,* 269.

151. See Joyce N. Sprafkin and L. Theresa Silverman, "Update: Physically Intimate and Sexual Behavior on Prime-Time Television, 1978–1979," *Journal of Communication* 31 (Winter 1981): 34–40.

152. Michael J. Robinson, "Prime Time Chic: Between Newsbreaks and Commercials the Values are L.A. Liberal," *Public Opinion* 2 (March–May, 1979): 42.

153. Mary Lewis Coakley, *Rated X: The Moral Case against TV* (New Rochelle, N.Y.: Arlington House, 1977), 37.

154. S. Robert Lichter, Linda S. Lichter, and Stanley Rothman, *Prime Time: How TV Portrays American Culture* (Washington, D.C.: Regnery, 1994), 109–10.

155. Harry F. Waters et al., "The New Right's TV Hit List," *Newsweek*, 15 June 1981, 101–3. Wildmon would go on to head Christian Leaders for Responsible Television and the American Family Association.

156. Waters et al., "The New Right's TV Hit List," 103.

157. Orlik, *Electronic Media*, 220.

158. For some of the relevant plotlines, see Chunovic, *One Foot on the Floor*, 84–87.

159. Chunovic, *One Foot on the Floor*, 146. Some of the content of the show is found on pages 145–47.

160. Chunovic, *One Foot on the Floor*, 91–92.

161. Marjorie Heins, *Sex, Sin, and Blasphemy: A Guide to America's Censorship Wars*, rev. ed. (New York: New Press, 1998), xx.

162. For a sampling of the sexual content of the programming, see Heins, *Sex, Sin, and Blasphemy*, 113–16. Fox had quickly distinguished itself from the older networks by treating sex in "an up-front and matter-of-fact manner." Casteman and Podrazik, *Watching TV*, 334.

163. Schneider, *Gatekeeper*, 42–45.

164. Chunovic, *One Foot on the Floor*, 22–23.

165. Some of the sexual content is summarized in Chunovic, *One Foot on the Floor*, 117–18.

166. Sharon Waxman, "'Simpsons' Animates Gay Nuptials, and a Debate," *New York Times*, 21 February 2005.

167. Chunovic, *One Foot on the Floor*, 126–28.

168. Castleman and Podrazik, *Watching TV*, 364.

169. David Whitman and Dorian Friedman, "The War over 'Family Values,'" *U.S. News & World Report*, 8 June 1992, 35.

170. Only in 1992 did NBC embrace the novel idea "that marriage could be sexy and fun" when it put *Mad about You* on its fall schedule. It would run for seven years. Castleman and Podrazik, *Watching TV*, 363.

171. Barry S. Sapolsky and Joseph O. Tabarlet, "Sex in Primetime Television: 1979 versus 1989," *Journal of Broadcasting & Electronic Media* 35 (Fall 1991): 505.

172. Eleanor Blau, "Study Finds Barrage of Sex on TV," *New York Times*, 27 January 1988.

173. Heins, *Sex, Sin, and Blasphemy*, 42–47.

174. Castleman and Podrazik, *Watching TV*, 362.

175. Jennifer Harper, "TV Viewers Choose Spice," *Insight on the News* 18 (April 22, 2002): 28.

176. Rhonda Gibson, "From Zero to 24-7: Images of Sexual Minorities on Television," in *News and Sexuality*, ed. Laura Castañeda and Sharon Campbell (Thousand Oaks, Calif.: Sage, 2006), 265.

177. Ron Becker, *Gay TV and Straight America* (New Brunswick, N.J.: Rutgers University Press, 2006), 141–46.

178. Becker, *Gay TV and Straight America*, 11, 148, 154–55, 164–66, 213.

179. See Jane Arthurs, *Television and Sexuality: Regulation and the Politics of Taste* (New York: Open University Press, 2004), 128–44, for a treatment of the show as postfeminist drama.

180. Arthurs, *Television and Sexuality*, 55.

181. Barbara Kantrowitz, "Mom, What's Oral Sex?" *Newsweek*, 21 September 1998, 44.

182. At least that was the decision of CBS in passing on an episode of *The Practice*. Chunovic, *One Foot on the Floor*, 153.

183. Schneider, *Gatekeeper*, 115–16.

184. Johnson, "TV Sex in the 1990s," *World and I*, 15 (December 2000): 60.

185. The Parents Television Council (PTC) tapes every hour of prime-time network TV to monitor indecency. James Poniewozik, "The Decency Police: A Year after Janet Jackson, Activists and Congress Are Revving Up Their Drive to Clean Up the Airwaves," *Time*, 28 March 2005, 24.

186. For instance, see the survey of the 2001–2002 season in Deborah A. Fisher et al., "Sex on American Television: An Analysis across Program Genres and Network Types," *Journal of Broadcasting & Electronic Media* 48 (December 2004): 529, 542, 551.

187. Alessandra Stanley, "The TV Watch: It's a Fact of Life: Prime Time Shows Are Getting Sexier," *New York Times*, 5 February 2003.

188. Pondillo, "Censorship," 594.

189. Walter Kirn, "The Way We Live Now: 11-16-03; Sex-Ed Night School," *New York Times*, 16 November 2003.

190. Karl Zinsmeister and Eli Lehrer, "Real-Life Results of TV Sex," *American Enterprise* 15 (December 2004): 15. The journal summarizes a study in *Pediatrics*.

191. Bill Carter, "Many Who Voted for 'Values' Still Like Their Television Sin," *New York Times*, 22 November 2004.

192. Lisa de Moraes, "Dropped-Towel Skit Earns Scolding but No Penalty for ABC," *Washington Post*, 15 March 2005.

193. "No 'Amen' for House Bill," *Broadcasting & Cable* 135 (February 28, 2005): 52.

194. Frank Ahrens, "FCC's New Standards-Bearer: Bush Picks Vocal Indecency Opponent to Head Commission," *Washington Post*, 17 March 2005.

195. David Ho, "FCC Fines CBS over Indecency," *News & Observer* (Raleigh, N.C.), 16 March 2006.

196. David Zurawik, "FCC Slaps CBS with $3.5 Million Record Fine: Spate of Sanctions Signals Tough Stance," *Baltimore Sun*, 16 March 2006, Telegraph, 1A.

197. Broadcast Decency Enforcement Act of 2005, Pub. L. No. 109–235, 120 Stat. 491 (2006). For early reaction, see Frank Ahrens, "Six-Figure Fines for Four-Letter Words Worry Broadcasters," *Washington Post*, 11 July 2006.

198. James Poniewozik, "The Decency Police: A Year after Janet Jackson, Activists and Congress are Revving Up Their Drive to Clean Up the Airwaves," *Time*, 28 March 2005.

199. *Turner Broadcasting System, Inc. v. F.C.C.*, 512 U.S. 622 (1994).

200. Marjorie Heins, *Not in Front of the Children: 'Indecency,' Censorship, and the Innocence of Youth* (New York: Hill and Wang, 2001), 190.

201. *United States v. Playboy Entertainment Group, Inc.*, 529 U.S. 803 (2000).

202. Jennifer C. Kerr, "Comcast, Time Warner to Offer Packaged 'Family Choice' Channels," *Herald-Sun* (Durham, N.C.), 13 December 2005.

203. Pew Research Center for the People and the Press, "Support for Tougher Indecency Measures, but Worries about Government Intrusiveness: New Concerns

about Internet and Reality Show," 19 April 2005, http://people-press.org/reports/pdf/241.pdf.

204. Walt Howe, "A Brief History of the Internet," www.walthowe.com/navnet/history.html.

205. Ted Schadler, "What It Will Take to Reach PC Have-Nots," research excerpt, June 17, 2005, www.forrester.com/Research/Document/Excerpt/0,7211,37051,00.html.

206. "Innovations: Many Americans Are Still Resisting the Web," *News & Observer* (Raleigh, N.C.), 9 October 2005.

207. Electronic Communications Privacy Act of 1986, Pub. L. 99–508, 100 Stat. 1848.

208. By late 1999 approximately one billion dollars or 25 percent of the total pornographic industry was generated online. See Tom Samiljan, "Digitaletc," *Rolling Stone*, 28 October 1999, 109. For more current statistics and support for the role of pornography in furthering technological development, see Mike Musgrove, "Internet Is Indebted to Porn," *News & Observer* (Raleigh, N.C.), 22 January 2006.

209. Paul Saffo quoted in Musgrove, "Internet Is Indebted to Porn," *News & Observer*.

210. Cooperman, "Role of the Pornography Industry," 178–79.

211. Whether new law is needed, especially regulation that limits access to information, when the existing criminal law makes certain conduct punishable under existing law is worth considering.

212. Jonathan Wallace, "The Religious Right Hits the Internet," *Freedom Writer*, May 1996, www.publiceye.org/ifas/fw/9605/internet.html. *Freedom Writer* was a publication of the Institute for First Amendment Studies that ran from 1989 to 2001. Its full text archives can be found at www.spectacle.org/cda/rr.html.

213. The shift in political control was dramatic. In the House the number of Republicans increased from 176 to 230, and the number of Democrats declined from 258 to 204. In the Senate, fifty-seven Democrats now became forty-eight, as Republicans increased their presence from forty-three to fifty-two.

214. Wallace and Mangan, *Sex, Laws, and Cyberspace*, 177–80.

215. Philip Elmer-Dewitt and Hannah Bloch, "On a Screen Near You: Cyberporn," *Time*, 3 July 1995, 38–40.

216. Marty Rimm, "Marketing Pornography on the Information Superhighway," *Georgetown Law Journal* 83 (June 1995): 1849–1934.

217. Elmer-Dewitt and Bloch, "On a Screen Near You."

218. Wallace and Mangan, *Sex, Laws, and Cyberspace*, 188.

219. Norman Solomon, "Media Beat (7/19/95)," www.fair.org/index.php?page=2272.

220. Wallace and Mangan, *Sex, Laws, and Cyberspace*, 125–52. The chapter summarizes the entire episode quite well.

221. Solomon, "Media Beat."

222. Wallace, "Religious Right."

223. Communications Decency Act of 1996, Pub. L. 104–104, 110 Stat. 56, 133.

224. Wallace and Mangan, *Sex, Laws, and Cyberspace*, 187–88.

225. *ACLU v. Reno*, 929 F. Supp. 824, 881, 882 (1996).

226. *Mutual Film Corp. v. Industrial Commission of Ohio*, 236 U.S. 247 (1915).

227. *Olmstead v. United States*, 277 U.S. 438 (1928).

228. *Estes v. Texas*, 381 U.S. 532 (1965).

229. *Sable Communications of California, Inc. v. F.C.C.*, 492 U.S. 115, 131 (1989).

230. *Reno v. ACLU*, 521 U.S. 844, 874 (1997).

231. Child Pornography Prevention Act of 1996, Pub. L. 104–208, 110 Stat. 3009, 3009–26, 3009–28.

232. Sue Ann Mota, "The United States Supreme Court Addresses the Child Pornography Prevention Act and Child Online Protection Act in *Ashcroft v. Free Speech Coalition* and *Ashcroft v. American Civil Liberties Union*," *Federal Communications Law Journal* 55 (December 2002): 89–90.

233. *Ashcroft v. Free Speech Coalition*, 535 U.S. 234, 253–54 (2002).

234. *Ashcroft v. ACLU*, 542 U.S. 656 (2004). In the interim the Third Circuit Court had for the second time in March 2003 found COPA unconstitutional. Further appeal by the government seemed doomed. *ACLU v. Ashcroft*, 322 F. 3d 240 (2003).

235. *Ashcroft v. ACLU*, 542 U.S. 656, 660 (2004).

236. Pub. L. 106–554, 114 Stat. 2376, 2763A–335 (2000).

237. *United States v. American Library Assn., Inc.*, 539 U.S. 194 (2003).

238. The ALA's position on filtering can be found in Electronic Privacy Information Center, *Filters and Freedom 2.0: Free Speech Perspectives on Internet Content Control* (Washington, D.C.: Electronic Privacy Information Center, 2001), 43–50. The publication also includes a wide variety of articles on the subject including a history dealing with worldwide filtering attempts to control the Internet. A variation of the historical essay can be found in Marjorie Heins, *Not in Front of the Children: 'Indecency,' Censorship, and the Innocence of Youth* (New York: Hill and Wang, 2001), 180–200.

239. Electronic Privacy Information Center, *Filters and Freedom 2.0*, 200.

EPILOGUE

1. Arthur Schlesinger Jr., preface to *Censorship: 500 Years of Conflict*, by the New York Public Library (New York: Oxford University Press, 1984), 7.

2. Adolf Hitler, *Mein Kampf*, trans. Ralph Manheim (Boston: Houghton Mifflin, 1943), 255.

3. Philip Slater, *Pursuit of Loneliness: American Culture at the Breaking Point*, rev. ed. (New York: Beacon, 1976), 67.

4. Marjorie Heins, *Sex, Sin, and Blasphemy: A Guide to America's Censorship Wars*, rev. ed. (New York: New Press, 1998), 164.

5. Heins, *Sex, Sin, and Blasphemy*, 200. In the most thorough report on the subject, the editors lament "the lack of reliable and valid science-based information for many dimensions of the problem it was addressing." Dick Thornburg and Herbert S. Lin, eds., *Youth, Pornography, and the Internet* (Washington, D.C.: National Academy Press, 2002), 386.

6. Marjorie Heins, *Not in Front of the Children: "Indecency," Censorship, and the Innocence of Youth* (New York: Hill and Wang, 2001), 259. For an even stronger argument against protecting children from sex, see Judith Levine, *Harmful to Minors: The Perils of Protecting Children from Sex* (Minneapolis: University of Minnesota Press, 2002).

7. For a treatment of this initiative and its outcome, see Donald Alexander Downs, *The New Politics of Pornography* (Chicago: University of Chicago Press, 1989). For a comprehensive look at the literature in the area, see Betty-Carol Sellen and Patricia A. Young, *Feminists, Pornography, & the Law: An Annotated Bibliography of Conflict, 1970–1986* (Hamden, Conn.: Library Professional Publications, 1987).

8. The argument was first developed in Andrea Dworkin, *Pornography: Men Possessing Women* (New York: Dutton, 1979). In 1942 in *Chaplinsky v. New Hampshire*, 315 U.S. 568, 572, the Supreme Court said that "fighting words" were not protected by the First Amendment, since they obviously were "no essential part of any exposition of ideas." The Court has wisely avoided building upon this decision.

9. See Donald Alexander Downs, *The New Politics of Pornography* (Chicago: University of Chicago Press, 1989), 34–94.

10. *Caught Looking: Feminism, Pornography & Censorship* (East Haven, Conn.: LongRiver Books, 1992), 29. The slim volume contains a wide range of pornographic images.

11. For the most fully developed argument challenging the MacKinnon-Dworkin view, see Nadine Strossen, *Defending Pornography: Free Speech, Sex, and the Fight for Women's Rights* (New York: Scribner, 1995). For a view that the attack on pornography, either from the left or the right, is based on a misunderstanding of the genre and is political in its thrust, see Alan Soble, *Pornography Sex and Feminism* (Amherst, N.Y.: Prometheus Books, 2002.)

12. *American Booksellers Assn., Inc. v. Hudnut*, 598 F. Supp. 1316, 1320, 1337 (1984).

13. *American Booksellers Assn., Inc. v. Hudnut*, 771 F. 2d 323, 329, 330 (1985).

14. *Hudnut v. American Booksellers Association*, 475 U.S. 1001 (1986).

15. Heins, *Sex, Sin, and Blasphemy*, 160.

16. For instance, Lawrence Soley, *Censorship, Inc.: The Corporate Threat to Free Speech in the United States* (New York: Monthly Review Press, 2002) documents considerable corporate censorship but none directed toward sexual matters.

17. Rochelle Gurstein, *The Repeal of Reticence: America's Cultural and Legal Struggles over Free Speech, Obscenity, Sexual Liberation, and Modern Art* (New York: Hill and Wang, 1996), 179, 212.

18. Alexis de Tocqueville, *Democracy in America*, ed. J. P. Mayer and Max Lerner, trans. George Lawrence (New York: Harper & Row, 1966), 174–80.

19. For a treatment of the unifying beliefs that hold the nation together, referred to as the civil religion, and the role of the United States Supreme Court in reinforcing those beliefs, see John E. Semonche, *Keeping the Faith: A Cultural History of the U.S. Supreme Court* (Lanham, Md.: Rowman & Littlefield, 1998).

20. 18 U.S.C. § 1460–1470 (2000).

21. The seven states without such laws are Alaska, Hawaii, Montana, New Mexico, Oregon, Vermont, and West Virginia.

22. Morality in Media Inc.'s website is www.moralityinmedia.org, through which citizens can report alleged obscenity violations and lawyers can access materials at the National Obscenity Law Center.

23. The National Coalition Against Censorship maintains a website, www.the fileroom.org, at which incidents of censorship are collected from the earliest recorded to those of the present day.

Index

ABC, 157, 197–99, 203, 206
abortion on TV, 202
abstract art, 70
ACLU (American Civil Liberties Union): on art exhibits, censorship of, 88, 91–92; on the Communications Decency Act, 217; on the Internet, 219, 272n234; on movies, censorship of, 129; on printed materials, censorship of, 29, 31, 50; on radio, censorship of, 181–83, 190; on warning labels for albums, 166
ACLU v. Reno, 217
Adam & Eve (PHE Inc.), 46
Adams, Jane, 99
adolescents, 48
adultery, 203, 204
advertising, 42, 118, 160–61, 180, 196, 203–5, 208, 210, 228
Advertising Code, 111
"Advice to a Young Man on the Choice of a Mistress" (Franklin), 14
"After the Ball" (song), 142
Agee, James, 117
age restrictions, 42, 74, 87, 100–101, 124–26, 129–33, 254n185
AIDS in art, 85

Alabama, censorship in, 244n138, 261n150
Albee, Edward, 124
Alberts v. California, 37
Albright Art Gallery, 64
album cover art, 157–58
Alexandria (LA), 86–87
Alfie (movie), 124
Alice Alone/Alice in April/Alice on the Outside (Naylor), 49
Aliso Niguel High School (California), 174–75
Aliso Viejo (CA), 174–75
Allen, Fred, 183, 185
Allen, Gracie, 183, 185
Allen, Woody, 198
Alley, Rick, 162
All in the Family (TV show), 202
Alloway, Lawrence, 78
Ameche, Don, 184
American Artists Professional League, 66
American Bandstand (TV show), 146–47
American Birth Control League, 183
American Booksellers' Association, 11, 226
American Broadcasting System. *See* ABC

American Civil Liberties Union. *See* ACLU

American Family Association, 85, 179, 207

American Library Association (ALA), 48–49, 217, 219–20, 238n183, 272n239

American Mercury (magazine), 27

American Mothers' Committee, 157

American Pie (movie), 132

American Purity Alliance, 63

Americans, unifying beliefs of, 273n19

An American Tragedy (Dreiser), 27, 109

Andrews, William S., 23

Anglo-Irish traditional ballads, 140

Annapolis (MD), 79

"Annie Had a Baby" (song), 153, 259n85

Annie Hall (movie), 198

anticensorship campaigns, 22–27, 50

Antonioni, Michelangelo, 125

The Arabian Nights (book), 18, 30

Arbuckle, Fatty, 107

Aristophanes, 19

Aristotle's Master-piece (book), 12

Arizona, censorship in, 166

Arkansas, censorship in, 161

Arlington County (VA), 86

Armey, Dick, 83

Arnaz, Desi, 194

Arno, Peter, 68

Arnold, William, 33–34

The Arrow Show (TV show), 195

art: abstract, 70; and AIDS, 85; censorship generating interest in, 3, 66, 81, 84, 87, 93; censorship of, 5–7, 55–93; Customs Service on, 64–68, 72–73, 75; erotic, 73–75, 78, 88; homosexuality in, 85; nudity in, 62–63, 66, 68, 71–73, 79–80; as political statement, 70, 91–92; and public access to, 80–81; public support of, 67, 83–86, 89, 245n144; street art and artists, 90–91. *See also* paintings; photography; sculpture

artifacts, ancient, 57–59, 72

artistic freedom, 68–69, 126, 133, 254n186. *See also* creative process

Artists and Models (magazine), 32

Art Journal (magazine), 44

art schools and students, 63, 68, 93

As Clean As They Wanna Be (album), 168

Ashcroft, John, 54, 56

Ashcroft v. ACLU, 272n234

As Nasty As They Wanna Be (album), 168

Atlanta Christian Film and Television Commission, 207

Atlantic City (NJ), 98

Austin (TX), 50

Authors Supporting Intellectual Freedom, 50

automatic language rule, 132

Babcock, Barbara, 206

Baby Doll (movie), 122

Baccante and the Infant Fawn (sculpture), 63

Back Seat Dodge—'38 (sculpture), 74

Baehr, Ted, 207

Baker, Norman, 181

Baker, Susan, 163–64

Bakker, Jim, 191

Balance, Bill, 190

Baldwin, Roger, 31

Ball, Lucille, 194

Ballard, Hank, 153

Baltimore (MD), 72

Balzac, Honoré de, 19

banned books, 11, 21, 28, 39, 48–52, 238n183

Banned Books Week, 48–49, 238n183

banned in Boston, 21

banned songs, 152, 157, 182

Bara, Theda, 104–5

Bardot, Brigitte, 36

Barker, Sarah Evans, 227

Barnard, George Grey, 68

Barnes and Noble, 244n138

Barnwell County Museum (SC), 89

Barnwell County (SC), 89

Barr, Roseanne, 208

Barrie, Dennis, 85
Barrymore, John, 105
Bartolo, Rita, 86
Barton County Community College, 87
baseball, 108
Basic Instinct (movie), 130, 133
Bazelon, David, 159
Beardsley, Aubrey, 128
The Beatles, 157
Beaton, Wilford, 112
"Behind Closed Doors" (song), 160
Belán, Kyra, 79–80
Benny, Jack, 185
Benton Harbor (MI), 139
Bergen, Edgar, 184
Bergman, Ingrid, 114
Berle, Milton, 193
Berlin, Irving, 145
Bernstein, Judith, 78
Berry, Richard, 137–38
bestiality, references in music, 169
Beverly Hills (CA), 73
Beware (movie), 99
"Bewitched, Bothered, and Bewildered"
    (song), 115, 153
Biafara, Jello, 158
big bands, 146
Big 8, 108
Billboard (magazine), 150, 153, 157
Bill Haley and the Comets, 144
"A Bird in a Gilded Cage" (song), 150
Bird in Space (sculpture), 67
Birth Control (movie), 104
birth control information: censored,
    183; in movies, 102, 104; in music
    videos, 161; in printed material, 16,
    30, 60; on TV, 202, 207
The Birth of a Baby (documentary
    movie), 114
Birth of a Baby (exploitation movie),
    107
Birth of a Nation (movie), 103
Black, Hugo, 38, 41
Blackboard Jungle (movie), 144
Blackmun, Harry A., 51
black music, 149, 153, 167–69,
    261n147

Blair, Linda, 199
Blecha, Peter, 1
Blow-Up (movie), 125
Bluemont Park Sculpture Project, 86
blues music, 146
Blume, Judy, 49
BMG Music Group, 171
Boccaccio, Giovanni, 30
Body Double (movie), 130
Boise, Ron, 73
Bok, Curtis, 35, 37
Bonaparte, Charles J., 15
books: banned or prohibited, 11, 21,
    28, 39, 48–52, 238n183; censorship
    generating interest in, 47;
    censorship of, 5–6, 9–52; hardback
    vs. paperback, 39; lesbianism in,
    50–51; masturbation in, 28;
    pornographic, 15–16; pulp novels,
    42–43. *See also* specific titles
Boone, Pat, 167
Bork, Robert, 200
Born Innocent (television movie), 199
Born to be Made (book), 42
Boston (MA), 20–21, 26–27, 41, 64,
    129
Boston Bookseller's Committee, 27
Boston Public Library, 63
Boston Women's Health Collective, 44
The Bounty of the West (sculpture), 68
Bow, Clara, 105, 107, 233n50
bowdlerization, 14
Boykin, Charles, 158
Bradenton (FL), 90
Brancusi, Constantin, 67–68
Brando, Marlon, 127
Brave New World (Huxley), 48
breasts shown on TV and in movies,
    113, 115–17, 125, 178, 195–96
Breen, Joseph I., 113–19, 152
Breezy Stories (magazine), 34
Brennan, William J., Jr., 38–39, 41, 45,
    51, 189
Brigham Young University, 90
Brinkley, John, 181
British invasion, 157
Broadway (newspaper), 63

Broadway Open House (TV show), 196
Brokeback Mountain (movie), 133, 173, 255–56nn229–230
Brokeback Mountain (Proulx), 50
Brooklyn Museum of Art, 78
Broun, Elizabeth, 87–88
Broward County (FL), 168
Bruce, Robert, 153
Brueghel the Elder, Pieter, 71
Bryan, Frederick Van Pelt, 39–40
Bryant, Anita, 82
Buchmeyer, Jerry, 51
Buffalo (NY), 63–64
the bunny hug (dance), 144–45
Burch, Dean, 190
Burger, Warren, 43–45, 51
Burns, George, 185
Burress, Phil, 134
Burroughs, William, 41
Burstyn, Joseph, 119
Bush, George W., 83, 134, 212

Cabell, James Branch, 23–24
cable TV, 160–63, 198, 206, 208, 212
Cain, James, 118
Cairns, Huntington, 31, 67–68
the cakewalk (dance), 144
Caldwell, Erskine, 34
California: art, censorship of, 67–69, 73–75, 81–82, 88; and dancing, 174–75; music, censorship of, 158; and obscenity, 37, 44, 73; and printed material, 41, 50; radio, censorship of, 169, 181, 189–90
Campus Mistress (book), 42
Canaday, John, 74
Cantor, Eddie, 183, 185, 193
Capitol Records, 157
Carlin, George, 188
Carnal Knowledge (movie), 128
Carnegie Mellon University, 215
Carter, Jack, 196
Casanova, Giacomo, 30
A Case of Rape (television movie), 199
Castle, Vernon and Irene, 145–46
the Castle Walk (dance), 145

Catholic Church, 97, 112–13. *See also* Legion of Decency
Catholic World (magazine), 70
CBS, 178, 181, 191, 202, 210–11
CBS Music, 166
censorship: and anti-drug legislation, 173–74; of classical art, 57–59, 71–72; in colonial America, 12–13, 232n19; and democracy, 134; history of, 11–52, 232n19; prior restraint, 99. *See also under* art; books; magazines; movies; music; photography; pornography; radio; sculpture; self-censorship; television
centerfolds, 36
Center for Media and Public Affairs, 207
Cerf, Bennett, 30–31
Chabas, Paul, 64
Chap Book (magazine), 98
Chaplin, Charlie, 107
the Charleston (dance), 146
Charlie's Angels (TV show), 204
"Charlotte the Harlot" (song), 140
Chase, Ilka, 195
Chase & Sandborn Radio Hour (radio show), 184
chat rooms, 214
Checker, Chubby, 147
Cheney, Lynn, 172
Cher, 161
Chicago (IL): art, censorship of, 64, 74, 79, 157; magazines, censorship of, 32; movies, censorship of, 98–101, 120; radio, censorship of, 169, 190
Chicago, Judy, 78
Chicago Art Institute, 74
Chicago Tribune (newspaper), 99
child abuse on TV, 199
childbirth in movies, 109
Child Online Protection Act, 219, 272n234
child pornography, 81–82, 130–32, 214, 217–18, 244n138
Child Pornography Prevention Act, 218
children: art, protection from works of, 77, 79; Internet, protection from,

214–15, 217–21, 272n234; lessons learned from TV, 210; movies, protection from, 100, 112; music, protection from, 162–64, 166; printed materials, protection from, 2, 5, 42, 47–51; radio and TV, protection from, 178, 188–89; as sexual beings, 47, 238nn174–75; used as standard for obscenity, 37, 223–25
Children's Internet Protection Act, 219–21
The Children's Society, 100
The Chocolate War (Cormier), 49
Christian Coalition, 215
CIA, art exhibit in building, 88
Cincinnati (OH), 59, 85, 162
Cincinnati Contemporary Arts Center, 85
Cincinnati Inquirer (newspaper), 162
Cinderella (movie), 99
Citadel Broadcasting, 169–70
Citizen Kane (movie), 115–16
citizens' commission (Rhode Island), 39
Citizens for Community Values, 134
Citizens for Decent Literature, 44
Civil War, 60
Clairol, 196
Clark, Russell, G., 147
class bias and censorship, 58, 61–62
classic literature, 17–18, 30
Clean Books Bill (New York), 8, 9
Clean Books League, 10
clear and present danger test, 35
Clear Channel Communications, 191
Cleland, John, 13, 41
Clem, Todd, 191
Cleopatra (movie), 104
Cleveland (OH), 145
Clinton, Bill, 172, 208–9
"Club Drug Campaign," 173
Coalition for Better Television, 205
Coats, Daniel R., 216
Cockburn, Alexander, 17
Cocteau, Jean, 95
Code and Rating Administration (CARA), 126, 128

Cold War, 70
colonial America, censorship in, 12–13, 232n19
Colorado, censorship of music in, 169
Colorado Springs (CO), 169
Columbia Broadcasting Company. *See* CBS
Columbia Pictures, 108, 127
Comcast, 212
Commission of Obscenity and Pornography, 76
Committee for Public Information, 65
Committee of Five for the Betterment of Radio, 151–52
Communications Act (of 1934), 151, 183, 217–18
Communications Decency Act (of 1996), 212, 216–18
communism and artists, 70
community standards, 22, 38, 40, 44, 72, 84, 120–21, 127
Comstock, Anthony, 5, 20, 21, 55, 60–65
Comstock, Barbara, 57
Comstock Act, 60
Comstockery, 65
Concerned Women for America, 134
concerts and performances, 155, 172
Conference of Catholic Bishops, 133
The Confessional Unmasked (Scott), 17
Congressional hearings: on the Internet, 215–20, 218; on pornography, 32; on ratings systems, 209; on television, 196, 197, 211–12; on white slavery, 104. *See also* Senate hearings
Congressional Record, 215
Connecticut, censorship in, 88
Connecticut Workers' Compensation Commission Office, 88
conservatives. *See* social conservatives
contemporary community standards. *See* community standards
Continuity Acceptance Department, 195
Contract with America, 215
Copps, Michael J., 210

Corcoran Gallery of Art, 83–86
Cormier, Robert, 49
Cortland (NY), 169
country-western music, 153, 160
court records, "purity of," 58, 63
Covington, Lorenze Dow, 65
"Cowboys Are Frequently, Secretly . . ." (song), 173
Cox, Kenneth A., 188
"crack house" law, 173–74
Craddock, Ida, 16
Crafts, Wilbur Fisk, 106
Crane, Stephen, 17
Crash (movie), 131
Crawford, Joan, 111
Cray, Ed, 138–41
creative process, 4, 113–14. *See also* artistic freedom
Creel, George, 65
Crimes of Passion (movie), 128
criminal behavior and obscene materials, 35, 37, 77
Cronenberg, David, 131
crooners, 152, 155
Crosby, Bing, 152
crossover of music genres, 143–44
Crossroads of Lust (book), 42
Crowther, Bosley, 118
"Crying in the Chapel" (song), 144
Crystal, Billy, 212
Cumia, Anthony, 192–93
Cushing, Richard J., 196
Customs Service: and books, 28, 30; and foreign movies, 102, 115, 129; and obscenity, 15, 64–68, 75; and works of art, 58–59, 64–68, 72–73, 75
Cutting, Bronson M., 28–29
cybersex, 214
Cypress (CA), 75

Daddy's Roommate (Willhoite), 51
Dagmar, 196
Daily News (newspaper), 57
Dallas (TV show), 206
Dallas (TX), 70, 80
Dalzell, Stewart, 217

Damaged Goods (movie), 106
D'Amato, Alfonse, 83
dance clubs, 173–74
dance halls, regulation of, 144–45
dancing, 6, 143–48, 174–75. *See also* specific dance names
Danforth, John, 165
d'Annunzio, Gabriele, 20
"Darling Nikki" (song), 163
David (sculpture), 75
Davies, Marion, 115
daytime soap operas, 196, 200
Dead Kennedys, 157
Dean, Abner, 68
The Decameron (Boccaccio), 16, 18, 30
decoy letters, 19, 29
Deep Throat (movie), 127
Defoe, Daniel, 19
DeGeneres, Ellen, 208
De Grazia, Edward, 129
DeLacey, James A., 27
Delaware, censorship in, 166
Dell, Floyd, 25
Deluxe Coffee House (Wilmington, NC), 89
DeMille, Cecile B., 105
DeMille, William C., 95
Dennett, Mary Ware, 28–29
"Den of Iniquity" (song), 153
Denver (CO), 187
Denver, John, 158
De Palma, Brian, 130
Department of Justice, 173
Department of Justice building, *54*, 55–57
Derek, Bo, 129
Derek, John, 129
Des Moines (IA), 74–75
Des Moines Art Center, 74–75
Desperate Housewives (TV show), 210
Detroit (MI), 131, 153–54
The Devil in Miss Jones (movie), 127
Devils and Dust (album), 172–73
DeVito, Danny, 132
Diamond Lil (musical), 95–96
Dietrich, Marlene, 115
digital-delay systems, 179

The Dinner Party (installation), 78
A Dirty Shame (movie), 134
disco, 147
disk jockeys, 186–87
display laws, 52
distribution of movies, 98, 119
diversity in America, 229–30
Dolorita in the Passion Dance
  (Kinetoscope show), 98
Dondero, George A., 70
"Don't be Cruel" (song), 155
"Don'ts and Be Carefuls" (NAMPI),
  109–10
The Doors, 155–56
Doubleday and Company, 22, 37
Douglas, William O., 33, 38, 41, 44
Dowling, Paula, 138
The Drag (play), 95
Dreiser, Theodore, 17, 22, 25, 27, 109
Dressed to Kill (movie), 130, 133
Dr. Kildare (TV show), 201
Droll Stories (Balzac), 19
Drug Enforcement Administration,
  173–74
drug use, 158, 167, 173–74
Dubuque (IA), 71
Dubin, Al, 150
Duchamp, Marcel, 64
Duchess of Alba (painting), 71
Duel in the Sun (movie), 118
Duncan, Robert, 182
Durgnat, Raymond, 137
Dworkin, Andrea, 226
Dynasty (TV show), 206

"Earth Angel" (song), 154
Eastman Kodak Company, 71
Easton, Sheena, 163
"Eat Me Alive" (song), 163
Ecstasy, 173–74
Ecstacy (movie), 115
Ecstasy Prevention Act, 174
Ed Sullivan Show, 155
educational function of movies and TV,
  99, 102, 201
Edwards, Jonathan, 12
Egnor, Virginia Ruth, 196

Electric Ladybird (album), 157
electronic media, 6, 178–80. *See also*
  Internet; radio; television
Electronic Music Defense & Education
  Fund, 173–74
Ellen (TV show), 208
Ellington, Duke, 149
Elmer Gantry (Lewis), 27
Ely, Jack, 138
Emerson, Faye, 195
Emerson, Ralph Waldo, 14
Eminem, 169–70, 172
The Eminem Show (album), 172
Emmanuelle (movie), 127
End as a Man (Willingham), 35
Entertainment Weekly (magazine), 207
entrapment, 63. *See also* decoy letters
Erie (PA), 148
Ernst, Morris, 30, 181–82
Eros (magazine), 42
erotic art, 73–75, 78, 88
"Erotic City" (song), 159
erotic magazines. *See* girlie magazines
Escape from the Asylum, 248n34
Esquire (magazine), 32–33, 235n107
E.T. (movie), 126
Evanston (IL), 79
Events (painting), 74
"Everybody's Doing It Now" (song),
  145
"Every Little Movement Has a Meaning
  All Its Own" (song), 150
"Everything Old is Nude Again"
  (photo), 89
Exon, James J., 215–16
exotic dancing, 148
explicit lyrics warning label, 166–67,
  171–72
exploitation films, 106
"Express Yourself" (music video), 162
expurgation, 14
Eyes Wide Shut (movie), 132

failure to inform, 58, 63
Fairbanks, Douglas, 105, 107
Fairness & Accuracy in Reporting, 216
Fall River (MA), 71

Falwell, Jerry, 44, 205
family hour, 202–3
Family Research Council, 134
Family Viewing Policy, 202–3
Fand, Daria, 91
Fanny Hill (Cleland), 13, 41
A Farewell to Arms (Hemingway), 48
Farrell, James T., 35
Farrow, Mia, 200
Fatal Attraction (movie), 130
Fatima, 98
Faulkner, Thomas A., 143
Faulkner, William, 35, 114
FBI. *See* Federal Bureau of Investigation
FCC: cable TV free from regulations, 212; creation of, 180; music, indecency standards for, 169–70; radio, regulation of, 151, 158, 183–93; radio and TV, indecency standards for, 178–80, 188–89, 211–12, 225–26; U.S. Supreme Court on, 159, 188
Fear of Flying (Jong), 83
Federal Bureau of Investigation (FBI), 63, 81–82, *136*, 139
Federal Communications Act (of 1934), 180
Federal Communications Commission. *See* FCC
Federal Radio Commission, 180–83
Federal Trade Commission, 171
Feminine Forum (radio show), 190
feminist art, 78, 80, 85–86
feminists against pornography, 130, 226
Femme Forum (radio show), 190
Ferguson, Warren J., 202
fig leaves, 56, 68
Film Comment (magazine), 130
films. *See* movies
filters and the Internet, 219–20, 272n239
"Filthy Words" (monologue), 188
The Financier (Dreiser), 22
Finley, Karen, 86
First Amendment. *See* freedom of speech and expression; freedom of the press

First Amendment Center, 259n85
First Great Awakening, 12
Fischl, Eric, 73
Five Dollar Billie (sculpture), 74
Florida: art, censorship of, 80, 90; dance clubs in, 174; movies, censorship of, 103; music, censorship of, 166, 168–69; radio, censorship of, 191
Flying Blind (TV show), 207
Folio (magazine), 43–44
folk music, 142
Forcade, Thomas, 76
Ford, Charles Henri, 31
Ford, John, 10, 11
foreign movies, 102, 115, 118, 122–23, 129
Forever (Blume), 49
Forever Amber (movie), 118
Forever Amber (Windsor), 34
Forman, Henry James, 112
For Men Only (radio show), 185
42 Street (musical), 150
forum shopping, 46
Foster, Sally, 87
Fox Network, 206–7, 269n162
fox trot (dance), 145
Frank, Jerome, 37
Frankenshrist (album), 157
Franklin, Benjamin, 12–14
freaking (dance), 174–75
freedom of speech and expression: broadcast media discriminated against, 191; and dancing, 148; and democracy, 134; financial burden of fighting for, 92; and the Internet, 218–21; on military bases, 48; and movies, 103–4, 119–20, 217, 249n52; and obscenity, 35–38, 43–44, 72, 230; and performance art, 86; and popular music, 168, 171; and pornography, 227; and radio, 180–93; and sexual speech, 7; and state interests, 249n52; and TV, 202–3; U.S. Supreme Court on, 224, 236n126
freedom of the press, 103, 249n52
Freedom Sings (album), 259n85

Freidman, Robert, 1
Friends (TV show), 207
Frisco (TX), 93
Fritts, Eddie, 163–64
Frohnmayer, John, 55, 84–85
From the Ballroom to Hell (Faulkner, T.), 143
Fruits of Philosophy (Knowland), 16
FTC (Federal Trade Commission), 171
Fuck Me, Fuck You (photograph), 86
fundamentalists, religious, 50, 147–48. *See also* social conservatives
Funt, Allen, 124

Gaieties of Divorce (movie), 99
"gansta" rap, 168
Garbo, Greta, 115
Garcia, Jerry, 187
Gargantua and Pantagruel (Rabelais), 18, 30
Gates, Henry Louis, Jr., 168
Gathers, Ezekiel Candler, 196
The Gay Lesbian Alliance Against Defamation, 208
gays. *See* homosexuality
General Federation of Women's Clubs, 106, 109
The Genius (Dreiser), 22, 25
Gensen-Gerber, Judianne, 82
Georgetown Law Journal, 215
George Washington (sculpture), 59
Georgia, censorship in, 128, 171
Gergen, David, 164
Gilman, Catheryne Cooke, 109
Gilmore, Jim, 82
Gingrich, Arnold, 32–33
Gingrich, Newt, 215, 217
Ginsberg, Allen, 188
Ginsberg, Sam, 42
Ginsberg v. United States, 254n185
Ginzburg, Ralph, 42
girlie magazines, 32–33, 236n122. *See also* names of specific magazines
Girls Concentration Camp Ordeals (book), 43
"Girls Just Want to Have fun" (music video), 161

Girls on the Beach (painting), 88
Giuliani, Rudolph, 90–91
Glyn, Elinor, 20–21, 233n50
And God Created Woman (movie), 36
Godfrey, Arthur, 193
God's Little Acre (Erskine), 34–35
Golden Globes Awards, 179
Goldstein, Al, 130
Goldwater Amendment, 43
Gone with the Wind (movie), 116
Goodman, Daniel Carson, 21
Goodman, Theodosia, 104
"Good Rockin' Tonight" (song), 155
Gordon, George N., 55
Gore, Albert, 165
Gore, Tipper, 137, 163–66
Gortikov, Stan, 164–65
Gotham Book Mart, 66
Goya, Francisco, 71
G. P. Putnam's Sons, 41
Grable, Betty, 70
Grant, Cary, 94, 96–97, 114
The Grapes of Wrath (Steinbeck), 48
Grassley, Charles, 215–16
Grauer, Ben, 186
Great American Nudes (Wesselmann), 73
Great Awakenings, First and Second, 12–13
Great Bend (KS), 87
The Great Train Robbery (movie), 99
Grecian Guild Pictorial (magazine), 40
Greek Slave (sculpture), 59
Greenough, Horatio, 59
Griffiths, D. W., 103
Grove Press, 39–41, 128–29
Guerilla Girls, 80
Guerney, Bernard Guilbert, 26
Gurstein, Rochelle, 229
Gutenberg, Johannes, 1, 11
"A Guy What Takes His Time" (song), 96

Hagar Revelly (Goodman), 21
Hahn, Jessica, 191
Haines, William, 16
Hair (movie and musical), 123

Hairspray (movie), 134
Halsey, Raymond D., 23
Hand, Augustus N., 29
Hand, Learned, 21, 31
Happiness (movie), 132
Harcourt, Alfred, 27
hardback books, 39
Hari, Eugene, 196
Harlan, John Marshall, 38
Harlow, Jean, 96, 107, 115
Harmful to Minors (Levine), 47, 238n175
Harris, Robie H., 49
Harry Potter books, 48
Hart, Lorenz (Larry), 115, 153
Hawley-Smoot Tariff, 28, 66
Hawthorne, Nathaniel, 13
Hays, William H., 96–97, 108–11, 116, 119
Hays Office. *See* Production Code Administration (PCA)
Hayworth, Rita, 70
HBO, 208
Hearst, William Randolph, 115–16
"Heartbreak Hotel" (song), 155
Heather Has Two Mommies (Newman), 51
Hefner, Hugh, 36
Heidenry, John, 1
Heins, Majorie, 1, 223, 238n174
Helena (MT), 44
Helffrich, Stockton, 195
Heller, Marvin, 197
"Help Me Make It Through the Night" (song), 160
Hemingway, Ernest, 32, 48
Hendrix, Jimi, 157
Henry and June (movie), 131
The Heptameron (Marguerite of Navarre), 18
Hermaphrodite (drawing), 88
Hicklin, Henry, 17
Hicklin test, 17–21, 31, 37–38
Hill Street Blues (TV show), 206
Himber, Richard, 151
hip-hop, 168–69
history of censorship, 11–52, 232n19

Hitchcock, Alfred, 114
Hitler, Adolf, 223
Hoffman, Donna, 216
Holden, William, 121
Hollings, Ernest, 165
Holmes, Peter, 13
Holocaust, 199
Holt, Guy, 24
home as protected space, 181
homosexuality: in art, 85; in movies, 123, 128, 133, 255–56nn229–230; in music videos, 161–62; in printed material, 31–32, 49–51; on the radio, 182, 185, 188; on TV, 198–99, 202–3, 205–6, 208
Honolulu (HI), 91
"Hoochie Coochie Man" (song), 152
Hooper, Janette, 91
Hoover, J. Edgar, 157
Hope, Bob, 185
Hot Dog (magazine), 32
hotels and movies, 134
Hotshot (album), 172
"Hound Dog" (song), 155
The Housewife's Handbook on Selective Promiscuity (book), 42
Houston (TX), 155
Howar, Pam, 164
"Howl" (poem), 188
How to Marry a Millionaire (movie), 197
How to Write and Sell a Hit Song (Silver and Bruce), 153
Hughes, Gregg, 192–93
Hughes, Howard, 116–18, 252n139
Hughes, Linda, 51
human anatomy, study of, 58
Huxley, Aldous, 48

"I Ain't Gonna Give Nobody None of My Jelly Roll" (song), 149–50
I am Curious—Yellow (movie), 129
Idaho State University, 87
I Dream of Jeannie (TV show), 201
"If I Could Turn Back Time" (music video), 161
"I Get Ideas" (song), 154
"I know it when I *See* it," 240n14

Illicit Drug Anti-Proliferation Act, 174
Illinois: art, censorship of, 64, 68, 79; censorship of radio stations, 190; movies, censorship of, 99, 120–21; music, censorship of, 157, 166, 169; obscenity trials in, 42–43
Illinois Citizens Committee for Broadcasting, 190
Illinois State University, 85
"I Love Louisa" (song), 150
I Love Lucy (TV show), 193
images, power of, 99
immigration and censorship, 3, 16, 61, 224
The Immoral Mr. Teas (movie), 123
I'm No Angel (movie), 97
impotence on TV, 202–3
Imus, Don, 192
indecency standards, 169–70, 178–80, 188–89, 211–12, 225–26
Index Librorum Prohibitorum (Index of Prohibited Books), 11
Indiana: and dancing, 148; music, censorship of, 168, 172; pornography, censorship of, 226
Indiana University, 72
Infinity Broadcasting, 192–93
the Ink Spots, 153
Instant Love (book), 42
Institute for Sex Research, 72
Institute for the Future, 214
integration of popular music, 167–68
intentions (of author), 21
Intercourse (PA), 42
Internet: children, protection of, 214–15, 217–21, 272n234; Congressional hearings on, 215–20, 218; development of, 213; and filters, 219–20, 272n239; and freedom of speech and expression, 218–21; internationality of, 214–15, 220; and Janet Jackson Superbowl episode, 179; pornography on, 214–18, 271n208; ratings system for, 220; regulation of, 6, 272n234; and sexually explicit materials, 214–21; U.S. Supreme Court on, 218–21

Interstate Circuit, Inc. v. Dallas, 254n185
interstate commerce and obscenity, 46, 103, 229–30
Iowa, censorship in, 71, 74–75, 166, 181
irresponsible sex on TV, 207, 210
Irwin, May, 97
Isle of Pines (fictional journal), 12
"It" girl, 105
It's Perfectly Normal (Harris), 49–50
"It Wasn't Me" (song), 172

Jackson, Janet, *176*, 177–79, 211
Jackson, Jesse, 159, 167
Jackson, Michael, 160, 167
Jagger, Mick, 157
"Jailhouse Rock" (song), 155
James, John, 90
James Bond movies, 123
James Boys (movie), 99
Jane's Addiction, 158
Janet Marsh (Dell), 25
Janis, Sidney, 74
jazz, 146, 149
Jazz from Hell (album), 166
The Jazz Singer (movie), 110
Jeffress, Robert, 51
jelly roll (slang), 149–50
Jenkintown (PA), 80
Jennewein, C. Paul, 55–56
Jessup, Morris K., 16
Jews in the movie industry, 102, 106, 114
the jitterbug, 146
The Joe Pyne Show (radio show), 189
John, Olivia Newton, 159
John Lane Company, 22
Johnson, Eric, 119, 124
Johnson, Hugh S., 186
Johnson, Lyndon, 76–77
Johnson, Nicholas, 158, 190, 203, 268n143
Jones, Grandpa, 160
Jones, Sarah, 170
Jong, Erica, 83
Joyce, James, 25, 30–31
jungle music, 149

Jurgen: A Comedy of Justice (Cabell), 24
"Justify My Love" (music video), 162

Kaiser Family Foundation, 209
Kallen, Horace M., 1
Kaltenborn, H. V., 9
Kama Sutra, 73
Kankakee (IL), 68
Kansas, censorship in, 32, 51, 87,
   102–3, 125, 161, 181
Kaplan, Norma, 86
Karlson, Julie Kay, 88
Kaufman, Frank A., 75
Keating, Charles H., Jr., 44, 76–77
"Keep Your Skirt Down, Mary Ann"
   (song), 152
Keisler, Hedy, 115
Kemp, Shana, 175
Kennedy, Anthony, 218–19
Kentucky, censorship in, 134
Keyhole (magazine), 36
"Kiddie Porn" (song), 169
Kienholz, Edward, 74
kinetoscope shows, 98
the Kingsmen, 138
Kingstree (SC), 187
Kinsey, Alfred, 72, 195
The Kiss (sculpture), 90
The Kiss (Vitascope film), 97
kissing, 97–98, 109, 114, 251n121
Knopf, Alfred A., 25
Knowland, Charles, 16
Koop, C. Everett, 161
Korell, Franklin, 182
Kosik, Edwin M., 81
Kreutzer Sonata (Tolstoy), 20
Krug, Judith, 49
Kubrick, Stanley, 132

Ladies' Home Journal (magazine), 149
Ladies' Visitor (magazine), 13
Lady Chatterley's Lover (Lawrence), 27,
   39–40
Lamarr, Hedy, 115
Lambert, Kenneth, 89
Landis, Kenesaw Mountain, 108
Lane, Thomas, 196

language: in movies, 132; on radio and
   TV, 179, 181–84, 187, 193–96. *See
   also* lyrics
LaPrade, Ernest, 152
The Lascivious London Beauty (book), 16
Last Tango in Paris (movie), 127
Lauper, Cyndi, 161
Law, Patricia, 175
Lawrence, D. H., 10, 27, 39–40
Leahy, Patrick, 215
Lear, Norman, 202, 205
Leaves of Grass (Whitman), 13–14, 16, 18
Leaving Town Alive (Frohnmayer), 85
Lederman, Robert, 91
Leeds, Josiah W., 62
Legion of Decency, 97, 112–13, 118,
   121–24, 250n95
leisure time, increase in, 142
Lennon, John, 157
lesbianism, 50–51, 133, 161–62, 206,
   208
Lester, Jerry, 196
"Let Me Be Your Teddy Bear" (song),
   155
"Let's Do It" (song), 150
"Let's Make a Baby" (song), 167
Let's Make Love (movie), 122
"Let's Pretend We're Married" (song),
   162
"Let's Spend the Night Together"
   (song), 155, 157
Levine, Judith, 47, 238n175
Lewinsky, Monica, 209
Lewis, Sinclair, 23, 27
LeWitt, Sol, 87–88
Lewitzky, Bella, 84
Lexington (VA), 82
Liason (newsletter), 42
libraries, 48–52, 219–21
licensing laws for radio and TV, 11,
   181–86, 193, 211
Life (magazine), 69, 71
The Life Millennium (Friedman), 1
Lifestories (TV show), 208
"Light My Fire" (song), 155–56
"Like a Virgin" (song and music video),
   162, 164

Lillie, Bea, 185
literary community against censorship, 22–27, 50
literary reputation, 40
literature of disillusion, 23
The Little Girl Next Door (movie), 101
Little Review (magazine), 25
Liveright, Horace, 25, 27
local censorship: of dance halls, 144–45; of movies, 106, 124–25, 127–28, 131; of music, 153–54, 167
local standards, 127, 230
LodgeNet, 134
Loews Theatres, 108, 119
Lolita (movie), 123, 131
Lombardo, Guy, 151
Lord, Daniel, 110
Lord, Joseph S., 79
Los Angeles (CA): art, censorship of, 69, 74, 158; books, censorship of, 41; obscenity trials, 75; radio, censorship of, 169, 181; talk radio and, 189–90
Los Angeles Art Museum, 69
Los Angeles County (CA), 88
Los Angeles County Art Museum, 74
Los Angeles County Fire Department, 88
Los Angeles Times, 47
Loudoun (VA), 87
"Louie Louie" (song), *136*, 138–39
Louisiana, censorship in, 71, 86, 103
"Love for Sale" (song), 150
Love on the Sly (book), 16
The Lovers (movie), 121
Lovers in the Cornfield (painting), 71
"Love to Love You Baby" (song), 159
Lowell (MA), 71
Lust Campus (book), 42
The Lustful Turk (book), 16
Lust Pool (book), 43
Lyman, Abe, 151
Lynch, James L., 177
lyrics: explicit lyrics warning label, 166–68, 171–72; printing of, 164, 166–68; ribald, 138–41; Senate

hearings on, 165; sexually explicit, 115, 149–60, 162–68, 169–73
Lysistrata (Aristophanes), 19

MacKinnon, Catharine, 226
Macmillan, 34
MacMonnies, Frederick, 63
MacRorie, Janet, 185
Mad About You (TV show), 269n170
made-for-TV movies, 198–99
Mademoiselle de Maupin (Gautier), 23
Madonna, 162, 164
magazines, 32–33, 36, 40, 42–43, 236n122. *See also* names of specific magazines
Maggie: A Girl of the Streets (Crane), 17
The Maid of Orleans (Voltaire), 18
mail. *See* Post Office Department
Majesty of Justice (sculpture), 56
Mangan, Mark, 177
Mann, Sally, 82
Mann Act, 104
Mansfield, Jane, 40–41
Manton, Martin T., 31
MANual (magazine), 40
Mapplethorpe, Robert, 44, 83–85
Marcus Welby, M.D. (TV show), 202
Married . . . With Children (TV show), 206
Married Love and Contraception (Stopes), 30
Marshall, Thurgood, 45, 51, 189
Martin, Kevin J., 211–12
Martin, Nora, 193
Maryland, censorship in, 72, 79, 102, 125, 129, 166
Mary Tyler Moore Show (TV show), 201
M*A*S*H (TV show), 202
Massachusetts: censorship in, 12–16, 27–28, 34–35, 71, 103, 109, 161, 232n19; and dancing, 145; obscenity trials, 34–35, 41, 58. *See also* Boston
masturbation: in books, 28, 49; in movies, 130; in popular music, 156, 163, 169; on the radio, 191; on TV, 198–99, 207

Mata, Ruth, 196
Mathers, Marshall Bruce, III. *See*
    Eminem
Maud (TV show), 202
Maugham, Somerset, 110
Mauro, Tony, 170
May, Lady, 171
May Day (album), 171
MCA Records, 166
McCain, John, 197
McCall's (magazine), 112
McCarthy, Charlie, 184
McCartney, Paul, 178
McClellan, George B., 101
McGee, Sydney, 93
McKenna, Joseph, 103–4
McLendon, Gordon, 157
MC Lyte, 169
McNamara, Maggie, 121
Meese, Edwin, 45, 56, 77
Meese Commission on Pornography,
    77
Memoirs (Casanova), 30
Memoirs of a Woman of Pleasure
    (Cleland), 13, 41
Memoirs of Hecate County, 37
Memphis (TN), 125
Mencken, H. L., 23, 25, 27
Men in the Ladies Room (book), 43
Metalious, Grace, 39, 200
Metro-Goldwyn-Mayer, 108, 119
Metropolitan Museum of Art, 63
Meyer, Russ, 127
MGM Television, 201
Miami (FL), 156, 169
Miami Vice (TV show), 206
Michelangelo, 66, 75
Michigan, censorship in, 88, 172
Mid-Columbia Arts Council, 91
Milan, Lorenzo W., 187
military, 23, 47–48, 60, 69, 106
Military Honor and Decency Act,
    47–48
Miller, Henry, 40, 42, 131
Miller, Marvin, 44
Miller, Wes, 92
Miller v. California, 44, 127

Mills, Irving, 149
Mills Brothers, 153
Mill Valley (CA), 88
Milsom, Robin, 80–81
Milwaukee Art Institute, 68
Mingo, Norman, 8
Minneapolis (MN), 226
Minnesota, censorship in, 29–30
Minnow, Newton N., 201
minors. *See* children
The Miracle (movie), 119
Miracle at Morgan's Creek (movie), 117
miscegenation in movies, 109
Mishawaka (IN), 172
Mississippi, censorship in, 161
Missouri, censorship in, 147–48, 166
M. Knoedler & Company, 62
modern art, 64, 66, 70
modern dance, 196
Modern Romance (magazine), 34
Mom and Dad (movie), 107
Monday Night Football (TV show), 210
Monroe, Marilyn, 36, 122
Montand, Yves, 122
Montgomery, Elizabeth, 199
Montgomery High School (California),
    174
The Mooche, 149
the Moonlighters, 153
Moore, Marianne, 190
Morality in Media, Inc., 230
The Morals of the Movie (Oberholtzer),
    107
Morals vs. Art (Comstock), 62
Moran, Terrence, 137
Morgenthau, Hans, 67
Morrison, Jim, 155–56
Morrow, Elizabeth Cutter, 69
Morton, James M., 27
Mother Earth's Fertility (sculpture), 71
Motion Picture Association of America
    (MPAA), 108, 124, 198
Motion Picture Producers and
    Distributors of America (MPPDA),
    108
Motion Picture Research Council, 112
Motown Records, 167, 261n147

movie industry: and competition with television, 118–19; distribution of movies, 98, 119; Jews in, 102, 106, 114; movies as a business, 103–4; and self-censorship, 101, 108–9, 126

movies: age restrictions, 100–101, 124–26, 129–33, 254n185; and artistic freedom, 126, 133, 254n186; birth control information in, 102, 104; censorship generating interest in, 98, 118, 130; censorship of, 6, 96–134; childbirth in, 109; child pornography in, 129–31; desexualization of, 115; and freedom of speech and expression, 103–4, 119–20, 217, 249n52; hard-core pornography, 127, 132; homosexuality in, 123, 128, 133, 255–56nn229–230; kissing in, 109; language in, 132; lesbianism in, 133; miscegenation in, 109; nudity in, 104–5, 108–9, 125, 128–29; pornographic, 126–27; pregnancy in, 102; prostitution in, 101, 106, 108–9; rape in, 109; ratings system for, 6, 126, 128–34, 228, 254n186; sex hygiene films, 106, 109; sexually explicit material in, 101–2, 104–12, 124–34; songs in, 152–53; on TV, 197–98; U.S. Supreme Court on censorship of, 103–4, 119–20, 125; violence in, 101; X-rated movies, 126–27. *See also* specific titles

movie stars and scandals, 107

MPAA (Motion Picture Association of America), 108, 124, 198

Mr. Novak (TV show), 201

MTV, 160–63, 177–79

multiple prosecutions, 46

Munsey's (magazine), 32

Munson, Lynne A., 89

Museum of Art (Alexandria, LA), 86–87

museums, 63–64, 85. *See also* specific names of museums

music: black, 149, 153, 167–69, 261n147; censorship generating interest in, 165, 168, 172; censorship of, 137–75; piracy of, 165; as political statement, 169–70; ratings system for, 171–72; transportability of, 142. *See also* popular music

Musical Courier (magazine), 144

Musical Majority, 166

Music Publishers' Protective Association, 156

music videos, 160–63

Mutual Film Corporation v. Industrial Commission of Ohio, 103–4

"My God, How the Money Rolls In" (song), 140

"My Heart Belongs to Daddy" (song), 150

My Husband Comes (movie), 99

Nabokov, Vladimir, 123, 131

Naked Lunch (Burroughs), 41

The Naked Maja (movie and painting), 71

National Academy of Design, 59

National Association of Broadcasters, 159, 163–64, 182, 186, 190, 194

National Association of Record Manufacturers, 167

National Association of Secondary School Principles, 175

National Association of the Motion Picture Industry (NAMPI), 108–9

National Board of Censorship, 101

National Board of Review, 101

National Book Foundation, 49

National Broadcasting Company. *See* NBC

National Catholic Office of Motion Pictures (NCOMP), 124, 253n176

National Citizens Committee for Broadcasting, 203

National Council on Freedom from Censorship, 29, 183

National Council to Protect Freedom of Art, Literature and the Press, 65

National Endowment for the Arts (NEA), 83–86

National Football League, 178
National Guard Armory Show (NY), 64
National Institute on Drug Abuse, 173
National Law Center for Children, 215
National Museum of Art (Washington,
   D.C.), 87–88
National Obscenity Enforcement Unit,
   45–46
National Organization for Decent
   Literature, 34
National Religious Broadcasters, 211
naturalism, 17, 21
Naylor, Phyllis Reynolds, 49–50
NBC, 152–54, 181–83, 197, 199, 207
NC-17, 129–33
NEA (National Endowment for the
   Arts), 83–86
Near, Jay M., 29
Nelson, Willie, 173
Nesbitt, Evelyn, 100
network affiliates, 153–54
Never Love a Stranger (Robbins), 35
Never on Sunday (movie), 122
A New Day in Eden (TV show), 206
New Deal, 67
New England Society for the
   Suppression of Vice, 20
New Jersey, censorship in, 87, 98
Newman, Leslea, 51
New Mexico, censorship in, 71, 81, 166
New Orleans, 71
New Republic (magazine), 29, 114
Newsletter on Intellectual Freedom (ALA),
   238n183
Newsweek, 164, 169, 202, 205, 209
New York: anti obscenity programs,
   60–61; art, censorship of, 65–66;
   and child pornography, 130; movies,
   censorship of, 100–101, 103–4,
   108, 114, 119–21, 125, 127; music,
   censorship of, 157, 169; obscenity
   trials, 34–35, 37, 43, 61; printed
   material, censorship of, 9–11,
   18–20, 24, 28, 32, 68; radio,
   censorship of, 150–51, 188, 192–93
New York City (NY): art, censorship of,
   157; Comstock and censorship, 20,

60–61; magazines, censorship of,
   32; and modern art, 64; as moral
   cesspool, 9–10; movies, censorship
   of, 100–101, 104; radio, censorship
   of, 150–51, 192–93; and street
   artists, 90–91; Sumner and
   censorship, 9–10, 65–66. *See also*
   New York Society for the
   Suppression of Vice
The New Yorkers (musical), 150
New York Society for the Suppression
   of Vice, 10, 23–25, 34, 61–65
New York Telegram (newspaper), 62
New York Times, 10, 20, 169
New York World (newspaper), 150
New York World-Telegram (newspaper),
   71
nickelodeons, 98–101
Nicklas, Trina, 90
Nightline (TV show), 162, 215
Night Riders (movie), 99
Nikki D, 169
1999 (album), 162
nipples, 178
Nix, Robert N. C., 76
Nixon, Richard M., 70
nonprotected speech, child
   pornography as, 130
nonrepresentational art, 70
nonspeech, obscenity as, 37–38, 72,
   224
Noon (painting), 71
Norris, Frank, 17
Northern Virginia Community College
   (Loudoun, VA), 87
Northhampton (MA), 12
nose art, 69
Notice of Apparent Liability for
   Forfeiture, 170
Not in Front of the Children (Heins),
   238n174
Notorious (movie), 114
Nott, Charles D., 25
Novak, Thomas, 216
nude dancing, 148
Nude Descending a Staircase (painting),
   64

nude models, 68
nudity: in album cover art, 157–58; censorship of, 86–87; and children, 81–82; discomfort with, 57; in magazines, 36, 40; male vs. female, 79–80, 87; in movies, 104–5, 108–9, 125, 128–29; nude dancing, 148; in paintings and pictorial art, 62–63, 66, 71–73, 79–80; in photographs, 6, 59, 79–81, 86–87, 90; and the Post Office Department, 68; and public schools, 93; in sculpture, 56–58, 63–64, 68, 71; on television, 199; vs. obscenity, 68
nudity, female: in magazines, 36; in movies, 104–5, 129; in photography, 86; in sculpture, 56–58, 63–64; vs. male nudity, 79–80, 87
nudity, male: and homosexuality in art, 85; in movies, 128; in photography, 86, 89; in sculpture, 57, 68; U.S. Supreme Court on, 40; vs. female nudity, 79–80, 87
nuisance laws and censorship, 29–30, 127, 247n22
NYPD Blue (TV show), 206

Oakland (CA), 67
Oberholtzer, Ellis Paxson, 107
Oberwager, Charles A., 25
O'Brien, Morgan J., 18
obscenity: and criminal behavior, 35, 37; and the Customs Service, 64–68, 75; definition of, 17–19, 37–45, 72, 120–21, 240n14; and freedom of speech and expression, 35–38, 43–44, 72, 230; "I know it when I *See* it," 240n14; and interstate commerce, 46, 103, 229–30; mailing of, 28–29; as nonspeech, 37–38, 72, 224; and the Post Office Department, 33, 35–37, 39–43, 60–62; private possession of, 75–76, 127; on the radio, 187–91; recommendation to eliminate laws, 76–77; Senate hearings on, 28, 77;

and state interests, 45; as subject of scientific inquiry, 72; U.S. Supreme Court on, 18–19, 37–45, 72, 75–76, 120–21, 127–28; vs. nudity, 68; vs. sexual speech, 37–38, 45
obscenity trials: and art, 58, 61, 62, 73, 75, 85; *Forever Amber*, 34; *God's Little Acre*, 34–35; jurisdiction of decision, 66; of Lawrence Covington, 65; *Memoirs of Hecate County*, 37; and PHE Inc., 46; and popular music, 168; and printed materials, 17–20, 42–43; *Strange Fruit*, 34; 2 Live Crew, 261n150. *See also* Hicklin test
O'Connor, Sandra Day, 51, 218
Office of Censorship, 186
Oglive, Lloyd John, 215
Oh! Calcutta! (musical), 123
Ohio: art, censorship of, 81, 88; and dance halls, 81; movies, censorship of, 102, 120–21, 134; music, censorship of, 162, 168; obscenity trials, 85
Oklahoma, censorship in, 166
Oldenburg, Claes, 78
Old Man's Darling (movie), 99
Omaha (NB), 32
OnCommand, 134
Ono, Yoko, 157
The Opening of Misty Beethoven (movie), 127
Open Mind (TV show), 196
Operation PUSH, 159
Opie and Anthony (radio shock jocks), 192–93
oral sex: and Bill Clinton, 208–9; in movies, 125, 128, 132; in popular music, 168; on the radio, 190, 191; on TV, 198–99, 207
Orange Blossoms (play), 247n22
the Orioles, 154
Orlando (FL), 80
Orr-Cahall, Christina, 85
Our Movie Made Children (Forman), 112
The Outlaw (movie), 116–18, 252n139
Owens, Terrell, 210

Pacifica Foundation, 188, 265n56
paintings: censorship of, 58–59, 64, 79; nudity in, 62–63, 71–73, 79–80
Pal Joey (movie), 114, 153
Panama City Beach (FL), 174
Pandering Act, 43
Panse, Peter, 93
paperback books, 39
Paramount Pictures, 108, 119
parental control, 209, 220
parental guidance and movies, 126
Parents' Music Resource Center (PMRC), 163–66
Parents Television Council, 179, 209, 270n185
Parent Teacher Associations, 162, 165–66, 204
Parisi, Mark, *136*
Parker, Isaac, 13
Parker, Trey, 132
parody songs, 140
Pasco (WA), 91
Passion Bride (book), 42
Passion Play (movie), 99
Pastore, Joseph O., 177
Pawlenty, Tim, 47
The Pawnbroker (movie), 123
Payne Study and Experiment Fund, 112
Peale, Charles Wilson, 58
Peale Museum, 72
Pearlstein, Philip, 80, 89
pedophilia. *See* child pornography
Peek-a-Boo Bookstore, 44
Peep behind the Curtains of a Female Seminary (book), 16
the Penguins, 144
"Penis Envy" (song), 169
penises: in movies, 125; in popular music, 169; on the radio, 189–90; on TV, 198–99; in works of art, 78, 81, 86, 88–90
Pennsylvania: censorship in, 78–80, 102, 107, 166, 168; obscenity trials, 35, 58, 62; restrictions on dancing, 148
Pennsylvania Academy of Fine Arts, 58
Penthouse, 45, 48, 191

People for the American Way, 170, 205
The Perfect Moment (exhibit of Mapplethorpe's works), 83–84
performance art, 85–86
Petty, George, 32
Petty Girl, 32
Pew Research Center, 213
Peyton Place (Metalious), 39
Peyton Place (TV show), 200
the Pharaohs, 138
PHE Inc., 46
Philadelphia (PA): art, censorship of, 62, 78, 79; censorship trials, 20; obscenity trials, 58; radio, censorship of, 187
Philadelphia Academy of Art, 62
Philadelphia Inquirer, 62–63
Philosophical Dictionary (Voltaire), 18
phone sex, 217
"Phonograph Blues" (song), 150
photography: and child pornography, 244n138; of nude children, 81–82; nudity in, 6, 59, 79–81, 86–87, 90; and the Post Office Department, 36; of works of art, 61, 65, 71
"Physical" (song), 159
Picasso, Pablo, 80
Picket Fences (TV show), 208
Pickford, Mary, 107
pictorial art, 5–6, 58–93, 66. *See also* paintings; photography
Picture Fun (magazine), 36
"The Pill" (song), 158
Pilot Point (TX), 91–92
pinups, 33, 69–70
piracy, music, 165
Pirandello, Luigi, 193
Pittsfield (MA), 71
Pius XII, 70
Planned Parenthood Federation, 207
Plato, 137
Playboy, 36–37, 40–41, 43–45, 48, 88
Plummer, Elmer, 69
PM (magazine), 68
The Pocket Book of Old Masters, 71
Police Gazette (magazine), 32
police shows on TV, 206

political statements, art and music as, 70, 91, 169–70

popular music, 139–43; banned songs, 152, 157, 182; censorship of, 67, 150; concerts and performances, 155, 172; FCC indecency standards, 169–70; and glorification of drug use, 158; integration of, 167–68; in movies, 152–53; obscenity trials, 168; pregnancy in, 259n85; protests against, 163–67; publishing of, 153, 259n82; as rebellion against the status quo, 6, 154, 175; and ribald song lyrics, 138–40; self-censorship of, 151, 156–57; and sexually explicit song lyrics, 115, 149–60, 162–68, 169–73; as threat to status quo, 149; violence in, 172; warning labels on albums, 166–67, 171–72. *See also* lyrics

pornography: in books and magazines, 15–16, 32–33; censorship generating interest in, 244n138; Congressional hearings on, 32; and degradation of women, 87–88, 226; FBI as major purchasers, 63; feminist protests against, 130; and freedom of speech and expression, 227; hard and soft core, 127, 132; on the Internet, 214–18, 271n208; and movies, 126–27; as protected speech, 227; and sex crimes, 77; studies on, 45, 272n5; U.S. Supreme Court on, 227; underground book industry, 15; and VCRs, 200. *See also* child pornography

Pornography Victims Compensation Act, 227

Porter, Cole, 150, 152

Portland (OR), 170

postage. *See* Post Office Department

Postal Reorganization Act, 43

Postal Revenue and Federal Salary Act, 43

postcards, 71

posters and record albums, 157

The Postman Always Rings Twice (movie), 118

Post Office Department: censorship of printed materials by, 15, 28–29; and nudity, 68; and obscenity, 33, 35–37, 39–43, 60–62; and private possession of obscenity, 76; second class mailing rate, 32–33, 36, 235n107; U.S. Supreme Court on, 60

Poulsbo (WA), 133

Powell, Lewis F., 51

Powell, Michael K., 178

Powers, Hiram, 59

pregnancy references, 102, 193, 202, 259n85

Preminger, Otto, 121–22

Presley, Elvis, 155

Priest, Judas, 163

Prince, 159, 162, 163

printers, 11, 43–44

Priority Records, 169

private individuals, power of, 51–52, 61, 229

Private Parts (Stern), 191

private possession of obscenity, 75–76, 127

private viewing of art, 75

Production Code, 6, 95–97, 110–11, 121, 123, 152

Production Code Administration (PCA), 113–19, 123–24, 251n121

Progressive Era, 100, 224

prolonged passion, scenes of, 102, 108

propaganda, 65

prostitution in movies, 101, 106, 108–9

prostitution in music, 173

Proulx, Annie, 50

Providence (RI), 79

prurient interest, appealing to, 38, 41–42, 72, 120–21, 188

PTAs, 162, 165–66, 204

public access and art displays, 80–81

publication of censored items, 12

public display of art, 75

public interest, defined, 183

public libraries, 48–52, 219–21

public morals, protection of, 59–62

public support of the arts, 67, 83–86, 89, 245n144
publishers, self-censorship by, 17, 21–22
Publishers Weekly, 11, 26
pulp novels and magazines, 42–43
Purdy (MO), 147–48
purity crusaders, 3, 17–20, 61–65
Purple Rain (album), 163

Quantum Leap (TV show), 208
Quigley, Martin, 110, 250n95

Rabelais, François, 18, 30
race music. *See* black music
racism, 202
Racketeer Influenced and Corrupt Organization Act (RICO), 46
racketeering, 46
radio: censorship generating interest in, 191; censorship of, 6, 151–52, 169–70, 181–82, 190–91; competition from TV, 186; discriminated against, 191; FCC regulation of, 151, 158, 178–93, 225–26; and homosexuality, 182, 185, 188; language on, 179, 181–84, 187; obscenity on, 187–91; satellite, 173, 192–93, 266n81; self-censorship, 182, 186; sexually explicit materials on, 189–91, 193; "shock jocks," 191–93; talk radio, 189–91; "topless radio," 190; and vaudeville comedians, 183
Radio Acts (of 1912 and 1927), 180
Radio-Keith-Orpheum (RKO), 108
ragtime, 144
Raiders, 138
Rain (movie), 110
Raising PG Kids in an X-Rated Society (Gore, T.), 166
Ramayo, Rufino, 69
Rand, Sally, 185
Rand Corporation, 210
Random House, 30–31
rape in movies, 109
rap music, 167–69

Raspberry, William, 164
ratings systems: and the Internet, 220; for movies, 6, 126, 128–34, 228, 254n186; for music, 171–72; and self-censorship, 228; for TV, 198, 209
rave culture, 173–74
Ray, Joseph, 81
Reagan, Ronald, 45, 77
"The Real Slim Shady" (song), 169–70
The Record Bar, 168
Recording Industry Association of America (RIAA), 163–67, 171
The Red Badge of Courage (Crane), 17
redeeming social importance test, 41–42, 44, 120, 127, 190
Redrup v. New York, 43
Reed, Ralph, 216
Reefer Madness (movie), 107
Rehnquist, William, 218
Reichenbach, Harry, 64
religious fundamentalists, 50, 147–48, 215. *See also* social conservatives
Renton (WA), 131
"repeal of reticence," 104
Resale Activities Board of Review, 48
responsible sex on TV, 207, 210
Revelle, Barbara Jo, 90
Reynolds, Jock, 87–88
Rhenquist, William H., 51
Rhode Island, censorship in, 39, 79
Rhode Island School of Design, 79
rhythm and blues (R&B), 153
RIAA (Recording Industry Association of America), 163–67, 171
Rice, John C., 97
Riggs, Marlon, 199
right to be informed of the charges, 19
right to privacy, 75
Rimm, Martin, 216
Ritual de lo Habitual (album), 158
RKO radio, 158
Robbins, Harold, 35
rock and roll, 138–39, 144–59
"Rock around the Clock" (song), 144
"Rocky Mountain High" (song), 158
"Rock Your Body" (song), 177

Rodin, August, 90
Rolling Stones, 155, 157, 178
"Roll Me Over" (song), 141
Room at the Top (movie), 122
Roosevelt, Franklin D., 68
Roseanne (TV show), 208
Rosen, Hilary, 170, 171
Rosen, Lew, 63
Ross, Edward A., 106
Roth v. United States, 37
Rowan & Martin's Laugh-In (TV show), 201
"Ruby, Don't Take Your Love to Town" (song), 160
Run-D.M.C. (album), 168
Rupp, Sharon, 91
Russell, Jane, 117
Ryan, Meg, 212

safe harbor, 189
safe sex on TV, 210
sale of censored items, 12, 45–46
Salle, David, 73
salsa, 147
Salter, Charles, 174–75
Salt Lake City (UT), 133
Salt-N-Pepa, 169
same-sex marriage, 50
Sammons Communications, 161
Sanctuary (Faulkner), 35, 114
San Francisco (CA), 68, 73, 81–82, 188
Sanger, Margaret, 16, 102, 104
Santa Fe (NM), 71, 81
Santa Rosa (CA), 174
satellite radio, 173, 192–93, 266n81
"Satisfaction (I Can't Get No)" (song), 157
Saturday Night at the Movies (TV show), 197
Saturday Press (magazine), 29
Scalia, Antonin, 86
scandals, movie stars, 107
Scarlet Confessions (magazine), 34
The Scarlet Letter, 13
Scarlet Street (movie), 119
Schaeffer, William, 182
Schatz, Aaron, 179

Schlafly, Phyllis, 44
Schlessinger, Arthur, 223
Schneider, Alfred R., 197–98
School Protective League, 64
schools: dances, 174–75; libraries, 44, 48–52, 219–21; school boards, 50–51; school buses and music, 172
Schroeder, Theodore, 9
Schumach, Murray, 95
scientific inquiry, 72
Scott, Henry, 17
Scranton (PA), 81
sculpture: ancient, 57–59; censorship of, 74–75, 86, 91; erotic, 73; nudity in, 56–58, 63–64, 68, 71
Seabury, Samuel, 18
Seagle, William, 9
Sears, Roebuck and Company, 204
Seattle (WA), 131
second class mailing rate, 32–33, 36, 235n107
Second Great Awakening, 12–13
Second Serve (television movie), 199
Seinfeld (TV show), 207
self-censorship, 4; and the Internet, 220; and the movie industry, 101, 108–9, 126; by orchestra leaders, 151–52; of popular music, 151, 156–57; by printers, 43–44; by publishers, 17, 21–22; of the radio, 6, 182, 186; and ratings systems, 228; and textbooks, 50; of TV, 6, 194, 202–3
Seltzer, Thomas, 25
Selznick, David O., 116, 118
Senate hearings: on obscenity, 28, 77; on song lyrics, 165; on television, 197. *See also* Congressional hearings
September Morn (painting), 64
Serrano, Andres, 83
sex: in movies, 101–2, 104–12, 124–34; on TV, 200–201, 203–11
The Sex Addicts (book), 42
Sex and the City (TV show), 208
sex hygiene films, 106, 109
sexism, 80, 168–69
Sex Orgies Illustrated (book), 44

The Sex Side of Life (Dennett), 28–29
sexual harassment vs. art, 88
sexual intercourse: in art, 73; in movies, 125, 129; in music, 172; in printed materials, 28, 34; references in popular music, 149–60, 162–67, 169–73; references on the radio, 191, 193; on TV, 206, 211
sexually explicit materials: children, protection from, 223–25; and the Internet, 214–21; and lyrics, 115, 139–40, 149–60, 162–67, 169–73; and magazines and printed materials, 36, 48–52; and music videos, 161–62; on the radio, 189–91, 193; and social conservatives, 45, 134, 162, 189, 224–25; on TV, 198–202, 203–11, 269n162. *See also* erotic art; Post Office Department
sexual speech: and child pornography, 130; in colonial America, 13; and freedom of expression, 7; in magazines and printed materials, 5, 32–33; sexual information, 16; U.S. Supreme Court on, 224; vs. obscenity, 37–38, 45; and zoning laws, 52, 80, 131
"Sexy Lady" (song), 160
Seymour, Jane, 199
Shaggy, 172
"Shake Your Booty" (song), 167
Shame Agent (book), 43
Shaw, George Bernard, 65
She Done Him Wrong (movie), 94, 96–97
sheet music, 142
Sherer, Robert, 89
Sheridan, Nicolette, 210
Shipman, David, 95
"shock jocks," 191–93
Showgirls (movie), 131
Showtime, 132, 206
show tunes, 153
Shreves, Leanne, 74
Shuler, Robert, 181–82
Shurlock, Geoffrey, 122–24, 253n169

Silver, Abner, 153
Silvers, Phil, 195
Silverstein, Max, 39
Simmons, Marc, 88
Simpson, George W., 25
The Simpsons (TV show), 206–7
Sinatra, Frank, 155, 200
Sirius Satellite Radio, 192, 266n81
Sister Carrie (Dreiser), 22
Six Characters in Search of an Author (Pirandello), 193
skin songs, 160
Slater, Philip, 223
Smith, Lillian, 34
Smith College, 69
Smothers Brothers, 201
Snappy Stories (magazine), 32
Soap (TV show), 203
soap operas, 196, 200
social benefit rationale for censorship, 3–4
social conservatives and sexually explicit materials, 45, 76, 134, 162, 189, 204–5, 224–25. *See also* fundamentalists
social dancing. *See* dancing
Society for the Suppression of Vice, 22
soft-core pornography, 127, 132
soldiers' songs, 141
Something about Amelia (television movie), 199
Sonderling Broadcasting, 190
songs: Anglo-Irish traditional ballads, 140; bawdy songs, 139–41; in movies, 152–53; parody, 140; show tunes, 153; soldiers' songs, 141; Tin Pan Alley songs, 153, 259n82; "Undergraduate Coarse" songs, 141. *See also* banned songs; lyrics; specific titles
Songwriter's Protective Organization, 156
Sousa, John Philip, 144
Souter, David, 86, 148, 219
South Carolina, censorship in, 89, 172, 187
South Charleston (WV), 79

Southern Baptist Convention, 159
South Park: Bigger, Louder and Uncut
(movie), 132
South Salt Lake (UT), 148
Spielberg, Steven, 126
The Spirit of Freedom (sculpture), 69
Spirit of Justice (sculpture), *54*, 56–57
Splendor in the Grass (movie), 123
The Spreading Evil (movie), 106
Springsteen, Bruce, 172–73
Sprinkle, Annie, 86
stag films, 126–27
Stanley v. Georgia, 75–76
Stanwyck, Barbara, 111
Starbucks, 172–73
State Department building, 73–74
Statement of Principles of Radio and
Television Broadcasting, 194
statues. *See* sculpture
status quo: desire to maintain, 2–3,
149; rebellion against, 6, 144–45,
154, 175
Steinbeck, John, 48
Steinberg, David, 201
Stern, Howard, 191, 266n81
Stevens, John Paul, 51, 188, 218
Stevens, Ted, 212
Stewart, Potter, 41, 45, 189, 240
Stewart, Rod, 158
Stone, Herbert S., 98
Stone, Matt, 132
Stopes, Marie C., 30
The Story of Temple Drake (movie), 114
Strange Fruit (Smith), 34
street art and artists, 90–91
A *Streetcar Named Desire* (movie),
121–22
Stuart, David, 75
studies: on the Internet, 214–16; of
movies, 112, 131; of popular music,
139–41; of pornography, 45, 47,
76–77, 272n5; of TV, 207, 210, 213
Studio Relations Committee, 109–10
Studs Lonigan Trilogy (Farrell), 35
Sturges, Jock, 81–82, 244n138
"Sugar Walls" (song), 163
Sullivan, Ed, 155, 193

Summer, Donna, 159
Summerfield, Arthur E., 36
Sumner, John, 10–11, 22–27, 34,
65–66
Sunland (CA), 175
Super Bowl XXXVIII, *176*, 177–79,
211–12
Supreme Court. *See* U.S. Supreme
Court
Susanna (painting), 65–66
Swanson, Gloria, 110
sweater shots, 115–16
The Sweet Smell of Success (movie), 122
"Sweet Violets" (song), 154
synchronized sound, 110, 152

"Take Your Girlie to the Movies"
(song), 107
talk radio, 189–91
the tango (dance), 145
Tariff Acts, 58, 64. *See also* Customs
Service
Tarzan, the Ape Man (movie), 129
Taylor, Bruce, 215
Taylor, William Desmond, 107–8
Tea and Sympathy (movie), 122
Team America (movie), 132
teenage rebellion and music, 144
Telecommunications Act (of 1996),
209, 216–18
Tele-Community Antenna, 161
television: birth control references, 202,
207; and breasts, 178, 195–96; cable
TV, 160–63, 198, 206, 208, 212;
censorship generating interest in,
209–10; censorship of, 6, 179,
209–10; child abuse on, 199;
competition with movies, 118–19,
252n148; competition with radio,
186; Congressional hearings on,
196, 211–12; controversial issues
on, 202–3; discriminated against,
191; educational function of, 201;
family hour, 202–3; FCC regulation
of, 193, 211, 225–26; and freedom
of speech and expression, 202–3;
and homosexuality, 198–99, 202–3,

205–6, 208; indecency standards on, 211–12; language used, 193–96; lesbianism on, 206, 208; modern dance on, 196; movies on, 197–98; and music videos, 160–63; nudity on, 199; pregnancy references, 194, 202; ratings system for, 198, 209; self-censorship of, 6, 194, 202–3; Senate hearings on, 197; sexually explicit materials on, 198–211, 269n162; violence on, 203–4. *See also* ABC; CBS; Fox; NBC
10 (movie), 129
Tennessee, censorship in, 80, 168, 170–71
Terry, Randall, 244n138
Texaco Star Theater (TV show), 193
Texarkana, 161
Texas: art, censorship of, 80, 91–93; movies, censorship of, 120, 254n185; music, censorship of, 155; music videos, censorship of, 161; printed materials, censorship of, 50–51, 239n193
Texas Fine Arts Association, 80
textbooks, self-censorship of, 50
That Certain Summer (television movie), 198
That Girl (TV show), 201
That '70s Show (TV show), 206
Thaw, Harry K., 100, 248nn33–34
Thayer, Martin R., 20
theater owners, liability of, 127, 247n22
thirteen points (NAMPI), 108
Thirtysomething (TV show), 206, 208
This Film Is Not Yet Rated (documentary movie), 133
Thomas, Clarence, 86
Thomas, Marlo, 201
Thomas, Roxie, 90
Thompson, Jack, 168
Thompson, Ruth, 156
Three's Company (TV show), 204
Three Weeks (Glyn), 20–21
Throw Mama From the Train (movie), 132

Thurmond, Strom, 165
Tice, Clara, 66
Timberlake, Justin, *176*, 177–78
Time (magazine), 71, 159, 215–16
Time Warner, 212
Tin Pan Alley songs, 153, 259n82
Tintoretto, 65–66
The Titan (Dreiser), 22
Toast of the Town (TV show), 193
Toledo (OH), 81
Tolstoy, Leo, 20
Tom Jones (Fielding), 18
Tongues United (television movie), 199
"Tonight's the Night" (song), 158
"topless radio," 190
To the Democrats, Republicans, and Bipartisans (sculpture), 91
Traffic in Souls (movie), 104
transportation of censored items, 12. *See also* Customs Service
transsexualism and transvestitism, 203
Treasury Department. *See* Customs Service
Trenton (NJ), 69
Trim (magazine), 40
Triumph of Death (d'Annunzio), 20
Tropic of Cancer (Miller), 40, 42
Tropic of Capricorn (Miller), 40
True Love (magazine), 34
Trujillo, Carmen, 88
Tucker, Sophie, 150
turkey trot (dance), 144–45
Turner, Brian, 169
Turner, Lana, 115
Turner, Ted, 131, 161
TV. *See* television
Twentieth Century Fox, 108
the Twist (dance), 147
2 Live Crew, 168, 261n150
two-step, 143–44
Two Virgins (album), 157
Tyler, Parker, 31

Ulysses (Joyce), 25, 30–31
"Undergraduate Coarse" songs, 141
unifying beliefs and Americans, 273n19

United Artists Corporation, 71, 108, 122, 127
Universal Studios, 108
University of California, 210
University of Florida, 90
University of Michigan, 88
University of Minneapolis Press, 47
University of North Carolina, 76
University of Southern California, 68, 139
University of Tennessee, 80
University of the District of Colombia, 78
University of Wisconsin, 106
Unspeakable Acts (television movie), 199
The Unwritten Law (movie), 100
Upton, Fred, 211
USA Today (newspaper), 134, 170
U.S. Supreme Court: on age restrictions, 254n185; and banning of books by school boards, 50–51; on cable TV, 212; and censorship by the Post Office Department, 60; on censorship of movies, 103–4, 119–20, 125; on the Communications Decency Act, 217–18; on FCC restrictions, 159, 188; on freedom of speech and expression, 224, 236n126; on the Internet, 218–21; on local standards of judgment, 230; and NEA restrictions, 86; on nudity, 40, 148; on obscenity, 18–19, 37–45, 72, 76, 120–21, 127–28; on pornography, 227; and private possession of obscenity, 75–76; on second class mailing rate, 33; on using children as standard for obscenity, 37, 42; on zoning laws, 131
Utah, 46, 133, 148
"Uterus Guy" (song), 169

Valenti, Jack, 124–25, 133
Valentino, Rudolph, 105
Vallee, Rudy, 151, 152
vamp, 104–5

Vandergrift, Kay E., 177
Varga Girl, 32–33, 69–70
Vargas, Alberto, 33, 69–70
Variety (magazine), 116, 152, 156, 182
vaudeville comedians and the radio, 183
V-chip, 209
VCRs, 199–200
venereal disease, 201–2
Viacom, 191, 193
Victoria's Secret Fashion Show Special (TV show), 210
videocassette recorders, 199–200
videocassettes and video stores, 132
Video Privacy Protection Act (of 1988), 200
violence, 101, 167, 172, 203–4
Virginia, censorship in, 82, 87, 103, 125, 166
Virginia Museum of Fine Arts, 82
Vitascope films, 97
Vixens (movie), 127
"Vogue" (music video), 162
Voltaire, 18

Walker, Cindy, 160
Walker, Frank C., 33
Walker, Jimmy J., 9
"Walk with an Erection" (song), 169
Wallace, Jonathan, 177
Wal-Mart, 167
the waltz, 143
War and Remembrance (television movie), 199
"wardrobe malfunction," 176, 178
Warner Brothers, 108, 163
warning labels on albums, 166–67, 171–72
Warren, Earl, 38, 121
Warren, Harry, 150
Washington, censorship in, 32, 91, 131, 133, 171
Washington, D.C., 78, 83–85; art, censorship in, 87
Washington Post (newspaper), 78, 164
Washington Project for the Arts, 84
Watch and Ward Society, 20, 26–28

Waters, John, 134
Wayne (NJ), 87
The Wayne King Show (TV show),
    153–54
The Wedding Dance (painting), 71
The Wedding Night (Craddock), 16
Welles, Orson, 115–16
Wenger, Jane, 79
"We're Having a Baby" (song), 193
Wesselmann, Tom, 73
West, Mae, 94, 95–97, 111, 184–85
West Virginia, censorship in, 79
"We Want Our MTV" advertising
    campaign, 160–61
Weymouth (MA), 161
What Do You Say to a Naked Lady?
    (movie), 124
What Price Glory? (movie), 109
"When Harry Met Sally" law, 212
Where Are My Children (movie), 102
Whistler, James Abbott McNeil, 66
White, Byron R., 51, 130
White, Stanford, 100
Whiteman, Paul, 151
white slavery, 104, 106, 109
Whitman, Walt, 13–14, 16, 18
Whitney, Anne, 59
Who's Afraid of Virginia Woolf? (movie),
    124
Wichita Falls (TX), 51
The Widow Jones (musical), 97
Wildmon, Donald, 205–6, 207
Wiley, Richard E., 202
Wilkinson, Raylene, 87
Will and Grace (TV show), 206
Willhoite, Michael, 51
William Patterson College, 87
Williams, Grace, 145
Williams, Tennessee, 122
Willingham, Calder, 35
Willis, Kent, 55
Wilmington (NC), 89
Wilson, Edmund, 37
Wilson, Woodrow, 103
Windsor, Kathleen, 34

Windsor High School (California),
    175
Wink (magazine), 36
Wisconsin, censorship in, 156, 168
Without a Trace (TV show), 211
Wojnarowicz, David, 85
Wollaston, Justine, 92
women: artists, 59, 78; degradation of,
    87–88, 170, 226; effect of movies
    on, 112; moral welfare of, 69;
    objectification of, 73; and sexual
    harassment, 88; single women on
    TV, 201
Women against Pornography, 130
Women in Love (Lawrence), 10
Women's Christian Temperence Union
    (WCTU), 63
Wonders of Canada (movie), 99
Woolsey, John M., 30
"Work with Me Annie" (song), 153
A World I Never Made (Farrell), 35
The World is Blue (movie), 121–22
Wouk, Herman, 199
The Writers Guild, 202

XM Satellite Radio, 193
X-rated movies, 126–27

Yale Broadcasting Company, 158
Yellow Springs (OH), 88
YMCA's Committee for the Suppression
    of Vice. *See* New York Society for the
    Suppression of Vice
"Yodeling in the Valley" (song), 169
The Young and Evil (Ford and Tyler), 31
"Young and Healthy" (song), 150
Your Hit Parade (TV show), 154
Your Show of Shows (TV show), 196
"You Suck" (song), 169
Yo-Yo, 169

Zanuck, Darryl F., 118
Zappa, Frank, 160, 165–66, 261n144
zoning laws, 52, 80, 131
Zorn, Anders, 66

About the Author

John E. Semonche is professor of history at the University of North Carolina, Chapel Hill. An authority on American constitutional and legal history, he is the author of numerous articles and books, including *Keeping the Faith: A Cultural History of the U.S. Supreme Court* and *Religion and Constitutional Government in the United States*.